THE COMPLETE

SEARCH FOR SIGNIFICANCE

Rapha Resources offers a variety of books and other materials . . .

By Robert S. McGee:
- *The Search for Significance 4-Part Video Seminar with Study Guide & Promotion Kit*
- *The Search for Freedom* (Book)
- *Discipline with Love* (Book)
- *Father Hunger* (Book)
- *Rapha's 12-Step Program for Overcoming Chemical Dependency*

Co-authored by Robert S. McGee:
- *The Search for Significance Youth Discussion Manual* (Book), with Dawson McAllister
- *Your Parents and You* (book/workbook), with Pat Springle and Jim Craddock
- *Getting Unstuck*, with Pat Springle

. . . and much more!

THE COMPLETE
SEARCH FOR SIGNIFICANCE

ROBERT S. MCGEE

INCLUDING:

THE SEARCH FOR SIGNIFICANCE BOOK/WORKBOOK

THE SEARCH FOR SIGNIFICANCE DEVOTIONAL

THE SEARCH FOR SIGNIFICANCE 22-DAY GUIDED STUDY

THE SEARCH FOR SIGNIFICANCE SMALL GROUP LEADERS' GUIDE

Rapha

PUBLISHING

HOUSTON, TEXAS

The Complete Search for Significance

Unless otherwise indicated, Scripture references in this volume are from the New American Standard Bible, © The Lockman Foundation, 1960, 1962, 1963, 1968, 1971, 1972, 1975, 1977.

First Printing, 1994
Printed in the United States of America

ISBN: 0-945276-54-0

To my wife, Marilyn, who has given of herself so that I might minister these truths, both personally and now by the written word.

CONTENTS

THE SEARCH FOR SIGNIFICANCE BOOK/WORKBOOK

ACKNOWLEDGMENTS
THE SEARCH FOR SIGNIFICANCE BOOK/WORKBOOK

The concepts presented in this book have been utilized at our counseling centers and seminars for many years. The results have been so phenomenal that we were compelled to produce this book.

Many have contributed to *The Search for Significance.* I want to especially thank my staff, whose great dedication to the spreading of these truths is immeasurable. I also want to thank Rick Hove, Ray Anderson, Melanie Ahlquist, Dan Hayes, Dr. Steve Spotts, Conrad Koch, Richard Price, Sandy Ballard-Rote, Jay Hamman, Becky Blount, and especially my mother, Minerva McGee, all of whom have made significant contributions to this book. Finally, I would like to thank Pat Springle and Susan Joiner, who were instrumental in bringing clarity and insight to this material.

INTRODUCTION

When Christ told His disciples, *You shall know the truth, and the truth shall make you free* (John 8:32), He was referring not only to an intellectual assent to the truth, but also to the application of truth in the most basic issues of life: our goals, our motives, and our sense of self-worth. Unfortunately, many of us give only lip-service to the powerful truths of the Scriptures without allowing them to affect the basis of our self-esteem in a radical way. Instead, we continue to seek our security and purpose from worldly sources: personal success, status, beauty, wealth, and the approval of others. These rewards may fulfill us for a short time, but they soon lead us to a sense of urgency to succeed and be approved again.

To meet these compelling needs, we drive ourselves to achieve, doing virtually anything to make people happy with us, and spend countless hours and dollars trying to look "just right." Often, we avoid situations and people where the risks of failure and rejection are high. It's a rat race that can't be won by simply running faster. We need to get off of this hopeless treadmill, and learn to apply the foundational truths that can motivate us to live for Christ rather than for the approval of other people.

Christ's death paid the penalty for our sins, and His resurrection gives us new life, new goals, and new hope. He has given us complete security and challenging purpose. These are not based on our abilities, but on His grace and the power of His Spirit. Yes, Christ wants us to be zealous and ambitious, but not about our sucess or status. If we understand His forgiveness and acceptance, we will pursue the right things—Christ and His cause—and we will be free to enjoy His love.

The principles and insights in this book have been gleaned from years of counseling experience and also, from the writings of many psychologists and Bible teachers. I am indebted to their scholarship and wisdom.

This book focuses on how our thoughts affect our emotional, relational and spiritual development. It is not a textbook for professionals. Instead, the goal of this book is to enable a wide range of people to apply the Scriptures specifically and deeply to real issues in their lives. The scope of this material does not include some factors. For instance, some emotional problems have a physiological source (e.g. schizophrenia, learning disabilities, chemical imbalances, etc.); some disorders have their roots in emotional and relational pain but are complicated by physiological symptoms (e.g. chronic fatigue, mood swings, weight loss or gain, migraines, etc.). These factors should certainly be addressed by a competent, qualified physician or psychotherapist if they exist.

This is the revised and expanded version of *The Search for Significance*. The response from those who have read the book and used the workbook has been overwhelming. It is my prayer that the Lord will use these materials to convince you of His love, forgiveness, and purposes for your life.

> *For the love of Christ controls us, having concluded this,*
> *that one died for all, therefore all died;*
> *and He died for all, that they who live should no longer*
> *live for themselves, but for Him who died and rose again on*
> *their behalf.*
>
> 2 CORINTHIANS 5:14–15

One
Turning on the Light

Tim Woodall is a young regional sales representative for a company that manufactures building materials. He travels by car, covering a large section of East Texas as he visits building supply stores in the many small towns there.

Almost a year ago, after his last appointment in the day, Tim decided to drive home instead of spending another night in a motel. At about midnight, driving down a lonely, two-lane country highway, he dozed off. His car ran off the road, hit an embankment, and flipped over.

Tim was dazed, and when he moved, seemed to hurt all over. He managed to struggle out of his car, and then lay on the grass trying to grasp what had happened to him. *I'm okay,* he kept telling himself. *It's really not that bad.*

About forty-five minutes later, Tim, barely conscious, heard the sound of an approaching car. He tried to raise himself up, but it was useless; he was too weak. The car zoomed past, and then braked. Bob and Natalie Johnson were driving through the night from El Paso, Texas, to Montgomery, Alabama, to visit their daughter. In the moonlight, Natalie had spotted the overturned car from the corner of her eye. Now, her husband backed down the road and pulled over onto the shoulder. Beyond their headlights, they could clearly see the wrecked car, and lying next to it, Tim.

Tim lay in a pool of blood. Beneath the light, the Johnsons discovered that his head and arm were badly cut, and as they tried to help him to his feet, realized that his left leg was probably fractured.

Seeing his own blood-stained shirt; the dirt, wet beside him; and the concern on the Johnsons' faces, Tim began to shake uncontrollably, suddenly aware that he was badly hurt. He was, in fact, slowly bleeding to death, but due to shock, wasn't fully able to comprehend the extent of his wounds.

The Johnsons lifted Tim into their car and sped him toward the county hospital, where his cuts were stitched and his fractured leg put into a splint. This would be replaced with a cast when the swelling went down.

If the Johnsons hadn't been driving to Alabama that night; if Natalie had been looking another way; if the headlights of their car hadn't enabled them to find Tim in the darkness, he might have died.

This story illustrates a reality in many of our lives: We are hurt, emotionally, relationally, and spiritually, but because we aren't aware of the extent of our wounds, we can't take steps toward healing and health. Our problem is not stupidity, but a lack of objectivity. Because of this, we fail to see the reality of pain, hurt, and anger in our lives.

A college student was considered "the life of the party." She was intelligent, witty, and sociable, but when she was alone, she experienced deep loneliness and seething resentment.

A businessman who, as a child, was neglected by his ambitious father thought, *If I can just get that promotion, then I'll be happy. Success is what really counts in life!* He got many promotions and raises because he was driven to perform well, but happiness continued to elude him.

A housewife with three children painfully wonders, *Why is it that I don't feel close to my husband?* Having grown up with an alcoholic father and a demanding mother, this woman has never felt lovable, and so isn't able to receive her husband's love.

An articulate pastor speaks powerfully about the unconditional love and grace of God, yet he is plagued by guilt. He is driven to succeed in his public ministry, but is passive and withdrawn around his family. He has never understood how to apply his own teaching to *his* life and relationships.

We all have experienced the inability to be objective about our experiences, thoughts, and behavior in different circumstances. This objective "light" didn't begin to penetrate my own life until shortly after I had entered the business world. Before that time, whenever I felt the pain of rejection, the sting of sarcasm, or anything less than the complete approval of others, I tried to shrug it off. I reasoned that because of my status as a Christian, I should exude an attitude of happiness and contentment in all things. When something didn't go the way I'd hoped or planned it would, I simply told myself it didn't really matter. Though I was able to fool myself in these instances, my gloomy countenance told those who were closest to me another story.

On one such occasion, a good friend of mine inquired about what was wrong. "You seem troubled," he said. "Is anything bothering you?"

"Me? No, I'm fine."

"You don't seem fine to me," he persisted. "You're acting as though you might be depressed about something."

I stuck to my time-tested text. "No, really, I *am* fine. I guess I've just been a little pressured lately."

The truth was that an idea I'd presented in a business meeting the week before had been challenged and later, shot down. I didn't think it really mattered at first, but after hearing my friend's remarks, I began to wonder if I were being honest with myself.

Several weeks later, I phoned this friend to thank him for confronting me about my behavior. I briefly told him about the business meeting and said, "Realizing I was hurt because my idea was rejected has enabled me to be honest with the Lord about my feelings and begin working through them."

"I'm sorry about what happened," he said, "but I appreciate your honesty, and think it's great that you're doing something constructive with a difficult situation."

Over time, I began to confide in this friend about other problems I

3

encountered. He helped me a great deal. At times, he would say, "Here's how I'd feel in your situation. I'd be angry because.... Do *you* feel angry?" Or, "I'd be hurt because.... Do *you* feel hurt?"

In the light of his honesty and love, and through the gracious work of the Holy Spirit, I began to be honest with myself and with God. The tough exterior I had developed started cracking, and I began to experience the pain I had neither wanted nor allowed myself to feel. This was hardly pleasant, but acknowledging the presence of hurt in my life was my first step toward finding comfort.

Why do some of us lack objectivity? Why can't we see the reality of our lives? Why are we afraid to "turn on the lights"?

There are a number of answers to these questions, and they vary for each person. Perhaps we think that our situations are "normal," that experiencing loneliness, hurt, and anger is really all there is to life. Perhaps we want to be "good Christians," and believing that *good* Christians don't have problems or feelings like ours, we deny the existence of our painful emotions. Perhaps our lack of objectivity is a learned response from childhood. All of us desperately want our parents to be loving and supportive. If ours aren't (or weren't), we may protect our concept of them by blaming ourselves for their lack of love, and deny that we have been hurt by their behavior.

Human beings develop elaborate defense mechanisms to block pain and gain significance. We suppress emotions; we are compulsive perfectionists; we drive ourselves to succeed, or withdraw and become passive; we attack people who hurt us; we punish ourselves when we fail; we try to say clever things to be accepted; we help people so that we will be appreciated; and we say and do countless other things.

A sense of need usually propels us to look for an alternative. We may have the courage to examine ourselves and may desperately want to change, but may be unsure of how and where to start. We may refuse to look honestly within for fear of what we'll find, or we may be afraid that even if we can discover what's wrong, nothing can help us.

It is difficult—if not impossible—to turn on the light of objectivity by ourselves. We need guidance from the Holy Spirit, as well as the honesty, love, and encouragement of at least one other person who's willing to help us. Even then, we may become depressed as we begin to discover the effects of our wounds. Some of us have deep emotional and spiritual scars resulting from the neglect, abuse, and manipulation that often accompany living in a dysfunctional family (alcoholism, drug abuse, divorce, absent father or mother, excessive anger, verbal and/or physical abuse, etc.), but all of us bear the effects of our own sinful nature and the imperfections of others.

Whether your hurts are deep or relatively mild, it is wise to be honest about them in the context of affirming relationships so that healing can begin.

Many of us mistakenly believe that God doesn't want us to be honest about our lives. We think that He will be upset with us if we tell Him how we really feel. But the Scriptures tell us that God does not want us to be superficial—in our relationship with Him, with others, or in our own lives. David wrote, *Surely you desire truth in the inner parts; you teach me wisdom in the inmost place* (Ps. 51:6, NIV).

The Lord desires truth and honesty at the deepest level, and wants us to experience His love, forgiveness, and power in *all* areas of our lives. Experiencing His love does not mean that all of our thoughts, emotions, and behaviors will be pleasant and pure. It means that we can be *real*, feeling pain and joy, love and anger, confidence and confusion.

The Psalms give us tremendous insight about what it means to be honest with the Lord. David and other psalmists wrote and spoke honestly about the full range of their responses to situations. For example, David expressed his anger with the Lord because he felt abandoned by Him:

> *I say to God my Rock, "Why have you forgotten me?*
> *Why must I go about mourning, oppressed by the enemy?"*
> Ps. 42:9-10, NIV

At times, David was very angry with others, and expressed that anger to the Lord in terms that reveal the depth of his feelings:

> *Break the teeth in their mouths, O God; tear out, O Lord, the fangs of the lions!*
> *Let them vanish like water that flows away; when they draw the bow, let their arrows be blunted.*
> *Like a slug melting away as it moves along, like a stillborn child, may they not see the sun.*
> *Before your pots can feel the heat of the thorns—whether they be green or dry—the wicked will be swept away.*
>
> Ps. 58:6-9, NIV

David wrote of his despair about difficult situations:

> *My heart is in anguish within me; the terrors of death assail me.*
> *Fear and trembling have beset me; horror has overwhelmed me.*
>
> Ps. 55:4-5, NIV

And he communicated his despair to the Lord:

> *Why do you hide your face and forget our misery and oppression?*
> *We are brought down to the dust; our bodies cling to the ground.*
>
> Ps. 44:24-25, NIV

Sometimes, he was confused:

> *How long, O Lord? Will you forget me forever? How long will you hide your face from me?*

How long must I wrestle with my thoughts and every day have sorrow in my heart?

Ps. 13:1-2, NIV

Sometimes, David communicated his love for the Lord:

As the deer pants for streams of water, so my soul pants for you, O God.

My soul thirsts for God, for the living God. When can I go and meet with God?

Ps. 42:1-2, NIV

At times, David trusted in the Lord:

The Lord is my light and my salvation—whom shall I fear? The Lord is the stronghold of my life—of whom shall I be afraid?

When evil men advance against me to devour my flesh, when my enemies and my foes attack me, they will stumble and fall.

Though an army besiege me, my heart will not fear; though war break out against me, even then I will be confident.

Ps. 27:1-3, NIV

At other times, he was filled with praise for God:

I will exalt you, my God the King; I will praise your name for ever and ever.

Every day I will praise you and extol your name for ever and ever.

Great is the Lord and most worthy of praise; his greatness no one can fathom.

Ps. 145:1-3, NIV

These passages demonstrate that God, who spoke of David as a man after His own heart, wants us to be open and honest with Him about *all* of our emotions, not just the pleasant ones.

Some people can read passages like these and begin moving toward healing and health rather quickly. Others, however, may read and study, go to seminars and meetings—they may even be in relationships where they are loved and encouraged—but they may not see substantive change in their lives and patterns of behavior. One reason for this spiritual and emotional inertia is a sense of hopelessness. For various reasons (family background, past experiences, poor modeling), we may have negative presumptions which determine our receptivity to love and truth. In some cases, God's light may have revealed our pain and wall of defenses, but it may not yet have penetrated to our deepest thoughts and beliefs about ourselves. These beliefs may not be clearly articulated, but often reflect misperceptions such as these:

- *God doesn't really care about me.*
- *I am an unlovable, worthless person. Nobody will ever love me.*
- *I'll never be able to change.*
- *I've been a failure all my life. I guess I'll always be a failure.*
- *If people really knew me, they wouldn't like me.*

When the light of love and honesty shines on thoughts of hopelessness, it is often very painful. We begin to admit that we really do feel negatively about ourselves—and have for a long time. But God's love, expressed through His people, and woven into our lives by His Spirit and His Word can, over a period of time, bring healing even to our deepest wounds and instill within us an appropriate sense of self-worth.

The purpose of this book is to provide clear, biblical instruction about the basis of your self-worth by helping you:

1. Identify and understand the nature of man's search for significance.

2.   Recognize and challenge inadequate answers.
3.   Apply God's solutions to *your* search for significance.

This is a process which we will examine throughout the following pages. At this point, simply ask the Lord to give you the courage to be honest. Give Him permission to shine His Spirit's light on your thoughts, feelings, and actions. You may be surprised by additional pain as you realize the extent of your wounds, but our experience of healing can only be as deep as our awareness of the need for it. This takes the power of God's light. Ask Him to turn on the light.

Author's Note:

With the proliferation of books on both secular and Christian psychology, it is helpful to get a perspective of the biblical principles taught in *The Search for Significance*.

Some Christian counselors and authors observe the pain caused by low self-esteem, and try to inflate a person's ego so that he will feel better about himself. Often, this is simply "positive mental attitude" material in Christian lingo.

Some authors and counselors abhor the shallowness of this "let's all feel good about ourselves" approach, but their response takes them to the other extreme. They camp on Christ's teaching that we should hate our lives in order to be His disciples, excluding the abundant and clear teaching of Christ's love, forgiveness, and acceptance. This harsh, out-of-balance approach may be stimulating to someone who is very secure in Christ, but it is devastating to most of us.

A healthy, positive self-esteem is not attained by "feel good" superficiality. On the other hand, a Christ-centered view of ourselves is not detrimental to true discipleship; it is the result of understanding and applying the truths of the Scriptures. A proper view of God and of ourselves enables us to love, obey, and honor Christ with full hearts. Paul wrote, *For through the grace given to me I say to every man among you not to think more highly of himself than he ought to think; but to think so as to have sound judgment* ... (Rom. 12:3). This sound judgment is not based on either pop psychology or spiritual masochism. Sound judgment is based squarely on God's truth. *The Search for Significance* is designed to present His truth clearly.

Two
Our Search for Significance

Relatively few of us experience the blend of contentment and godly intensity that God desires for each person. From life's outset, we find ourselves on the prowl, searching to satisfy some inner, unexplained yearning. Our hunger causes us to search for people who will love us. Our desire for acceptance pressures us to perform for the praise of others. We strive for success, driving our minds and bodies harder and farther, hoping that because of our sweat and sacrifice, others will appreciate us more.

But the man or woman who lives only for the love and attention of others is never satisfied—at least, not for long. Despite our efforts, we will never find lasting, fulfilling peace if we have to continually prove ourselves to others. Our desire to be loved and accepted is a symptom of a deeper need—the need that often governs our behavior and is the primary source of our emotional pain. Often unrecognized, this is our need for self-worth.

The case of Mark and Beth aptly demonstrates this great need. During their final semester at Cornell University, Mark and Beth fell in love. Beth's eyes sparkled, her walk had that certain lightness, and she found it difficult to concentrate on her studies. As she and Mark gazed into each other's eyes, Beth saw the special affection she had always desired. She felt that her need to feel valued and loved would be fulfilled through their relationship. Likewise, Mark was encouraged and motivated by

Beth's acceptance and admiration of him. With her support, Mark thought he could boldly begin a successful career after graduation.

The summer after they graduated from Cornell, Mark and Beth married, believing their love would provide them both with a permanent sense of self-worth. Unfortunately, they were depending on each other to fill a void that could only be filled by their Creator. Each expected the other to always be loving, accepting, and forgiving, but soon both were disillusioned and even felt betrayed by the other. As the years passed, affirmation was replaced by sarcasm and ridicule. Because each had anticipated that the other would consistently provide love and acceptance, each failure to do so was another brick in their wall of hurt and separation. Recently, Mark and Beth celebrated their tenth wedding anniversary. Sadly, although they had shared ten years with each other, they had experienced very little true, unconditional love for each other. Their search for self-worth and significance ended in despair.

Another example illustrates how the promise of fulfillment through success is an empty one, often resulting in tragic consequences for ourselves and those around us:

Brad and Lisa had been married for twelve years. Brad was a successful lawyer, and Lisa was a homemaker extensively involved in church activities. Their two sons, six-year-old Kyle and eight-year-old David, were well-behaved boys. Although their family appeared to be a model of perfection to those around them, Brad and Lisa were beginning to experience some real problems. True, Brad's law practice was flourishing, but at the expense of Lisa and the boys. He arrived home later and later each evening, and often spent the weekend locked in his office. Brad was driven to succeed, believing that satisfaction and contentment were always just one more trial victory away. But each success gave him only temporary fulfillment. *Maybe the next one....*

Brad would not allow anything to interfere with his success, not even the needs of his family. At first, Lisa seemed to understand. She knew Brad's work was important and hated to protest when he was so busy. Not wanting to burden him, she began to feel guilty for talking to him about family problems. But as the weeks turned into months, and Brad remained obsessed with his work, Lisa became resentful. Even though it was painful, she could overlook her own needs, but the boys needed their father. The family never had time to be together any more, and Brad's promises had begun to sound hollow. "When this big case is over, the pressure will be off," he'd say, but there was always another case. Brad was continually solving other people's problems, but never those of his own family. Realizing that she and the boys weren't important to him, Lisa became bitter and depressed.

As Brad and Lisa's problems persisted, they became obvious to others. Friends began asking Lisa what was wrong. Finding it difficult at first to be honest about the situation, Lisa eventually shared her feelings. She was both hurt and surprised by the glib responses she received from well-meaning but insensitive friends. "Just trust the Lord," one said. Another close friend advised, "You shouldn't have any problems, Lisa. You're a Christian. With God's help, you can work it out."

Like falling on a jagged rock, these comments hurt deeply. Lisa began to doubt herself and wonder if she were capable of building a successful marriage and family. Feeling like a failure, she reasoned that perhaps she deserved a broken marriage; perhaps her problems with Brad were her fault and God was punishing her for her sins.

Confused and frustrated, both Brad and Lisa were searching for significance in their own ways—Brad in his success as an attorney, and Lisa in her success as a wife and mother. Their lives began to reflect that strange combination of hopelessness and compulsion. Sadly, neither Brad nor Lisa realized that their search should both begin and end with God's Word.

In the Scriptures, God supplies the essentials for discovering our true significance and worth. The first two chapters of Genesis recount man's creation, revealing man's intended purpose (to honor God) and man's value (that he is a special creation of God). John 10:10 also reminds us of how much God treasures His creation, in that Christ came so that man might experience "abundant life." However, as Christians, we need to

13

realize that this abundant life is lived in a real world filled with pain, rejection, and failure. Therefore, experiencing the abundant life God intends for us does not mean that our lives will be problem-free. On the contrary, life itself is a series of problems that often act as obstacles to our search for significance, and the abundant life is the experience of God's love, forgiveness, and power in the midst of these problems. The Scriptures warn us that we live within a warfare that can destroy our faith, lower our self-esteem, and lead us into depression. In his letter to the Ephesians, Paul instructs us to put on the armor of God so that we can be equipped for spiritual battle. However, it often seems that unsuspecting believers are the last to know this battle is occurring, and that Christ has ultimately won the war. They are surprised and confused by difficulties, thinking that the Christian life is a playground, not a battlefield.

As Christians, our fulfillment in this life depends not on our skills to avoid life's problems, but on our ability to apply God's specific solutions to those problems. An accurate understanding of God's truth is the first step toward discovering our significance and worth. Unfortunately, many of us have been exposed to inadequate teaching from both religious and secular sources concerning our self-worth. As a result, we may have a distorted self-perception, and may be experiencing hopelessness rather than the rich and meaningful life God intends for us.

Christian psychologist, Lawrence J. Crabb, Jr., describes our need for self-esteem this way: "The basic personal need of each person is to regard himself as a worthwhile human being." And, according to William Glasser, "Everyone aspires to have a happy, successful, pleasurable belief in himself."

Some secular psychologists focus on self-worth with a goal of simply feeling good about ourselves. A biblical self-concept, however, goes far beyond that limited perspective. It is an accurate perception of ourselves, God, and others based on the truths of God's Word. An accurate, biblical self-concept contains both strength and humility, both sorrow over sin and joy about forgiveness, a deep sense of our need for God's grace and a deep sense of the reality of God's grace.

14

Whether labeled "self-esteem" or "self-worth," the feeling of significance is crucial to man's emotional, spiritual, and social stability, and is the driving element within the human spirit. Understanding this single need opens the door to understanding our actions and attitudes.

What a waste to attempt to change behavior without truly understanding the driving needs that cause such behavior! Yet, millions of people spend a lifetime searching for love, acceptance, and success without understanding the need that compels them. We must understand that this hunger for self-worth is God-given and can only be satisfied by Him. Our value is not dependent on our ability to earn the fickle acceptance of people, but rather, its true source is the love and acceptance of God. He created us. He alone knows how to fulfill *all* of our needs.

In order to fully understand the provisions that God has made for our self-worth, we must look back to man's beginning—to the first man and woman, and their search for significance.

Three
The Origin of the Search

The Old Testament depicts the original incident of sin and the Fall of Man:

> *When the woman saw that the tree was good for food, and that it was a delight to the eyes, and that the tree was desirable to make one wise, she took from its fruit and ate; and she gave also to her husband with her, and he ate.*
> *Then the eyes of both of them were opened, and they knew that they were naked; and they sewed fig leaves together and made themselves loin coverings.*
>
> Gen. 3:6-7

To understand the devastating effects of this event properly, we need to examine the nature of man before sin caused him to lose his security and significance.

The first created man lived in unclouded, intimate fellowship with God. He was secure and free. In all of God's creation, no creature compared to him. Indeed, Adam was a magnificent creation, complete and perfect in the image of God, designed to reign over all the earth (Gen. 1:26-28). Adam's purpose was to reflect the glory of God. Through man, God wanted to demonstrate His holiness (Ps. 99:3-5); love and patience (1 Cor. 13:4); forbearance (1 Cor. 13:7); wisdom (James 3:13, 17); comfort (2 Cor. 1:3-4); forgiveness (Heb. 10:17); faithfulness (Ps. 89:1, 2, 5, 8); and grace (Ps. 111:4). Through his intellect, free will, and emotions, man was to be the showcase for God's glorious character.

Adam was, therefore, a very important creation to God. To meet his needs for companionship and understanding, God created a woman for Adam and gave her to him as his wife. In keeping with their perfect character, God placed Adam and Eve in a perfect environment—a lush, beautiful garden where the Creator Himself provided for their physical needs. Adam and Eve had the challenge and responsibility of supervising this paradise of vegetation and animal life. To satisfy Adam and Eve's spiritual needs, God visited them and talked with them personally. Adam and Eve were perfect in body, mind, and spirit.

Like Adam and Eve, Satan also was created in perfection. At the time of his creation, his name was Lucifer, which means "morning star." He was an angel of the highest rank, created to glorify God. He was clothed with beauty and power, and was allowed to serve in the presence of God. Sadly, Lucifer's pride caused him to rebel against God, and he was cast from heaven with a third of the angels (Is. 14:12-15). When he appeared to Adam and Eve in the garden, it was in the form of a serpent, *more crafty than any beast of the field which the Lord God had made* (Gen. 3:1).

Adam had been given authority over the earth, but if he, like Lucifer, rebelled against God, he would lose both his authority and perfection. He would become a slave to Satan and to sin (Rom. 6:17), and a child of God's wrath (Eph. 2:3). Therefore, destroying man was Satan's way to reign on earth and, he apparently thought, to thwart God's glorious plan for man.

To accomplish his goal, Satan began by deceiving Eve, who fell to the temptation. Eve ate of the tree of the knowledge of good and evil, believing it would make her wise and like God. Adam, however, was not deceived. He deliberately chose to forsake the love and security of God and follow Eve in sin. Paul explained this fact to Timothy:

And it was not Adam who was deceived, but the woman being quite deceived, fell into transgression.

1 Tim. 2:14

In doing this, Adam not only lost the glory God had intended for mankind, but he also forfeited his close communion and fellowship with God. Adam's deliberate rebellion also aided Satan's purpose, giving him power and authority on earth. From that moment on, all history led to a single hill outside of Jerusalem, where God appointed a Savior to pay the penalty for man's sin of rebellion.

Though we justly deserve the wrath of God because of that deliberate rebellion (our attempts to find security and purpose apart from Him), His Son became our substitute, experienced the wrath our rebellion deserves, and paid the penalty for our sins. Christ's death is the most overwhelming evidence of God's love for us. Because Christ paid for our sins, our relationship with God has been restored, and we are able to partake of His nature and character, to commune with Him, and to reflect His love to all the world.

Spread the good news! Man is not lost forever! God has not given up on us! He has bought us out of slavery to sin by the payment of Christ's death on the cross. Satan's rule can be broken and we can reign with Christ. We can be restored to the security and significance for which we have been created—not simply in eternity, but here and now as well.

We must never forget that God wants His children to bear His image and to rule with Him. Adam's sin has had tragic consequences, but through God's plan of redemption, we can still have the unspeakable privilege of relating to Him. God has provided the solution, but the question is this: Will we accept Christ's death as the payment for our sins and discover the powerful implications of our salvation, or will we continue to follow Satan's lies and deceptions?

Perhaps you are unsure of your relationship with God and need to deal conclusively with this choice now. We cannot pay for our sins; Christ has already done this for us as a free gift. Paul wrote to the Ephesian Christians:

> *For by grace* (unmerited favor) *you have been saved* (rescued from spiritual death—hell) *through faith* (trust); *and that not of yourselves, it is the gift of God;*
>   *not as a result of works, that no one should boast.*
> Eph. 2:8-9

Are you trusting in your own abilities to earn acceptance with God, or are you trusting in the death of Christ to pay for your sins, and the resurrection of Christ to give you new life? Take a moment to reflect on this question: On a scale of 0-100 percent, how sure are you that you would spend eternity with God if you died today? An answer of less than 100 percent may indicate that you are trusting, at least in part, in yourself. You may be thinking, *Isn't it arrogant to say that I am 100 percent sure?* Indeed, it would be arrogance if you were trusting in yourself—your abilities, your actions, and good deeds—to earn your salvation. However, if you are no longer trusting in your own efforts, but in the all-sufficient payment of Christ, then 100 percent certainty is a response of humility and thankfulness, not arrogance.

Reflect on a second question: If you were to die today and stand before God, and He were to ask you, "Why should I let you into heaven?" what would you tell Him? Would you mention your abilities, church attendance, kindness to others, Christian service, abstinence from a particular sin, or some other good deed? Paul wrote to Titus:

> *But when the kindness of God our Savior and His love for mankind appeared,*
>   *He saved us, not on the basis of deeds which we have done in righteousness, but according to His mercy....*
> Titus 3:4-5

We must give up our own efforts to achieve righteousness, and instead believe that Christ's death and resurrection alone are sufficient to pay for our sin and separation from God.

Perhaps you have intellectually believed that Jesus Christ lived 2,000 years ago, performed miracles, died on the cross, and was raised from the dead. Perhaps you have even felt close to God at times in your life. But biblical faith is more than intellectual assent or warm emotions.

Consider the analogy of a wedding: An engaged couple may intellectually know they want to marry each other, and probably feel very close to one another, but until they willfully say, "I do" to each other, they are not married. Many people are at this point in their relationship with Christ. They need to say, *I do* to Him.

If there is any question about whether you have conclusively accepted Christ's substitutionary death to pay for the wrath you deserve for your sins, take some time to think about the two questions we have examined, and reflect on His love and forgiveness. Then, respond by trusting in Christ and accepting His payment for your sins. You can use this prayer to express your faith:

> *Lord Jesus, I need You. I want You to be my Savior and Lord.*
> *I accept Your death on the cross as the complete payment for*
> *my sins. Thank You for forgiving me and for giving me new life.*
> *Help me to grow in my understanding of Your love and power*
> *so that my life will bring honor to You. Amen.*

The moment you trust Christ, many wonderful things happen to you:

All your sins are forgiven: past, present, and future
(Col. 2:13-14).
You become a child of God (John 1:12; Rom. 8:15).
You receive eternal life (John 5:24).
You are delivered from Satan's domain and transferred into the kingdom of Christ (Col. 1:13).

Christ comes to dwell within you (Col. 1:27; Rev. 3:20).
You become a new creation (2 Cor. 5:17).
You are declared righteous by God (2 Cor. 5:21).
You enter into a love relationship with God (1 John 4:9-11).
You are accepted by God (Col. 1:19-22).

Think on the implications of these truths in your life. Then, thank God for His wonderful grace and experience *the love of Christ which surpasses knowledge* (Eph. 3:19).

Some people may ask, "How does baptism relate to this conversion experience?" Water baptism is a visible demonstration of a believer's internal conversion to Christ. It enables the believer to identify himself with Christ in his culture. The act of baptism symbolizes his being dead, buried, and raised with Christ. In the early church and in some countries today, this identification is a dramatic statement of being severed from the world and being bonded to the body of Christ. In our society, it is still an important step of obedience as we identify ourselves publicly with Christ and His people. (For a sample of passages on Spirit baptism and water baptism, see Acts 8:26-39; Rom. 6:1-4, and 1 Cor. 12:13.)

Four
The Saving Solution vs. Satan's Snare

Satan, the father of lies, twists and distorts the truth so that his deceptions appear to be more reasonable and attractive than the truth. Notice how Satan snared Eve. He told her:

> *For God knows that in the day you eat from it your eyes will be opened, and you will be like God, knowing good and evil.*
>
> Gen. 3:5

Here, Satan directly questioned God's truthfulness, implying that Eve could have greater significance apart from God, and that eating the forbidden fruit would reveal hidden knowledge, enabling her to know good from evil like God Himself.

Being deceived, Eve traded God's truth for the serpent's lie. She ate the forbidden fruit. Then, Adam followed her in sinful rebellion against God, and he, too, ate the forbidden fruit. One of the tragic implications of this event is that man lost his secure status with God and began to struggle with feelings of arrogance, inadequacy, and despair, valuing the opinions of others more than the truth of God. This has robbed man of his true self-worth and has put him on a continual, but fruitless, search for significance through his success and the approval of others.

In one form or another, Satan's lie still thrives today. For example, humanism, the central philosophy of our schools and society, teaches that man is above all else, that he alone is the center of meaning. Teaching that man has meaning totally apart from God, humanism leaves morality, justice, and behavior to the discretion of "enlightened" man and encourages people to worship man and nature rather than God. Living without God's divine truth, humanity sinks lower and lower in depravity, blindly following a philosophy that intends to heighten the dignity of man, but which instead lowers him to the level of animals. Rather than a spiritual and emotional being, man has been classified as merely natural phenomena of time plus chance, no greater than rocks, animals, or clouds. The Apostle Paul described this foolish and demeaning perspective of man in Rom. 1:20-25:

> *For since the creation of the world His invisible attributes, His eternal power and divine nature, have been clearly seen, being understood through what has been made, so that they are without excuse.*
>
> *For even though they knew God, they did not honor Him as God, or give thanks; but they became futile in their speculations, and their foolish heart was darkened.*
>
> *Professing to be wise, they became fools,*
>
> *and exchanged the glory of the incorruptible God for an image in the form of corruptible man and of birds and four-footed animals and crawling creatures.*
>
> *Therefore God gave them over in the lusts of their hearts to impurity, that their bodies might be dishonored among them.*
>
> *For they exchanged the truth of God for a lie, and worshiped and served the creature rather than the Creator, who is blessed forever. Amen.*

In the beginning, God declared that man was created to reign with Him; however, man rejected God's truth and chose instead to believe Satan's lie. Today, man continues to reject God's truth and offer of salvation through Jesus Christ. He chooses instead to trust in his success and the opinions of others to give him a sense of self-worth, though the Scriptures clearly teach that apart from Christ, man is enslaved to sin and condemned to an eternity in hell.

Since the Fall, man has often failed to turn to God for the truth about himself. Instead, he has looked to others to meet his inescapable need for self-worth. *I am what others say I am,* he has reasoned. *I will find my value in their opinions of me.*

Isn't it amazing that we turn to others who have a perspective as limited and darkened as our own to discover our worth! Rather than relying on God's steady, uplifting reassurance of who we are, we depend on others who base our worth on our ability to meet their standards.

Because our performance and ability to please others so dominates our search for significance, we have difficulty recognizing the distinction between our real identity and the way we behave, a realization crucial to understanding our true worth. Our true value is not based on our behavior or the approval of others, but on what God's Word says is true of us.

Our behavior is often a reflection of our beliefs about who we are. It is usually consistent with what we think to be true about ourselves (Prov. 23:7). If we base our worth solidly on the truths of God's Word, then our behavior will often reflect His love, grace, and power. But if we base our worth on our abilities or the fickle approval of others, then our behavior will reflect the insecurity, fear, and anger that comes from such instability.

Though we usually behave in ways that are consistent with our beliefs, at times, our actions may contradict them. For example, we may believe that we are generous and gracious, when we are actually very selfish. Sometimes, our behavior changes what we believe about ourselves. If, for instance, we succeed in a task at which we initially believed we would fail, our confidence may begin to grow and expand to other areas of our lives. Our feelings, behavior, and beliefs all interact to shape our lives.

Our home environment plays a central role in forming our beliefs and emotions, and these can have a powerful impact on our outlook and behavior.

This truth is evident in the case of Scott. Scott grew up in a home without praise, discouraged by his parents whenever he attempted anything new and challenging. After twenty years of hearing, "You'll never be able to do anything, Scott, so don't even try," he believed it himself. Neither Scott nor his parents could later understand why he had flunked out of college and was continually shuffling from one job to another, never able to achieve success. Believing he was doing the best he could do, but suspecting he would always fail, Scott consistently performed according to his self-perception.

Separated from God and His Word, people have only their abilities and the opinions of others on which to base their worth, and the circumstances around them ultimately control the way they feel about themselves.

Take the case of Stacy, a young girl who became pregnant when she was seventeen. Stacy gave her baby up for adoption, and only her family and a few close friends knew of the incident. Several years later, Stacy fell in love with a compassionate man named Ron and married him. Fearing his reaction, she didn't tell Ron about the baby.

Over the years, Stacy concealed her guilt and grief until the pressure finally became so overwhelming that she admitted the entire episode to him.

Surprisingly, Ron did not respond in anger. He understood the agony his wife had carried for so many years and loved her in spite of her past. It was Stacy who could not cope at this point. Unable to accept Ron's forgiveness, and knowing she had failed according to society's standards, Stacy felt unworthy of his love. Stacy refused to forgive herself and chose to leave her husband.

In this case, Stacy fell victim to one of Satan's most effective lies: *Those who fail are unworthy of love and deserve to be blamed and condemned.* Because she failed in her own eyes, Stacy's perception of herself was detrimentally affected.

Each of us has probably failed badly at some point in our lives. Perhaps some particular sin or weakness has caused us to feel condemned and unworthy of love. Without the hope and healing that God can provide, our evaluation of ourselves will eventually lead to despair.

In spite of Adam and Eve's sin, God's plan is to bring man back to the destiny for which he was originally created—to bear His image. To accomplish this, God gives a new nature to all who believe in Christ. This new nature is able to reflect God's character and rule His creation. In Luke 10:19, Jesus spoke of the authority of this new nature when He said, *Behold, I have given you authority to tread upon serpents and scorpions, and over all the power of the enemy, and nothing shall injure you.*

Satan, however, continues to deceive people, including many Christians, into believing that the basis of their worth is their performance and their ability to please others. The equation below reflects Satan's lie:

SELF-WORTH = PERFORMANCE + OTHERS' OPINIONS

Can we overcome Satan's deception and reject this basis of our self-worth? Can we trust God's complete acceptance of us as His sons and daughters, and allow Him to free us from our dependency on success and the approval of others? Rejecting Satan's lie and accepting God's evaluation of us leads to a renewed hope, joy, and purpose in life.

We all have compelling, God-given needs for love, acceptance, and purpose, and most of us will go to virtually any lengths to meet those needs. Many of us have become masters at "playing the game" to be successful and win the approval of others. Some of us, however, have failed and have experienced the pain of disapproval so often that we have given up and have withdrawn into a shell of hurt, numbness, or depression. In both cases, we are living by the deception that our worth is based on our performance and others' opinions—some of us are simply more adept at playing this game than others.

Our attempts to meet our needs for success and approval fall into two broad categories: compulsiveness and withdrawal.

Some people expend extra effort, work extra hours, and try to say just the right thing to achieve success and please those around them. These people may have a compelling desire to be in control of every situation. They are perfectionists. If a job isn't done perfectly, if they aren't dressed just right, if they aren't considered "the best" by their peers, then they work harder until they achieve that coveted status. And woe to the poor soul who gets in their way! Whoever doesn't contribute to their success and acclaim is a threat to their self-esteem—an unacceptable threat. They may be very personable and have a lot of "friends," but the goal of these relationships may not be to give encouragement and love; it may be to manipulate others to contribute to their success. That may sound harsh, but people who are driven to succeed will often use practically everything and everybody to meet that need.

The other broad category is withdrawal. Those who manifest this behavior usually try to avoid failure and disapproval by avoiding risks. They won't volunteer for the jobs that offer much risk of failure. They gravitate toward people who are comforting and kind, skirting relationships that might demand vulnerability, and consequently, the risk of rejection. They may appear to be easygoing, but inside they are usually running from every potential situation or relationship that might not succeed.

Obviously, these are two broad categories. Most of us exhibit some combination of the two behaviors, willing to take risks and work hard in the areas where we feel sure of success, but avoiding the people and situations that may bring rejection and failure.

Rob and Kathy had dated for three years. Kathy was a perfectionist. Her clothes, her hair, her work, her car...and her boyfriend had to be perfect. Rob, a good-natured, fun-loving fellow, was not as concerned with such details. Predictably, the more intense Kathy became about having everything and everybody "just right," the more passive and easygoing Rob became. This spiral of intensity and passivity continued until Rob and Kathy hit rock bottom.

After several weeks of counseling, Kathy saw that her perfectionism came from a misplaced base of security: her performance instead of Christ. But Rob said that he didn't have a problem with performance. He certainly didn't have a compelling drive to succeed, and he didn't pressure people around him to "get their act together." In the midst of these explanations, I asked, "But Rob, what about your tendency to withdraw? Why do you think you do that?" It still didn't compute.

Finally, after several months, Rob understood. He based his security on his performance just as much as Kathy did, but he handled it differently. She became more compulsive to have things "just right," while he withdrew to avoid failure. Both slowly began to recognize the root of their problems, and through months of encouragement and honest interaction, they started believing that their worth is secure in Christ. Today, Kathy is less intense about her performance, and Rob doesn't run from failure as much as he used to. They are learning to channel their intensity toward the right things: Christ and His kingdom.

When we base our security on success and others' opinions, we become dependent on our abilities to perform and please others. We develop a *have-to* mentality: *I have to do well on this exam (or my security as a "good student" will be threatened); I have to make that deal (or it will mean that my boss will think I am a failure); My father (or mother, spouse, or friend) has to appreciate me and be happy with my decisions (because I cannot cope with his disapproval).*

Our self-esteem and view of God are usually a mirror of our parents' attitudes toward us. Those who are loved and affirmed by their parents tend to have a fairly healthy self-concept, and usually find it easy to believe that God is loving and powerful. Those whose parents have been neglectful, manipulative, or condemning usually seem to feel that they have to earn a sense of worth, and that God is aloof, demanding, and/or cruel.

Our parents are our models of the character of God. When we do not have that fundamental sense of feeling lovable and protected by them, then we tend to base our self-worth on how well we perform and please others, instead of on what the sovereign God of the universe, our all-wise, omniscient Savior says of us.

We do not *have to* be successful or *have to* be pleasing to others to have a healthy sense of self-esteem and worth. That worth has freely and conclusively been given to us by God. Failure and/or the disapproval of others can't take it away! Therefore, we can conclude, *It would be nice to be approved by my parents* (or whomever), *but if they don't approve of me, I'm still loved and accepted by God.* Do you see the difference? The *have-to* mentality is sheer slavery to performance and the opinions of others, but we are secure and free in Christ. We don't *have to* have success or anyone else's approval. Of course, it would be nice to have success and approval, but the point is clear: Christ is the source of our security; Christ is the basis of our worth; Christ is the only One who promises and never fails.

The transition from the slavery and compulsion of a *have-to* mentality to the freedom and strength of a *want-to* motivation is a process. Bondage to such thinking is often deeply rooted in our personalities, patterns of behavior, and ways of relating to other people. These patterns of thinking, feeling, and responding—learned over time—flow as naturally as the course of rainwater in a dry desert riverbed. Changing them requires time, the encouragement of others, the truth and application of God's Word, and the power of God's Spirit.

This book is dedicated to the process of understanding, applying, and experiencing the foundational truths of God's Word. In the remaining chapters, we will examine the process of hope and healing. We will also identify four specific false beliefs generated by Satan's deception. In addition, we will discover God's gracious, effective, and permanent solution to our search for significance.

Five
The Process of Hope and Healing

In the first chapter of this book, we saw that Tim Woodall had a car accident late in the evening on a lonely country highway in East Texas. Tim was broken and bleeding, but because he was in shock, he was completely unaware of the extent of his injuries.

Aided by their car's headlights, the Johnsons realized that Tim needed immediate attention, and took him to the nearest hospital. Tim stayed there for three days. The doctors waited for the swelling in his leg to go down before putting it in a cast, and then kept him for observation, knowing that the blow to his head might have caused a concussion.

Tim's wife took him home from the hospital, and after a week or so, the pain in his leg began to subside, and the stitches were removed from his head and arm. Tim wasn't sure which was worse: limping around on his crutches, or looking at himself in the mirror. The nurse had shaved a portion of his scalp for the stitches, and his new appearance took some getting used to for everyone—but especially for Tim.

Three months later, Tim's cast was removed, and a new hairstyle gave him a far more presentable appearance. It was several more months before he was able to build strength back into his leg muscles again, but after awhile, the only marks left from the accident were the scars, which weren't readily noticeable.

Tim's rehabilitation was a process. It wasn't spontaneous. His injuries required attention and expert care. Emotional, spiritual, and relational healing is a process, too. It doesn't happen overnight, but it can happen.

Several elements are required for emotional healing. These are not consecutive steps to be accomplished one after the other. They are ingredients which promote healing by working together simultaneously over a period of time. These elements are honesty; affirming relationships; right thinking; the Holy Spirit's power, strength, and wisdom; and time. If any of these is missing, then the healing process will be hindered, if not completely stifled.

Let's examine these ingredients:

Honesty

As we noted in chapter 1, we can apply and experience healing only to the depth that we are aware of our need for it. If we are completely unaware of our need, we won't seek a solution. If we are only superficially aware of our need and honest about it, we may only seek (and find) superficial remedies. But if we are encouraged to be honest about our painful needs at a deeper level, then we can experience the power of healing and comfort at that level.

Affirming Relationships

People seldom have the objectivity and the courage to be honest about reality in their lives without some affirmation from others. The love, strength, and honesty we find in other people are tangible expressions of those traits that are characteristic of God. A friend, a small group, a pastor, or a counselor who won't be frustrated by our slow progress—and who won't give us quick and easy solutions—is a valuable find! (Of course, it is always wise to use discretion and discernment regarding what and with whom we share. The act of sharing is a responsibility.) Pray that God will provide a person or group of persons with whom you can be open and honest, who can objectively listen to you and share with you, and who will encourage you to make real, rather than superficial progress.

Right Thinking

Many of us are unaware of what we really believe about God and about ourselves. We often say what we don't mean, and mean what we don't say. God's Word is our guide. It is truly *a lamp for our feet and a light for our path* (Ps. 119:105). And yet, we often experience difficulty in applying scriptural concepts to our lives because of the elaborate array of defenses we have structured over the years to protect ourselves. It is important to understand that Scripture can be used to identify and attack these defensive barriers, enabling us to experience an open and honest relationship with God:

> *For the word of God is living and active and sharper than any two-edged sword, and piercing as far as the division of soul and spirit, of both joints and marrow, and able to judge the thoughts and intentions of the heart.*
>
> *And there is no creature hidden from His sight, but all things are open and laid bare to the eyes of Him with whom we have to do.*
>
> Heb. 4:12-13

The Holy Spirit

Deep, spiritual healing requires giving attention to the whole man, to his emotional, relational, physical, and spiritual needs. The Holy Spirit is given by God to communicate His love, light, forgiveness, and power to our deepest needs. This spiritual aspect of healing is perhaps the most fundamental, because our view of God (and subsequent relationship with Him) can determine the quality and degree of health we experience in every other area of our lives.

Some of us believe that the Holy Spirit's ministry is characterized only by positive, pleasant emotions like love and joy. However, one of the miracles of the Holy Spirit's work is that of producing honesty and courage in our lives as we grapple with the reality of pain. He is the Spirit of truth, not denial, and He enables us to experience each element of the healing process as He gives us wisdom, strength, and encouragement through God's Word and other people.

Time

If we were computers, solutions to our problems would be produced in microseconds. People, however, don't change that quickly. The agrarian metaphors given in the Scriptures depict *seasons* of planting, weeding, watering, growth, and harvesting. Farmers don't expect to plant seeds in the morning and harvest their crops that afternoon. Seeds must go through a complete cycle of growth, receiving plenty of attention in the process, before they mature. In this age of instant coffee, microwave dinners, and instant banking, we tend to assume that spiritual, emotional, and relational health will be instantaneous. These unrealistic expectations only cause discouragement and disappointment.

Although this book's primary focus is on the cognitive, or right-thinking, aspect of our spiritual growth, we need to remember that all of these elements are required to produce growth and health. Our growth will be stunted and superficial if we don't give proper emphasis to honesty about our emotions, affirming relationships, right thinking promoted through biblical study and application, the ministry of the Holy Spirit, and time.

Some of us seem to respond to this environment of growth very quickly; others, after a few weeks or months; and still others, never at all. Why the difference? Why are some of us able to apply principles of growth so much more readily that others?

Again, differing factors will produce a variety of responses from different people. Those who respond quickly may not be as wounded as others, or they may already be in an environment which has prepared them for relatively rapid growth.

Some of us are in situations where one or more elements of growth are in some way missing or lacking. We may be trying to deal with our difficulties alone. We may be depending on a rigid structure of discipline for positive change, instead of blending a healthy combination of our responsibility with the Holy Spirit's enabling power. We may be expecting too much too soon, and may be experiencing disappointment with our slow results. Some of us may, in fact, be ready to quit the growth process entirely.

Those of us who can't seem to get the light turned on have the greatest difficulty in beginning this process. We can't see our problems. We may recognize that something is wrong, but can't pinpoint exactly what. Or, our defense mechanisms of denial may be so strong that we're unable to see any needs in our lives at all.

A young man asked me, "What about people from very stable backgrounds? They don't wrestle with the difficulties you're talking about, do they?"

"All of us have a fallen, sinful nature," I responded. "Because of that, we all wrestle to some degree with the fears of failure and rejection, and with feelings of inadequacy, guilt, and shame. Those from stable, loving families are usually better able to determine what their difficulties are, and be honest about them, than those who are shackled by the defense mechanisms that are often developed in dysfunctional families.

"Those from abusive, manipulative, or neglectful families have far more to overcome than those from a healthier home environment," I explained. "Alcoholism, divorce, sexual abuse, physical abuse, workaholism, drug abuse, and other major family disorders leave deep wounds. Many people from backgrounds like these have suppressed their intense hurt and anger for so long that they are simply out of touch with the reality in their lives. Therefore, just as a broken arm requires more time, attention, and therapy for healing than does a small abrasion, people suffering from deep emotional, spiritual, and relational injuries need more time, attention, love, and encouragement than those with more minor wounds. Though the process for recovery may take longer, enjoying health in these areas is still possible if all the elements of healing are applied over its duration."

Another person asked, "Why doesn't just understanding these issues work? Why isn't knowledge enough to produce change?"

"Man is a relational, physical, emotional, and spiritual being," I said. "We develop and learn and grow best in an environment of honesty, love, and affirmation, where all aspects of our nature are given the encouragement to heal."

A woman asked me, "What do I need to do to begin seeing some results?"

"Put yourself in an environment of growth, which includes all the elements of honesty, affirming relationships, right thinking, the ministry of the Holy Spirit, and time. I can't tell you how or when growth will come—but I know that it will come if you are patient and persistent."

A businessman asked, "Why do I not see much change in my life?"

After talking with him for awhile, three issues surfaced which can be common to many of us: First, this gentleman had advanced significantly in his profession by performing well and pleasing people. Although he had received promotions, raises, prestige, and comfort, he still wasn't happy. Yet, it was difficult for him to consider living by a pattern of behavior other than that which had seemingly brought him so far.

In addition, this man was afraid of how he might respond to the generosity of God's love and freedom. He feared that he would either abuse God's grace or be so changed by it that some of his friends and business associates might make fun of him and ultimately reject him.

Finally, he feared that if he did respond wholeheartedly to God's love, the Lord might test his faith by making his life miserable. "I couldn't stand that," he told me. "My life is painful now, but at least I'm used to it. If I surrender completely to God, my life might get totally out of control."

These and many other reasons make the process of spiritual, relational, emotional, and mental health elusive to many people. But again, honesty is our starting point. When we are willing to be open about our thoughts
and fears, we generally find that others have thought and felt much the same way.

Our growth toward wholeness and maturity is a journey which won't be completed until we join the Lord in heaven. The Apostle Paul understood this, and saw himself as being in the middle of this process. He wrote to the Philippian believers:

> *Not that I have already obtained it, or have already become perfect, but I press on in order that I may lay hold of that for which I was laid hold of by Christ Jesus.*
>
> Phil. 3:12

If Paul, the foremost missionary and writer of much of the New Testament, saw himself as being "in the process," we can be encouraged to continue in the process toward change as well. It will help to have reasonable expectations about our progress. Sometimes, we will experience flashes of insight and spurts of growth, but the process of healing and renewal will more often be slow and methodical. Our emotions, too, may occasionally be very pleasant and positive, but when God's light shines on another area of hurt in our lives, we will likely experience another round of pain and anger. Remember that healing can only continue as we put ourselves in an environment characterized by honesty, affirming relationships, right thinking, the Holy Spirit's love and power, and time.

Introduction to Chapters Six, Seven, Eight, and Nine

It is often helpful to see a general outline when attempting to grasp new concepts. In the next four chapters, we will examine four false beliefs resulting from Satan's deceptions with some of the consequences that accompany these beliefs. Finally, we will examine God's specific solution for our false belief system, and apply this through some practical exercises.

Remember that the specific consequences of false beliefs and resulting actions vary from person to person, depending on family background, personality traits, other relationships, and many other factors. Likewise, the application of biblical truths will vary according to the perception of the individual, the degree of his or her emotional, spiritual, and relational health, and the process by which the cognitive, relational, spiritual, and emotional elements are incorporated into his or her life. All of this takes time, but health and hope are worth it!

The chart on the following pages provides an overview of the next four chapters:

Chapter	False Beliefs
Six The Performance Trap	*I must meet certain standards in order to feel good about myself.*
Seven Approval Addict	*I must be approved (accepted) by certain others to feel good about myself.*
Eight The Blame Game	*Those who fail are unworthy of love and deserve to be punished.*
Nine Shame	*I am what I am. I cannot change. I am hopeless.*

Consequences	God's Answer
The fear of failure; perfectionism; driven to succeed; manipulating others to achieve success; withdrawal from risks.	**Justification** *Justification means that God has not only forgiven me of my sins, but has also granted me the righteousness of Christ. Because of justification, I bear Christ's righteousness and am, therefore, fully pleasing to the Father* (Rom. 5:1).
The fear of rejection; attempting to please others at any cost; overly sensitive to criticism; withdrawing from others to avoid disapproval.	**Reconcilation** *Reconciliation means that although I was at one time hostile toward God and alienated from Him, I am now forgiven and have been brought into an intimate relationship with Him. Consequently, I am totally accepted by God* (Col. 1:21-22).
The fear of punishment; punishing others; blaming others for personal failure; withdrawal from God and others; driven to avoid failure.	**Propitiation** *Propitiation means that Christ satisfied God's wrath by His death on the cross; therefore, I am deeply loved by God* (1 John 4:9-11).
Feelings of shame, hopelessness, inferiority; passivity; loss of creativity; isolation; withdrawal from others.	**Regeneration** *Regeneration means that I am a new creation in Christ* (John 3:3-6).

One man asked me, "Why do you include only *four* false beliefs? Doesn't Satan also use many others?"

"Yes," I replied, "he uses an endless variety of deceptions to confuse and distort the truth of God; yet, in my study of the Scriptures and through my interaction with people, these four seem to represent the central issues we struggle with in our desire for significance."

"Can a person experience more than one false belief in a given situation?" he asked.

"Yes, of course," I said. "Many of life's circumstances reveal that we are basing our response to a situation on more than one of Satan's lies. Usually, however, close examination will reveal that one may be more foundational. For example, I may be afraid to fail, but the real reason I fear failure could be that I'm afraid that my failure might result in the disapproval of others."

We will explore the interrelationship of misconceptions after we've identified the false beliefs in the following chapters.

Six
The Performance Trap

Most of us are unaware of how thoroughly Satan has deceived us. He has led us blindly down a path of destruction, captives of our inability to meet our standards consistently, and slaves of low self-esteem. Satan has shackled us in chains that keep us from experiencing the love, freedom, and purposes of Christ.

In Col. 2:8, Paul warns:

> *See to it that no one takes you captive through philosophy and empty deception, according to the tradition of men, according to the elementary principles of the world, rather than according to Christ.*

Indeed, we've reached a true mark of maturity when we begin testing the deceitful thoughts of our minds against the Word of God. We no longer have to live by our fleshly thoughts; we have the mind of Christ (1 Cor. 2:16). Through His Spirit, we can challenge the indoctrinations and traditions that have long held us in guilt and condemnation. We can then replace those deceptions with the powerful truths of the Scriptures.

A primary deception all of us tend to believe is that success will bring fulfillment and happiness. Again and again, we've tried to measure up, thinking that if we could meet certain standards, we would feel good about ourselves. But again and again, we've failed and have felt miserable. Even if we succeed on a fairly regular basis, occasional failure may be so devastating that it dominates our perception of ourselves.

Consciously or unconsciously, all of us have experienced this feeling that we must meet certain arbitrary standards to attain self-worth. Failure to do so threatens our security and significance. Such a threat, real or perceived, results in a fear of failure. At that point, we are accepting the false belief: *I must meet certain standards in order to feel good about myself.* When we believe this about ourselves, Satan's distortion of truth is often reflected in our attitudes and behavior.

Because of our unique personalities, we each react very differently to this deception. As we saw in a previous chapter, some of us respond by becoming slaves to perfectionism—driving ourselves incessantly toward attaining goals.

Perfectionists can be quite vulnerable to serious mood disorders, and often anticipate rejection when they believe they haven't met the standards they are trying so hard to attain. Therefore, perfectionists tend to react defensively to criticism and demand to be in control of most situations they encounter. Because they are usually more competent than most, perfectionists see nothing wrong with their compulsions. "I just like to see things done well," they claim. There is certainly nothing inherently wrong with doing things well; the problem is that perfectionists usually base their self-worth on their ability to accomplish a goal. Therefore, failure is a threat and is totally unacceptable to them.

Karen, a wife, mother, and civic leader, seemed ideal to everyone who knew her. She was a perfectionist. Her house looked perfect, her kids were spotless, and her skills as president of the Ladies' Auxiliary were superb. In each area of her life, Karen was always in charge, always successful. However, one step out of the pattern she had set could lead to a tremendous uproar. When others failed to comply with her every demand, her condemnation was quick and cruel.

One day, her husband decided that he couldn't stand any more of Karen's hypercritical behavior. He wanted an understanding wife to talk and share with, not an egocentric, self-driven perfectionist. Friends later could not understand why he chose to leave his seemingly perfect wife.

Like Karen, many high achievers are driven beyond healthy limitations. Rarely able to relax and enjoy life, they let their families and relationships suffer as they strive to accomplish often unrealistic goals.

On the other hand, the same false belief *(I must meet certain standards to feel good about myself)* that drives many to perfectionism sends others into a tailspin of despair. They rarely expect to achieve anything or to feel good about themselves. Because of their past failures, they are quick to interpret present failures as an accurate reflection of their worthlessness. Fearing more failure, they often become despondent and stop trying.

Finally, the pressure of having to meet self-imposed standards in order to feel good about ourselves can result in a rules-dominated life. Individuals caught in this trap often have a set of rules for most of life's situations, and continually focus their attention on their performance and ability to adhere to their schedule. Brent, for example, made a daily list of what he could accomplish if everything went perfectly. He was always a little tense because he wanted to use every moment effectively to reach his goals. If things didn't go well, or if someone took too much of his time, Brent got angry. Efficient, effective use of time was his way of attaining fulfillment, but he was miserable. He was constantly driven to do more, but his best was never enough to satisfy him.

Brent believed that accomplishing goals and making efficient use of his time were what the Lord wanted him to do. Due to stress, he occasionally thought that *something* wasn't quite right, but his solution was to try harder, make even better use of his time, and be even more regimented in his adherence to self-imposed rules.

Brent's focus was misdirected. The focus of the Christian life should be on Christ, not on self-imposed regulations. Our experience of Christ's lordship is dependent on our moment-by-moment attention to His instruction, not our own regimented schedule.

As these cases demonstrate, the false belief, *I must meet certain standards in order to feel good about myself,* results in a fear of failure. How affected are you by this belief? Take the following test to determine how strongly you fear failure.

FEAR OF FAILURE TEST

Read each of the following statements; then, from the top of the test, choose the term which best describes your response. Put the number above that term in the blank beside each statement.

1	2	3	4	5	6	7
Always	Very Often	Often	Sometimes	Seldom	Very Seldom	Never

____ 1. Because of fear, I often avoid participating in certain activities.

____ 2. When I sense that I might experience failure in some important area, I become nervous and anxious.

____ 3. I worry.

____ 4. I have unexplained anxiety.

____ 5. I am a perfectionist.

____ 6. I am compelled to justify my mistakes.

____ 7. There are certain areas in which I feel I *must* succeed.

____ 8. I become depressed when I fail.

____ 9. I become angry with people who interfere with my attempts to succeed, and as a result, make me appear incompetent.

____ 10. I am self-critical.

____ Total (Add up the numbers you have placed in the blanks.

Interpretation of Score
If your score is...

57-70
God has apparently given you a very strong appreciation for His love and unconditional acceptance. You seem to be freed from the fear of failure that plagues most people. (Some people who score this high are either greatly deceived, or have become callous to their emotions as a way to suppress pain.)

47-56
The fear of failure controls your responses rarely, or only in certain situations. Again, the only major exceptions are those who are not honest with themselves.

37-46
When you experience emotional problems, they may relate to a sense of failure or to some form of criticism. Upon reflection, you will probably relate many of your previous decisions to this fear. Many of your future decisions will also be affected by the fear of failure unless you take direct action to overcome it.

27-36
The fear of failure forms a general backdrop to your life. There are probably few days that you are not affected in some way by this fear. Unfortunately, this robs you of the joy and peace your salvation is meant to bring.

0-26
Experiences of failure dominate your memory, and have probably resulted in a great deal of depression. These problems will remain until some definitive action is taken. In other words, this condition will not simply disappear; time alone cannot heal your pain. You need to experience

deep healing in your self-concept, in your relationship with God, and in your relationships with others.

EFFECTS OF THE FEAR OF FAILURE

The fear of failure can affect our lives in many ways. The following list is not an exhaustive discussion of its resulting problems, nor are these problems explained completely by the fear of failure. However, recognizing and confronting the fear of failure in each of these experiences could result in dramatic changes.

Perfectionism

Again, one of the most common symptoms of the fear of failure is perfectionism, an unwillingness to fail. This tendency suffocates joy and creativity. Because any failure is perceived as a threat to our self-esteem, we develop a propensity to focus our attention on the one area in which we failed rather than those in which we did well. Areas where we often tend to be perfectionistic include work, punctuality, house-cleaning, our appearance, hobbies and skills—practically anything and everything!

Perfectionists often appear to be highly motivated, but their motivations usually come from a desperate attempt to avoid the low self-esteem they experience when they fail.

Avoiding Risks

Another very common result of the fear of failure is a willingness to be involved in only those activities that can be done well. New, challenging activities are avoided because the risk of failure is too great. Avoiding risks may seem comfortable, but it severely limits the scope of our creativity, self-expression, and service to God.

Anger, Resentment

When we fail, when others contribute to our failure, or when we are injured or insulted in some way, anger is a normal response. Feeling angry isn't wrong. In fact, the Apostle Paul encouraged the Ephesians to *be angry*, but quickly followed that encouragement with the admonition to avoid expressing anger in a sinful, or hurtful, way (Eph. 4:26).

Unfortunately, rather than using our anger constructively, many of us either vent our fury without a thought of its result, or we suppress it. Repressed anger eventually leads to retaliatory outbursts, deep and seething resentment, and/or depression.

Anxiety and Fear

Failure is often the source of self-condemnation and the disapproval of others, both of which are severe blows to a self-worth based on personal success and approval. If failure is great enough or occurs often enough, it can harden into a negative self-concept in which we will expect to fail at virtually every endeavor. This negative self-concept perpetuates itself and leads to a downward spiral of anxiety about our performance and fear of disapproval from others.

Pride

When we base our self-worth on our performance and are successful, we often develop an inflated view of ourselves: pride. Some of us may persist in this self-exaltation through any and all circumstances; for most of us, however, this sense of self-esteem lasts only until our next failure (or risk of failure). The self-confidence that most of us try to portray is only a facade to hide our fear of failure and insecurity.

Depression

Depression is generally a result of anger turned inward and/or a deep sense of loss. Experiencing failure and fearing subsequent failure can lead to deep depression. Once depressed, many become emotionally numb and passive in their actions, believing there is no hope for change. Occasionally, depressed people may also exhibit outbursts of anger resulting from failure. Generally, depression is the body's way of blocking psychological pain by numbing physical and emotional functions.

Low Motivation

Much of what is known as low motivation or laziness is better understood as hopelessness. If people believe they will fail, they have no reason to exert any effort. The pain they endure for their passivity seems relatively minor and acceptable compared to the agony of genuinely trying and failing.

Sexual Dysfunction

The emotional trauma caused by failure can cause disturbances in sexual activity. Then, rather than experience the pain of failing sexually, many tend to avoid sex altogether.

Chemical Dependency

Many people attempt to ease their pain and fear of failure by using drugs or alcohol. Those who abuse alcohol often do so with the false notion that it will increase their level of performance, thus enhancing their attempts at being successful. Alcohol, however, is a depressant, and actually decreases the user's performance ability.

Stimulants also are often used to increase productivity. Users of these drugs are likely to consume larger doses on an increasingly regular basis until they are addicted. This is because natural physiological processes deplete bodily resources during drug binges, so that when users come down from the chemical's "high" effect, they crash and are unable to rise to any occasion without it.

Taking a drink—like playing tennis, jogging, seeing a movie, or reading a book—can be a refreshing means of temporary escape. The problem is that chemical substances are addictive, and often, easily abused. For those who find themselves trapped by chemical dependency, what may have begun as a pleasurable means of temporary escape, or an effort to remove pressures to perform, ends with the despair of realizing an inability to cope without the substance. This pain-pleasure cycle continues, slowly draining the life from its victim.

Because of their euphoric effect, alcohol or drugs may give us an illusion that we are "on top of the world." But success, or the idea of success, regardless of how it is achieved, cannot dictate our sense of self-esteem.

In the case of chemical substances, cocaine users provide a clear example of this truth. A major reason for cocaine's popularity is its ability to produce feelings of greater self-esteem. However, it is interesting to note that a number of highly successful people use this drug. If success truly provided a greater sense of self-esteem, these people would probably not be in the market for the drug in the first place.

As long as we operate according to Satan's lies, we are susceptible to the fear of failure. Our personal experience of this fear is determined by the difference between our performance standards and our ability to meet those standards.

Although we all will continue to experience the fear of failure to some degree, we must realize that as Christians, we have the power provided by the Holy Spirit to lay aside deceptive ways of thinking, and be renewed in our minds by the truth of God's Word (Rom. 12:2; Eph. 4:21-25). For our benefit, God often allows us to experience circumstances which will enable us to recognize our blind adherence to Satan's deceptions. Many times, these circumstances seem very negative, but through them, we can learn valuable, life-changing truths. In Ps. 107:33-36, we see a poetic example of this:

> *He changes rivers into a wilderness, and springs of water into a thirsty ground;*
> *A fruitful land into a salt waste, because of the wickedness of those who dwell in it.*
> *He changes a wilderness into a pool of water, and a dry land into springs of water;*
> *And there He makes the hungry to dwell, so that they may establish an inhabited city.*

51

Has your fruitful land become a salt waste? Maybe God is trying to get your attention to teach you a tremendously important lesson: that success or failure is not the basis of your self-worth. Maybe the only way you can learn this lesson is by experiencing the pain of failure. In His great love, God leads us through experiences that are difficult but essential to our growth and development.

The more sensitive you become to the fear of failure and the problems it may cause, the more you will understand your own behavior as well as that of others.

GOD'S ANSWER: JUSTIFICATION

If we base our self-worth on our ability to meet standards, we will try to compensate, either by avoiding risks, or by trying to succeed no matter what the cost. Either way, failure looms as a constant enemy.

As I reflect on my life, I recall being especially fearful of failure during my teenage years. This fear was apparent in many areas of my life, but particularly in athletics.

Because I was, from an early age, taller than most children, many perceived that I would be a basketball player. I practiced a lot during that time, and became a very skilled player. In the process, I learned that I could do many things on the court in practice, or while playing with friends, that I would never even attempt to try during a game, when the pressure was intense. I was afraid of failure, and that fear prevented me from doing many things in basketball which I had the ability to do.

The same fear, I now realize, has prevented me from attempting achievement in several other areas of my life. Although God has enabled me to conquer this fear on many occasions, there are still times when I struggle with the risk of failing. This may be surprising to some who have known me and have thought of me as being successful. Yet, those who have experienced great success know that making an important achievement is often followed by the fear of losing that attainment.

Success truly does not reduce the amount of fear we experience in our lives. In fact, success often causes our fears to escalate because we perceive that we have more to lose.

Thankfully, God has a solution for the fear of failure! He has given us a secure self-worth totally apart from our ability to perform. We have been *justified*, placed in right standing before God through Christ's death on the cross, which paid for our sins. But God didn't stop with our forgiveness; He also granted us the very righteousness of Christ (2 Cor. 5:21)!

Visualize two ledgers: on one is a list of all your sins; on the other, the righteousness of Christ. Now exchange your ledger for Christ's. This exemplifies justification—transferring our sin to Christ and His righteousness to us. In 2 Cor. 5:21, Paul wrote:

> *He made Him* (Christ) *who knew no sin to be sin on our behalf, that we might become the righteousness of God in Him.*

I once heard a radio preacher berate his congregation for their hidden sins. He exclaimed, "Don't you know that someday you're going to die and God is going to flash all your sins upon a giant screen in heaven for all the world to see?" How tragically this minister misunderstood God's gracious gift of justification!

Justification carries no guilt with it, and has no memory of past transgressions. Christ paid for all of our sins at the cross—past, present, and future. Hebrews 10:17 says, *And their sins and their lawless deeds I will remember no more*. We are completely forgiven by God!

As marvelous as it is, justification means more than forgiveness of sins. In the same act of love through which God forgave our sin, He also provided for our *righteousness*: the worthiness to stand in God's presence.

By imputing righteousness to us, God attributes Christ's worth to us. The moment we accept Christ, God no longer sees us as condemned sinners. Instead, we are forgiven, we receive Christ's righteousness, and God sees us as creatures who are fully pleasing to Him.

God intended that Adam and his descendants be righteous people, fully experiencing His love and eternal purposes. But sin short-circuited that relationship. God's perfect payment for sin has since satisfied the righteous wrath of God, enabling us to again have that status of righteousness, and to delight in knowing and honoring the Lord.

God desires for those of us who have been redeemed to experience the realities of His redemption. We are forgiven and righteous because of Christ's sacrifice; therefore, we are pleasing to God in spite of our failures. This reality can replace our fear of failure with peace, hope, and joy. Failure need not be a millstone around our necks. Neither success nor failure is the proper basis of our self-worth. Christ alone is the source of our forgiveness, freedom, joy, and purpose.

God works by *fiat*, meaning that He can create something from nothing by simply declaring it into existence. God spoke and the world was formed. He said, "Let there be light," and light appeared. The earth is no longer void because God sovereignly created its abundance.

In the same way, we were condemned, but now we are declared righteous! Romans 5:1 refers to us as *having been justified by faith*, a statement in the past perfect tense. Therefore, if we have trusted in Christ for our salvation, we each can say with certainty, *I am completely forgiven, and am fully pleasing to God.*

Some people have difficulty thinking of themselves as being pleasing to God because they link *pleasing* so strongly with performance. They tend to be displeased with anything short of perfection in themselves, and suspect that God has the same standard.

The point of justification is that we can never achieve perfection on this earth; even our best efforts at self-righteousness are as filthy rags to God (Is. 64:6). Yet, He loves us so much that He appointed His Son to pay for our sins and give to us His own righteousness, His perfect status before God.

This doesn't mean that our actions are irrelevant, and that we can sin all we want. Our sinful actions, words, and attitudes grieve the Lord, but our status as beloved children remains intact. In His love, He disciplines and encourages us to live godly lives—both for our good and for His honor.

The Apostle Paul was so enamored with his forgiveness and righteousness in Christ that he was intensely motivated to please God by his actions and his deeds. In 1 Cor. 6:19-20; 2 Cor. 5:9; Phil. 3:8-11, and in other passages, Paul strongly stated his desire to please, honor, and glorify the One who had made him righteous.

Some people may read these statements and become uneasy, believing that I am discounting the gravity of sin. As you will see, I am not minimizing the destructive nature of sin, but am simply trying to elevate our view of the results of Christ's payment on the cross. Understanding our complete forgiveness and acceptance before God does not promote a casual attitude toward sin. On the contrary, it gives us a greater desire to live for and serve the One who died to free us from sin. Let's look at some strong reasons to obey and serve God with joy:

REASONS FOR OBEDIENCE

The love of God and His acceptance of us is based on grace, His unmerited favor. It is not based on our ability to impress God through our good deeds. But if we are accepted on the basis of His grace and not our deeds, why *should* we obey God? Here are six compelling reasons to obey Him:

Christ's Love

Understanding God's grace compels us to action because love motivates us to please the One who has so freely loved us. When we experience love, we usually respond by seeking to express our love in return. Our obedience to God is an expression of our love for Him (John 14:15, 21), which comes from an understanding of what Christ has accomplished for us on the cross (2 Cor. 5:14-15). We love because He first loved us and clearly demonstrated His love for us at the cross (1 John 4:16-19). Understanding this will highly motivate us to serve Him.

This great motivating factor is missing in many of our lives because we don't really believe that God loves us unconditionally. We expect His love to be conditional, based on our ability to earn it.

Our experience of God's love is based on our perception. If we believe that He is demanding or aloof, we will not be able to receive His love and tenderness. Instead, we will either be afraid of Him or angry with Him. Faulty perceptions of God often prompt us to rebel against Him.

Our image of God is the foundation for all of our motivations. As we grow in our understanding of His unconditional love and acceptance, we will be better able to grasp that His discipline is prompted by care, not cruelty. We will also be increasingly able to perceive the contrast between the joys of living for Christ and the destructive nature of sin. We will be motivated to experience eternal rewards *where neither moth nor rust destroys* (Matt. 6:20). And we will want our lives to bring honor to the One who loves us so much.

Sin Is Destructive

Satan has effectively blinded man to the painful, damaging consequences of sin. The effects of sin are all around us, yet many continue to indulge in the sex, status- and pleasure-seeking, and rampant self-centeredness that cause so much anguish and pain. Satan contradicted God in the Garden when he said, *You surely shall not die!* (Gen. 3:4). Sin is pleasant, but only for a season. Sooner or later, sin will result in some form of destruction.

Sin is destructive in many ways. Emotionally, we may experience the pain of guilt and shame and the fear of failure and punishment. Mentally, we may experience the anguish of flashbacks. We may also expend enormous amounts of time and energy thinking about our sins and rationalizing our guilt. Physically, we may suffer from psychosomatic illnesses or experience pain through physical abuse. Sin may also result in the loss of property, or even the loss of life. Relationally, we can alienate ourselves from others. Spiritually, we grieve the Holy Spirit, lose our testimony, and break our fellowship with God. The painful and destructive effects of sin are so profound that why we don't have an aversion to it is a mystery!

The Father's Discipline

Our loving Father has given us the Holy Spirit to convict us of sin. Conviction is a form of God's discipline, and serves as proof that we have become sons of God (Heb. 12:5-11). It warns us that we are making choices without regard to either God's truth or sin's consequences. If we choose to be unresponsive to the Holy Spirit, our heavenly Father will discipline us in love. Many people do not understand the difference between discipline and punishment. The following chart shows their profound contrasts:

	PUNISHMENT	DISCIPLINE
SOURCE:	God's Wrath	God's Love
PURPOSE:	To Avenge a Wrong	To Correct a Wrong
RELATIONAL RESULT:	Alienation	Reconciliation
PERSONAL RESULT:	Guilt	A Righteous Lifestyle
DIRECTED TOWARD:	Non-Believers	His Children

Jesus bore all the punishment we deserved on the cross; therefore, we no longer need to fear punishment from God for our sins. We should seek to do what is right so that our Father will not have to correct us through discipline, but when we are disciplined, we should remember that God is correcting us in love. This discipline leads us to righteous performance, a reflection of Christ's righteousness in us.

His Commands for Us Are Good

God's commands are given for two good purposes: to protect us from the destructiveness of sin, and to direct us in a life of joy and fruitfulness. We have a wrong perspective if we only view God's commands as restrictions in our lives. Instead, we must realize that His commands are guidelines, given so that we might enjoy life to the fullest.

God's commands should never be considered as a means to gain His approval.

In today's society, we have lost the concept of doing something because it is the right thing to do. Instead, we do things in exchange for some reward or favor, or to avoid punishment. Wouldn't it be novel to do something simply because it is the right thing to do? God's commands are holy, right, and good, and the Holy Spirit gives us the wisdom and strength to keep them. Therefore, since they have value in themselves, we can choose to obey God and follow His commands.

Eternal Rewards

Yet another compelling reason to live for God's glory is the fact that we will be rewarded in heaven for our service to Him. Two passages clearly illustrate this fact:

> *For we must all appear before the judgment seat of Christ, that each one may be recompensed for his deeds in the body, according to what he has done, whether good or bad.*
>
> 2 Cor. 5:10

> *Now if any man builds upon the foundation with gold, silver, precious stones, wood, hay, straw,*
> *each man's work will become evident; for the day will show it, because it is to be revealed with fire; and the fire itself will test the quality of each man's work.*
> *If any man's work which he has built upon it remains, he shall receive a reward.*
> *If any man's work is burned up, he shall suffer loss; but he himself shall be saved, yet so as through fire.*
>
> 1 Cor. 3:12-15

Through Christ's payment for us on the cross, we have escaped eternal judgment; however, our actions will be judged at the judgment seat of Christ. There, our performance will be evaluated, and rewards presented for service to God. Rewards will be given for deeds that reflect a desire to honor Christ, but deeds performed in an attempt to earn God's acceptance, earn the approval of others, or meet our own standards will be rejected by God and consumed by fire.

Christ Is Worthy

Our most noble motivation for serving Christ is simply that He is worthy of our love and obedience. The Apostle John recorded his vision of the Lord and his response to His glory:

> *After these things I looked, and behold, a door standing open in heaven, and the first voice which I had heard, like the sound of a trumpet speaking with me, said, "Come up here, and I will show you what must take place after these things."*
>
> *Immediately I was in the Spirit; and behold, a throne was standing in heaven, and One sitting on the throne.*
>
> *And He who was sitting was like a jasper stone and a sardius in appearance; and there was a rainbow around the throne, like an emerald in appearance.*
>
> *And around the throne were twenty-four thrones; and upon the thrones I saw twenty-four elders sitting, clothed in white garments, and golden crowns on their heads. . . .*
>
> *And when the living creatures give glory and honor and thanks to Him who sits on the throne, to Him who lives forever and ever,*
>
> *the twenty-four elders will fall down before Him who sits on the throne, and will worship Him who lives forever and ever, and will cast their crowns before the throne, saying,*
>
> *"Worthy art Thou, our Lord and our God, to receive glory and honor and power; for Thou didst create all things, and because of Thy will they existed, and were created."*
>
> Rev. 4:1-4, 9-11

Christ is worthy of our affection and obedience. There is no other person, no goal, no fame or status, and no material possession that can compare with Him. The more we understand His love and majesty, the more we will praise Him and desire that He be honored at the expense of everything else. Our hearts will reflect the psalmist's perspective:

> *Whom have I in heaven but Thee? And besides Thee, I desire nothing on earth. . . .*
>
> *But as for me, the nearness of God is my good; I have made the Lord God my refuge, that I may tell of all Thy works.*
>
> Ps. 73:25, 28

A SUMMARY

We obey God because...

1. Christ's love motivates us to live for Him.
2. Sin is destructive and should be avoided.
3. Our Father lovingly disciplines us for wrongdoing.
4. His commands for us are good.
5. We will receive eternal rewards for obedience.
6. He is worthy of our obedience.

Obeying Christ for these reasons is not a self-improvement program. The Holy Spirit gives us encouragement, wisdom, and strength as we grow in our desire to honor the Lord.

A BEGINNING EXERCISE

How can we begin to experience God's freedom from our fear of failure? How can we begin to live in the light of our justification? Reflecting on the following passage of Scripture will help us to get started:

For as he thinks within himself, so he is.

Prov. 23:7

From this passage of Scripture, and from what we know about ourselves, we can draw the following conclusions and applications:

1.   Though some of us are more reflective than others, most of us spend a great deal of time thinking about our performance.

2.   We have a choice: We can use the same method we have always used to evaluate ourselves and others (Our Self-Worth = Performance + Others' Opinions), or we can adopt God's evaluation (Our Self-Worth = God's Truth About Us).

3.   If we want our lives to be what God has designed them to be, then we must use His truth as our standard of evaluation, rather than our own judgment.

4.   To accomplish this change in mindset, we need to apply the following action points:

     a)   Memorize this statement: *I have great worth apart from my performance because Christ gave His life for me, and therefore, imparted great value to me. I am deeply loved, fully pleasing, totally forgiven, accepted, and complete in Christ.* Repeat this statement to yourself several times each day for two or three weeks.

     b)   Each day, tell those in your family whom you know are Christians, "You are deeply loved, fully pleasing, totally forgiven, accepted, and complete in Christ."

61

5. As you do this, these truths can begin to positively reinforce your view of yourself, your relationship with God, and your relationships with others.

6. Failures, both in your own life and in the lives of your family, can be seen as opportunities to apply this biblical value system. The affirmation of God's love and acceptance can be powerful in shaping a healthy self-concept!

God has given us the Bible as a guidebook. By understanding biblical truths, we will be able to identify the deceptions of Satan; then, we can begin to reject these lies and replace them with the eternal truths of God's Word. This process is not easy, but it is essential to our sense of self-worth and our desire to honor Christ.

Seven
Approval Addict

Our self-concept is determined not only by how we view ourselves, but by how we think others perceive us. Basing our self-worth on what we believe others think of us causes us to become addicted to their approval.

Randy felt like a vending machine. Anyone wanting something could pull an invisible lever and get it. On the job, Randy was always doing other people's work for them. At home, his friends continually called on him to help them with odd jobs. His wife had him working weekends so that she could continue in the lifestyle to which she had grown accustomed. Even people in Randy's church took advantage of him, knowing that they could count on "good old Randy" to head a number of the programs they planned. What was the problem? Was Randy simply a self-sacrificing saint? On the surface, yes; in reality, no. Randy deeply resented those people who, by demanding so much from him, left him little time for himself. Yet, he just couldn't say no. He longed for the approval of others and believed that by agreeing to their every wish, he would win that approval.

Randy typifies many of us. We spend much of our time building relationships, striving to please people and win their respect. And yet, after all of our sincere, conscientious effort, it takes only one unappreciative word from someone to ruin our sense of self-worth. How quickly an insensitive word can destroy the self-assurance we've worked so hard to achieve!

The world we live in is filled with people who demand that we please them in exchange for their approval and acceptance. Such demands often lead us directly to a second false belief: *I must be approved by certain others to feel good about myself.*

We are snared by this lie in many subtle ways. Believing it causes us to bow to peer pressure in an effort to gain approval. We may join clubs and organizations, hoping to find a place of acceptance for ourselves. We often identify ourselves with social groups, believing that being with others like ourselves will assure our acceptance and their approval.

Many people have admitted that their experimentation with drugs or sex is a reaction to their need to belong. However, drugs and sexual promiscuity promise something they can't fulfill, and experimentation only leaves these people with pain, and usually, a deeper need for self-worth and acceptance.

Another symptom of our fear of rejection is our inability to give and receive love. We find it difficult to open up and reveal our inner thoughts and motives because we believe that others will reject us if they know what we are really like. Therefore, our fear of rejection leads us to superficial relationships or isolation. The more we experience isolation, the more we need acceptance. Psychologist Eric Fromm once wrote, "The deep need of man is the need to overcome separateness, to leave the prison of his aloneness."

The fear of rejection is rampant, and loneliness is one of the most dangerous and widespread problems in America today. Some estimate that loneliness has already reached epidemic proportions, and say that if it continues to spread, it could seriously erode the emotional strength of our country. Loneliness is not relegated only to unbelievers. Ninety-two percent of the Christians attending a recent Bible conference admitted in a survey that feelings of loneliness were a major problem in their lives. All shared a basic symptom: a sense of despair at feeling unloved and a fear of being unwanted or unaccepted. This is a tragic commentary on the people about whom Christ said:

> *By this all men will know that you are my disciples, if you have love for one another.*
>
> John 13:35

For the most part, our modern society has responded inadequately to rejection and loneliness. Our response has been outer-directed, meaning that we try to copy the customs, dress, ideas, and behavioral patterns of a particular group, allowing the consensus of the group to determine what is correct for us. But conforming to a group will not fully provide the security we are so desperately seeking. Only God can provide that through His people, His Word, His Spirit, and His timing. Turning to others for what only God can provide is a direct result of our acceptance of Satan's lie:

Self-Worth = Performance + Others' Opinions

Living according to the false belief, *I must be approved by certain others to feel good about myself,* causes us to fear rejection, conforming virtually all of our attitudes and actions to the expectations of others. How are you affected by this belief? Take the test on the following page to determine how strongly you fear rejection.

FEAR OF REJECTION TEST

Read each of the statements below; then, from the top of the test, choose the term which best describes your response. Put the number above that term in the blank beside each statement.

1	2	3	4	5	6	7
Always	Very Often	Often	Sometimes	Seldom	Very Seldom	Never

_____ 1. I avoid certain people.

_____ 2. When I sense that someone might reject me, I become nervous and anxious.

_____ 3. I am uncomfortable around those who are different from me.

_____ 4. It bothers me when someone is unfriendly to me.

_____ 5. I am basically shy and unsocial.

_____ 6. I am critical of others.

_____ 7. I find myself trying to impress others.

_____ 8. I become depressed when someone criticizes me.

_____ 9. I always try to determine what people think of me.

_____ 10. I don't understand people and what motivates them.

_____ Total (Add up the numbers you have placed in the blanks.)

Interpretation of Score
If your score is...

57-70
God has apparently given you a very strong appreciation for His love and unconditional acceptance. You seem to be freed from the fear of rejection that plagues most people. (Some people who score this high are either greatly deceived, or have become callous to their emotions as a way to suppress pain.)

47-56
The fear of rejection controls your responses rarely, or only in

certain situations. Again, the only major exceptions are those who are not honest with themselves.

37-46

When you experience emotional problems, they may relate to a sense of rejection. Upon reflection, you will probably relate many of your previous decisions to this fear. Many of your future decisions will also be affected by the fear of rejection unless you take direct action to overcome it.

27-36

The fear of rejection forms a general backdrop to your life. There are probably few days that you are not in some way affected by this fear. Unfortunately, this robs you of the joy and peace your salvation is meant to bring.

0-26

Experiences of rejection dominate your memory and have probably resulted in a great deal of depression. These problems will persist until some definitive action is taken. In other words, this condition will not simply disappear; time alone cannot heal your pain. You need to experience deep healing in your self-concept, in your relationship with God, and in your relationships with others.

EFFECTS OF THE FEAR OF REJECTION

Virtually all of us fear rejection. We can fall prey to it even when we've learned to harden our defenses in anticipation of someone's disapproval. Neither being defensive nor trying to please another person's every whim is the answer to this problem. These are only coping mechanisms which prevent us from dealing with the root of our fear.

Rejection is a type of communication. It conveys a message that someone else is unsatisfactory to us; that he or she doesn't measure up to a standard we've created or adopted. Sometimes, rejection is willfully used as an act of manipulation designed to control someone else. Usually, rejection is manifested by an outburst of anger, a disgusted look, an impatient answer, or a social snub. Whatever the form of behavior, it communicates disrespect, low value, and lack of appreciation. Nothing hurts quite like the message of rejection.

If this is true, why do we reject others so frequently? Again, rejection can be a very effective, though destructive, motivator. Without raising a finger, we can send the message that our targeted individual doesn't meet our standards. We can harness this person's instinctive desire for acceptance until we have changed and adapted his or her behavior to suit our tastes and purposes. This is how rejection enables us to control the actions of another human being.

Many misguided preachers have used rejection and guilt as a forceful means of motivation. They expound upon our weaknesses, our failures, our unworthiness, and our inability to measure up to Christ's high standards. Not only is our performance declared unworthy, but we are left feeling denounced, devalued, and devastated. As a result, thousands who have been broken by this rejection have left the Church without understanding Christ's accepting, unconditional love—a love that never uses condemnation to correct behavior.

However, rejection and guilt are only effective motivators as long as people are near us. This is why certain parental techniques of guilt motivation produce results only until the child matures and gains more freedom. With freedom, he is able to remove himself physically from his parents. Unrestrained, he then can do as he pleases.

In this instance, both the parents and the child need to experience God's love and forgiveness. His grace and power can give understanding and strength, so that they can forgive each other, forgive themselves, and exhibit strong, loving relationships.

Another damaging result of rejection is isolation. Michael, for example, was raised in a broken home and had lived with his father since he was six years old. It wasn't that Michael's father wanted him, but his mother was too busy to care for him. Shortly after the divorce, Michael's father married another woman with three children. She began to resent spending any time or effort on Michael. She favored her own children at his expense.

It was no surprise, then, that when Michael grew up and married a beautiful girl who truly loved him, he was cautious about sharing his love with her. Michael had experienced the pain of rejection all of his life and now, because he feared rejection, he withheld his love from someone he truly cared for. Michael was afraid of becoming too close to his wife, because if she rejected him, the pain would be too much for him to bear.

How do you react to the fear of rejection? Some of us project a cool, impervious exterior, and consequently, never develop deep, satisfying relationships. Some of us are so fearful of rejection that we withdraw and decline almost everything, while others continually say yes to everyone, hoping to gain their approval. Some of us are shy and easily manipulated; some of us are sensitive to criticism and react defensively. A deep fear of rejection may prompt hostility and promote the development of nervous disorders.

Our fear of rejection will control us to the degree by which we base our self-worth on the opinions of others rather than on our relationship with God. Our dependence on others for value brings bondage, while abiding in the truths of Christ's love and acceptance brings freedom and joy.

In Gal. 1:10, Paul clearly draws the line concerning our search for approval:

> *For am I now seeking the favor of men, or of God? Or am*
> *I striving to please men? If I were still trying to please men, I*
> *would not be a bond-servant of Christ.*

According to this passage, we can ultimately seek either the approval of men or the approval of God as the basis of our self-worth. We cannot seek both. God wants to be the Lord of our lives, and He is unwilling to share that rightful lordship with anyone else. Therefore, the only way we can overcome the fear of rejection is to value the constant approval of God over the conditional approval of people.

My desire for the approval of others has often been so great that I sometimes joke about having been born an "approval addict." Growing up, I had the feeling that I didn't fit in; that I was "different" from others; that there was, therefore, something inherently wrong with me. I felt inadequate and tried to win the approval of others, desperately hoping that this would compensate for the negative feelings I had about myself.

But ironically, the conditional approval of others was never enough to satisfy me. Instead, being praised only reminded me of the disapproval I might encounter if I failed to maintain what I had achieved. I was thus compelled to work even harder at being successful. I occasionally find myself falling into this pattern of behavior even now, despite my improved knowledge, experience, and relationship with God.

Many people may be surprised to learn this, perhaps assuming that reading this book and completing its exercises will forever liberate them from the propensity to base their self-worth on the approval of others.

I don't believe that any of us will gain complete freedom from this tendency until we see the Lord. Our God-given instinct to survive compels us to avoid pain. Knowing that rejection and disapproval bring pain, we will continue our attempts to win the esteem of others whenever possible. The good news is that because we are fully pleasing to God—a fact we will examine later in this chapter—we need not be devastated when others respond to us in a negative way.

As we grow in our relationship with God, the Holy Spirit will continue teaching us how to apply this liberating truth to different aspects of our lives at an increasingly deeper level. In fact, one evidence of His work within us is the ability to see new areas of our lives in which we are allowing the opinions of others to determine our sense of worth. With spiritual maturity, we will more often be able to identify these areas and choose to find our significance in God's unconditional love for us and complete acceptance of us. However, profound changes in our value system take honesty, objectivity, and prolonged, persistent application of God's Word.

Before we examine God's solution to our fear of failure, we must first identify and understand how this fear is manifested in our lives. Similar to the fear of failure, the fear of rejection can affect us in many ways. The explanations of the following symptoms are not exhaustive, but are intended to demonstrate how rejection can trigger certain problems in our lives:

Anger, Resentment, Hostility

Anger is usually our most common response to rejection. Some of us are not honest about our anger. We may deny its existence, suppress it, and assume that it will go away. We may vent our anger in destructive explosions of wrath. Or, we may use sarcasm or neglect to express anger in a more subtle way. If we don't resolve our anger through honesty and forgiveness, we can become deeply hostile and resentful. One motive for retaining anger is the desire for revenge.

Being Easily Manipulated

Those who believe that their self-worth is based on the approval of others are likely to do virtually anything to please people. They truly believe they will be well-liked if they agree to every request of those who are, consciously or not, manipulating them. Many of these people often despise those who are being manipulative, and resent what they feel they have to do to earn their approval.

Codependency

In families affected by dependency on alcohol, drugs, work, or any other compulsion, family members often develop behavioral patterns to rescue the dependent person from the consequences of his or her behavior. This compulsive rescuing, called *codependency*, effectually allows the dependent person to continue acting destructively, and keeps him or her in need of being habitually rescued, so that the pattern continues.

Avoiding People

Among the most common ways people react to their fear of rejection is to avoid others, thereby avoiding the risk of rejection. Some people avoid others overtly, spending most of their time alone, but most people try to lower the risk of rejection by having superficial relationships. They may be around people much of the time, and they may be considered socially adept because they know how to make friends easily, but their friends are never really able to know them because they hide behind a wall of words, smiles, and activities. These people are usually quite lonely in the midst of all their "friends."

Control

In an effort to avoid being hurt, many people constantly try to maintain control of others and dominate most situations. They have become adept in exercising control by dispensing approval or disapproval, unwilling to let others be themselves and make their own decisions without their consent. Because such people are actually very insecure, lack of control is an unacceptable threat to them.

Depression

Depression is the result of a deep sense of loss or repressed, pent-up anger. When anger is not handled properly, the body and mind respond to its intense pressure, and the person's emotions and sense of purpose become dulled.

The reason we experience the fear of rejection and its accompanying problems is because we believe Satan's lie that our *Self-Worth = Performance + Others' Opinions.* We crave love, fellowship, and intimacy, and turn to others to meet those needs. However, the problem with basing our worth on the approval of others is that God is the only One who loves and appreciates us unconditionally. He has provided a solution to the fear of rejection.

GOD'S ANSWER: RECONCILIATION

God's solution to the fear of rejection is based on Christ's sacrificial payment for our sins. Through this payment, we find forgiveness, reconciliation, and total acceptance through Christ. *Reconciliation* means that those who were enemies have become friends. Paul described our transformation from enmity to friendship with God:

> *And although you were formerly alienated and hostile in mind, engaged in evil deeds,*
> *yet He has now reconciled you in His fleshly body through death, in order to present you before Him holy and blameless and beyond reproach.*
>
> Col. 1:21-22

As I talked with Pam, it became obvious that she did not understand this great truth of reconciliation. Three years after she married, Pam had committed adultery with a coworker. Although she had confessed her sin to God and to her husband, and had been forgiven, guilt continued to plague her, making it difficult for her to feel acceptable to God. Four years after the affair, she still could not forgive herself for what she had done.

Sitting in my office, we explored her reluctance to accept God's forgiveness.

"It sounds as though you believe that God can't forgive the sin you committed," I said.

"That's right," she replied. "I don't think He ever will."

"But God doesn't base His love and acceptance of us on our performance," I said. "If any sin is so filthy and vile that it makes us less acceptable to Him, then the cross is insufficient. If the cross isn't sufficient for all sin, then the Bible is in error when it says that He forgave *all* your sins (Col. 2:13-15). God took our sins and cancelled them by nailing them to Christ's cross. In this way, God also took away Satan's power to condemn us for sin. So you see, nothing you will ever do can nullify your reconciliation and make you unacceptable to God."

Our unconditional acceptance in Christ is a profound, life-changing truth. Salvation is not simply a ticket to heaven. It is the beginning of a dynamic new relationship with God. *Justification* is the doctrine that explains the judicial facts of our forgiveness and righteousness in Christ. *Reconciliation* explains the relational aspect of our salvation. The moment we receive Christ by faith, we enter into a personal relationship with Him. We are united with God in an eternal and inseparable bond (Rom. 8:38-39). We are bound in an indissoluble union with Him, as fellow heirs with Christ. The Holy Spirit has sealed us in that relationship, and we are absolutely secure in Christ. Ephesians 1:13-14 states:

> *...Having also believed, you were sealed in Him with the Holy Spirit of promise,*
> *who is given as a pledge of our inheritance, with a view to the redemption of God's own possession, to the praise of His glory.*

Recently, in a group prayer meeting, someone prayed, "Thank you, God, for accepting me when I am so unacceptable." This person understood that we cannot earn God's acceptance by our own merit, but seemed to have forgotten that we are unconditionally accepted in Christ. We are no longer unacceptable—the point of the cross. Through Christ's death and resurrection, we have become acceptable to God. This did not occur because God decided He could overlook our sin, but because Christ forgave all of our sins so that He could present us to the Father, holy and blameless.

There is no greater theme in Scripture than the reconciliation of man to God. Open your Bible and read for yourself. The following passages are taken from the New American Standard Version of Scripture. Study them, and then answer the question after each one:

Ps. 103:12—What happens to our transgressions? HE
REMOVES THEM

Matt. 26:28—Why was Christ's blood shed?
FOR FORGIVENESS OF SIN

John 3:16—What is God's promise? ETERNAL LIFE

John 5:24—What is the promise to the person who knows and believes?

John 10:27-29—What do His sheep have? Will they perish?

Acts 10:43—Of what did the prophets bear witness?

Acts 13:39—What does belief do?

Rom. 3:23, 24—By what are we justified?

Rom. 4:7—Who is blessed?

Rom. 5:10—Through what are we reconciled?

Rom. 8:15-17—Describe the nature of our relationship with God:

Rom. 8:33—Who shall accuse us?

Rom. 8:38-39—Of what is Paul convinced?

2 Cor. 5:17,19,21—Describe what we are in Christ:

Gal. 2:16—On what basis are we justified?

Gal. 2:16—What part do works play in justification?

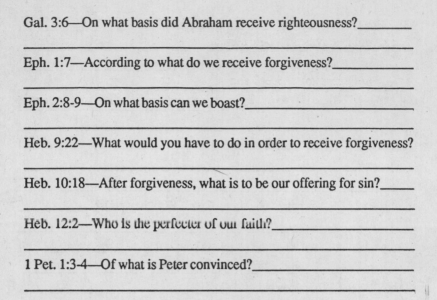

Gal. 3:6—On what basis did Abraham receive righteousness?_____
_____

Eph. 1:7—According to what do we receive forgiveness?_____
_____

Eph. 2:8-9—On what basis can we boast?_____
_____

Heb. 9:22—What would you have to do in order to receive forgiveness?
_____

Heb. 10:18—After forgiveness, what is to be our offering for sin?_____
_____

Heb. 12:2—Who is the perfecter of our faith?_____
_____

1 Pet. 1:3-4—Of what is Peter convinced?_____
_____

Because of reconciliation, we are completely acceptable to God and are completely accepted by God. As these passages illustrate, we enjoy a full and complete relationship with Him, and in this relationship, His determination of our value is not based on our performance.

However, we may question what this relationship means as we attempt to apply it in our day-to-day experience. Let's analyze this issue:

When we are born again as spiritual beings in right standing with God, we are still tilted toward the world's way of thinking. Because we have been conditioned by the world's perspective and values, we find it hard to break away. Indeed, when Paul wrote the Christians at Corinth, he called them *men of flesh*. Though born of the Spirit, and equipped with all provisions in Christ, these individuals had yet to develop into the complete, mature believers God intended them to be (1 Cor. 3:1-4).

Many of us are like the Christians at Corinth. We still try to obtain our significance the world's way, through success and approval. Often, we look only to other believers rather than to Christ Himself. We learn to use the right Christian words, claim divine power and guidance, and organize programs, and yet so often, our spiritual facade lacks depth and substance. Our spiritual activities become human efforts lacking the real touch of the Master. In effect, we live a lie.

The desire for success and approval constitutes the basis of an addictive, worldly self-worth. Certainly, withdrawal from this dependency may cause us some pain as we change the basis of our self-worth, yet we will begin to discover true freedom and maturity in Christ only when we understand that our lives mean much more than what success or the approval of others can bring.

We can do nothing to contribute to Christ's free gift of salvation; furthermore, if we base our self-worth on the approval of others, then we are actually saying that our ability to please others is of greater value than Christ's payment. We are the sinners, the depraved, the wretched, and the helpless. He is the loving Father, the seeking, searching, patient Savior who has made atonement for the lost, and has extended to us His grace and sonship. We add nothing to our salvation. It is God who seeks us out, convicts us of sin, and reveals Himself to us. It is God who gives us the very faith with which to accept Him. Our faith is simply our response to what He has done for us.

So then, our worth lies in the fact that Christ's blood has paid for our sins; therefore, we are reconciled to God. We are accepted on that basis alone, but does this great truth indicate that we don't need other people in our lives? On the contrary, God very often uses other believers to demonstrate His love and acceptance to us. The strength, comfort, encouragement, and love of Christians toward one another is a visible expression of God's love. However, our acceptance and worth are not *dependent* on others' acceptance of us, even if they are fellow believers! Whether they accept us or not, we are *still* deeply loved, completely forgiven, fully pleasing, totally accepted, and complete in Christ. *He alone* is the final authority on our worth and acceptance.

THE ROLE OF RELATIONSHIPS

For many of us, the unconditional love, forgiveness, and acceptance of Christ seems abstract, and is difficult to comprehend. We may understand the premise of these character traits, but may still be unable to incorporate them into our personal experience. Often, we can trace this difficulty to our parental relationships.

God intends for parents to model His character to their children. According to Scripture, parents are to give their children affection, compassion, protection, provision, and loving discipline. When parents provide this kind of environment in their home, children are usually able to transfer these perceptions to the character of God, and believe that He is loving, compassionate, protective, gracious, and a loving disciplinarian. In turn, they are often able to model these characteristics to their own children.

Many of us, however, have not received this parental model of God's character. On an extremely wide spectrum, some of us have had relatively healthy relationships with our parents, while others have experienced various forms of neglect, condemnation, and manipulation. Still others have suffered the deeper wounds of sexual abuse, physical abuse, or abandonment. The greater the degree of dysfunction (or poor modeling) in a family, the greater the potential for emotional, spiritual, and relational wounds. Put another way, the poorer the parental modeling of God's love, forgiveness, and power, the greater our difficulty in experiencing and applying these characteristics in our lives.

Instead of being refreshed by the truth of God's love, if we have been deeply wounded, we may recoil from it, believing that we are unlovable. We may be fearful of reaching out and being hurt again. Whatever the cause, the result is withdrawal from the very idea of being loved and accepted.

Those who have received poor parental modeling need new models— loving Christian friends—to experience the love and grace of God. Through His body of believers, God often provides us with models of His love, so that our perception of His character can be slowly reshaped into one that is more accurate, resulting in a healthier relationship with Him. Then, our deep emotional, spiritual, and relational wounds can begin to heal, and we can more fully experience God's unconditional love.

Some of us are already involved in strong relationships with people who are understanding and patient with us; some of us haven't yet been able to cultivate relationships like these, and are still looking. If this is your situation, you may need to find a pastor or counselor who can help you get started, possibly by directing you to one or more believers who can minister to you. A small fellowship group or Bible study is often an excellent resource for intimate sharing, comfort, and encouragement. If you have tried to cultivate healthy relationships, but haven't found any yet, don't give up! The Lord wants all of us to be in an environment where we can experience more of His love through our relationships with other believers.

If you ask God for guidance, and are willing to continue putting forth the effort, He will lead you to some people who can provide this kind of an environment for you in His perfect time.

Healthy vs. Unhealthy Relationships

Because many of us are so vulnerable when we begin allowing ourselves to experience the pain that usually accompanies growth, it is wise to have a basic understanding of healthy and unhealthy relationships.

We must first understand that while God often demonstrates His love and affirmation for us through believers and non-believers alike, His desire is that our relationships with others will enable us to know Him more fully. His work through others is, in part, to serve as a channel by which we can better understand His divine love and acceptance of us. Sadly, we are all prone to miss His message and mistake His messenger(s) as the source of our fulfillment. When this misperception is carried to an extreme, we can fall into *emotional dependency*, "the condition resulting when the ongoing presence and/or nurturing of another is believed necessary for personal security."[1]

In his book, *The Four Loves*, C.S. Lewis described the difference between lovers and friends:

> *Lovers are always talking to one another about their love; Friends hardly ever about their Friendship. Lovers are normally face to face, absorbed in each other; Friends, side by side, absorbed in some common interest. Above all, Eros (while it lasts) is necessary between two only. But two, far from being the necessary number for Friendship, is not even the best.*[2]

This well describes the difference between healthy and unhealthy friendship, whether sex comes into the picture or not. Healthy relationships are turned outward, rather than inward. Healthy relationships encourage individuality rather than conformity, and are concerned with independence, rather than emotional dependence. Healthy relationships point one's focus to the Lord and pleasing Him, rather than toward the friendship and pleasing one another.

How do we know when we've crossed the line from a healthy relationship to one that is emotionally dependent? When either party in a relationship:[3]

- experiences frequent jealousy, possessiveness and a desire for exclusivism, viewing other people as a threat to the relationship.
- prefers to spend time alone with this friend and becomes frustrated when this does not happen.
- becomes irrationally angry or depressed when this friend withdraws slightly.
- loses interest in a friendship other than this one.
- experiences romantic or sexual feelings leading to fantasy about this person.
- becomes preoccupied by the person's appearance, personality, problems, and interests.

- is unwilling to make short- or long-range plans that do not include the other person.
- is unable to see the other's faults realistically.
- becomes defensive about this relationship when asked about it.
- displays physical affection beyond what is appropriate for a friendship.
- refers frequently to the other in conversation; feels free to "speak for" the other.
- exhibits an intimacy and familiarity with this friend that causes others to feel uncomfortable or embarrassed in their presence.

Our relationships with one another are very important to God; so much so, that He has placed unity among the brethren as a priority in our relationship with Him (see Matt. 5:23-24). This is because God has reconciled us to Himself as a *body* in Christ (Eph. 2:16), and therefore intends for us to interact as *members of one another* (Eph. 4:25).

Pray that God will guide you to relationships which will encourage you to be honest; practice the truth of His Word; affirm you, and thereby help you develop an appropriate love for yourself; and compel you to focus on Him as the gracious provider of your needs. Eventually, your gratitude will motivate you to practice pleasing Him rather than other people.

A BEGINNING EXERCISE

How do we learn to reject Satan's lie, *I must be approved by certain others to feel good about myself*? How can we begin to practically apply the great truth of our reconciliation to Almighty God? The following exercise will help you begin to experience the freedom and joy of reconciliation.

The thirteenth chapter of First Corinthians describes God's unconditional love and acceptance of us. To personalize this passage, replace the word *love* with *My Father*. Then, memorize the following, and when fear comes to you, recall the love and kindness of God:

My Father is very patient and kind.

My Father is not envious, never boastful.

My Father is not arrogant.

My Father is never rude, nor is He self-seeking.

My Father is not quick to take offense.

My Father keeps no score of wrongs.

My Father does not gloat over my sins, but is always glad when truth prevails.

My Father knows no limit to His endurance, no end to His trust.

My Father is always hopeful and patient.

As you memorize this passage, ask God to show you if your perception of Him is in error in any way. This will enable you to have a more accurate perception of God, and will help you to experience more of His unconditional love and acceptance.

Eight
The Blame Game

Our perception of success and failure is often our primary basis for evaluating ourselves and others. If we believe that performance reflects one's value, and that failure makes one unacceptable and unworthy of love, then we will usually feel completely justified in condemning those who fail, including ourselves. Self-condemnation may include name-calling *(I'm so stupid! I can't do anything right!),* making self-deprecating jokes or statements, or simply never allowing any room for error in our performance. With others, we may be harsh (physically or verbally abusive), or relatively subtle (sarcastic or silent). But any form of condemnation is a powerfully destructive force which communicates, *I'll make you sorry for what you did.*

Matt made a serious mistake early in his life and was never able to overcome it. At age fourteen, he and several friends from school stepped inside a downtown department store and tried to slip out with some cassette tapes without paying for them. They made it to the glass doors past the cashier's stand before a security guard caught them and escorted all of them into the manager's office.

Matt never heard the end of the incident. Every time he made a mistake at home, his father reminded him of what he had done. "You're a colossal failure!" his father would scream. "You've got no values whatsoever! You're a liar and a thief, and you'll never amount to anything!"

Matt was never able to forget his humiliation. At age twenty, he sat in my office and told me very seriously that on some days, he was happy until he realized that he was feeling good. Believing that he had no right to feel good about himself, he would then begin to feel depressed again.

"After all," he reflected, "no one as worthless as I am should feel good about himself."

Like so many others, Matt had been brainwashed and broken by the false belief: *Those who fail are unworthy of love and deserve to be punished.*

Whether consciously or unconsciously, we all tend to point an accusing finger, assigning blame for virtually every failure. Whenever we fail to receive approval for our performance, we are likely to search for a reason, a culprit, a scapegoat. More often than not, we can find no one but ourselves to blame, so the accusing finger points right back at us. Self-condemnation is a severe form of punishment.

If possible, we will often try to place the blame on others and fulfill the law of retribution—that people should get what they deserve. For most of our lives, we have been conditioned to make someone pay for failures or shortcomings. When a deadline is missed at work, we let everyone know it's not our fault: "I know the report was due yesterday, but Frank didn't get me the statistics until this morning." If a household chore is left undone, we quickly look to our other family members to determine who is responsible. For every flaw we see around us, we usually search for someone to blame, hoping to exonerate ourselves by making sure that the one who failed is properly identified and punished.

Another reason we seek to blame others is that our success often depends on their contribution. Their failure is a threat to us. When the failure of another blocks our goal of success, we usually respond by defending ourselves and blaming them, often using condemnation to manipulate them to improve their performance. Blaming others also helps put a safe distance between their failure and our fragile self-worth.

Whether our accusations are focused on ourselves or others, we all have a tendency to believe that someone has to take the blame. When Ellen discovered that her fifteen-year-old daughter was pregnant, she went a week without sleep, tossing and turning, trying to determine who was at fault. Was it her daughter, who had brought this reproach on the family, or was she to blame for failing as a mother? All Ellen knew was that someone had to take responsibility for the crisis.

Rather than being objective and looking for a solid, biblical solution to our problems, we often resort to either accusing someone else or berating ourselves.

Sometimes, we blame others to make ourselves feel better. By blaming someone else who failed, we feel superior. In fact, the higher the position of the one who failed (parent, boss, pastor, etc.), the farther they fall, and often, the better we feel. This desire to be superior, to be "one up" on someone, is at the root of gossip.

In other situations, however, just the opposite is true. When a parent fails, a child usually accepts the blame for that failure. Even as adults, we may readily assume blame in our relationships with those in authority. We have much invested in supporting those we depend upon. This is one reason why denial is so strong in abusive families. For example, one little girl said, "I never told anybody that Daddy was molesting me because I thought that somebody would take him away from our family."

How should we respond when another fails? If the person who failed is a Christian, we need to affirm God's truth about him or her: *He (or she) is deeply loved, completely forgiven, fully pleasing, and totally accepted by God, and complete in Christ.* This perspective can eventually change our condemning attitude to one of love and a desire to help. By believing these truths, we will gradually be able to love this person just as God loves us (1 John 4:11), forgive him or her just as God has forgiven us (Eph. 4:32), and accept him or her just as God has accepted us (Rom. 15:7). This does not mean that we will become blind to the faults or failures of others. We will continue to see them, but our response to them will change considerably over time, from condemnation to compassion. As we depend less on other people for our self-worth, their sins and mistakes will become less of a threat to us, and we will desire to help them instead of being compelled to punish them.

But what about our response to unbelievers? Although they haven't yet trusted in the cross of Christ for the removal of their condemnation before God, Jesus was very clear about how we are to treat them. In Matt. 22:37, 39, He told His disciples to *love the Lord your God, with all your heart, and with all your soul, and with all your mind,* and to *love your neighbor* (both believers and unbelievers) *as yourself.* Jesus was even more specific in Luke 6:27-28. He said, *But I say to you who hear, love your enemies, do good to those who hate you, bless those who curse you, pray for those who mistreat you.* Christ didn't come to love and die for the lovely, righteous people of the world. If He had, we would all be in trouble! Instead, He came to love and die for the unrighteous, the inconsiderate, and the selfish. As we grow in our understanding of His love for us, and continue to grasp that He has rescued us from the righteous condemnation we deserve because of our sins, we will gradually become more patient and kind to others when they fail. It can be very helpful if we compare the failure or sin of others with our sin that Christ died to forgive: *There is nothing that anyone can do to me that can compare with my sin of rebellion that Christ has completely forgiven.* That should give us a lot of perspective!

We tend to make two major errors when we punish others for their failures. The first is that we condemn people not only for genuine sin, but also for their mistakes. When people who have tried their best fail, they do not need our biting blame. They need our love and encouragement. Again, we often tend to blame others because their actions (whether they reflect overt disobedience or honest mistakes) make us look like failures, and our own failure is unacceptable to us. Husband–wife, parent–child, and employer–employee relationships are especially vulnerable to one's being threatened by the failure of another. A wife gets angry with her husband for his not-so-funny joke at an important dinner party; a parent erupts at a child for accidentally spilling milk; a manager scowls at an employee because an error in the employee's calculations has made him look foolish to his supervisor. People generally experience difficulty in dealing with their *sins*; let's not compound their problems by condemning them for their *mistakes*.

A second major error we often make by condemning others is believing that we are godly agents of condemnation. Unable to tolerate injustice, we seem to possess a great need to balance the scales of right and wrong. We are correct in recognizing that sin is reprehensible and deserves condemnation; yet, we have not been licensed by God to punish others for their sins. Judgment is God's responsibility, not man's.

Jesus dealt specifically with this issue when several men decided to stone a woman caught in adultery. He told them that the person without sin should throw the first stone. Beginning with the eldest, all of the accusers walked away as they remembered their own sins (John 8:3-9). In light of their own sinfulness, they no longer saw fit to condemn the sins of another.

As this incident clearly illustrates, we should leave righteous condemnation and punishment in the hands of the One worthy of the responsibility. Our response should be love, affirmation, and possibly, compassionate correction.

When others offend or insult us, should we tell them that they have made us angry or hurt our feelings? This question can be difficult to answer. Some psychologists tell us that we should vent all of our emotions because repression is unhealthy. Others tell us that our emotions will always be positive and controlled if we are truly walking with the Lord. We should avoid both of these extremes. Venting our anger uncontrollably is not a healthy solution, but neither is continued repression and denial.

We need a safe environment to express our emotions: a good friend or counselor who will help us get in touch with our true feelings, which we may have suppressed for years. We can also learn to express ourselves fully to the Lord and tell Him our true feelings, fears, hopes, and dreams. (The Psalms are filled with honest expressions of anger, pain, confusion, hope, and faith.) In this safe environment, we can slowly learn how to communicate appropriately with those who have hurt us. This requires wisdom because each situation and each person often requires a different form of communication.

As we learn to relate appropriately with those who have hurt or injured us in some way, we will begin to develop a healthy sense of assertiveness—an important component in shaping other people's behavior toward us. For example, if others are rude, but never realize it because we passively accept their behavior in an attempt to avoid upsetting them, at least two things usually happen: We develop resentment toward them, and they never have to come to terms with their negative impact on others. They then miss an important opportunity to change, and we effectually prolong their hurtful behavior. There are appropriate and inappropriate ways of communicating our sense of anger or resentment to others, but these feelings need to be spoken—for their benefit and for ours.

We also need to remember that learning how to express our feelings appropriately is a *process*. We can't expect to respond perfectly to everyone. It takes time to express years of repressed pain. It also takes time to learn how to respond firmly and clearly. Be patient with yourself.

We have a choice in our response to failure: We can condemn or we can learn. All of us fail, but this doesn't mean that we are failures. We need to understand that failing can be a step toward maturity, not a permanent blot on our self-esteem. Like children first learning to walk, we all stumble and fall. And, just like children, we can pick ourselves up and begin again. We don't have to allow failure to prevent us from being used by God.

There have been many times in my life when I felt that God was going to punish me by causing me to lose all that I had, either because I'd done something I shouldn't have, or because I'd failed to do something I should have. This erroneous perception of God has driven me away from Him on many occasions when I've needed Him most, and is completely contrary to the One whom Paul described as *the Father of mercies and God of all comfort* (2 Cor. 1:3).

If we have trusted Christ for our salvation, God has forgiven us, and wants us to experience His forgiveness on a daily basis. Moses was a murderer, but God forgave him and used him to deliver Israel from Egypt. David was an adulterer and a murderer, but God forgave him and made him a great king. Peter denied the Lord, but God forgave him, and Peter became a leader in the Church. God rejoices when His children learn to accept His forgiveness, pick themselves up, and walk after they have stumbled. But we must also learn to forgive ourselves. Rather than viewing our weaknesses as a threat to our self-esteem, it is God's desire that they compel us to move forward in our relationship with Him. As the author of Hebrews wrote:

> *Therefore, since we have a great high priest who has gone through the heavens, Jesus the Son of God, let us hold firmly to the faith we profess.*
>
> *For we do not have a high priest who is unable to sympathize with our weaknesses, but we have one who has been tempted in every way, just as we are—yet was without sin.*
>
> *Let us then approach the throne of grace with confidence, so that we may receive mercy and find grace to help us in our time of need.*
>
> Heb. 4:14-16, NIV

Some of us have a tendency to perceive of Jesus as our friend, and God as a harsh disciplinarian. Yet the author of Hebrews described Jesus as *the radiance of [God's] glory and the exact representation of His nature* (Heb. 1:3).

Studying passages like these and spending time with compassionate, forgiving Christians has enabled the Holy Spirit to reshape my perception of God over the years. I continue to experience remorse when I fail. But rather than hide from God, fearing His punishment, I more often approach Him with appreciation for what His love has accomplished for me.

Both assuming and assigning blame for failure can have a number of detrimental consequences. Many psychologists today adhere to a theory called Rational Emotive Therapy. This very helpful theory states that blame is the core of most emotional disturbances. The answer, they insist, is for each of us to stop blaming ourselves and others, and learn to accept ourselves in spite of our imperfections. How right they are! Christ's death is the complete payment for sin, and we can claim His complete forgiveness and acceptance daily.

A number of emotional problems are rooted in the false belief that we must meet certain standards to be acceptable, and that the only way to deal with inadequacies is to punish ourselves and others for them. There is no way we can shoulder such a heavy burden. Our guilt will overpower us, and the weight of our failures will break us.

The false belief, *Those who fail (including myself) are unworthy of love and deserve to be punished,* is at the root of our fear of punishment and our propensity to punish others. How deeply are you affected by this lie? Take the following test to determine how great an influence it has in your life:

FEAR OF PUNISHMENT/PUNISHING OTHERS TEST

Read each of the following statements; then, from the top of the test, choose the term which best describes your response. Put the number above that term in the blank beside each statement.

1	2	3	4	5	6	7
Always	Very Often	Often	Sometimes	Seldom	Very Seldom	Never

_____ 1. I fear what God might do to me.

_____ 2. After I fail, I worry about God's response.

_____ 3. When I see someone in a difficult situation, I wonder what he or she did to deserve it.

_____ 4. When something goes wrong, I have a tendency to think that God must be punishing me.

_____ 5. I am very hard on myself when I fail.

_____ 6. I find myself wanting to blame people when they fail.

_____ 7. I get angry with God when someone who is immoral or dishonest prospers.

____ 8.   I am compelled to tell others when I see them doing wrong.

____ 9.   I tend to focus on the faults and failures of others.

____ 10.   God seems harsh to me.

____Total (Add up the numbers you have placed in the blanks.)

Interpretation of Score

If your score is...

57-70

God has apparently given you a very strong appreciation for His unconditional love and acceptance. You seem to be freed from the fear of punishment that plagues most people. (Some people who score this high are either greatly deceived, or have become callous to their emotions as a way to suppress pain.)

47-56

The fear of punishment and the compulsion to punish others control your responses rarely or only in certain situations. Again, the only exceptions are those who are not honest with themselves.

37-46

When you experience emotional problems, they may tend to relate to a fear of punishment or to an inner urge to punish others. Upon reflection, you will probably relate many of your previous decisions to this fear. Many of your future decisions will also be affected by the fear of punishment and/or the compulsion to punish others unless you take direct action to overcome these tendencies.

27-36

The fear of punishment forms a general backdrop to your life. There are probably few days that you are not affected in some way by the fear of punishment and the propensity to blame others. Unfortunately, this robs you of the joy and peace your salvation is meant to bring.

0-26

Experiences of punishment dominate your memory, and you probably have suffered a great deal of depression as a result of them. These problems will remain until some definitive plan is followed. In other words, this condition will not simply disappear; time alone cannot heal your pain. You need to experience deep healing in your self-concept, in your relationship with God, and in your relationships with others.

EFFECTS OF THE FEAR OF PUNISHMENT AND THE COMPULSION TO PUNISH OTHERS

The logical result of Satan's deception, *Self-worth = Performance + Others' Opinions*, is fear—the fear of failure, rejection, and punishment. When we base our security and value on how well we perform and how we want others to perceive us, failure poses a tremendous threat to us. When threatened, we will often withdraw from the source of our fear and/or become very controlling of ourselves and others. For example, in an attempt to avoid failure, we may adhere to a fairly rigid schedule in which we're fairly certain of success, and avoid those activities which are less promising. Because we often perceive those closest to us as a reflection of ourselves, and are consequently threatened by their failures, we are likely to try to control their behavior as well. If we have also determined that those who fail deserve to be punished, we will tend to victimize ourselves and/or others for virtually any wrongdoing.

Because of our insecurity, some of us are so self-protective that we are rarely able to perceive of ourselves as being in the wrong. We may be quick to pinpoint—and condemn—the weaknesses of others, but in our own self-evaluation, we may be effectually blind to faults and frailties. This attitude may prompt us to turn others (who are "more needy") to God, but may prevent us from seeking Him because of our frequent inability to see our need for Him, or because when we do fail, we may believe that the fault is His.

Some of us may fall on the other end of the spectrum. We may be so absorbed in our performance and so demanding of ourselves that when failure enters our circumstances, we believe that we are solely responsible. Rather than laying blame on someone else, we inflict punishment on ourselves and protect those who hurt us by explaining their deficiencies: *She didn't mean what she said. I'm sure that he loves me; he just has a hard time showing it.* If we have a tendency to punish ourselves for failures, we may believe that we must feel remorse for a certain length of time before we can experience peace and joy again. In a twisted form of self-motivation, we may think that if we condemn ourselves enough, then perhaps we won't fail again.

Somewhere in the middle of this spectrum are those of us who are so hard on ourselves that we project our self-condemning attitude onto others. Passing judgment on others may be a response to our great need for consistency and justice. If we are going to punish failure in ourselves, we reason, then we must be consistent and punish failure in others. Insisting on justice, we may also take it upon ourselves to be God's instrument of correction. We normally don't like to see others getting away with something that they should be punished for (or perhaps, that we wish we could do ourselves).

Finally, there are those of us who determine that because punishment is inevitable, we may as well "live it up" and enjoy our sin before the Judgment comes.

The fear of punishment and the propensity to punish others can affect our lives in many ways. The following provides a brief description of common problems which often result from this deception:

Self-Induced Punishment

Many of us operate on the theory that if we are hard enough on ourselves, then God won't have to punish us. We fail to realize that God disciplines us in love and never punishes us in anger. Because God loves us unconditionally and does not punish us, we don't need to punish ourselves.

Bitterness

If we believe that God and others are always punishing us, we will soon become very angry. Harboring anger and continually questioning God's motives result in deep bitterness and pessimism.

Passivity

Fear of punishment is at the root of one of the most common problems in our society: passivity. *Passivity* is the neglect of our minds, time, gifts, or talents through inaction. God intends for us to actively cooperate with Him, but fear can have an immobilizing effect on our will. Passivity results in a dull life, avoiding risks, and missing opportunities.

Punishing Others

Our specific response to the failure of others depends on several factors: our personalities, the nature of their failure, and how their failure reflects on us (*His mistake makes me look like I'm dumb*, or ...*a bad parent*, or ...*a poor leader*, or ...*a rotten employee*). Our condemnation of those who fail may take the form of verbal abuse, physical abuse, nagging criticism, withholding appreciation and affection, or ignoring them. All of these responses are usually designed to "make them pay for what they did."

The fear of punishment and the desire to punish others can be overcome by realizing that Christ has borne the punishment we deserve. His motives toward us are loving and kind. His discipline is designed to correct us and protect us from the destruction of sin, not to punish us.

GOD'S ANSWER: PROPITIATION

When Christ died on the cross, He was our substitute. He took upon Himself the righteous wrath of God that we deserved. The depth of God's love for us is revealed by the extremity of His actions for us: the holy Son of God became a man and died a horrible death in our place. Two passages state this eloquently. The first was written by Isaiah, who anticipated the coming of Christ:

Surely our griefs He Himself bore, and our sorrows He carried; yet we ourselves esteemed Him stricken, smitten of God, and afflicted.

But He was pierced through for our transgressions, He was crushed for our iniquities; the chastening for our well-being fell upon Him, and by His scourging we are healed.

All of us like sheep have gone astray, each of us has turned to his own way; but the Lord has caused the iniquity of us all to fall on Him.

Is. 53:4-6

And from the New Testament:

By this the love of God was manifested in us, that God has sent His only begotten Son into the world so that we might live through Him.

In this is love, not that we loved God, but that He loved us and sent His Son to be the propitiation for our sins.

Beloved, if God so loved us, we also ought to love one another.

1 John 4:9-11

Propitiation means that the wrath of someone who has been unjustly wronged has been satisfied. It is an act that soothes hostility and satisfies the need for vengeance. Providing His only begotten Son as the propitiation for our sin was the greatest possible demonstration of God's love for man.

To understand God's wondrous provision of propitiation, it is helpful to remember what He has endured from mankind. From Adam and Eve's sin in the Garden of Eden to the obvious depravity we see in our world today, human history is mainly the story of greed, hatred, lust, and pride—evidence of man's wanton rebellion against the God of love and peace. If not done with a desire to glorify Him, even our "good" deeds are like filthy garments to God (Is. 64:6).

Our sin deserves the righteous wrath of God. He is the Almighty, the rightful judge of the universe. He is absolutely holy and perfect. *God is light, and in Him there is no darkness at all* (1 John 1:5). Because of these attributes, God cannot overlook sin, nor can He compromise by accepting sinful behavior. For God to condone even one sin would defile His holiness like smearing a white satin wedding gown with black tar.

Because He is holy, God's aversion to sin is manifested in righteous anger. However, God is not only righteously indignant about sin, He is also infinitely loving. In His holiness, God condemns sin, but in the most awesome example of love the world has ever seen, He ordained that His Son would die to pay for our sins. God sacrificed the sinless, perfect Savior to turn away, *to propitiate*, His great wrath.

And for whom did Christ die? Was it for the saints who honored Him? Was it for a world that appreciated His sinless life and worshipped Him? No! Christ died for *us*, while we were yet in rebellion against Him:

> *For while we were still helpless, at the right time Christ died for the ungodly.*
>
> *For one will hardly die for a righteous man; though perhaps for the good man someone would dare even to die.*
>
> *But God demonstrates His own love toward us, in that while we were yet sinners, Christ died for us.*
>
> *Much more then, having now been justified by His blood, we shall be saved from the wrath of God through Him.*
>
> *For if while we were enemies, we were reconciled to God through the death of His Son, much more, having been reconciled, we shall be saved by His life.*
>
> *And not only this, but we also exult in God through our Lord Jesus Christ, through whom we have now received the reconciliation.*
>
> Rom. 5:6-11

Who can measure the fathomless depth of love that sent Christ to the cross? While we were the enemies of God, Christ averted the wrath we deserved so that we might become the sons of God.

What can we say of our holy heavenly Father? Surely, He did not escape seeing Christ's mistreatment at the hands of sinful men—the scourgings, the humiliation, the beatings. Surely, He who spoke the world into being could have delivered Christ from the entire ordeal. And yet, the God of heaven peered down through time and saw you and me. Though we were His enemies, He loved us and longed to rescue us from our sins, and designated the sinless Christ to become our substitute. Only Christ could avert God's righteous wrath against sin, so in love, the Father kept silent as Jesus hung from the cross. All of His anger, all of the wrath we would ever deserve, was poured upon Christ, and Christ became sin for us (2 Cor. 5:21). Because he paid the penalty for our sins, and God's wrath was avenged, God no longer looks upon us through the eyes of judgment, but instead, He now lavishes His love upon us. The Scriptures teach that absolutely nothing can separate us from God's love (Rom. 8:38-39). He has adopted us into a tender, intimate, and powerful relationship with Him (Rom. 8:15).

Because we are His children, performance is no longer the basis of our worth. We are unconditionally and deeply loved by God, and we can live by faith in His grace. We were spiritually dead, but the Lord has made us alive and has given us the high status of sonship to the Almighty God. It will take all of eternity to comprehend the wealth of His love and grace. Paul explains this incomprehensible gift this way:

> *But God, being rich in mercy, because of His great love with which He loved us,*
> *even when we were dead in our transgressions, made us alive together with Christ (by grace you have been saved),*
> *and raised us up with Him, and seated us with Him in the heavenly places, in Christ Jesus,*

in order that in the ages to come He might show the surpassing riches of His grace in kindness toward us in Christ Jesus.

For by grace you have been saved through faith; and that not of yourselves, it is the gift of God;

not as a result of works, that no one should boast.

Eph. 2:4-9

Propitiation, then, means that Christ has satisfied the holy wrath of God through His payment for sin. There was only one reason for Him to do this: He loves us; infinitely, eternally, unconditionally, irrevocably, He loves us. God the Father loves us with the love of a father, reaching to snatch us from harm. God the Son loves us with the love of a brother, laying down His life for us. He alone has turned away God's wrath from us. There is nothing we can do, no amount of good deeds we can accomplish, and no religious ceremonies we can perform that can pay for our sins. Instead, Christ has conclusively paid for them so that we can escape eternal condemnation and experience His love and purposes both now and forever.

Christ not only paid for our sins at one point in time, but continues to love us and teach us day after day. We have a weapon to use against Satan as he attacks us with doubts about God's love for us. Our weapon is the fact that Christ took our punishment upon Himself at Calvary. We no longer have to fear punishment for our sins because Christ paid for them all—past, present, and future. This tremendous truth of propitiation clearly demonstrates that we are truly and deeply loved by God. His perfect love casts out all fear as we allow it to flood our hearts (1 John 4:18).

A BEGINNING EXERCISE

How do we begin to experience freedom from Satan's lie: *Those who fail are unworthy of love and deserve to be punished*? We will be increasingly freed as we understand and apply the truth of propitiation in the context of loving and supportive relationships, where we can express ourselves honestly and receive both the warmth of affirmation and the challenge of God's Word.

The Scriptures indicate that Satan accuses believers of being unworthy of God's grace. It is his desire that we cower under the fear of punishment. Consider this passage from Rev. 12:10-11:

> *And I heard a loud voice in heaven, saying, "Now the salvation, and the power, and the authority of His Christ have come, for the accuser of our brethren has been thrown down, who accuses them before our God day and night.*
>
> *And they overcame him because of the blood of the Lamb and because of the word of their testimony, and they did not love their life even to death.*

How are we to overcome Satan, the accuser, and experience our acceptance in Christ? According to this passage of Scripture, there is only one way: by the sacrificial blood of Christ on the cross, the blood of the Lamb. To do this, we must first stop trying to overcome our feelings of condemnation and failure by penitent actions. Defending ourselves or trying to pay for our sins by our actions leads only to a guilt-and-penance spiral because we can never do enough on our own to justify our sins.

There have been times when I thought that I couldn't feel forgiven until I had experienced remorse about my sin for a certain period of time. These occasions led to depression, because I could hardly complete my penance for one sin before I had sinned again. Then, I would have to feel badly about *that* for a period of time, only to sin again...and again...and again...and....

Eventually, I began to realize that I had one of three options: I could continue trying to make up for my sin by mourning over it for however long it seemed necessary (although that wasn't getting me very far); I could try to deny that I had sinned (even though I knew that I had); or I could give up on the idea of using my guilt as a form of penance, and trust in Christ's forgiveness. Initially, of course, these options were not as clear as they've become with time and reflection.

No matter how much we do to make up for our sin, we will continue to feel guilty and believe that we need to do more unless we resist Satan, the accuser of the brethren. This can only be accomplished because Christ's blood has completely paid for our sins and delivered us from guilt.

Secondly, we need to verbalize what the blood of Christ has done for us: *We are deeply loved, completely forgiven, fully pleasing, totally accepted, and complete in Christ.*

As the Bible says in Rev. 12:11, we should not love our lives (the excitement, comfort, prestige, and status) to the point of spiritual deadness. Love for the world and its pleasures renders us spiritually impotent. We must decide that our minds are no longer the source of truth, and instead gain our knowledge, wisdom, and direction from the Scriptures. There are two practical steps that will help make these truths a reality in our lives:

1. On one side of a 3x5 card, write the following:
    Because of Christ and His redemption, I am completely forgiven and fully pleasing to God. I am totally accepted by God.

2. On the other side of the card, write the words of Rom. 5:1 and Col. 1:21-22.

Carry this card with you for the next twenty-eight days. Every time you get something to drink, or do some other routine activity, look at it and remind yourself of what Christ has done for you. This exercise will help you develop a habit of reflecting on these liberating truths. As you read and memorize these statements and passages, think about how they apply to you. Memorization and application of these truths will have profound effects on your life as your mind is slowly transformed by God's Word.

Nine
Shame

When we base our self-worth on past failures, dissatisfaction with personal appearance, or bad habits, we often develop a fourth false belief: *I am what I am. I cannot change. I am hopeless.* This lie binds people to the hopeless pessimism associated with poor self-esteem.

"I just can't help myself," some people say. "That's the way I've always been, and that's the way I'll always be. You can't teach an old dog new tricks." We assume that others should have low expectations of us, too. "You know I can't do any better than that. What do you expect?"

If we excuse our failures with an attitude of hopelessness too often, our personality can become glued to them. Our self-image becomes no more than a reflection of our past.

When Leslie approached Janet about serving a term as president of the Ladies' Auxiliary, Janet's outward poise and confidence vanished.

"Are you serious?" she stuttered. "You know I've never been a leader, and have never even gotten along well with people. No, no, I'd simply be an embarrassment to you. No, I can't do it, don't you see?"

Janet was suffering from low self-esteem. Her opinions of herself were based on her past failures, and those failures kept her from enjoying new experiences.

A young man named Jeff once questioned me when I told him that he needed to separate his past from the present, and that no natural law dictated his having to remain the same individual he had always been. I told Jeff that he could change, that he could rise above his past and build a new life for himself.

"But how?" Jeff asked. "I'm more of a realist than that. I know myself. I know what I've done and who I am. I've tried to change, but it hasn't worked. I've given up now."

I explained to Jeff that he needed a new perspective, not just new efforts based on his old, pessimistic attitude. He needed to develop a new self-concept based on the unconditional love and acceptance of God. Both Jeff's past failures and God's unconditional love were realities, but the question was which one Jeff would value more. If he continued to value his failures, he would continue to be absorbed in self-pity. Instead, he needed to be honest. He needed someone he could talk to openly, so that he could express his feelings without the fear of being rejected. And he needed to be encouraged to study and apply the truths of God's Word. As he persisted in this process, his sense of self-worth would begin to change. In addition to a changed self-worth, he would eventually experience changes in every area of his life: his goals, his relationships, and his outlook.

Too often, our self-image rests solely on an evaluation of our past behavior, being measured only through a memory. Day after day, year after year, we tend to build our personalities upon the rubble of yesterday's personal disappointments.

Perhaps we find some strange kind of comfort in our personal failings. Perhaps there is some security in accepting ourselves as much less than we can become. That minimizes the risk of failure. Certainly, if we expect little from ourselves we will seldom be disappointed!

But nothing forces us to remain in the mold of the past. By the grace and power of God, we can change! We can persevere and overcome! No one forces us to keep shifting our feet in the muck of old failures. We can dare to accept the challenge of building a new life.

Dr. Paul Tournier once compared life to a man hanging from a trapeze. The trapeze bar was the man's security, his pattern of existence, his lifestyle. Then God swung another trapeze into the man's view, and he faced a perplexing dilemma. Should he relinquish his past? Should he reach for the new bar? The moment of truth came, Dr. Tournier explained, when the man realized that to grab onto the new bar, he must release the old one.

Our past relationships may involve the intense pain of neglect, abuse, and manipulation, but if we do not begin the process of healing, we will be unable to experience the joy, challenge, and yes, the potential for failure in the present.

I have struggled with this process of change for the greater part of my life. It may have been that I was raised in a poor family. It may have been that while I was growing up, I often felt very awkward. It may have been that there were some inadequacies in my home life. For whatever reasons, I grew up with a sense of shame about myself and my circumstances.

As I've mentioned previously, I often felt inadequate during my childhood. I had the impression that I just didn't measure up. Others might not have thought I felt this way, but my sense of inadequacy was often intense.

Being exceptionally tall and lanky, I was uncomfortable with the way I looked, and felt out of place among my peers. My feelings of inferiority prevented me from pursuing dating relationships for a number of years. The threat of potential rejection prompted me to withdraw from social gatherings, preferring instead to spend time with the few friends I felt most comfortable with.

The truth that I am deeply loved, fully pleasing, and totally accepted by the God of the universe has taken me a lifetime to comprehend. But gradually, by studying God's Word and by experiencing loving relationships with other believers who genuinely care for me and appreciate me, I have continued to gain a better understanding of the way God values me. This has improved my sense of self-worth considerably.

Many of my past memories are still painful for me, and I imagine they always will be. But through Christ, my present attitude about myself is continually changing. Knowing that I have no reason to feel ashamed has motivated me to pursue a number of challenges that I wouldn't have even considered pursuing a number of years ago. In the process, I have experienced failure and success. God has used each instance to teach me that despite my circumstances, my worth is secure in Him.

We need to be honest about the pain, the anger, the disappointment, and the loneliness of our past. We need to put ourselves in relationships that will encourage us to feel what we may have suppressed for many years. This will enable us to begin (or continue) to experience hope, and eventually, healing. Change is possible, but it is a process.

Does this seem strange? Does it seem difficult? We may have difficulty relinquishing what is familiar (though painful) for what is unfamiliar because our fear of the unknown often seems stronger than the pain of a poor self-concept. It seems right to hang on. Proverbs 16:25 says, *There is a way which seems right to a man, but its end is the way of death.*

Any change in our behavior requires a release from our old self-concept, which is often founded in failure and the expectations of others. We need to learn how to relate to ourselves in a new way. To accomplish this, we must begin to base our self-worth on God's opinion of us and trust in His Spirit to accomplish change in our lives. Then, and only then, can we overcome Satan's deception that holds sway over our self-perception and behavior.

By believing Satan's lie, *I am what I am, I cannot change, I am hopeless,* we become vulnerable to pessimism and a poor self-concept. Take the test on the following page to determine how strongly you are affected by this false belief:

SHAME TEST

Read each of the following statements; then, choose the term from the top of the test which best describes your response. Put the number above that term in the blank beside each statement.

1	2	3	4	5	6	7
Always	Very Often	Often	Sometimes	Seldom	Very Seldom	Never

_____ 1. I often think about past failures or experiences of rejection.

_____ 2. There are certain things about my past which I cannot recall without experiencing strong, painful emotions (i.e. guilt, shame, anger, fear, etc.).

_____ 3. I seem to make the same mistakes over and over again.

_____ 4. There are certain aspects of my character that I want to change, but I don't believe I can ever successfully do so.

_____ 5. I feel inferior.

_____ 6. There are aspects of my appearance that I cannot accept.

_____ 7. I am generally disgusted with myself.

_____ 8. I feel that certain experiences have basically ruined my life.

_____ 9. I perceive of myself as an immoral person.

_____10. I feel that I have lost the opportunity to experience a complete and wonderful life.

_____ Total (Add up the numbers you have placed in the blanks.)

Interpretation of Score

If your score is...

57-70

God has apparently given you a very strong appreciation for His love and unconditional acceptance. You seem to be freed from the shame that plagues most people. (Some people who score this high are either greatly deceived, or have become callous to their emotions as a way to suppress pain.)

47-56

Shame controls your responses rarely or only in certain situations. Again, the exceptions are those who are not honest with themselves.

37-46

When you experience emotional problems, they may relate to a sense of shame. Upon reflection, you will probably relate many of your previous decisions to feelings of worthlessness. Many of your future decisions will also be affected by low self-esteem unless you take direct action to overcome it.

27-36

Shame forms a generally negative backdrop to your life. There are probably few days that you are not affected in some way by shame. Unfortunately, this robs you of the joy and peace your salvation was meant to bring.

0-26

Experiences of shame dominate your memory, and have probably resulted in a great deal of depression. These problems will remain until some definitive action is taken. In other words, this condition will not simply disappear one day; time alone cannot heal your pain. You need to experience deep healing in your self-concept, in your relationship with God, and in your relationships with others.

EFFECTS OF SHAME

Susan was the product of heartless parents. Although she was a beautiful girl with dark brown eyes and long, silky hair, Susan never seemed quite as confident or as outgoing as her brothers and sisters. One reason for this was that by her eighth birthday, Susan had been approached by her father for sexual favors. Overcome by the shame this caused her, Susan withdrew from others and looked for an escape.

By the time she was sixteen, Susan was addicted to alcohol and drugs, and was frequently stealing as well as selling her body for money. She had accepted the belief that she was nothing more than sexual merchandise. Although she was ashamed of her lifestyle and wanted to change, she saw no way out. The only people who didn't seem to reject her were the ones who used her. She was not only ashamed, but was also trapped and alone.

Unlike Susan, Diana was raised by Christian parents. She had grown up in a conservative Protestant church and was very active in its youth group. Diana was diligent in witnessing to her friends at school, and her actions were always an example to those around her.

Unfortunately, Diana made a mistake one night that changed her life. Alone for the evening, she and her boyfriend went too far. Shocked and ashamed by their actions, they both agreed that they must admit the incident to their parents. Tearfully, Diana confided in her mother, looking for understanding and support. But Diana's mother lost control and bitterly told her how ashamed and disappointed she was. Diana's father couldn't believe what she had done, and refused even to speak to her.

Her relationship with her parents continued to worsen and six months later, Diana left home. Heartbroken and overcome by shame, she turned to her boyfriend. Soon, they began sleeping together regularly, and both began using drugs. Believing that her parents would never accept her again, Diana sought acceptance in the only way she knew how.

Both Susan and Diana suffered from the devastating effects of shame. Shame often engulfs us when a flaw in our performance is so important, so overpowering, or so disappointing to us that it creates a permanently negative opinion about our self-worth. Others may not know of our failure, but we do. We may only imagine their rejection, but real or imagined, the pain resulting from it cripples our confidence and hope.

Shame usually results in guilt and self-deprecation, but it can also lead us to search for God and His answers. Our inner, undeniable need for personal significance was created to make us search for Him. He alone can fulfill our deep need. In Him, we find peace, acceptance, and love. Through Him, we find the courage and power to develop into the men and women He intends us to be. Although Satan wants to convince us that we will always be prisoners of our failures and past experiences, by God's grace we can be freed from the guilt of our past, and experience a renewed purpose for our lives.

Shame can have powerful effects on our esteem, and it can manifest itself in many ways. The following is a brief list of common problems associated with shame:

Inferiority

By definition, *shame* is a deep sense of inferiority. Feelings of inferiority can result from prolonged patterns of failure, or they can stem from only one or two haunting instances. Either way, they can destroy our self-worth, and as a result, adversely affect our emotions and behavior. These perceptions of ourselves aren't easily altered, but they can change through honesty, the affirmation of others, the truths of God's Word, the power and encouragement of the Holy Spirit, and time. Because of Christ's redemption, we are worthy, forgiven, loved, accepted, and complete in Him.

Habitually Destructive Behavior

We often behave in a manner that is consistent with our perception of ourselves. Therefore, seeing ourselves through the eyes of shame usually results in a pessimistic outlook on life and a lifestyle of destructive behavior.

Self-Pity

Shame often prompts us to view ourselves as victims. Consequently, whether we blame others or condemn ourselves for our actions, we sink into the depths of feeling sorry for ourselves.

Passivity

Some of us try to compensate for gnawing feelings of shame through passivity, refusing to invest any part of ourselves in relationships and responsibilities. We may be compulsive perfectionists in some areas of our lives, but may avoid taking risks in relationships or circumstances. We may tend to become engrossed in peripheral activities (clipping coupons, cleaning the kitchen, filing papers, reading magazines), so that we are "too busy" to experience the reality of relationships and situations.

Isolation and Withdrawal

Isolation is often a corollary of passivity. Avoiding both the risks of rejection and failure, some of us withdraw from virtually all meaningful interaction. We develop facades, so that nobody can see our hurt. We may be socially active, but may not allow anyone to get really close to us. We are often afraid that if people *really* knew us, we would again experience hurt and rejection. Our deep sense of shame leads us to withdraw from others, feel isolated, and experience the pain of loneliness.

Loss of Creativity

When we are ashamed of ourselves over a period of time, the cutting edge of our creativity atrophies. We tend to become so preoccupied with our own inferiority that we are unable to come up with new ideas. Often believing that whatever we attempt will fail, we may choose to avoid doing anything that isn't a proven success and relatively risk-free.

Codependent Relationships

In an attempt to overcome their sense of shame, many people become *codependent*; that is, they depend on being needed by a family member or friend who has an addictive problem or compulsion. Codependents thus develop a need to "rescue" and take care of others. This caretaking is the codependent's subconscious way of trying to gain personal significance. Such attempts usually backfire, however, because dependent persons often use shame to manipulate the codependent. A frequent ploy is to tell the codependent that he or she is being "selfish" for taking care of personal affairs rather than those of the dependent person. This locks the codependent into a hopeless pattern of rescuing to gain approval and feeling ashamed because of his or her inability to develop a sense of personal value, regardless of how hard he or she tries to do so.

Despising Our Appearance

Beauty is highly valued in our society. Television commercials and programs, magazine ads and billboards all convey the message that beauty is to be prized. But very few of us compare to the beautiful people we see in these ads and programs, and most of us are ashamed of at least one aspect of our appearance. We spend hundreds of dollars and an inestimable amount of time and worry covering up or altering our skin, eyes, teeth, faces, noses, thighs, and scalps, refusing to believe that God, in His sovereignty and love, gave us the features He wants us to have.

GOD'S ANSWER: REGENERATION

Perhaps no passage in the Bible better illustrates God's regeneration than the story of Zaccheus in Luke 19:1-10. Zaccheus was a tax collector, despised by the people for overtaxing their meager earnings. There were few in the Roman world more despicable than tax collectors, who obtained their wealth at the expense of others.

One day, Zaccheus learned that Jesus was visiting his town, and climbed a sycamore tree to get a good look at the man who reportedly loved even sinners and outcasts. Jesus saw him in the tree, and to the astonishment of all—including Zaccheus—invited him to come down, and then went to his house to eat with him!

During dinner, Zaccheus experienced the unconditional love and acceptance of Christ. As a result, he became a different person. His self-concept was radically changed from a swindling, loathsome tax collector to a person who knew he was loved by God. His actions reflected this dramatic change. He pledged to repent of his sins and repay fourfold those he had swindled. He also promised to give half of his possessions to the poor. Through Christ, Zaccheus developed a new self-concept, new values, new goals, and new behavior.

Regeneration is not a self-improvement program, nor is it a clean-up campaign for our sinful natures. *Regeneration* is nothing less than the impartation of new life. As Paul stated in Eph. 2:5, we were once dead in our sins, but have since been made alive in Christ.

Paul also wrote about this incredible transformation process in his letter to the young pastor, Titus:

> *For we also once were foolish ourselves, disobedient, deceived, enslaved to various lusts and pleasures, spending our life in malice and envy, hateful, hating one another.*
>
> *But when the kindness of God our Savior and His love for mankind appeared,*
>
> *He saved us, not on the basis of deeds which we have done in righteousness, but according to His mercy, by the washing of regeneration and renewing by the Holy Spirit,*
>
> *whom He poured out upon us richly through Jesus Christ our Savior,*

> *that being justified by His grace we might be made heirs*
> *according to the hope of eternal life.*
>
> Titus 3:3-7

Regeneration is the renewing work of the Holy Spirit that literally makes each believer a new person at the moment he or she trusts Christ as Savior.

In that wondrous, miraculous moment, we experience more than swapping one set of standards for another. We experience what Jesus called a new birth (John 3:3-6), a Spirit-wrought renewal of the human spirit, a transforming resuscitation which takes place so that the Spirit is alive within us (Rom. 8:10).

Through the gift of God's grace, we are spiritually alive, forgiven, and complete in Him. Paul wrote the Colossian Christians:

> *For in Him* (Christ) *all the fullness of Deity dwells in bodily form,*
> *and in Him you have been made complete, and He is the head over all rule and authority.*
>
> Col. 2:9-10

In the church at Colossae, false teachers taught that "completeness" came through a combination of philosophy, good works, other religions, and Christ. Paul's clear message was that we are made complete *through Christ alone*. To attempt to find completeness through any other source, including success, the approval of others, prestige, or appearance, is to be taken captive through philosophy and empty deception (Col. 2:8). Nothing can add to the death of Christ to pay for our sins and the resurrection of Christ to give us new life. We are complete because Christ has forgiven us and given us life—the capacity for growth and change.

According to the theologian, Louis Berkhof, "Regeneration consists in the implanting of the principle of the new spiritual life in man, in a radical change of the governing disposition of the soul, which, under the influence of the Holy Spirit, gives birth to a life that moves in a Godward direction. In principle this change affects the whole man: the intellect...the will...and the feelings or emotions."[1]

When we trust Christ and experience new life, forgiveness, and love, our lives will begin to change. Still, regeneration does not affect an instantaneous change in the full realm of our performance. We will continue to stumble and fall at times, but the Scriptures clearly instruct us to choose to act in ways that reflect our new lives and values in Christ. As Paul wrote the Ephesians:

> *that, in reference to your former manner of life, you lay aside the old self, which is being corrupted in accordance with the lusts of deceit,*
> *and that you be renewed in the spirit of your mind,*
> *and put on the new self, which in the likeness of God has been created in righteousness and holiness of the truth.*
>
> Eph. 4:22-24

We are to *put on*, or envelop ourselves in, this new self that progressively expresses Christian character in our attitudes and behavior. We are marvelously unique, created to reflect the character of Christ through our individual personalities and behavior. Each believer, in a different and special way, has the capability to shine forth the light of God. No two will reflect His light in exactly the same way.

The truth of regeneration can dispel the specter of the past. Our sins have been forgiven, and we now have tremendous capabilities for growth and change because we are new people with the Spirit of God living in us. Yes, when we sin, we will experience its destructive effects and the Father's discipline, but our sin will never change the truth of who we are in Christ.

When we do sin, we should follow King David's example. When Nathan confronted David about his sin of adultery with Bathsheba, David confessed his sin to the Lord (2 Sam. 12:1-13). David did not run from his sin or its consequences. He married Bathsheba, and God was merciful: He enabled Bathsheba to give birth to Solomon, the wise king of Israel. Certainly, God could have brought Solomon into the world another way, but perhaps as a message to us, He chose Bathsheba.

What a message! Confess your sins, worship God, and get on with your life. You can experience the mercy of God no matter what you've been through.

A BEGINNING EXERCISE

Satan wants us to believe the lie: *I am what I am. I cannot change. I am hopeless.*

How can you begin to experience freedom from the fear of shame? Start by looking up the following verses and reflecting on who you are in Christ. Paraphrase each of the following passages about your new life in Him:

Matt. 5:13_____

_____

Matt. 5:14_____

_____

Rom.1:7_____

_____

Rom. 5:17-18_____

_____

Rom. 8:1_____

_____

Rom. 8:17_____

_____

Rom. 8:37_____

_____

2 Cor. 5:17_____

_____

2 Cor. 5:21_____

_____

Gal. 2:20_____

_____

Eph. 1:5_____

_____

Eph. 1:7_____

_____

Eph. 2:4-6_____

_____

_____

Eph. 2:10_____

_____

Eph. 6:10_____

_____

Col. 2:10_____

_____

Col. 3:12_____

_____

1 Pet. 1:16_____

_____

1 John 4:17_____

_____

These passages describe the stable and secure identity we have in Christ. It is our privilege to be His children; to experience His love, forgiveness, and power; and to express our appreciation of Him to others.

To summarize the last four chapters:

Because of *justification*, you are completely forgiven and fully pleasing to God. You no longer have to fear failure.

Because of *reconciliation*, you are totally accepted by God. You no longer have to fear rejection.

Because of *propitiation*, you are deeply loved by God. You no longer have to fear punishment; nor do you have to punish others.

Because of *regeneration*, you have been made brand new, complete in Christ. You no longer need to experience the pain of shame.

Ten
Obstacles to Growth

Our redemption was made complete at Calvary. When Jesus lifted up His eyes and cried, *It is finished!* (John 19:30), He told us that the provision for man's reconciliation with God was complete. Nothing more need be done, because the Word of life had been spoken to all mankind. Man needed only to hear the Word, accept it, and place his hope and trust in Christ.

But if the redemption we enjoy is complete, why do we so often fail to see the changes in our lives we long for? Why do we wrestle day after day with the same temptations, the same failings, and the same distractions we have always fought? Why can't we break free and move on toward maturity?

Christ illustrated the reasons for our lack of fruitfulness in the parable of the sower in Mark 4:3-20. In agriculture, productivity depends on the fertility of the soil, the climate, and the presence or absence of weeds. The reasons Christ gave for lack of fruit in the believer's life were: Satan's taking away the Word of God, persecution, and the worries of the world. For most of us, the worries of the world are the primary culprit for our lack of growth. Jesus described it this way:

> *And others are the ones on whom seed was sown among*
> *the thorns; these are the ones who have heard the word,*
> *and the worries of the world, and the deceitfulness of*
> *riches, and the desires for other things enter in and choke the*
> *word, and it becomes unfruitful.*
>
> Mark 4:18-19

In the context of honesty, affirmation, and patience, we can focus on the forgiveness we have received, and reject the deception and worldly desires that choke out the Word of life. We need to base our lives on God's Word and allow His character to be reproduced within us by the power of His Spirit:

> *And those are the ones on whom seed was sown on the*
> *good soil; and they hear the word and accept it, and bear fruit,*
> *thirty, sixty, and a hundredfold.*
>
> Mark 4:20

The moment we trust Christ, we are given *everything pertaining to life and godliness* (2 Pet. 1:2-4). Immediately, we become His sons and daughters, with all the provisions He has graciously given us. As we allow Him to reign over the affairs of our lives, He transforms our values, attitudes, and behavior so that we are able to glorify Him more and more. Of course, we are still chained to a mortal body, but we are reborn in righteousness and holiness of the truth (Eph. 4:24). We have within us the Christ who has authority over Satan. Christ has triumphed over him by the power of His blood to pay for sin, and by the power of His resurrection to give new life (Col. 2:15).

Now redeemed, our rightful purpose to rule in life will only be denied if we continue to allow Satan to deceive us. If we fail to recognize our true position of sonship, and fail to exercise our new power and authority, we will remain trapped in the world's system. Satan's lies and schemes are designed to keep us from recognizing and experiencing these wonderful truths.

In order to overcome Satan's lies and begin to enjoy freedom from false beliefs, we need to have a clear understanding of what Christ has done for us through His death on the cross. The more fully we understand the implications of Christ's sacrifice, the more we will experience the freedom, motivation, and power God intends for us. God's Word is the source of truth: the truth about Christ, the cross, and redemption.

The Apostle Peter wrote that the cross is not just the beginning of Christian life, but our constant motivation to grow spiritually and to live for Christ:

> *Now for this very reason also, applying all diligence, in your faith supply moral excellence, and in your moral excellence, knowledge;*
> *and in your knowledge, self-control, and in your self-control, perseverance, and in your perseverance, godliness;*
> *and in your godliness, brotherly kindness, and in your brotherly kindness, love.*
> *For if these qualities are yours and are increasing, they render you neither useless nor unfruitful in the true knowledge of our Lord Jesus Christ.*
> *For he who lacks these qualities is blind or shortsighted, having forgotten his purification from his former sins.*
> 2 Pet. 1:5-9

This passage clearly teaches that the absence of spiritual growth can be traced to a lack of understanding or a failure to remember the implications of Christ's forgiveness. The cross is central to our motivation and development.

I have given you a beginning exercise for each of four false beliefs in previous chapters, but this is only a start. In the closing chapters, we'll look at the basics of renewing the heart and mind: experiencing the power of the Holy Spirit, and replacing thought patterns that tell us our worth is based on *performance plus others' opinions* with those that focus on the truths of God's unconditional love for us.

The principles in this book can be life-changing, but they are applied most readily in an environment where we are encouraged to be honest about our hurt, anger, joys, and hopes. Most of us are not very perceptive about ourselves (though we may be very perceptive about other people), and we need both the objectivity and the affirmation of others as we continue the process of application. It is also important to realize that working through these principles once is not enough. Many whom I have counseled, and many who have read this material in its previous edition, report that they have experienced dramatic growth only as they have applied these truths at an increasingly deeper level of their lives.

Let's review for a minute. The chart on the following pages depicts the contrast between the rival belief systems. Use the chart to help you when you want to determine if any particular thought is based on a lie or on God's truth. If the thought is based on a lie, learn how to confront it and overcome it with the truth of God's Word.

FALSE BELIEFS	CONSEQUENCES OF FALSE BELIEFS
I must meet certain standards in order to feel good about myself.	The fear of failure; perfectionism; being driven to succeed; manipulating others to achieve success; withdrawing from healthy risks
I must have the approval of certain others to feel good about myself.	The fear of rejection; attempting to please others at any cost; being overly sensitive to criticism; withdrawing from others to avoid disapproval
Those who fail (including myself) are unworthy of love and deserve to be punished.	The fear of punishment; propensity to punish others; blaming self and others for personal failure; withdrawing from God and fellow believers; being driven to avoid punishment
I am what I am. I cannot change. I am hopeless.	Feelings of shame, hopelessness, inferiority; passivity; loss of creativity; isolation, withdrawing from others

GOD'S SPECIFIC SOLUTION	RESULTS OF GOD'S SOLUTION
Because of justification, *I am completely forgiven and fully pleasing to God. I no longer have to fear failure.*	Increasing freedom from the fear of failure; desire to pursue the right things: Christ and His kingdom; love for Christ
Because of reconciliation, *I am totally accepted by God. I no longer have to fear rejection.*	Increasing freedom from the fear of rejection; willingness to be open and vulnerable; able to relax around others; willingness to take criticism; desire to please God no matter what others think
Because of propitiation, *I am deeply loved by God. I no longer have to fear punishment or punish others.*	Increasing freedom from the fear of punishment; patience and kindness toward others; being quick to apply forgiveness; deep love for Christ
Because of regeneration, *I have been made brand new, complete in Christ. I no longer need to experience the pain of shame.*	Christ-centered self-confidence; joy, courage, peace; desire to know Christ

Eleven

The Holy Spirit:
Our Source of Change

The truths we have examined in this book can have tremendous implications on our every goal and relationship, but now we need to understand how to actually implement them in our lives. How can we begin to experience positive change? Jesus answered this question in His last time of intimate instruction with His disciples (John 13-16). He told them that He would soon be put to death, but that they would not be left alone: *And I will ask the Father, and He will give you another Helper, that He may be with you forever* (John 14:16). That Helper is the Holy Spirit, who came some fifty days later to direct and empower the believers at Pentecost. That same Holy Spirit indwells each believer today, and serves as our instructor, counselor, and source of spiritual power as we live for Christ's glory and honor.

Who is the Holy Spirit, and why did He come? The Holy Spirit, the third Person of the Trinity, is God and possesses all the attributes of deity. His primary purpose is to glorify Christ and bring attention to Him. Christ said, *He shall glorify Me; for He shall take of Mine, and shall disclose it to you* (John 16:14). The Holy Spirit is our teacher, and He guides us into the truth of the Scriptures (John 16:13). It is by His power that the love of Christ flows through us and produces spiritual fruit within us (John 7:37-39; 15:1-8). This spiritual fruit is described in many ways in the New

Testament, including: intimate friendship with Christ (John 15:14); love for one another (John 15:12); joy and peace in the midst of difficulties (John 14:27; 15:11); steadfastness (Eph. 5:18-21); and evangelism and discipleship (Matt. 28:18-20).

Obviously, this fruit is not always evident in the lives of Christians, but why not?

As we all know, the Christian life is not an easy one. It is not simply a self-improvement program. True, we may at times be able to make some changes in our habits through our own discipline and determination, but Christianity is not merely self-effort. The Christian life is a supernatural one in which we draw on Christ as our resource for direction, encouragement, and strength. In one of the most widely-known metaphors of the Bible, Christ described the Christian life in John 15, using the illustration of a branch and a vine. He said:

> *I am the true vine, and My Father is the vine dresser.*
> *... Abide in* (live, grow, and gain your sustenance from) *Me, and I in you. As the branch cannot bear fruit of itself, unless it abides in the vine, so neither can you, unless you abide in Me.*
> *I am the vine, you are the branches; he who abides in Me, and I in him, he bears much fruit; for apart from Me you can do nothing.*
>
> John 15:1, 4-5

Nothing? Yes, in terms of that which honors Christ, is spiritually nourishing to us, and is genuine Christian service, anything done apart from the love and power of Christ amounts to nothing. Although we may expend tremendous effort at a great personal cost, only that which is done for Christ's glory in the power of His Spirit is of eternal value.

The very power of God that was evident when Christ was raised from the dead (Eph. 1:19-21) is available to every believer who abides in Him, who desires that He be honored, and who trusts that His Spirit will produce fruit in his or her life.

Just as the cross of Christ is the basis of our relationship with God, it is also the foundation of our spiritual growth. Christ's death is the supreme demonstration of God's love, power, and wisdom. The more we understand and apply the truths of justification, propitiation, reconciliation, and regeneration, the more our lives will reflect His character. Spiritual growth is not magic. It comes as we apply the love and forgiveness of Christ in our daily circumstances—reflecting on the unconditional acceptance of Christ and His awesome power, and choosing to respond to situations and people in light of His sovereign purpose and kindness toward us. As noted in the previous chapter, the Apostle Peter stated very clearly that our forgiveness, bought by the death of Christ, is the foundation of spiritual growth:

> Now for this very reason also, applying all diligence, in your faith supply moral excellence, and in your moral excellence, knowledge;
> and in your knowledge, self-control, and in your self-control, perseverance, and in your perseverance, godliness;
> and in your godliness, brotherly kindness, and in your brotherly kindness, love.
> For if these qualities are yours and are increasing, they render you neither useless nor unfruitful in the true knowledge of our Lord Jesus Christ.
> For he who lacks these qualities is blind or shortsighted, having forgotten his purification from his former sins.
> 2 Pet. 1:5-9

Again, the clear implication from this passage is that the absence of spiritual growth signifies one's lack of understanding concerning forgiveness. Seeking an emotional experience, going to seminar after seminar, or looking for a "deeper life" may not be the solution. Emotional experiences, seminars, and studies are only valid if they are founded on the love, forgiveness, and power of the cross and resurrection of Christ.

There is nothing more motivating, nothing more comforting, nothing else that compels us more to honor Christ, and nothing else that gives us as much compassion for others as the sacrificial payment of Christ which has rescued us from eternal condemnation.

At least five obstacles stem from a misunderstanding of Christ's love and forgiveness, and often prevent us from experiencing His presence and power:

1. We have wrong motives.
2. Our approach to the Christian life is too mechanical, or regimented.
3. We are too "mystical."
4. We lack knowledge about the availability of Christ's love and power.
5. We are harboring sin which blocks our fellowship with Christ.

Let's take a closer look at these obstacles:

Wrong Motives

Determining where we err in our motivations is often difficult. We usually have a variety of motives for what we pursue, and probably do nothing with completely pure motives. However, we must examine some of the reasons we may be following Christ before we can consider whether or not our motivations might be hindering our walk with Him.

Many of us tend to approach Christian living as a self-improvement program. We may desire spiritual growth, or we may have one or more fairly serious problems from which we desperately want to be delivered. While there is certainly nothing wrong with spiritual growth or desiring to be rid of a besetting problem, what is our motivation in wanting to achieve goals like these? Perhaps we desire success or the approval of others. Perhaps we fear that God can't really accept us until we have spiritually matured, or until "our problem" is removed. Perhaps we just want to feel better without having to struggle through the process of making major changes in our attitudes and behavior.

Motivations such as these may be mixed with a genuine desire to honor the Lord, but it's also possible that deep within us is a primary desire to glorify ourselves. When self-improvement becomes the center of our focus, rather than Christ, our focus is displaced.

It is important to understand that fruitfulness and growth are the *results* of focusing on Christ and desiring to honor Him. When growth and change are our primary goals, we tend to be preoccupied with ourselves instead of with Christ. *Am I growing? Am I getting any better? Am I more like Christ today? What am I learning?*

This inordinate preoccupation with self-improvement parallels our culture's self-help and personal enhancement movement in many ways. Personal development is certainly not wrong, but it is misleading—and it can be very disappointing—to make it our preeminent goal. If it is our goal at all, it should be secondary. As we grasp the unconditional love, grace, and power of God, then honoring Christ will increasingly be our consuming passion. God wants us to have a healthy self-awareness and to periodically analyze our lives, but He does not want us to be preoccupied with ourselves. The only One worthy of our preoccupation is Christ, our sovereign Lord, who told the Apostle Paul, *My grace is sufficient for you, for power is perfected in weakness* (2 Cor. 12:9).

If, through affirming Christian relationships, the power of God's Word, His Spirit, and time, we can begin to realize that our needs for security and approval are fully met in Christ, we will gradually be able to take our attention and affections off of ourselves, and place them on Him. Only then can we begin to adopt Paul's intense desire to honor Christ: *Therefore also we have as our ambition...to be pleasing to Him* (2 Cor. 5:9).

Too Mechanical

Some of us are too mechanical in our approach to the Christian life. Although we may rigorously schedule and discipline our lives in an effort to conform to what we believe is a biblical lifestyle, our lives may exhibit little of the freshness, joy, and spontaneity of Christ.

One man had organized his life into hourly segments, each designated to accomplish some particular "biblical purpose." True, he was organized and accomplished some good things, but he was miserable. This man was trusting in himself, instead of the Holy Spirit, to produce a life that pleased God.

Eventually, this man joined a church Bible study on God's grace. One of the men leading the group began meeting with him regularly. He had a lot of questions, and slowly, he began to realize that Christ's foremost commandment is to love Him and others (Matt. 22:36-40), and that joy, peace, and kindness are much more important to God than adhering to strict rules (for which Jesus rebuked the Pharisees). Over the next few months, as he continued in this affirming relationship, he gained a new perspective which later resulted in a new lifestyle of love and joy. This man is still an organized person, but being organized no longer dominates his life.

Though we may not be as extreme, many of us do have certain Christian activities (church attendance, tithing, Bible studies, etc.) that we feel we *must* do to be "good Christians." These activities themselves are obviously not wrong, but a performance-oriented perspective is wrong. Christ wants us to receive our joy and acceptance from Him instead of merely following rules or schedules. He is the Lord; He alone is our source of security, joy, and meaning.

Too Mystical

A third obstacle to abiding in Christ is becoming too *mystical*, or depending on supernatural feelings to dictate our relationship with God. This dependence on feelings leads to two problems. The first occurs when we wait for feelings to motivate us, and the other occurs when we see virtually every emotion as a "sign" from God. Let's examine these:

Some of us won't get up in the morning until the Lord "tells us to." We may not want to share Christ with others until we feel that God is prompting us. What we may be forgetting is that Christianity is primarily faith in action. Our emotions are not the most reliable source of motivation. Yes, the Holy Spirit does sometimes prompt us through impressions, but He has already given us the vast majority of what He wants us to do through the Scriptures. Rather than waiting for a "holy zap" to get us going, we need to believe the truth of God's Word and take action for His glory. Must we wait until we *feel* like loving other Christians, praying, studying the Scriptures, sharing our faith, or serving His cause? No. We need to follow the examples recounted in Hebrews 11 of the men and women who acted on their faith in God, often in spite of their feelings. True, these people were often reflective, and prayed for God's direction, but they always acted on His truth.

The second problem with depending on our feelings occurs when we believe that our emotions are a primary means of God's communication with us and are, therefore, signs from God which indicate His leading. This conclusion may compel us to make authoritative statements about God's will (for both ourselves and others) that are based on little more than how we feel. As in the first extreme, the Scriptures may take a back seat as we sometimes justify foolish and even immoral acts by this false "leading from the Lord."

Though the Scriptures encourage us to be real and honest about our emotions, they never tell us to live by them. Biblical truths are the only reliable guide for our lives. Our feelings may reinforce these truths, but they may also reflect Satan's lies that God doesn't love us, that the fun of a particular sin is more satisfying than following God, or that God will never answer our prayers. The truth of God's Word is our authority, not our feelings.

Does this mean that we should repress our feelings or deny that we have them? No, but we need a safe environment (a friend or small group) with whom we can be honest about how we feel. We also should express our feelings to the Lord, fully and freely, and look at the Scriptures to determine what He would have us do. Then, with the encouragement of mature believers, the power of His Spirit, and in obedience to His Word, we should do what honors Christ. Many times, when we obey Christ in spite of our feelings, the emotions of joy and peace will follow sooner or later.

Again, our emotions are God-given; it is not wrong to have them, but by themselves, our feelings aren't enough to determine God's direction in our lives. Understanding God's leading requires that we blend a proper understanding of the Scriptures with a sensitivity to His Spirit. The Bible is our ultimate authority, and we need to become good students of it so that we will understand both the character and will of God. As Paul told Timothy:

> *All Scripture is inspired by God and profitable for teaching,*
> *for reproof, for correction, for training in righteousness,*
> > *that the man of God may be adequate, equipped for every*
> *good work.*
>
> 2 Tim. 3:16-17

We also need to develop a sensitivity to the Holy Spirit's leading that goes beyond emotionalism. This sensitivity takes time to develop, and is an awareness of His conviction of sin, what He wants us to say and do in certain situations, His prompting to share the gospel, etc. Discerning whether or not an impression is of God comes from three primary sources: the clear teaching of the Scriptures, previous experiences of learning, and the agreement of mature believers. If an impression is from God, it will not violate biblical principles.

Lack of Knowledge

Many of us are hindered in our walk with God because we do not realize the nature and depth of the love and power available to us in Christ.

We haven't yet fully comprehended the magnificent truths of the Scriptures—*that we are deeply loved, totally forgiven, fully pleasing, totally accepted, and complete in Christ,* with all the power of His resurrection available to us. We may be like the West Texas sheep rancher who lived in poverty even though vast resources of oil were under his property. He was fabulously rich but didn't even know it. Since its discovery many years ago, the Yates oil field has proven to be one of the richest and most productive in the world. Similarly, we have incredible resources available to us through the Holy Spirit, who enables us to experience the reality of Christ's love and power in many ways, including:

- Expressing Christ-like characteristics to us through other believers over a period of time (John 13:34-35; 1 John 4:7, 12).
- Revealing sin in our lives so that we can confess it and prevent our fellowship with God from being hindered (1 John 1:9).
- Helping us choose to honor Christ in our circumstances and relationships (2 Cor. 5:9).
- Enabling us to endure as we follow Christ (Rom. 5:1-5).
- Producing spiritual fruit in our lives (John 15:1-8; Gal. 5:22-23).

Harboring Sin

Willful sin is a fifth obstacle that clouds our fellowship with God. Indeed, sin may be pleasurable for a moment, but inevitably, its destructive nature will reveal itself in many ways: broken relationships, poor self-esteem, and a poor witness for Christ. Whether it is a blatant sin of immorality or the more subtle sin of pride, we must learn to deal with all sin decisively, for our benefit and for Christ's glory.

Christ's death paid for all of our sins; they are completely forgiven. Comprehending His love and forgiveness encourages us to admit that we have sinned and claim forgiveness for any and every sin as soon as we become aware of it. Again, this prevents our fellowship with Christ from being hindered, and enables us to continue experiencing His love and power.

Paul wrote to the Galatian Christians:

> *...The fruit of the Spirit is love, joy, peace, patience,*
> *kindness, goodness, faithfulness,*
> > *gentleness, self-control. ...*
> > Gal. 5:22-23

As we respond to the love of Christ and trust His Spirit to fill us, these characteristics will become increasingly evident in our lives. The filling of the Holy Spirit includes two major aspects: our purpose (to bring honor to Christ instead of to ourselves) and our resources (trusting in His love and power to accomplish results, instead of trusting in our own wisdom and abilities). Although we will continue to mature in our relationship with the Lord over the years, we can begin to experience His love, strength, and purpose from the moment we put Him at the center of our lives.

Spencer, a junior at the University of Missouri, had been a Christian for several years. He had trusted Christ as his personal Savior when a friend from his dorm shared the gospel with him during his first semester. Although he was growing in his relationship with Christ, intramural athletics and parties with his rowdy friends became the focus of Spencer's life by the middle of his sophomore year. He still went to church frequently, but he was confused and often felt guilty about his relationships with his friends and their activities. He tried talking with them about this, but they only laughed. Despite his occasional feelings of discomfort, Spencer felt like he needed these friends, and he continued spending time with them.

Then, in the fall of his junior year, Spencer went to several Christian meetings on campus. He began hearing about the love and power of Christ, and how the Holy Spirit can enable us to live for Him.

Another young man, Phil, took an interest in Spencer, and began to disciple him. Through Phil's supportive friendship, Spencer began to develop an eternal perspective, slowly recognizing that worldliness and sin are destructive, but that following Christ is eternally significant. One night, Spencer spent some time alone, praying and thinking about what he had learned. He realized that his life was confusing, frustrating, and dishonoring to the Lord. Spencer also realized that Christ is worthy of his love and obedience, and decided to live for Him. As he began to confess the specific sins the Holy Spirit brought to his mind, and as he asked Him for the power to live in a way that is pleasing to Christ, Spencer felt a surge of relief and joy. He was doing the right thing.

Phil was excited about the steps Spencer was taking, but Spencer was primarily concerned about his other friends. Realizing that he might be rejected, Spencer made plans to tell them about his decision to follow Christ. When he did, some of them laughed. Others were surprised, and a few were even angry. For the next year, Spencer still spent some time with these friends, but now at ball games instead of wild parties. He shared Christ with many of them, and had the joy of seeing two trust Christ. Spencer had plenty of struggles and spiritual growing pains, but his life began to reflect a new consistency, a new purpose, and a new attitude of thankfulness to the Lord.

Like Spencer, our own willingness to be filled with the Holy Spirit is a direct response to the magnificent truths centered in the cross and resurrection of Christ, and our participation in relationships in which we sense His love for us. *We are deeply loved and completely forgiven by God, fully pleasing to God, totally accepted by God, and complete in Him.*

Are you depending on God's Spirit to teach you, change you, and use you in the lives of others? If so, continue trusting Him! If not, review the five obstacles to following Christ and see if any of these are obstructing your relationship with Him. Are there specific sins you need to confess? *Confession* means to agree with God that you have sinned and that Christ has completely forgiven you. It also means "to repent," to turn from your sins to a life of love and obedience to God.

As you continue in the process of experiencing more of God's grace, take time to reflect on His love and power. Trust Him to guide you by His Word, fill you with His Spirit, and enable you to live for Him and be used by Him in the lives of others. Abiding in Christ does not mean deliverance from all of your problems, but it will provide a powerful relationship with the One who is the source of wisdom for difficult decisions, love to encourage you, and strength to help you endure.

Twelve
Renewing the Mind

In one of the most famous dialogues in the Bible, Jesus explained the profound truth of regeneration to Nicodemus:

> ...*unless one is born again, he cannot see the kingdom of God....*
>
> *That which is born of the flesh is flesh, and that which is born of the Spirit is spirit.*
>
> *Do not marvel that I said to you, "You must be born again."*
>
> John 3:3, 6-7

When we were born, we entered a world ruled by Satan, and we learned the ways of the world. *You are of your father the devil*, Jesus explained, *and you want to do the desires of your father* (John 8:44). Words like these make it easy for us to understand why we believe Satan's lies so readily!

However, at some point in our lives, the Holy Spirit drew us to Christ, and we trusted Him to forgive us and give us new purpose and meaning in our existence. The Holy Spirit baptized us into the body of Christ, a new spiritual family, the family of God. He plucked us from the family of Satan (Col. 1:13-14) and adopted us into God's eternal family as sons and daughters (Rom. 8:15). We were cursed to die as members of Satan's family, but as members of God's family, we were granted everything pertaining to life and godliness at the very moment of our new birth. We were not forced to qualify to receive God's provisions, but instead have received the rights and privileges of sons by His grace and mercy.

If an earthly father receives his newborn son into his arms and gives the child good things, how much more does our heavenly Father give to His children? When we are born into an earthly family, we are given a name, all the provisions of food, clothing, and shelter to sustain us, and perhaps we are even made the beneficiary of a savings account for our future. All of the father's abilities to provide for his child start to work on the child's behalf before he or she even begins to perform. Children are bound to their earthly fathers by the unconditional right of birth, not by their ability to perform.

How much more are newly-born children of God bound to their heavenly Father! As His children, we are endowed with the Holy Spirit to lead and convict us, and are given all the capability needed to honor God and live purposeful and meaningful lives. All of His provisions become ours at our spiritual birth, before we do good or evil.

And yet, as babes in Christ, we need to grow in our understanding and experience of Christ's life in us. We may rebel, but God is long-suffering and willing to give us loving correction and instruction. We may fail Him, but we are still His children.

It is interesting that when the Holy Spirit gave us a new spirit, He did not give us a totally renewed mind. Although the Spirit of Christ lives within us and enables us to evaluate our experiences, our minds tend to dwell on the worldly thoughts of our old nature instead of on God's truth. We are in conflict, torn between our new godly motivation to glorify Christ and our old motivations of lust and pride. Paul recognized this conflict. He wrote the Christians in Rome:

> *I find then the principle that evil is present in me, the one who wishes to do good.*
>
> *For I joyfully concur with the law of God in the inner man,*
>
> *but I see a different law in the members of my body, waging war against the law of my mind, and making me a prisoner of the law of sin which is in my members.*
>
> *Wretched man that I am! Who will set me free from the body of this death?*
>
> *Thanks be to God through Jesus Christ our Lord!...*
>
> Rom. 7:21-25

How then can we break free from the law of sin and begin to grow in Christ? How can we assist in the process that will enable us to follow Him?

To change our behavior, we usually need to see others who are being honest, and who are in the process of applying spiritual truths to their lives. In this environment, and through our personal study of God's Word, we can reject earthly thoughts and replace them with those that are spiritual. Solomon wrote, *As [a man] thinks within himself, so he is* (Prov. 23:7). Our thoughts usually affect the way we feel, the way we perceive ourselves and others, and ultimately, the way we act. The way we think can determine whether we will live according to God's truth or the world's value system. Still writing to the Christians in Rome, Paul explained the serious implications of how we think:

> *And do not be conformed to this world, but be transformed by the renewing of your mind, that you may prove what the will of God is, that which is good and acceptable and perfect.*
>
> Rom. 12:2

Although the way we think often affects the way we feel (and thus, the way we act), it is also true that feelings affect our thoughts and behavior, and that our behavior can affect our feelings and our thinking. In the verse preceding the one we just examined, Paul wrote, *I urge you therefore, brethren, by the mercies of God* (an appeal to their feelings about God's grace toward them) *to present your bodies a living and holy sacrifice, acceptable to God. . . .* This relationship of thinking, feeling, and acting is not always unidirectional. Our thoughts, emotions, and behaviors are dependent on each other; none exists in a vacuum. Changing how we think, feel, and act is a process that involves the supernatural work of the Holy Spirit, honesty, time, modeling, affirmation, and truth. As a starting point, however, we will use a model adapted from psychologist Albert Ellis's Rational Emotive Therapy. A simple explanation of this approach is:

Situations

⇩

Beliefs ⇨ Thoughts ⇨ Emotions ⇨ Actions

We often interpret the situations we encounter through our beliefs. Some of our interpretations are conscious reflections; most of them, however, are based on unconscious assumptions. These beliefs trigger certain thoughts, which, in turn, stimulate certain emotions, and from these emotions come our actions. In order for an emotion to persist, our belief system must continue to produce certain thoughts. For example, we often will not stay sad without continuing to think sad thoughts. Think of it in this way: Our minds contain deeply held beliefs and attitudes which have been learned through our environment, experiences, and education. These beliefs and attitudes produce thoughts which reflect how we perceive the events in our lives. These thoughts, then, combined with past experiences, relationships, and patterns of behavior, are often the source of our emotions, and our emotions are usually the launching pad for our actions.

Understanding ourselves and how we think can help us in two ways: we can learn how to manage our responses to current events, and we can learn how to experience healing from the damage of our past. Understanding that our thoughts are usually products of our beliefs gives us a tool for exposing those beliefs and identifying their source. Which false belief do the following thoughts expose?

- *He just has to like me.*
- *What can I do to make her like me more?*
- *I'm afraid he's given up on me.*

All of these thoughts reveal a belief in Satan's lie that we must be approved by certain people to have self-worth. In this same manner, many of our thoughts can be traced back to our beliefs—beliefs which are either founded on the truths of Scripture, or the lies of Satan.

False beliefs may be based on a partially accurate perception of circumstances. For example, it may be accurate that you failed to get a report in on time. You did actually fail, but that is only part of the truth. The other part is that your self-worth is not affected by that failure. To recognize your failure, but then believe that your failure has caused you to lose self-worth, is to believe both a truth and a lie. The facts may be true, but our interpretation of those facts may be based on the crafty deceit of Satan.

Sometimes, a completely accurate perception may trigger a whole array of emotions and unconscious thoughts, some of which are accurate, and some of which stem from false beliefs. For example, Kay's accurate perception, *My husband is drinking again*, actually represents many of the following unconscious thoughts:

- *I hate that inconsiderate bum!*
- *He'll start mistreating the children and me.*
- *I'll finally have to move out.*
- *I'll be forced to provide for the children and myself.*
- *I don't have any skills that qualify me to earn a living.*
- *I'm nothing but a failure.*
- *My friends won't have anything to do with me.*
- *Maybe God is punishing me.*

Kay was responding emotionally, not only to the conscious thought of her husband's drinking, but to her unconscious fears as well. The combination of her accurate perceptions and speculative assumptions formed a mental framework which spawned her emotions, and eventually, her actions.

We need to analyze our thoughts in each circumstance to determine which are valid and which are not.

I recall dealing with an ongoing sense of personal failure on several occasions when I experienced rejection. In one instance particularly, I felt consumed by feelings of hurt, anger, self-pity, and depression. I prayed about the situation as often as I could bring myself to face it; I read portions of the Scriptures at length, and several weeks after the relationship had ended, I talked with an objective friend about it.

Through this process, I gradually realized that my negative feelings were not only based on the pain of having been rejected by someone I cared for, but on the *implications* of that person's rejection. The implications, or false beliefs, I later identified were: *I will never have another relationship like the one that just ended. I will never be able to get over the pain this relationship has caused me. I'm just not any good at interpersonal relationships, and I never will be. I am obviously inferior because this person, whom I valued, has rejected me.*

Only as I began to realize that my emotions were largely the product of false beliefs—many of which stemmed from some misperceptions I had about myself during childhood—did I begin to recover from the injury of having been rejected. Granted, I still had to deal with painful feelings of loss caused by the ending of this relationship. But realizing that my negative emotions were primarily caused by my false beliefs—rather than the event itself—was enormously liberating for me.

For many of us, the majority of our beliefs were formed before we became Christians; therefore, it is easy to understand why many of our actions do not reflect Christ's character. Until those false beliefs are identified, ruthlessly rooted out, and replaced with biblical convictions, our lives will continue to be filled with destructive thoughts and actions.

Because of our fallen human nature, all of us experience false beliefs which contradict God's Word. Failure to recognize them can have devastating effects on our lives.

For example, a young girl named Dawn was sent to me by her parents, who hoped I could reason with her about her promiscuous behavior. But Dawn could not understand how something that felt so good and made her so happy could be wrong.

Over the course of several weeks, Dawn began to discuss her circumstances more openly with me. She explained that her father spent so much time working that he had little time for her and her mother. Dawn had been neglected, and after several meetings together, her wall of defenses eroded and she cried, "I just want to be loved, that's all!" Her behavior had been her unconscious attempt to feel close to someone. She had enjoyed it primarily because she finally felt loved, even though most of these men were really using her and not loving her at all.

Dawn eventually joined a support group, where she met other young women who were learning about the pain of their past and their hope for the future. These women could identify with Dawn's dreams and fears. They encouraged her and each other to gain a new sense of identity based on their love for each other and the truth of God's Word. This process hasn't been easy for Dawn, but her progress is real.

The case of Winston also provides a clear example of how we can experience progress in our circumstances by identifying our false beliefs. Winston was an older man with only a few years left until retirement. But he had become particularly anxious since he had gotten a new boss who was giving him degrading tasks seemingly designed to run him off. The pressure upset Winston so much that he was seriously considering an early retirement. When he came to me for advice and explained the situation, he was surprised when I told him that his problem wasn't his new boss, but the way he was perceiving the situation.

"What!" exclaimed Winston. "Are you trying to tell me that the awful way I'm being treated isn't really what's making me feel depressed?"

"Yes," I said. "Your anxiety comes from your perception of yourself and your job."

I explained to Winston that he was operating by the false belief that he must be approved by his boss in order to be happy. I also suggested that God was possibly allowing him to experience this situation so that he could begin learning how to be less dependent on the approval of others and more dependent on God. This would eventually enable him to count on what really matters in life: *that he is deeply loved by God, completely forgiven, fully pleasing, totally accepted, and complete in Christ,* resulting in a life of love and depth and meaning.

For the next several weeks, we talked about his anger toward his supervisor and the hurt he felt at the thought of being replaced. As Winston was honest about his emotions, he was better able to perceive God's unconditional love for him. He got involved in a prayer group at his church where he experienced the understanding and encouragement of others.

Several months later, I saw Winston again. He told me, "I still feel the sting of my boss's harassment, but at least I now have some friends who understand me. Their encouragement to be honest about my feelings has allowed me to experience more of God's love."

One of the greatest characteristics of personal maturity in Christ is the ability to be honest about how we really feel about a person or situation, and the willingness to accept full responsibility for our emotional and behavioral reactions in the disturbing circumstances of life. In realizing that our circumstances aren't the cause of our self-destructive reactions, and by applying God's truths to those situations, we can gain peace and perspective.

The world need not have control over us. Our spiritual battles may be intense, but we will be able to persevere if we can begin to analyze our circumstances through God's perspective and reject the false beliefs which often control our emotions and actions. Faith in God's Word prevents us from being buffeted by difficult situations, or having to live "under the circumstances." In Phil. 4: 8-9, Paul admonished the Christians in Philippi to focus their attention on truth:

> *Finally, brethren, whatever is true, whatever is honorable, whatever is right, whatever is pure, whatever is lovely, whatever is of good repute, if there is any excellence and if anything worthy of praise, let your mind dwell on these things.*
>
> *The things you have learned and received and heard and seen in me, practice these things; and the God of peace shall be with you.*

Identifying our false beliefs is the first step on our path toward new freedom in Jesus Christ. Once we recognize that many of our deeply-held beliefs are actually rooted in deception, we can begin using our emotions as a checkpoint to determine if we are basing our beliefs about a given circumstance on the truth or lies. Many of our painful emotions, such as fear, anger, and tension, are often the product of believing Satan's lies. Therefore, when we experience these emotions, we can ask ourselves, *What am I believing in this situation?* In almost every case, we will be able to trace our negative emotions back to one of Satan's false beliefs. We can then choose to reject the lie we have identified and replace it with the corresponding truth from the Scriptures. This process is amazingly simple, yet profound and applicable. Don's situation offers a good example:

Don was working hard on a mortgage loan proposal when his boss walked in to check on his progress. James, another man in the office who wanted a promotion very badly, made a joke about all the papers scattered on Don's desk. Their boss had a good laugh, and they walked out together.

Don was furious! He had worked diligently on that proposal, and it was excellent, yet James had made fun of him in front of his boss. But instead of fuming about the incident all day, Don used his anger as a gauge for his beliefs. He stopped and asked himself, *Why am I responding this way? What am I believing?* After a few minutes, he identified two false beliefs: *I must be approved by certain others to feel good about myself*, and *those who fail* (James and his boss had failed to treat Don the way he wanted to be treated) *are unworthy of love and deserve to be condemned.*

Don was honest about his anger, and determined to reject Satan's lies and focus on the truths that he is totally accepted by God and that he can love others with Christ's love. Though he was still unhappy about the incident, he felt encouraged that he was able to be honest about his emotions and apply God's Word to his thoughts and circumstances.

In examining our emotions, it is important to realize that not all distressing emotions reflect deception. For example, the emotion of remorse might be the Holy Spirit's conviction leading us to repentance. Anger with someone for molesting a child or beating an elderly person is righteous anger, just as a measure of fear while driving during rush hour is entirely justifiable!

In our problem-filled world, there are at least two ways that many of us choose to deal with our emotions and surrounding circumstances. One is to shut them out completely, refusing to acknowledge their presence or to be affected by them; the other is to become enslaved to them.

Switching off our emotions can cause us to become callous and insensitive to ourselves and those around us. Unfortunately, this is just what happened to Mike.

Over the years, Mike had deadened himself to his emotions, apparently not allowing anything to bother him. He had experienced a difficult childhood, first being abandoned by his parents, and then being shuffled from one relative to another. In an effort to stop the pain, Mike learned to block out his feelings and to ignore his circumstances.

Mike's success at suppressing his emotions had long-lasting consequences. First, by severing himself from his painful feelings, he missed out on many pleasant ones as well. Secondly, the longer Mike avoided dealing with his emotions, the more fearful he became of them. To combat this fear, he simply became more calloused and withdrawn. Third, and perhaps most importantly, Mike could not use his emotions to detect the false beliefs that were at the root of his problems, because he denied that he even had those emotions. He was helpless, unable to acknowledge his needs.

Melinda, on the other hand, wore her emotions on her sleeve. She wasn't difficult to figure out. Her flaring temper, her torrent of tears, and her jovial laughter were all indications of her rollercoaster emotions. Never knowing what to expect, Melinda's husband, Ken, became weary of trying to deal with his volatile wife.

Melinda's erratic mood swings affected her so much that they became, in effect, her lord. Her feelings seemed to be more real than anything else in her life and they clouded her perception of God and His purposes.

We often respond incorrectly to them, but our emotions are in fact a gift from God, intended to be used and enjoyed. Emotions are signals which tell us something about our environment. They can protect us by helping us to choose appropriate behavior. We can help ourselves (and others) by encouraging honesty and by allowing ourselves to fully experience both our positive and negative feelings. Emotions help us to determine what is really going on inside. In the same way that good parents allow their children to express hurt, and experience comfort and healing when they have fallen, we can do this for ourselves and others by advocating an honest expression of emotions and by applying comfort to the hurts each of us experience. In this way, we can avoid repression and denial, and encourage an appropriate expression of our emotions—within ourselves, with others, and with God.

The inability to experience and express feelings is as dangerous to our well-being as the inability to feel physical pain. As we become aware of painful emotions and destructive behavior, we need to acknowledge these feelings and actions to God in prayer, asking Him to reveal any false beliefs that may be hindering our fellowship with Him. Then, empowered by the Holy Spirit, and encouraged by the love and affirmation of others, we can learn to cast aside our false beliefs and choose to believe the truths of God's Word.

It is necessary to first expose our root emotions and the false beliefs which are triggering them. Then, by faith, we can allow God's Word to renew our minds.

Listed below are ten typical statements which reflect common false beliefs. Each is a reflection of the four false beliefs we have already studied:

1. *I must meet certain standards to feel good about myself.*
2. *I must be approved by certain others to feel good about myself.*
3. *Those who fail (including myself) are unworthy of love and deserve to be blamed and condemned.*
4. *I am what I am; I cannot change; I am hopeless.*

Examine each of these statements given below, asking, *What false belief(s) does this statement represent?* Then, beside each statement, place the number of one or more of the false beliefs:

1. *Tammy is right. I'll never be a successful husband and father.*_____
2. *I'm so undisciplined; I'll never be able to accomplish anything.*_____
3. *I just can't trust God.*_____
4. *My father never did accept me.*_____
5. *That's just the way I am.*_____
6. *Everything I do turns out badly.*_____
7. *I failed my college final. I'll never graduate now.*_____
8. *I can't overcome a particular sin.*_____
9. *I am going to fail financially.*_____
10. *I deserve all the misery I am experiencing.*_____

Compare your answers with these:

1.	1, 4	6.	1
2.	1, 4	7.	1, 3
3.	4	8.	4
4.	2	9.	1
5.	4	10.	3

Were you able to identify the false beliefs? If not, look at the statements again carefully, analyzing the root issue behind each one.

Sometimes, we tend to respond poorly to trying circumstances because we think we deserve better. Our society and media tell us that everybody should be happy, comfortable, healthy, and successful. The difficulty arises when we believe these statements, and equate orthodox Christianity with a comfortable, middle-class lifestyle. We think we deserve the best of everything, so when things don't go the way we'd like, we get upset.

What do you think you deserve? Appreciation from your friends, success in school or in your career, a clear complexion, good health, a promotion, leisure time, or freedom from whining children, an insensitive spouse, or inconsiderate neighbors? We sometimes are unable to identify the particular status or comfort we think we deserve, but are sure that we deserve better than what we're experiencing. One of the most obvious results of this perspective is a lack of thankfulness and contentment.

There are three principles from the Scriptures that can significantly help us understand what we deserve:

The Transcendent Purposes of God

The prophet Isaiah wrote that God's wisdom and purposes far surpass our own:

> *"For My thoughts are not your thoughts, neither are your*
> *ways My ways" declares the Lord.*
>
> *"For as the heavens are higher than the earth, so are My*
> *ways higher than your ways, and My thoughts than your*
> *thoughts."*
>
> Is. 55:8-9

One reason we may think we deserve better is that we believe we know what is best for ourselves and for others. But we are not omniscient. We are not sovereign, gracious, and good like God. Do we really deserve better than what the sovereign, Almighty God has for us?

A Humble View of Ourselves

Christ told a parable to explain our proper relationship to God:

> *But which of you, having a slave plowing or tending*
> *sheep, will say to him when he has come in from the field,*
> *"Come immediately and sit down to eat"?*
>
> *But will he not say to him, "Prepare something for me to*
> *eat, and properly clothe yourself and serve me until I have*
> *eaten and drunk; and afterward you will eat and drink"?*
>
> *He does not thank the slave because he did the things*
> *which were commanded, does he?*
>
> *So you too, when you do all the things which are*
> *commanded you, say, "We are unworthy slaves; we have done*
> *only that which we ought to have done."*
>
> Luke 17:7-10

Jesus is the Lord. He is the One who rightly deserves our affection and joyful obedience. Jesus said of the servant in this passage that if he did all that he was commanded, he was still to think of himself as an unworthy servant. *Unworthy? I thought we were deeply loved and accepted by God.* This passage does not contradict the biblical truths we have examined. It teaches a different issue than the basis of acceptance before God: that He is the sovereign Lord, and does not owe us anything. All that we have is by His grace. We are the thankful recipients; He is the gracious and loving Lord.

The problem with feeling deserving usually appears when we do something for the Lord: Bible study, church attendance, witnessing, or being kind to someone, and then think that He is obligated to bless us. God is never obligated to bless us, but does what is best for His honor and our growth.

Overwhelming Thankfulness for Our Forgiveness

In Luke 7:36-50, a woman who is overcome with thankfulness for her forgiveness is contrasted with a Pharisee who is not thankful:

> *Now one of the Pharisees was requesting Him to dine with him. And He entered the Pharisee's house, and reclined at the table.*
>
> *And behold, there was a woman in the city who was a sinner; and when she learned that He was reclining at the table in the Pharisee's house, she brought an alabaster vial of perfume,*
>
> *and standing behind Him at His feet, weeping, she began to wet His feet with her tears, and kept wiping them with the hair of her head, and kissing His feet, and anointing them with the perfume.*
>
> *Now when the Pharisee who had invited Him saw this, he said to himself, "If this man were a prophet He would know who and what sort of person this woman is who is touching Him, that she is a sinner."*
>
> *And Jesus answered and said to him, "Simon, I have something to say to you." And he replied, "Say it, Teacher."*
>
> *"A certain moneylender had two debtors: one owed five hundred denarii and the other fifty. When they were unable to*

repay, he graciously forgave them both. Which of them therefore will love him more?"

Simon answered and said, "I suppose the one whom he forgave more." And He said to him, "You have judged correctly."

And turning toward the woman, He said to Simon, "Do you see this woman? I entered your house; you gave Me no water for My feet, but she has wet My feet with her tears, and wiped them with her hair.

"You gave Me no kiss; but she, since the time I came in, she has not ceased to kiss My feet.

"You did not anoint My head with oil, but she anointed My feet with perfume.

"For this reason I say to you, her sins, which are many, have been forgiven, for she loved much; but he who is forgiven little, loves little."

And He said to her, "Your sins have been forgiven."

And those who were reclining at the table with Him began to say to themselves, "Who is this man who even forgives sins?"

And He said to the woman, "Your faith has saved you; go in peace."

Does your response to Christ resemble that of the Pharisee or that of the woman? The more we are able to grasp even a portion of the magnitude of Christ's love and forgiveness, the more we will tend to overflow with appreciation to Him.

Some of the influences on our minds have been very positive; some have been harmful. For good or bad, our thoughts have been shaped by years of parental modeling, friendships, past experiences, choices we have made, our culture, the media, and many other factors. Our perceptions about God and about ourselves do not usually change by reading a verse or two of Scripture. Renewing our minds is a lifelong process. It is often painfully slow, but diligent study of God's Word, trust in the Holy Spirit's power to change us, and the encouragement of other believers can produce minds and lives that are healthy, honest, and fruitful for the kingdom of God

Thirteen
The Weapons of Our Warfare

One of the biggest steps we can take toward consistently glorifying Christ and walking in peace and joy with our heavenly Father is to recognize the deceit which has held us captive. Satan's lies distort our true perspective, warp our thoughts, and produce painful emotions. If we cannot identify those lies, then it is very likely that we will continue to be defeated by them.

However, simply identifying the source of our problems will not free us from them. Once we recognize the tricks of the enemy, we must seize the offense. We must use the weapons God has provided to overcome incorrect thoughts, vain imaginations, and distorted beliefs. Paul describes the Christian's armor and weaponry this way:

Therefore, take up the full armor of God, that you may be able to resist in the evil day, and having done everything, to stand firm.

Stand firm therefore, having girded your loins with truth, and having put on the breastplate of righteousness, and having shod your feet with the preparation of the gospel of peace;

> *in addition to all, taking up the shield of faith with which you will be able to extinguish all the flaming missiles of the evil one.*
>
> *And take the helmet of salvation, and the sword of the Spirit, which is the word of God.*
>
> Eph. 6:13-17

Paul instructs us to put on the *full* armor of God. This armor is defensive, able to protect us from the attacks of Satan. Paul goes on to encourage us to take up *the sword of the Spirit, which is the word of God.* In contrast to the defensive armor, God's Word is an offensive weapon, and is used to attack the enemy and conquer him. Paul indicates that Christ does not intend for Christians to sit idly in their armor and absorb attack after attack from Satan. Instead, the wise warrior will reach for his offensive weapon and destroy the enemy's fortresses. Applying this to our study, we need to take the truths of God's Word and use them to attack and overcome Satan's lies.

Paul explains the nature of our warfare:

> *For though we walk in the flesh, we do not war according to the flesh,*
>
> *for the weapons of our warfare are not of the flesh, but divinely powerful for the destruction of fortresses.*
>
> *We are destroying speculations and every lofty thing raised up against the knowledge of God, and we are taking every thought captive to the obedience of Christ.*
>
> 2 Cor. 10:3-5

For many of us, our family backgrounds have been very painful. Alcoholism, drug abuse, divorce, workaholism, violence, or other family disorders have left us with deep emotional scars. We may feel neglected, lonely, angry, hurt, or numb. We may consequently believe that we are unlovable people who are unworthy of being cared for by others, and that

God is like our parents: harsh, condemning, manipulative, or aloof. These emotions and self-perceptions form a strong fortress that has been founded on Satan's lies and communicated to us by those who were supposed to love, protect, and provide for us. Concepts like these don't vanish quickly. Often, our first step toward progress is realizing that we have been hurting for a long time, but have refused to admit it, or perhaps, that our defense mechanisms of drivenness or withdrawal have been protecting us from the reality of our pain.

Through the process of being honest and experiencing comfort from the Lord and others, these fortresses can be slowly torn down. They are overcome by *destroying speculations and every lofty thing raised up against the knowledge of God;* that is, by identifying and rejecting specific lies, and then replacing them with the truth.

In the same letter to the Christians in Corinth, Paul shows how repentance can be a vital weapon in our warfare. If we have been deceived by the enemy, or if we have been involved in willful disobedience to God, we can repent by turning from our sin to God. Paul rejoiced that the Corinthians repented and experienced God's grace:

> *I now rejoice, not that you were made sorrowful, but that you were made sorrowful to the point of repentance; for you were made sorrowful according to the will of God, in order that you might not suffer loss in anything through us.*
>
> *For the sorrow that is according to the will of God produces a repentance without regret, leading to salvation; but the sorrow of the world produces death.*
>
> 2 Cor. 7:9-10

The Corinthians' example demonstrates repentance as a tactical weapon of our spiritual warfare. *Repentance* means "to change"; to change one's mind, purpose, and actions. It is more than just the experience of sorrow; it is the changing of our attitude and actions when we have realized that they are sinful and dishonoring to God.

157

As an offensive weapon, repentance has two sharp edges. The first allows us to discern and reject false beliefs. When situations occur which trigger certain beliefs that produce ungodly responses, we must:

1. Be honest about our emotions.
2. Trace the emotions back to their source and identify the false belief(s).
3. Consciously and assertively reject the false belief(s).

The following diagram illustrates this process:

Trace the emotions back to the false beliefs.

The second edge of repentance is the replacement of false beliefs with the truth of God's Word. By affirming God's truth about our worth, we will lodge it deep within our hearts and minds, and begin to reshape our thinking, feelings, and behavior. Then, the process of having the truth modeled to us, affirmed in us, taught to us, and applied by us over time will enable us to increasingly experience freedom in different areas of our lives.

If false beliefs remain in our minds, unchallenged and unrejected, they retain an unconscious influence on our emotions and reactions. Consequently, our warfare is a sustained and continuous battle. Every disturbing situation provides us with an opportunity to discover our incorrect thinking, to reject our world-acquired beliefs, and exchange them for the truth. This is a daily process for every Christian; only this aggressive, conscious, truth-seeking effort can reverse years of habitually wrong thinking.

Affirming God's truth is a weapon of great spiritual value. Through this process, we state God's truth as our own perspective. Continual affirmation gradually produces beliefs which result in correct thinking, which then result in godly responses. Affirming the truths of God's Word enables us to overcome the deception of the enemy (Rev. 12:10). The following diagram illustrates this process:

In practice, our actual experience may not be quite so neat and precise. Our emotions, beliefs, and behavior are the product of years of experiences and relationships. They can be very strong, very confusing, and very difficult to understand.

Although the above diagram is a general model, it is helpful in identifying some of the roots of our behavior and emotions, and can serve as an aid to direct us to follow God's truth in our growth process.

The circumstances of Stewart, a good friend of mine, may better illustrate how we can apply this double edge of repentance to our false belief system:

Stewart was raised in a dysfunctional family. His father, an alcoholic, was emotionally distant from his family, and disinterested in their concerns. His mother, in an effort to control her household, was manipulative and condemning. Nothing Stewart did as a child merited his father's interest or his mother's approval. The result was that Stewart felt unloved and incompetent. He responded by becoming a persistent people-pleaser, always hoping that by working a little harder, he would win his parents' approval and acceptance.

When Stewart became a Christian, he transferred his people-pleasing tendencies to his relationships with God and other believers. He joined a local church, and within a short time, became active in several of its ministry programs. Because he was responsible, conscientious, and sensitive to others, Stewart quickly became a valuable resource for assistance and advice. And he was happy to help. His role within the church gave him a special sense of significance and purpose. He felt highly esteemed by others and by God.

But as the years passed, Stewart's involvement with church activities became more demanding. Members were calling him at work and at home to attend meetings, lead studies, lend financial support, or more often, because they needed someone to listen. Wanting to gain approval from others, and striving to please God, Stewart dutifully complied to all of these demands and more. As a result, his output at work began to diminish. At home, his wife questioned whom he'd married: her or their church.

At first, Stewart reasoned that he was managing his time poorly, and compensated by cutting back on his sleep to get more done. But gradually, as the pressures around him increased, Stewart began to harbor feelings of resentment and anger toward members of his church. And, though he continued to adhere to his daily devotional schedule with God, he felt increasingly distant from Him. When his marriage became jeopardized and his boss confronted him with the possibility of losing his job, Stewart began to wonder if God really cared for him at all.

Feeling threatened and disillusioned, he finally sought the advice of a trusted friend. When this friend asked Stewart some pointed questions about his family background, he started taking an objective look at how he was raised for the first time. What he saw filled him with both pain and outrage.

In conversations with his parents over the next year, Stewart started recognizing that his hurt and anger were rooted in his fears of their rejection and perception of him as a failure. Through the help of his friend, he also began to notice patterns in his relationships with God and with others which indicated that he was basing his actions and self-worth on the beliefs that he must meet certain standards and be approved by certain others to feel good about himself.

When Stewart realized the degree to which he'd been affected by his family background, he was devastated and felt more incompetent than ever. Gradually, however, he began to understand that his new insights could be a driving force toward change in his life.

Over the next several years, as he identified false beliefs in his motivations to please and perform, he learned how to reject those beliefs and replace them with God's Word. Stewart's life slowly began to change. He started gaining a healthy sense of independence from his parents, and with it, self-respect. As a result, he began to assume responsibility for his own welfare. He resolved to put his wife and children first among his priorities, joined an athletic club, and began seeking supportive relationships. God has since used those relationships and others to convey His message of love for Stewart.

Today, Stewart is still active within his church, but he is more selective about the ways he involves himself there. Though he still desires to please others, and occasionally uses performance to measure his value, Stewart can now more easily recognize and reject false beliefs, and allow himself to feel affirmed by the truth of God's Word.

To effectively utilize affirmation as a weapon for change, remember these concepts:

• *Affirming the truths of the Scriptures does not mean that our natural mind will agree with what we are affirming.* The Bible teaches that the natural mind is antagonistic toward God:

> *But I say, walk by the Spirit, and you will not carry out the
> desire of the flesh.*
>
> *For the flesh sets its desire against the Spirit, and the
> Spirit against the flesh; for these are in opposition to one
> another, so that you may not do the things that you please.*
>
> Gal. 5:16-17

It may be uncomfortable to reflect on the truths of God's Word because they oppose the lies of the enemy. Don't be surprised by spiritual conflict when you confront these lies with God's truths.

• *Realize that we can't hope to achieve spiritual growth and change through self-effort.* The Holy Spirit is our Helper, and He will point out those circumstances in which we are believing Satan's lies; He will give us insight into the truth of the Scriptures; and He will give us strength to persevere in spiritual battle. Even our desire to honor Christ is due to the Holy Spirit's work in our lives. Through His wisdom and power, and through our moment-by-moment choice to follow Him, the Holy Spirit produces changes in our lives for the glory of Christ.

• *In order to become proficient at affirming these truths, we need to become students of God's Word, and allow its truth to lodge deep within our hearts and minds.* We should make it a regular practice to meditate upon the Scriptures so that the Holy Spirit can use them to change our beliefs, thoughts, emotions, and actions. David explained the power of applying God's Word:

> *Thy Word I have treasured in my heart, that I may not sin
> against Thee....*
>
> *If Thy law had not been my delight, then I would have
> perished in my affliction. I will never forget Thy precepts, for
> by them Thou hast revived me.*
>
> *Thy word is a lamp to my feet, and a light to my path.*
>
> *Therefore I love Thy commandments above gold, yes,
> above fine gold.*   Ps. 119:11, 92-93, 105, 127

• *Learn to confront each false belief with a specific truth from God's Word.* Once we have identified a specific false belief, we should claim God's corresponding truth in the situation. (See the chart at the end of chapter 10.)

• *Finally, take time to reflect on the marvelous biblical truths outlined in this book.* It is not the unthinking, mechanical utterance of these truths which produces freedom, but the conscious realization and application of them which changes our minds and actions. For example, when we want to affirm that we are deeply loved by God, we should think through the doctrine of propitiation; if possible, quoting 1 John 4:9-10 audibly. Through diligent study and application over a period of time, and in the context of affirming relationships, the power of God's Word will begin to conquer our false beliefs and liberate our minds.

The weapon of repentance, through rejection of false beliefs and affirmation of godly truth, has changed thousands of lives. Repentance can liberate the mind and *destroy speculations and every lofty thing raised up against the knowledge of God* (2 Cor. 10:5). And it can help us discover the wondrous significance we have in Jesus Christ: *We are deeply loved, completely forgiven, fully pleasing, totally acceptable, and complete in Him.* Our journey is a joyous and challenging adventure with Christ.

Now that we understand the value of the weapon of repentance, we will take a further look at guilt, conviction, affirmation, and faith.

Fourteen
Guilt vs. Conviction

There is no burden which produces pain, fear, and alienation quite like the feeling of guilt. Many of us know it as a constant burden. Some of us respond to it like a whipped puppy, beaten down and ashamed. Some of us avoid it through the numbing effects of denial. Our association with guilt may be prompted by many factors: poor parental modeling of Christ's love and forgiveness, divorce, neglect, a particular past sin, and the emphasis some believers place on the "ought's" and "should's" of Christianity. Regardless of these influences, guilt need not be a way of life for us.

In Rom. 8:1, Paul tells us, *There is therefore now no condemnation for those who are in Christ Jesus.* When I shared this important truth with a troubled Christian brother, his jaw dropped and his eyes filled with tears. He looked at me incredulously and exclaimed, "You mean, all this guilt I have been carrying for so long is unnecessary? I can be free from these tormenting feelings of condemnation? Why hasn't somebody told me this before?"

The Apostle Paul has been trying to tell us just that for centuries, but few of us have listened. We feel we deserve condemnation, and we fail to realize that Christ has freed us from the guilt and condemnation our sins deserve.

What exactly is guilt, anyway? Sigmund Freud said that guilt is a result of social restraint. To Freud, guilt was born in the mind of a child when his parents scolded him, and was rooted in his fear of losing the love of someone significant to him. Therefore, according to Freud, we experience guilt when we fear a loss of social esteem; when instinctive drives cause us to act in ways other than the accepted social norm.

Alfred Adler wrote that guilt arises from a refusal to accept one's inferiority. Therefore, he concluded, guilt feelings are those pangs of self-incrimination we feel anytime we think or behave inadequately.

Both Freud and Adler tried to explain the pain of guilt from a perspective that denies the righteous judgment of God and our personal responsibility for sin. To them, guilt could only be explained on a human, existential basis.

Christian authors, Bruce Narramore and Bill Counts, represent a more biblical perspective when they differentiate between true guilt and false guilt. True guilt, they explain, is an objective fact, but false guilt is a subjective feeling of pain and rejection. They emphasize that while the Bible discusses the fact of legal or theological guilt, it never tells the Christian to feel psychological guilt. These distinctions are helpful, but they may not clarify the issue for those who equate any guilt with condemnation. For this reason, we will use *guilt* and *conviction* to distinguish between the condemnation our sin deserves, and the loving motivation prompted by God to live in a way that brings honor to Him. Though many people confuse these two concepts, they are actually worlds apart. The comparisons given later in this chapter clearly illustrate their differences.

Perhaps no emotion is more destructive than guilt. It causes a loss of self-respect. It causes the human spirit to wither, and eats away at our personal significance. Guilt is a strong motivator, but it plays on our fears of failure and rejection; therefore, it can never ultimately build, encourage, or inspire us in our desire to live for Christ.

Some of us understand guilt as a sense of legal and moral accountability before God. We may try to distinguish it from low self-esteem by reasoning that guilt is the result of a sinful act or moral wrongdoing, while low self-esteem is derived from a feeling of social or personal inadequacy. Consequently, a lie makes us feel unacceptable to God and brings guilt, while bad table manners make us feel unacceptable to the people around us and bring low self-esteem.

This perspective shows some depth of thought, but it focuses on an emotional response to guilt rather than its root cause. At its root, guilt is the condition of being separated from God and of deserving condemnation for sin. Low self-esteem can be experienced by Christians or non-Christians—anyone who believes Satan's lies and feels like a failure, hopeless and rejected.

As we have determined, guilt has a restricted meaning in the New Testament. It refers only to man's condition prior to his salvation. Only the non-Christian is actually guilty before God. He has transgressed the law of God and must face the consequences. Guilt shakes its fist and says, "You have fallen short and must pay the price. You are personally accountable." Our condemnation is removed only through Christ. He took all of our guilt upon Himself when He accepted the penalty for our sins and suffered the full punishment for all sin. Because of His substitution, we need never face guilt's consequences. We are acquitted and absolved from guilt, free from our sentence of spiritual death.

Many of us have been told that we are still guilty even after we have trusted Christ to pay for our sins. And sadly, we have heard this in churches—places that should be loudly and clearly proclaiming the forgiveness and freedom found in the cross. Perhaps some people think that if they don't use guilt motivation, we won't do anything. Guilt may motivate us for a short while, until we adjust to being properly motivated. But a short period of waiting is well worth the long-term results of grace-oriented, intrinsic motivation.

Learn to identify incorrect teaching, guilt motivation, and the results of guilt in your own thoughts. Then, refuse to believe the lies any longer, and focus instead on the unconditional love and forgiveness of Christ. His love is powerful, and He is worthy of our intense zeal to obey and honor

Him. The result of proper motivation is an enduring, deepening commitment to Christ and His cause, rather than the prevalent results of guilt motivation: resentment and the desire to escape.

Christians are freed from guilt, but we are still subject to conviction. The Bible frequently speaks of the Holy Spirit's work to convict believers of sin. He directs and encourages our spiritual progress by revealing our sins in contrast to the holiness and purity of Christ.

Although the Holy Spirit convicts both believers and unbelievers of sin (John 16:8), His conviction of believers is not intended to produce pangs of guilt. Our status and self-worth are secure by the grace of God, and we are no longer guilty. Conviction deals with our behavior, not our status before God. Conviction is the Holy Spirit's way of showing the error of our performance in light of God's standard and truth. His motivation is love, correction, and protection.

While guilt is applicable to non-believers, and originates from Satan, conviction is the privilege of those who believe, and is given by the Holy Spirit. Guilt brings depression and despair, but conviction enables us to realize the beauty of God's forgiveness and to experience His love and power.

Perhaps the following will better illustrate the contrasting purposes and results of guilt and conviction:

Basic Focus:

GUILT focuses on the state of being condemned: *I am unworthy.*

CONVICTION focuses on behavior: *This act is unworthy of Christ and is destructive.*

Primary Concern:

GUILT deals with the sinner's loss of self-esteem and a wounded self-pride: *What will others think of me?*

CONVICTION deals with the loss of our moment–by–moment communication with God: *This act is destructive to me and interferes with my walk with God.*

Primary Fear:

GUILT produces a fear of punishment: *Now I'm going to get it!*

CONVICTION produces a fear of the destructiveness of the act itself: *This behavior is destructive to me and others, and it robs me of what God intends for me.*

Agent:

The agent of GUILT is Satan: *...the god of this world has blinded the minds of the unbelieving, that they might not see the light of the gospel of the glory of Christ* (2 Cor. 4:4).

The agent of CONVICTION is the Holy Spirit: *...but if by the Spirit you are putting to death the deeds of the body, you will live* (Rom. 8:13).

Behavioral Results:

GUILT leads to depression and more sin: *I am just a low-down, dirty, rotten sinner;* or to rebellion: *I don't care. I'm going to do whatever I want to do.*

CONVICTION leads to repentance, the turning from sin to Christ: *Lord, I agree with You that my sin is wrong and destructive. What do You want me to do?*

Interpersonal Result:

The interpersonal result of GUILT is alienation, a feeling of shame that drives one away from the person who has been wronged: *I can't ever face him again.*

The interpersonal result of CONVICTION is restoration, a desire to remedy the harm done to others: *Father, what would You have me do to right this wrong and restore the relationship with the one I have offended?*

Personal Results:

GUILT ends in depression, bitterness, and self-pity: *I'm just no good.*

CONVICTION ends in comfort, the realization of forgiveness:

Thank You, Lord, that I am completely forgiven and totally accepted by You!

Remedy:

The remedy for GUILT is to trust in Christ's substitutionary death to pay for the condemnation for sin.

The remedy for CONVICTION is confession, agreeing with God that our sin is wrong, that Christ has forgiven us, and that our attitude and actions will change.

Do you recognize any of your thoughts, feelings, and behaviors in these statements? Do they represent guilt or conviction?

Although Christians are no longer subject to condemnation, we will not be free from its destructive power until we learn to distinguish between guilt and conviction. The Holy Spirit wants us to be convinced that we are forgiven, accepted, and loved—totally secure—because of Christ. The Holy Spirit is the *paraclete*, or "one called along side," to lift us up and encourage us. As a part of His ministry, He faithfully makes us aware of any behavior that does not reflect the characteristics of Christ. He helps us understand both our righteousness before God and the failures in our performance.

From these observations, we can conclude that guilt is rooted in condemnation, but conviction leads us to confession and repentance, and to a renewed realization of God's grace and forgiveness.

Knowing this, how can we deal with feelings of guilt? First, we need to affirm that Christ has forgiven us and has made us judicially righteous before God. Our sin does not result in condemnation, but it is harmful and brings dishonor to God. We can confess our sin to God, claim the forgiveness we already have in Christ, and then move on in joy and freedom to honor Him. The following prayer expresses this attitude:

Father, I affirm that I am deeply loved by You, that I am fully pleasing to You, and that I am totally accepted in Your sight.

You have made me complete and have given me the righteousness of Christ, even though my performance often falls short. Lord, I confess my sins to You. (List them. Be specific.) *I agree with You that these are wrong. Thank You for Your grace and forgiveness. Is there anything I need to return, anyone I need to repay, or anyone I need to apologize to? Thank You.*

It is important to affirm our righteousness in Christ as well as to confess our sins. God does not need to be reminded of our right standing in Him, but we do. Therefore, we need to make this prayer a daily experience and allow it to pervade our thoughts and hearts. As we yield to the gentle prodding of God-given conviction, confess our sins, and affirm our true relationship with Him, we will be gradually shaped and molded in such a way that we will increasingly honor the One *who died and rose again on [our] behalf* (2 Cor. 5:15).

We may not experience joy and freedom immediately, especially if we have developed the painful habit of prolonged self-condemnation as a way of dealing with sin. Loving friends who listen to us and encourage us can be an example of God's forgiveness to us. As we become more honest about our feelings through these affirming relationships, we will be able to increasingly experience the freedom, forgiveness, and freshness of God's grace.

Fifteen
The Search Concluded

As we conclude our examination of the search for significance, we will touch on several issues to help clarify how we can apply scriptural truths to our thoughts and circumstances. These issues include the contrast between our old and new nature; how we can honor Christ; how to activate our faith, and finally, how to apply the concepts in this book to our lives. First, let's see how understanding the contrast between our old and new nature can help us grow in Christ and bring honor to Him.

Our Old and New Nature

Living freely and fully in Christ requires that we put ourselves in an environment of understanding and encouragement so that we can experience God's love through His people, His Spirit, and His Word. This healthy environment will encourage us to make obedient choices, rather than follow the enticing deceptions of the world. Time after time, Scripture instructs us to exercise our wills so that we can be freed from our old way of living. As Paul taught the believers in Ephesus:

> *...in reference to your former manner of life...lay aside the old self, which is being corrupted in accordance with the lusts of deceit,*

> *and...be renewed in the spirit of your mind,*
> *and put on the new self, which in the likeness of God has*
> *been created in righteousness and holiness of the truth.*
>
> Eph. 4:22-24

In this passage, Paul explains that Christians have two natures: one which he calls the "old self" and the other, the "new self."

What exactly is the old self that must be laid aside? The *old self* is the sinful, fallen nature we possess as descendants of Adam. Scripture tells us that the old self is corrupted by the lusts of deceit (Eph. 4:22); is involved in evil practices, such as lying, slander, abusive speech, idolatry, wrath, malice, immorality, impurity, passion, evil desire, and greed (Col. 3:5, 8-9); and is a body of sin (Rom. 6:6).

In contrast, the *new self* is the nature we receive from God when we trust Christ as our Savior. This nature bears the characteristics of Christ. It has been created in the likeness of God in righteousness and holiness (Eph. 4:24), and is strengthened according to God's power through His Spirit (Eph. 3:16). The new self is a reality for all individuals born of the Spirit.

As we know, man lost his ability to reflect God's image after the Fall. Now, through faith in Jesus Christ, we are released from the domination of the natural man, and are able to put on the new self and bear His image. Although we are free from sin's absolute domination, we are not free from the influence of our old nature. Until we die and leave our physical bodies to live with Christ, our new self will continually war against our old one. Our spiritual desires will battle against our lustful, worldly desires, and our natural mind will clash with the truths of the Scriptures (Gal. 5:16-24).

Unless we are diligent, we can grow weary of spiritual warfare, and succumb to the lusts and pride in which the world delights. When we acquiesce, we adopt our old emotions and habits again. Giving in may seem attractive at the time, but sin leads to feelings of failure and low self-esteem, and it dishonors the Lord. Clearly, momentary escape from the battle isn't worth it. Sin only *appears* to be escape; actually, it is exchanging one battle in which the Holy Spirit is our powerful ally for another in which He is our loving convictor.

The more we understand biblical truth about ourselves, the better we are able to wage spiritual warfare. The Apostle Paul clearly distinguished between the character and results of the old self and the new self. His delineation in the sixth chapter of Romans centers on four words: *know, consider, present,* and *obey.* Let's examine these:

To Know

In Rom. 6:3-10, Paul instructs us to *know* the basic facts about who we are in Christ:

> *Or do you not know that all of us who have been baptized into Christ Jesus have been baptized into His death?*
>
> *Therefore we have been buried with Him through baptism into death, in order that as Christ was raised from the dead through the glory of the Father, so we too might walk in newness of life.*
>
> *For if we have become united with Him in the likeness of His death, certainly we shall be also in the likeness of His resurrection,*
>
> *knowing this, that our old self was crucified with Him, that our body of sin might be done away with, that we should no longer be slaves to sin;*
>
> *for he who has died is freed from sin.*
>
> *Now if we have died with Christ, we believe that we shall also live with Him,*
>
> *knowing that Christ, having been raised from the dead, is never to die again; death no longer is master over Him.*
>
> *For the death that He died, he died to sin, once for all; but the life He lives, He lives to God.*
>
> Rom. 6:3-10

Our old self, which deserved the condemnation of God, was identified with Christ on the cross. It was crucified with Him, and we now live, identified with Christ's resurrection *so we too might walk in newness of life.* Paul wants us to be well aware of these facts so that we can draw definite conclusions from them.

To Consider

Romans 6:11 tells us to reflect on and *consider* the facts already presented: *Even so consider yourselves to be dead to sin, but alive to God in Christ Jesus.*

To consider means "to calculate," i.e., by adding up all the facts presented in Rom. 6:1-10.[1] Unless we take the time to reflect on the implications of our identity with Christ in His death and resurrection, these most important events will be like facts learned in a history class about a battle which was fought long ago. We may be able to recite the dates, names, and places, but those facts won't make a difference in our lives. The magnificent truths of our identity in Christ deserve far more attention than our ability to repeat the facts. They deserve deep reflection on their implications in our relationships, goals, and self-esteem, both personally, and in the context of strong, healthy relationships with people who are honest, and who are growing in their personal walk with Christ.

To Present

If we understand the implications of Christ's death and resurrection (that our old self died with Christ and our new self came to life in Him), then our logical, heart-felt response will be to *present* ourselves to Him:

Therefore do not let sin reign in your mortal body that you should obey its lusts,
and do not go on presenting the members of your body to sin as instruments of unrighteousness; but present yourselves to God as those alive from the dead, and your members as instruments of righteousness to God. Rom. 6:12-13

We have a choice: to present the members of our bodies (our thoughts, will, goals, desires, and actions) either to sin or to God. One results in more unrighteous behavior; it is harmful to us and to others, and it dishonors God. The other results in righteous behavior, enabling us to grow, to serve, and to bring glory to God. The choice is clear, isn't it? Note that Paul doesn't start the sixth chapter of Romans with the exhortation to present ourselves to God. The commitment to action *follows* understanding the facts and considering the implications of those facts. Then, the call to commitment seems reasonable, not forced. The Lord doesn't want us to commit ourselves to something we don't understand. Commitment must follow understanding or it will be shallow, and probably, short-lived.

To Obey

After presenting ourselves to God as a reasonable response to His grace, we then need to perpetuate that commitment through moment-by-moment obedience to Him:

> *What then? Shall we sin because we are not under law but under grace? May it never be!*
>
> *Do you not know that when you present yourselves to someone as slaves for obedience, you are slaves of the one whom you obey, either of sin resulting in death, or of obedience resulting in righteousness?*
>
> *But thanks be to God that though you were slaves of sin, you became obedient from the heart to that form of teaching to which you were committed,*
>
> *and having been freed from sin, you became slaves of righteousness.*
>
> Rom. 6:15-18

Paul indicates that because we have been freed from slavery to sin, it is foolish for us to disobey. It is right and proper to obey God because our new self in Christ is now our true source of identity. He uses *slaves* to signify obligation and mastery. Before we trusted Christ, we were slaves of sin, obligated to a lifestyle of unrighteousness, but now we are slaves of obedience to God, obligated to Christ, His teaching, and His righteousness.

As we identify our old selves with the fertile soil of Satan's deceptions, we will be better equipped to understand ourselves and deal properly with our ungodly thoughts, painful emotions, and unrighteous actions. Considering the old self to be dead does not mean that we deny the existence of distressing emotions. Indeed, they are very real, but now we can choose our response: either to allow them to run rampant, or to use them to identify and root out our false beliefs.

Honoring Christ

Following Christ is difficult because our culture, our old selves, and Satan fight against our desire to honor Him. Disobedience is difficult because of the painful and tragic consequences of sin. Some say that the world's way is easy; this is misleading. Others say that if we follow Christ, our lives will be free of problems, but these well-meaning people are misleading, too. We will be much better off if we realize that there is no easy way to live. Comfort is not to be our goal. Our goal, however difficult, is to honor Christ because He loves us and is worthy of our faith, love, and obedience.

But what does it mean to *honor* Christ? What can we do to bring glory to Him? Honoring Christ means accurately representing Him in every thought, action, relationship, and conversation—to bear His image. Some of the major categories of attitudes and activities that honor Christ include:

- *Love:* This love is unconditional affection for Christ, for other Christians, for unbelievers, and for ourselves. It means that we care enough to correct as well as to encourage.
- *Forgiveness:* Many of us think of forgiveness as an option, but Scripture explicitly commands us to forgive others as God through Christ has forgiven us (Matt. 18:21-35; Eph. 4:32; Col.

2:13-14). We are able to forgive more completely as we experience the Lord's forgiveness of us more deeply.

- *Holiness:* We may generally think of holiness in terms of what we don't do: abstinence from sin. But holiness also includes a positive side: zeal for Christ and His cause.

- *Biblical Values:* The more we understand the love and character of Christ, the more we will value the things that are important to Him. Prestige, money, success, and the approval of others will gradually lose their appeal, and instead, we will desire that Christ be honored, that people become Christians, that believers grow in their faith, and that missionaries be sent out to the world.

- *Giving:* Jesus said to Nicodemus, *For God so loved the world that He* gave... (John 3:16). The more we understand Him, the more we will be like Him. We have received so much from God, in both the temporal and eternal realms, that it becomes a joy to give to others in need. The measure of our lives should not be what we have, but how much we give.

- *Evangelism:* Christ has given us an example, a mission, and a command to reach others with the message of His love and forgiveness. The primary reason we don't tell more people about Him is because we fear their rejection, but His acceptance of us transcends the disapproval of others. The world (including our neighbors) desperately needs to hear a clear, loving presentation of the gospel. It is our privilege as His chosen ambassadors to share it with them.

- *Discipleship:* Christ discipled the people around Him by His example and by communicating truth to them. His love, humility, strength, and tenderness provided a powerful context for learning. If we want others to grow in their faith, we need to follow His example and model the life we study and teach.

- *Social Activism:* The influence of Christ should not be relegated only to the spiritual aspect of life. In the last century, William Wilburforce led the struggle against slavery in England, basing his arguments squarely on the Scriptures. In civil rights, politics, abortion, education, and in every other area of life, Christ is the source of truth, justice, and love. It is our privilege and our responsibility to represent Him in all aspects of our culture.

- *Prayer:* Christ said, *Apart from Me, you can do nothing* (John 15:5). Our programs and activities are unproductive in the eternal sense if we do not base them on the Word of Christ and accomplish them according to the power of Christ. Prayer reflects our dependence on Him.

- *Worship:* Perhaps our greatest expression of love for God is worship—speaking and/or singing of His greatness. Whether we worship on Sunday morning with hundreds of others, or alone, this expression properly reflects dependence, thankfulness, and praise.

Glorifying God is not limited to any given time or place. It is our privilege at every moment to accurately reflect our Creator and Savior to others, to ourselves, and to Him. Why? Because He rightly deserves it. As the following scene in heaven vividly illustrates, Christ is worthy of our praise and obedience:

> *And I looked, and I heard the voice of many angels around the throne and the living creatures and the elders; and the number of them was myriads of myriads, and thousands of thousands,*
>
> *saying with a loud voice, "Worthy is the Lamb that was slain to receive power and riches and wisdom and might and honor and glory and blessing."*
>
> *And every created thing which is in heaven and on the earth and under the earth and on the sea, and all things in them, I heard saying, "To Him who sits on the throne, and to the Lamb, be blessing and honor and glory and dominion forever and ever."*

> *And the four living creatures kept saying, "Amen." And*
> *the elders fell down and worshiped.*
>
> Rev. 5:11-14

Activating Our Faith

Throughout this book, we have seen how sin plunged man into spiritual darkness and how that darkness has blinded his eyes to truth. We have seen how every individual born in sin has been deceived by false beliefs, resulting in improper thoughts, emotions, and actions. Through this veil of darkness, it is impossible for the sinful man to earn the love and acceptance of God.

But in this darkness, we have discovered a light as God Himself has provided a path to an intimate relationship with Him. That light is Jesus Christ, from whom we freely receive salvation, forgiveness, justification, propitiation, and acceptance. By faith, in a miraculous instant, we have been adopted into a new family, have received an inheritance as sons and daughters of God, and have been given the purpose of representing the Lord to those around us. We can devote the rest of our lives to understanding and experiencing these incredible truths.

We have seen that our relationship with God, our security, and our self-worth are not earned by our efforts. They are obtained only by faith. This point is so important, let's take some time to analyze what faith is.

Faith has several synonyms: *trust, dependence, reliance,* and *belief.* The focus is on the object of faith, not the faith itself. For example, if I believe that a certain chair will hold me when I sit in it, the primary issue is the construction and quality of the chair—the *object* of my faith, not the *amount* of faith I have. Even if I believe very strongly that the chair will support me, if the chair is a rotten, broken-down piece of junk, then it will break if I try to sit in it. My faith will not make it a good chair. But if the chair is of quality construction, it takes very little faith to sit comfortably in it. Again, it is the quality of the object, not the quantity of my faith, that is of primary importance.

In Christianity, Christ is the object of faith, and faith is our trust in in His character and abilities. The more we know Him, the more we will trust Him. Faith, then, requires our knowing God, and knowing Him requires a relationship. To know God, we need to talk to Him through prayer, listen to His voice, see Him at work in our lives and the lives of others, and search out His will and deeds through the Scriptures He has given us. *So faith comes by hearing, and hearing by the word of Christ* (Rom. 10:17).

Make no mistake about it, faith is not a magic formula for manipulating God to grant us the wishes of our hearts. We cannot motivate God to act contrary to His sovereign will. Faith enables us to be partakers with Him, to gain wisdom from Him, and to bring His love and power to bear on human situations with lasting impact.

Let me explain it this way. Suppose Rusty needs $1,000 by Saturday to pay off an important obligation. Today is Wednesday, and Rusty has yet to raise the money.

Rusty decides to call John, a trusted friend. John is more than happy to supply the need, but tells Rusty to wait until Saturday, the very day the money is due. "Give me until Saturday," John says. "I'll have the money for you by noon."

Rusty can relax, realizing that his need has been met. Although he has yet to actually see the money, he has confidence in his close friend. After all, John has always been reliable, and is a person of means. If he says he wants to help meet Rusty's need and will supply the $1,000, certainly he will do so. Knowing that, Rusty can wait patiently until Saturday without anxiety. He has faith that John can and will deliver as promised because he has an intimate knowledge of John's proven character and ability.

Likewise, our faith in God lies in what we know of His character and ability. His character is one of love, revealed to us as a benevolent Father who desires to bestow good gifts to His children. And yet, a good Father knows that not all of the requests of His children are beneficial to them; therefore, some of them cannot be granted.

We often find situations in life when we want something that seems very good and reasonable to us, but either God's Word opposes it, or our prayers seem fruitless. There are at least three questions we must ask in these situations:

- *Is it God's will?* Do the Scriptures prohibit it, allow it, or promise it?
- *Is it for God's glory?* What is our motive: pleasure, prestige, or to honor Christ?
- *Is it in God's timing?* Are there conditions to be met? Does He want us to wait?

It is then that we must exercise our faith to trust in His character alone, even without visible evidence to support our trust. As the psalmist wrote:

> *I would have despaired unless I had believed that I would*
> *see the goodness of the Lord in the land of the living.*
> *Wait for the Lord; be strong, and let your heart take*
> *courage; yes, wait for the Lord.*
>
> Ps. 27:13-14

When we know God and realize from His Word that He is both powerful and compassionate, we can then trust in Him despite what our feelings or human perceptions tell us.

Too often, however, we presume upon the will of God by rationalizing that what we are asking is beneficial for us. We think that God should be more than willing to grant our request; however, we must remember that God sees a bigger picture than we do. He can see the future, other relating circumstances, and all of the events that will affect our lives. Though we may ask a specific request according to His will, we must not despair if we do not see an immediate response. And we must remember that a creative God can take all of His children's best interests in interrelated events and resolve the matter in a way we least expect. God's timing and methods are a mystery, and require our faith in His love and sovereignty:

> *Oh, the depth of the riches both of the wisdom and knowledge of God! How unsearchable are His judgments and unfathomable His ways!*
>
> Rom. 11:33

We need to dispel another common misunderstanding about faith. Some people believe that true faith exists only in the absence of doubt, but this is not necessarily the case. Biblical faith often exists in spite of our doubts. If we think that we need to be freed of conflicting thoughts and emotions for our faith to be honoring to the Lord, we will become introspective and be disappointed. Conflicting thoughts and emotions will be a normal part of our lives until we go to be with the Lord. Learn to be honest in conflict rather than deny its existence.

The account of Abraham and Isaac is an example of God-honoring faith in spite of doubts and conflicting emotions. In Gen. 12:1-3 and 17:1-5, God established and repeated a solemn covenant with Abraham which included the promise to *make [him] the father of a multitude of nations* (Gen. 17:5).

It probably didn't take Abraham long to figure out that if he was to be the father of many nations, he would have to have at least one child! When he was eighty-six years old and Sarah, his wife, was seventy-six years old, Abraham had his first child, but there was a problem. This child was not Sarah's. It was the child of Hagar, Sarah's maid. God indicated that the child, Ishmael, wasn't exactly what He had in mind as the first heir of the father of many nations. So, after fourteen long years, Abraham and Sarah (now 100 years old and ninety years old, respectively) miraculously had a son, Isaac. You can imagine how happy they were that God had given them this boy, the answer to His promise, when they were so far beyond the childbearing age!

But God was not through with Abraham. The twenty-second chapter of Genesis records God's command to him:

> *Now it came about after these things, that God tested Abraham, and said to him, "Abraham!" And he said, "Here I am."*
>
> *And He said, "Take now your son, your only son, whom you love, Isaac, and go to the land of Moriah; and offer him there as a burnt offering on one of the mountains of which I will tell you."*
>
> Gen. 22:1-2

Do you think Abraham had some conflicting thoughts and emotions? The miracle-child, the first-born son, the heir to the promise of God to be sacrificed as a burnt offering? We get a glimpse of the reasoning of Abraham's heart in the following verses:

> *So Abraham rose early in the morning and saddled his donkey, and took two of his young men with him and Isaac his son; and he split wood for the burnt offering, and arose and went to the place of which God had told him.*
>
> *On the third day Abraham raised his eyes and saw the place from a distance.*
>
> *And Abraham said to his young men, "Stay here with the donkey, and I and the lad will go yonder; and we will worship and return to you."*
>
> Gen. 22:3-5

"*We* will worship and return to you," Abraham said. Hebrews 11:19 states that Abraham *considered that God is able to raise men even from the dead.* Yes, Abraham would kill his only son if that was what God required, but God surely would raise Isaac from the dead so that His promise would not be broken.

As it turned out, God stopped Abraham from killing Isaac, and Isaac did not have to be raised from the dead. But there is an important point for us to learn about dealing with conflicting thoughts and emotions: We need to act on the revealed will of God as explained in the Scriptures, and focus on His love, promises, and power. Abraham did not focus on his conflicting thoughts and emotions, though he probably had many. Nor did he deny having them; rather, he simply didn't let them determine his actions. The promise of God to provide an heir and the command of God to kill Isaac looked mutually exclusive, but the sovereign Almighty God is able to accomplish far more than we can understand. We can have faith in His greatness, wisdom, and love, even when we don't understand what He is doing.

Application

Christ, His Word, and His work to accomplish our redemption are worthy of our faith. At this point you may be wondering, *How do I start applying these principles?*

First, you need to understand the four truths of redemption and the four corresponding false beliefs that we often mistake for truth. The ability to understand truth and recognize deception is a vital first step.

Secondly, learn to reject lies and replace them with their biblical truths so that your mind will be in the process of renewal. Along with renewing your mind, look for opportunities to represent Christ accurately and actively in your every situation and relationship. *The Search for Significance Workbook* has been developed to help you apply these truths so that your self-concept, your ambitions, and your relationships will begin to reflect the character of Christ.

Then, third, teach these truths to others. Teaching is the best way to learn because we pay more attention and study more diligently when we are going to communicate scriptural truths to someone else.

And fourth, endure. Develop a godly tenacity and keep following Christ. You will make mistakes, someone may disapprove of you, you may blame someone, you may sometimes fail to apply these truths, and you will occasionally dishonor the Lord, but realize that you are *deeply loved, completely forgiven, fully pleasing, totally accepted, and complete* because Christ died for you and was raised from the dead to give you new life. You are free! Free to *proclaim the excellencies of Him who has called you out of darkness into His marvelous light* (1 Pet. 2:9).

THE SEARCH FOR SIGNIFICANCE
WORKBOOK

Specially Designed Bible Studies & Applications

Introduction

General Douglas MacArthur said that one of the most important rules of war is to "know your enemy." If we are unaware of Satan's schemes and lies, we will be ineffective in spiritual warfare. The purpose of this workbook is twofold: to help you uncover Satan's deceptions in your thoughts and beliefs, and then to replace those lies with the powerful Word of God.

The goal of going through this workbook is not simply to "fill in the blanks," but to understand and apply God's truth. Don't rush through it. Take time to think. It is very important that you allow the Holy Spirit to show you those specific thoughts, emotions, relationships, or events that you need to deal with. This will take time and concentration.

Although self-analysis is a part of this workbook, the material presented here is designed to focus your attention primarily on Christ, not yourself. If you tend to be introspective (which comes from trying to find error in ourselves to blame, or good in ourselves to justify our existence), the truth brought out in this workbook will help you begin to experience freedom from that bondage. You will learn how to use Scriptural truth as the basis of your value, rather than your performance or the opinions of others. You will see that you do not have to get angry or disgusted when you fail, or when someone else does. You will realize that you are not in a hopeless rut. And you will discover the potential for a far deeper, more intimate relationship with Christ and with others, and a genuine appreciation for yourself. You will want to serve Christ and live for Him more than ever.

The workbook is divided into three sections:

I. Background (steps 1-4): How have Satan's deceptions affected mankind?

II. Satan's Lies vs. God's Truth (steps 5-14): How does the world system tell us we can obtain significance? What do the Scriptures say about our significance and worth?

III. Application (steps 15-25): How can we replace destructive beliefs with God's truth so that our thoughts, words, and actions reflect the love and purposes of God?

Each step includes questions for personal reflection and application, followed by a discussion for additional insight.

Special Note: There are many wonderful truths outlined in the workbook, but application is a critical part of the process of seeing the truths become a part of daily life. Steps 20 and 21 are a pivotal point! Learn to master the process of tracing painful emotions back to their root false belief and replacing them with God's Word. If you don't learn to do this, the workbook may become just a collection of "nice material" without profoundly affecting your life.

After you begin this workbook, it will be helpful for you to reread certain chapters of *The Search for Significance* as you go along. It's a good idea to do the workbook exercises as a regular part of your devotions. You may want to go through the material with a friend or teach the steps to a group. However you choose to proceed, be persistent. Don't let the enemy of our souls get you off track. And, again, don't hurry. Reflect. Think. Consider.

It is my heartfelt prayer that God will use this workbook to *enlighten the eyes of your heart* so that you will *proclaim the excellencies of Him who has called you out of darkness into His marvelous light* (1 Pet. 2:9).

Section I

Background

How have Satan's deceptions affected mankind?

Beginning the Search

Read chapters 1 and 2 from *The Search for Significance*.

This step is designed to help you understand the compelling need people have for self-worth. Let's examine two systems that we can use to meet this need.

1. How do you define *self-worth*?

    _____

    _____

2. Take several minutes to consider each of the following questions:

    a) Are you glad you are you?

    b) Do you have a healthy sense of self-worth?

    If you answered no to either of these questions, your sense of self-worth is lower than that which God wants you to have.

3. *a)*   Read Eph. 1:3-14 and list what God has done to you and for you:

_____

_____

_____

_____

_____

   b)   What phrases does Paul use to show you the extent of God's love?

_____

_____

_____

_____

   c)   How do you feel about these truths?

_____

_____

_____

4. Why do we have a basic desire for personal significance? Why does man wrestle with the basic questions, *Who am I?* and, *Why am I here?*

_____

_____

_____

5. There are two possible options we can choose to determine our self-worth:

   • The world's system: *Self-Worth = Performance* (what you do) + *Others' Opinions* (what others think or say about you).
   • God's system: *Self-Worth = God's Truth About You.*

a) List some activities, relationships, or achievements which make you feel better about yourself:

_____

_____

_____

_____

_____

_____

_____

b) List some activities, poor relationships, or failures which make you feel badly about yourself:

_____

_____

_____

_____

_____

_____

_____

6. What difference would it make in your attitude, relationships, and goals if you grasped the reality that your worth is not conditional (i.e., based on performance), but is based on the truth of the unconditional love, forgiveness, and acceptance of God?

_____

_____

7. *a)* Whose opinion of you do you value most?

_____

b) What is your most common response to that person?

_____

8. Think of the person you know who loves you most. How does that love make you feel?

_____

_____

9. Why does *others' opinions = self-worth* cause us to be concerned about our performance?

_____

_____

10. Is it difficult to view yourself in terms other than your performance or others' opinions of you? If so, why?

_____

_____

11. *a)* A number of the major problems in our lives originate from how we value ourselves—our self-worth. However, many of the answers to these problems are superficial "bumper-sticker" solutions. What are some examples of these, e.g., "Just have faith," "Just trust God"?

_____

_____

_____

b) How are these answers inadequate?

_____

_____

Most of the steps in this workbook include a section called "For Additional Insight." Compare your answers with these observations to get a deeper understanding of the questions presented in each step.

FOR ADDITIONAL INSIGHT

1. *Self-worth,* often called self-esteem or personal significance, is characterized by a quiet sense of self-respect and a feeling of satisfaction with who we are. True self-worth, unlike pride, is not based on an evaluation of our performance.

2. *a)* Are you glad you are you? If you aren't, you probably think that you would be happier if you could perform like someone else.

    b) Do you have a healthy sense of self-worth? This is not a neutral feeling about yourself, but a prevailing sense of value which is not related to your performance.
    A healthy self-concept is the recognition of one's value and worth: the understanding that as a unique human being, one has certain gifts and abilities unlike anyone else, and can contribute to the world in a special way. Success is both pleasing and encouraging, but it is the by-product of stability, rather than the source of self-esteem. One with a healthy self-concept will experience the pain of failure and defeat, but won't be devastated by it. One with a positive sense of self-esteem can enjoy personal strengths and tolerate the awareness of weaknesses. This is a wholesome love for oneself.
    Do you love yourself this way? Do you enjoy being you?

3. *a)* God has blessed you with every spiritual blessing, chosen you, declared you holy and blameless, adopted you, redeemed you, forgiven you, made known to you the mystery of His will, and sealed you with the Holy Spirit.

    b) Some of the phrases Paul used in Eph. 1:3-14 to describe what God has done for us are:

...according to the kind intention of His will to the praise of the glory of His grace, which He freely bestowed on us in the Beloved...

...according to the riches of His grace, which He lavished upon us...

...according to His kind intention which He purposed in Him...

and*...to the praise of His glory.*

c) You may feel very happy and thankful, you may be overwhelmed with the magnitude of God's love, or you may be thinking, *This can't be true. I don't feel like this at all.* That's okay. It's better to be honest, and feel pain, than to deny it and try to convince yourself that you are happy. Remember, your feelings are not the basis of truth. God's Word is our authority. What it says is true, whether we *feel* it or not. The more we understand God's Word and live by it, the more our feelings will reflect His character and love.

4. When God created man, He gave him a sense of purpose. When man rebelled against God, he lost that God-given sense of significance. Since then, he has tried to find purpose and meaning apart from God. But God has made us in such a way that He is the only One who can meet our needs. Money, fame, fine houses, sports cars, and prestige in a given profession are only counterfeits of the true significance we have in Christ. Though these counterfeits promise to meet our need for fulfillment, that which they provide is always short-lived. God and His purposes alone can give us a profound, lasting sense of significance.

5. *a)* You may feel better about yourself as a result of academic, athletic, or professional achievements, or even Christian activities (i.e., devotional time, prayer, witnessing, Bible study, church attendance).

b) Failure to meet our standards (or the standards of others) in any area can cause us to feel poorly about ourselves.

6. Realizing that your worth is not conditional will increasingly free you from the fears of failure and rejection, and give you joy, thankfulness, and a desire to honor the One who loves you so much.

7. *a)* Perhaps you most value the opinions of a parent, girlfriend, boyfriend, spouse, peer group, or boss.

   b) Possible responses to that person or group could include loyalty, obedience, fear, hard work, depression, or anger.

8. One of the many ways God communicates His love for us is through the committed and accepting love of another person. Love conveys the message that we are significant; that we have value and worth. This is exactly the way God wants us to feel! Recognizing this truth is a major step toward positive change in how we perceive ourselves, and in how we relate to God and other people.

9. The opinions others have of us are primarily based on our performance. If we are seeking our self-worth from others, peer pressure can cause us to conform to a certain standard. We learn acceptable behavior through a socialization process. Peer pressure conforms the behavior of each individual to fit the acceptable norm of the group—whether the behavior is best for that individual or not.

10. It is usually difficult to evaluate ourselves without considering our performance and the opinions of others. This standard of evaluation is primarily the input we receive from our society: radio, television, friends, clubs, work, school, billboards,

magazines. It is no wonder, then, that changing our value system is an uphill, but very necessary struggle.

11. *a)* • "Jesus is the answer."
  • "Give it to God."
  • "Just trust God and it will work out."
  • "Just pray about it."

b) The reason these answers are inadequate is because our problems are made up of specific elements. Unless we apply God's specific answers to our specific problems, we have nothing but a hollow ritual. Inadequate religious answers to life's problems may be more devastating than secular answers. If we apply what we think is God's answer and fail to find a solution, we are truly without hope. Unfortunately, some religious leaders give inadequate answers, and then blame those who seek their advice when the answers fail to yield solutions. Those of us who have received inadequate answers most of our lives may have a tendency to accept second-rate experiences and even defend the answers which have led us nowhere.

A FINAL WORD

The central questions man must face in life are, *Who am I?* and, *Why am I here?* These questions relate directly to man's search for self-worth and significance. The world has programmed us with a specific system of evaluating ourselves. This system is contrary to God's system, no matter what our standard of performance is, or whose approval we are seeking. The world's system will allow us fleeting moments of success and pride, but it will never let us enjoy lasting personal significance. Success and approval cannot ultimately fulfill our need for self-worth.

The Fall of Man: How Sin Has Affected Our Relationship with God

Read chapter 4 from *The Search for Significance*.

This step will help you to understand God's purpose for creating man, and how man's rebellion caused him to be separated from God and His purposes.

THE CREATION OF MAN

1. Read Gen. 1:25-31 and answer the following questions:

   a) What do you think it means for man to bear God's image?

   _____

   _____

   b) What are two responsibilities that God gave to Adam?

   _____

   _____

   c) What was God's evaluation of creation before Adam was created? What was it after he was created?

_____

_____

   d)   Was the basis of this evaluation based on Adam's performance
   or God's declaration?

_____

THE FALL OF MAN

2.   Read Gen. 3:1-10 and answer the following questions:

   a)   How did Satan tempt Eve?

_____

_____

_____

   b)   Where was Adam when Eve ate of the fruit (Gen. 3:6)?

_____

   c)   When Adam rebelled, did he know what he was doing? (See
   1 Tim. 2:14.)

_____

   d)   How did the Fall affect man's desire for significance?

_____

_____

THE EFFECTS OF MAN'S REBELLION

3.   Consider man's relationship with God:

   a)   Read Is. 59:2. How has sin, resulting from the Fall, affected
   man's relationship with God?

_____

b) Read 1 Cor. 6:9-10; Gal. 5:19-21; and Eph. 2:1-3. List some characteristics of fallen man:

_____   _____

_____   _____

_____   _____

_____   _____

_____   _____

_____

c) Read John 8:44; Eph. 2:2; and 1 John 3:8. Fallen man is dominated by whom?_____

d) Read John 8:34 and Rom. 6:12-17. Fallen man is a slave of...

_____

e) Read Matt. 25:46; 2 Thess. 1:6-10; Rev. 14:9-11; 20:11-15. What is fallen man's final outcome?

_____

_____

f) What effects of the Fall were evident in this morning's newspaper stories or last night's TV news programs? List specific events:

_____

_____

_____

_____

g) On a scale of 0-100 percent, how sure are you that you would go to heaven if you died tonight?

0%___10%___25%___35%___50%___75%___85%___95%___100%___

h) If you died tonight and stood before God and He asked you, "Why should I let you into heaven?" what would you say?

_____

_____

Review your answers with the following:

FOR ADDITIONAL INSIGHT

1. *a)* Man is to represent God on the earth by demonstrating His love, integrity, compassion, forgiveness, wisdom, joy, patience, goodness, and gentleness, among His other characteristics. This doesn't mean that man has all the capacities of God, but that there is a uniqueness about man which separates him from the rest of creation. In the same way that two spheres of different sizes are both similar and different, so man, created in the image of God, is uniquely similar to God, and yet, vastly different from Him.

   b) Man was created to bear God's image and exhibit His glory. In that role, he was given the two responsibilities of dominion over the earth and procreation, filling the earth with people who would also bear the image of God.

   c) Genesis 1:31 reveals that God's view of creation changed from "good" to "very good" after man was created.

   d) Since Adam's creation was said to be "very good" before he did anything, the basis of God's evaluation could not have been his performance. Adam was acceptable because God said he was.

2. *a)* Satan tempted Eve to *be like God, knowing good and evil* (Gen. 3:5). He accomplished this by causing Eve to question God's Word when he said, *You surely shall not die* (Gen. 3:4).

b)   Adam was with Eve, well aware of what was happening.

c)   Adam knew what he was doing. He was not deceived.

d)   The Fall isolated man from his true source of significance: God. Since then, man has sought success, wealth, prestige, and/ or the approval of others to meet his need for significance.

3.   *a)*   Sin has separated man from God.

b)   Fallen man is dead in his trespasses and sins, walks according to the course of the world, is led by the prince of the power of the air (Satan), is disobedient, lives in fleshly lust.

c)   Satan.

d)   Sin.

e)   Fallen man is denied heaven, and instead receives eternal punishment in hell.

f)   Effects of the Fall may be seen today in personal problems: sickness, loneliness, suicide; interpersonal problems: murder, rape, war; or natural disasters: drought, famine, earthquakes.

g)   If your response is less than 100 percent, it may indicate that your assurance of salvation is at least partially dependent on your performance, or good deeds, to earn God's acceptance.

h)   Read Rom. 3:19-28 and Titus 3:4-7. We do not gain a right standing before God based on our good works. There is no amount of good deeds, religious or otherwise, we can do that will obligate God to accept us into His eternal kingdom.

Romans 3:24-26 reveals the only certain basis for us to be

accepted by God: We are brought into a right relationship with Him based on our trust in what Jesus Christ accomplished for us on the cross. Christ's death was a substitutionary death for us. Even though we deserve death as punishment for our sins, Christ took our punishment upon Himself and died on the cross to pay for our sins.

If you have never trusted in Christ to pay for your sins and to give you new life, you can do so by expressing to Him your desire for a personal relationship with Him. The following is a suggested prayer that might help you communicate your attitude to God:

Lord Jesus, I need you. I want You to be my Savior and Lord. I accept Your death on the cross as the complete payment for my sins. Thank you for forgiving me and giving me new life. Help me to grow in my understanding of Your love and power so that my life will bring honor to You. Amen.

A FINAL WORD

The Shorter Version of the Westminster Catechism says, "The chief end of man is to glorify God and enjoy Him forever." Man, however, rejected God's purpose and chose to go his own way. Because of that rebellion, he experienced spiritual death, separation from God. Cut off from God, man had to find a new source of worth, so he turned to his performance and the approval of others. Still, God didn't give up on man. The loving Father offered His own Son as a sacrifice to bear the punishment we deserve. *For the wages of sin is death, but the free gift of God is eternal life in Christ Jesus our Lord* (Rom. 6:23).

Step Three
Satan's Deceptions

This step is designed to explain the implications of attempting to gain our self-worth through the world's system.

Man has been sadly deceived since the Fall. His mind has been darkened (Eph. 4:17-19), and he has chosen to believe the lies of Satan instead of God's truth.

Satan's lies are a direct result of his character:

> ...*He* (Satan) *was a murderer from the beginning, not holding to the truth, for there is no truth in him. When he lies, he speaks his native language, for he is a liar and the father of lies.*

> John 8:44, NIV

1. You may have heard that Satan is the father of lies, but have you ever considered what his lies are? List some of the lies you've been told by Satan:

   _____
   _____
   _____
   _____

2. The following are four general beliefs that many of us apply daily in our relationships and circumstances. To what extent are you affected by these? From chapters 6, 7, 8, and 9 of *The Search for Significance*, estimate the percentage you live by each of these beliefs, from zero to 100 percent:

_____% *I must meet certain standards in order to feel good about myself.*

_____% *I must have the approval of certain people (boss, friends, parents, etc.) in order to approve of myself. Without their approval, I cannot feel good about myself.*

_____% *Those who fail (including myself) are unworthy of love, and therefore, must be blamed and condemned.*

_____% *I am what I am. I cannot change. I am hopeless. In other words, I am the sum total of all my past successes and failures, and I'll never be significantly different.*

(Note: When we first begin to examine and confront these lies, our percentage scores may fluctuate. This is normal; the beginning of change. In time, the percentage to which we're affected by these lies will decrease.)

3. Proverbs 23:7 says, *As [a man] thinks within himself, so he is.* Our lifestyle is usually a reflection of what we think about ourselves. Analyze your lifestyle. Describe...
   a) The things you talk about:

   _____

   _____

   _____

b)   The places you like to go:

_____

_____

_____

c)   The people you spend time with:

_____

_____

_____

_____

d)   Your ambitions and dreams:

_____

_____

_____

_____

e)   How you spend your time:

_____

_____

_____

_____

f)   How you spend your money:

_____

_____

_____

g)   What are the main reasons you do these things (to gain the approval of others, to be a success, to avoid failure, to honor Christ, to fulfill someone's expectations, to help people...)?

_____

_____

_____

_____

Your attitudes, values, goals, and actions are primarily a reflection of what you believe about yourself. Paul writes that our lives are to be transformed by the renewing of our minds (Rom. 12:2). If you believe you must please people to be acceptable, you will be dominated by others' opinions. If, however, you believe that you are loved and accepted by God, you will grow to be a more secure, loving, and accepting person.

This diagram illustrates how our beliefs affect our thoughts, emotions, and actions:

Event

⇩

Beliefs ⇨ Thoughts ⇨ Emotions ⇨ Actions

Each of us has a set of beliefs through which we evaluate life. Any given event may trigger thoughts that evoke certain emotions and lead to actions. Therefore, our emotions and actions are usually a reflection of our belief system.

4. Think of the last situation that really angered you or made you feel afraid. What was the situation? What were your feelings? How did you act on those feelings?

    a) Situation:

    _____

    _____

    _____

    _____

    b) Emotion(s):

    _____

_____
_____

   c) Action(s):

_____
_____
_____

5. *a)* Which of the four beliefs in question 2 most apply to that situation? (It may be more than one.) How were the emotions you experienced and your subsequent actions a reflection of this belief?

_____
_____
_____
_____

  b) Is this belief based on God's truths or Satan's lies?_____

6. Reflect on the situation you described in question 4. If you had replaced the false belief with God's truth about you—*that you are deeply loved, completely forgiven, fully pleasing, totally accepted, and absolutely complete in Christ*—how do you think your emotions and actions would have been different?

_____
_____
_____
_____

7. God has provided love, peace, acceptance, and purpose through Christ's payment on the cross for us. He has made us so that He is the only One who can provide these in a lasting and fulfilling

way. Yet, virtually every TV commercial and magazine ad claims that a product or service will provide either love, happiness, comfort, or status. Will it? Think about this. How many people who start using a certain toothpaste are suddenly asked for a date by the person of their dreams? Will using a certain credit card suddenly make people happy, comfortable, and desirable...or in debt? Few of us are aware of the many deceptions we encounter each day.

a) What commercials or magazine ads promise love, happiness, comfort, or status? (Consider ads for beer, investment firms, computers, credit cards, cars, perfume, toothpaste.) Be specific.

• Love:
_____
_____

• Happiness:
_____
_____

• Comfort:
_____
_____

• Status:
_____
_____

Satan has enslaved most of mankind by convincing us that:

OUR SELF-WORTH = PERFORMANCE + OTHERS'
OPINIONS

Many of his lies can be summarized by these four false beliefs, each of which results in a specific fear:

False Belief: *I must meet certain standards to feel good about myself. If I fail to meet these standards, I cannot really feel good about myself.* This belief results in the fear of failure.

False Belief: *I must be approved* (accepted) *by certain people to accept myself. If I do not have the approval of these people, I cannot accept myself.* This belief results in the fear of rejection.

False Belief: *Those who fail are unworthy of love and deserve to be blamed and condemned.* This belief leads to the fear of punishment and the propensity to punish others.

False Belief: *I am what I am. I cannot change. I am hopeless. This means that I am simply a total of all my past performances, both good and bad. I am what I have done.* This belief leads to a sense of shame.

At this point in our study, many of us will have recognized the influence of these false beliefs in several different areas of our lives, but some of us may still be struggling to see the correlation between these lies and our attitudes and behavior.

You may be one who doesn't seem to be affected by others' opinions or by the fear of failure. If this seems to describe your situation, consider the fact that you live in the same world system as everyone else, and have, like everyone else, been taught to evaluate yourself on the basis of what you do and what others think of you. How have you been able to deal with this method of evaluation so well that the opinions of others seem to have no effect on you?

Perhaps you feel that you have already overcome these lies and fears, and are living by the truths of God's Word. However, it's also possible that you have deceived yourself, and only *think* that you've overcome these issues.

Deception of this nature may stem from a number of possible factors, two of which are given below:

Talent

Recall the rich young man who came to Jesus, wanting to follow Him (Matt. 19:16-24). When Christ told him that being complete in Him would mean giving up what he had been depending upon (in this case, wealth), the young man was tremendously disappointed. He had wanted to meet Christ on his own terms.

You, too, may have a wealth of skills in your work, studies, or relationships. You may be making a number of contributions and high achievements, even within the scope of Christian service. If this is the case, success may be preventing you from seeing the impact of Satan's lies on your attitudes and behavior, and hindering you from a more complete life in Christ.

Regardless of our talents or vocation, outward success can deceive us into believing that we have overcome the lies of the world.

Fear

There is nothing more personal than our self-worth, and it is frightening to admit that we have been basing our value on the wrong things. Success and the opinions of others are precarious sources of self-esteem. If making achievements and gaining approval are our primary means for obtaining self-worth, we will tenaciously hold to them until we are absolutely convinced that only God's love and acceptance of us can ultimately meet this need.

A young woman who came for counseling provides a good example of how we can seek fulfillment our way rather than God's way.

Due to a difficult relationship with her father, this woman found herself continually trying to gain the approval of men. She would even enter into obviously terminal relationships (such as with married men), and excuse her behavior by stating that she "just had to have someone to hold and love her." She would not allow herself to even consider that this need for acceptance could be met by the love of God and fellow believers.

If you have difficulty recognizing Satan's lies in your life, ask someone you trust to take the tests in chapters 6, 7, 8, and 9 in *The Search for Significance* book, and record his or her observations of you. This might give you further insight.

Review your answers to the previous questions in this step with the following:

FOR ADDITIONAL INSIGHT

1. By the very nature of deception, we are often unable to recognize those times when we are being deceived. These are a few of the lies Satan tells us:

   - *If you obey God, you'll be miserable.*
   - *The abundant life is trouble-free.*
   - *Unbelievers don't want to hear the gospel.*
   - *You couldn't help yourself . . . the temptation was too great.*
   - *If you fail, you're a failure.*
   - *You are what others think of you.*
   - *God can't use you.*
   - *You can't obey God.*
   - *If you do certain things, God will be pleased with you, and you will earn His affection.*

   It is interesting that Satan lies to unbelievers to convince them that they are *not* guilty, while he lies to believers to convince them that they *are* guilty.

217

2. To the extent (percentage) that you believe these lies, your life will be influenced by the world's system. Each belief stems from the concept that your *self-worth = performance + others' opinions*. We will continue to discover solutions to these lies in the remainder of this workbook.

3. Your actions and emotions are usually indicative of your belief system. Why do you do what you do, say what you say, and go where you go? How much of what you do is to honor God, and how much is to please people? We may say that we believe one thing, but our lifestyles often reveal that we believe something quite different.

4. Be specific in describing the situation and your feelings.

5. Realize that your emotions are integrally related to your belief system. Note that if you believe something that is false, it will affect your life as powerfully as if it were true. For instance, if you believe you are unwanted and a bother to God, you will probably be lonely and depressed, even though the truth is that you are precious to God and deeply loved by Him (Is. 43:4; Zeph. 3:17). Your beliefs, true or false, can dictate your emotions, actions, and ultimately, your life.

6. If you had replaced the false belief with God's truth, you most likely would have had a dramatically different emotional response. Also, your actions would probably have been much different. For example, rather than feeling depressed and unloved, you might have felt more secure and hopeful in light of God's love and acceptance. But remember that such a drastic change in attitude is a process, and that it's important to be honest about your emotions. Don't try to feel what you don't feel. Put yourself in an environment of honesty and encouragement so that you can experience the process of growth.

7. Learn to recognize deception. Instead of just sitting through television commercials, try to analyze what they are communicating. Are the ads deceptive? What does the product or service promise? Being an astute observer of the world around you will enable you to see how many lies are communicated to you each day. If you can't view the world's deceptions objectively, you are much more likely to believe them and be adversely affected by them.

A FINAL WORD

One of the most tragic results of the Fall is that man's mind became darkened. Satan has deceived the world into believing that **SELF-WORTH = PERFORMANCE + OTHERS' OPINIONS.** Satan continues to lie because he is the *father of lies* (John 8:44). But God has a solution! He has given us His Word, so that we don't have to be enslaved by the deceiver's schemes (2 Cor. 2:11). By learning to recognize deception in the world around us, and by confronting it with the truth of God's Word, we will increasingly experience the liberation He intends for us in the many aspects of our lives.

The Process of Hope and Healing

Read chapter 5 in *The Search for Significance*.

In this step, we will examine the process of healing so that we can increasingly experience hope and health in our lives.

FIVE ELEMENTS OF HEALING

Honesty

1. *a)* Describe your need for healing. What is your family background? How did (does) your relationship with your parents affect you? Have you experienced deep wounds, mild abrasions, or something in-between?

   _____

   _____

   _____

   _____

   _____

   _____

   _____

   _____

b) Read Ps. 51:6. From this passage, and from chapter 5 in *The Search for Significance* book, why do you think that the Lord wants us to be honest?

_____

_____

_____

c) To what extent has the Holy Spirit's light of truth shone on your life?

_____

_____

_____

Affirming Relationships

2. *a)* Name some people who have affirmed and encouraged you in the past:

_____   _____

_____   _____

_____   _____

b) How did their affirmation affect you?

_____

_____

c) Who is affirming you now?

_____   _____

_____   _____

_____   _____

d) What effect does this person (or group) have on you?

_____

_____

e) Do you need to find someone who will encourage and affirm you? If so, how do you plan to find that person or group of people?

_____

_____

Right Thinking

3. *a)* Describe how your thoughts and beliefs have been developed. (Include the influences of society, your family background, experiences, relationships):

_____

_____

_____

_____

b) Read 2 Tim. 3:16-17 and explain how the Scriptures can affect our thinking and our lives:

_____

_____

_____

_____

The Holy Spirit

4. *a)* Read John. 7:37-39; 14:16-17; 16:13-15, and describe the Holy Spirit's role in the healing process:

_____

_____

_____

_____

Time

5. *a)* Name some reasons why we often tend to expect fast results when we begin to seek growth and change in our lives:

_____

_____

_____

Are these realistic? Why, or why not?

_____

_____

b) Read Phil. 3:12-14. Paul had a process-perspective about life. Why is it important for us to have this same outlook?

_____

_____

_____

c) Describe how your emotions might change over the course of a year or two of healing:

_____

_____

_____

6. *a)* Are these five elements a part of your life right now?_____

b) Which are stronger than others?

_____

_____

c) Which need more attention?

_____

_____

d)   How can you experience all five of these elements to the extent that you need to?

_____

_____

_____

_____

Review your answers with the following:

FOR ADDITIONAL INSIGHT

1.   *a)*   Those of us from relatively stable backgrounds usually find it easy to be honest about the joys and pains in our lives. Some of us, however, come from dysfunctional families, and have experienced tragedies which have caused deep wounds. These experiences may have prompted us to erect defenses designed to block pain. Defensive barriers often prohibit us from seeing problem areas in our lives.

b)   The Lord wants us to be honest with ourselves, with Him, and with at least one other person, because honesty is the first crucial step toward healing and maturity.

c)   Most of us believe that we are completely honest and objective about ourselves because none of those around us are willing to tell us otherwise. If we are from a dysfunctional background, and haven't yet seen much damage in our lives, our defensive barriers may be blocking our objectivity. We may need to be asking God for increased light in order to determine what in our lives needs changing.

2. *a)* You have probably felt loved and valued by either your parents, a friend, teacher, spouse, child, or group.

   b) Perhaps you have gained a sense of confidence and courage. Or, you may have withdrawn from affirmation because you didn't feel that you deserved it.

   c) Perhaps you are now receiving positive reinforcement from your parents, a counselor, pastor, close friend, or group.

   d) This person or group probably listens to you appreciatively, encourages your honesty, accepts your strengths and weaknesses, and gives you love, support, and respect.

   e) It may be relatively easy to find someone to encourage you in the process of emotional healing, but it may also prove to be very difficult. A pastor or counselor may be able to steer you to a person or group with whom you can experience warmth and love.

3. *a)* All of these influences have a profound effect on our thoughts and beliefs, but our family background probably dominates the development of our belief system. Books, television programs, movies, and friends also strongly influence our current thoughts about God, other people, and situations.

   b) The Scriptures are a gift from God, designed to teach us about life, to show us where our views are in error, and to correct our faulty perceptions so that we can continually experience the process of growth, as well as God's love, forgiveness, and power.

4. *a)* The Holy Spirit is the source of spiritual wisdom, insight, and power. He uses the Word of God and the people of God to instruct us and model the character of Christ to us.

5. *a)* There are many reasons. Among the possibilities: we don't want to experience hurt; others tell us that a seminar, book, or something else helped them instantly; technological advances in society encourage us to expect dramatic results at the push of a button; we may experience a spurt of insight and healing, and conclude that the rest of the process should be as quick and easy.

b) A process-perspective will enable us to be realistic about our ups and downs. We won't think that we've completed the growth process the first time we feel better, and we won't give up when honesty and objectivity reveal deeper pain than we'd even imagined.

c) In the healing process, our emotions vary widely. We may experience exhilaration, then depression, then hope, then despair, anger, hurt, and a host of other feelings. We may feel worse than ever before, and/or better than before. This graph may be typical for many of us:

Feelings

Time

Try to be realistic—and honest—about your emotions.

6. These elements are most effective when they are employed together over a long period of time. Take steps to find people who will provide an environment in which all of these ingredients will produce a strong and healthy place for you to grow.

A FINAL WORD

A good understanding of the healing process can provide us with hope and realistic expectations. Without hope, we may go through some of the motions, but we probably won't develop deep relationships based on honesty because we lack the courage to take the risks of intimacy. If we lack realistic expectations, we may expect rapid and complete relief from years of hurt and anger. This will only lead to disappointment.

Section II

Satan's Lies vs. God's Truth

*How does the world system tell us
we can obtain significance?*

*What do the Scriptures say about our
significance and worth?*

Overview

In section II, we will study two conflicting belief systems: one based on Satan's lies, and the other based on God's truth about us.

Being able to identify Satan's lies and then confront them with a specific truth is crucial! Become a master of the relationships between these lies and their corresponding truths. It will help you tremendously as you start to apply them. In fact, most people find that their ability to apply these truths on a daily basis is directly related to their ability to recognize the lies. Recognition is the vital first step of application; for that reason, I encourage you to stop at this point and memorize the four false beliefs we have studied previously with God's corresponding truths. You will find the exercises in steps 5-14 to be much more productive if you can recognize Satan's deceptions in your life and refute them with scriptural truth. Learning these is a small investment of time and effort that will pay a handsome spiritual and emotional return!

BELIEF SYSTEMS

SATAN'S LIE:	GOD'S TRUTH:
Your Worth = Your Performance Plus Others' Opinions.	Your Worth = What God Says About You.
Those who fail are unworthy of love and deserve to be blamed and condemned. (Fear of punishment; propensity to punish others).	Propitiation (1 John 4:9-10): *I am deeply loved by God.*
I must meet certain standards to feel good about myself. If I don't...(Fear of failure).	Justification (Rom. 3:19-25; 2 Cor. 5:21): *I am completely forgiven and fully pleasing to God.*
I must be approved (accepted) by certain others to feel good about myself. If I'm not approved...(Fear of rejection).	Reconciliation (Col. 1:19-22): *I am totally accepted by God.*
I am what I am; I cannot change; I am hopeless. (Shame).	Regeneration (2 Cor. 5:17): *I am absolutely complete in Christ.*

We can renew our minds by using our emotions to analyze our belief system.

Step Five
The Fear of Failure

Read chapter 6 in *The Search for Significance*.

In this step, you will examine the effects of the fear of failure, which stems from the false belief, *I must meet certain standards in order to feel good about myself.*

1. *a)* List three recent situations in which your performance did not measure up to the standard you had set for yourself. Identify the standard you felt you needed to meet. Then, try to remember what thoughts and emotions accompanied each occasion, and the actions you took that reflected those thoughts and feelings. (Use a separate sheet of paper if necessary.)

Example:

Situation: *I failed a test.*

Standards: *I must make at least a B in the class to feel good about myself.*

Thoughts: *I'll never make it through this class. I'll flunk, and my friends will think I'm stupid. My parents will be so ashamed of me.*

Emotions: Anger, depression

Actions: *I yelled at my professor and blamed my roommate for making so much noise that I couldn't study for this test. I then withdrew from my friends.*

(1) Situation:_____

Standards:_____

Thoughts:_____

Emotions:_____

Actions:_____

(2) Situation:_____

Standards:_____

Thoughts:_____

_____

Emotions:_____

_____

_____

Actions:_____

_____

_____

(3) Situation:_____

_____

_____

Standards:_____

_____

_____

Thoughts:_____

_____

_____

Emotions:_____

_____

_____

Actions:_____

_____

_____

b) Do you see any patterns reflected in your emotions and actions? If so, what are they?

_____

_____

2. Why do people use performance as a measurement of personal worth?

_____

_____

3. *a)* Do you have to be successful in order to feel good about yourself? What would you have to be or do to feel like you are a "success"?

_____

_____

b) In what area(s) would you *never* allow yourself to fail?

_____

_____

_____

_____

_____

_____

4. *a)* What Christian activities do you use to evaluate yourself spiritually?

_____

_____

b) Does performing these activities make you more pleasing to God?

_____

_____

5. How does your desire to meet your performance standard affect your relationships with others?

_____

_____

_____

6. How do you feel toward those who hinder your ability to meet your standard?

_____

_____

_____

_____

7.   What things do you do in order to avoid failure?

_____

_____

_____

_____

8.   How do you think your life would be different if you did not
     experience the fear of failure?

_____

_____

_____

Compare your answers with the following:

FOR ADDITIONAL INSIGHT

1.   *a)*   Your list may include occasions dealing with academic
     responsibilities, professional activities, relationships, daily tasks,
     scheduling, etc.

     b)   In almost any activity or relationship, we are susceptible to
     the fear of failure. When we fail, we usually experience anger,
     resentment, worry, anxiety, fear, depression, and other negative
     emotions. In turn, these emotions express themselves through
     actions like withdrawal, hostility, being rude, and blaming others.
     If we analyze our responses to failures, we can usually see that
     they have a pattern. How do you tend to respond to failure?

2. When our performance meets our standard, it can give us a sense of pride that we might mistake for self-worth. We feel good; we feel significant. We will then want to meet another standard so that we can feel good about ourselves again.

   We use performance to evaluate our self-worth because the system reinforces itself: When we perform well, we feel good. This "success" makes us feel that the system works, so we continue to use it. (Please note: It is not wrong to be glad about being successful at something. The issue is not primarily how we feel, but the basis of our self-worth. Either our performance leads us to pride, or God's truth leads us to true joy and the desire to honor Him.)

   If you reject God's provision for self-worth, and instead embrace the world's false promises, then your performance is your only alternative for meeting this deep, almost all-encompassing need. You usually act according to your beliefs. If you believe that you are a failure, you will probably either withdraw from activities that involve a risk of failure, or drive yourself to succeed to prove that you're not a failure.

   Again, your performance often reflects your belief system. If your belief system is based on false beliefs, then your thoughts, emotions, and actions will usually reflect those false beliefs.

3. Be honest! You may be trying to gain a sense of worth from your participation in academics, athletics, your relationships, your job, club memberships, the cleanliness of your house or car, teaching Sunday School, tithing, or from some other activity or form of Christian service.

4. *a)* Your list may include daily devotions, Bible study, witnessing, fellowship, church involvement, and giving.

   b) Any standard of performance, even a Christian standard, used to obtain a more positive sense of self-worth is contrary to

God's truth, and is, therefore, an ungodly means to fulfill your need for significance. If this is the case, then you are still trapped in the world's system.

Once we realize that our self-worth is secure in Christ, we will begin wanting to do things that bring honor to Him. Our efforts then, coming from that motivation, are pleasing to God.

5. You might enter some relationships with selfish personal goals, which could prompt you to manipulate others in an effort to reach those goals. Sometimes, we even use kind and encouraging remarks to get others to do what we want them to. Sooner or later, these people usually realize that our kind remarks are actually being used as manipulative devices. This leads to alienation and bitterness in our relationships.

6. If people hinder you from meeting your standards, you might become angry, enraged, or resentful; you might blame them, reject them, or withdraw from them. They have kept you from meeting one of your deepest needs!

7. Some of the coping methods we use are: avoiding situations where failure is likely, working only in areas of strength, offering excuses, explaining away failure, trying harder to perform, lowering our standards, blaming others, and becoming lazy.

8. As you become less influenced by the fear of failure, you will probably be happier, more loving, more spontaneous, and more thankful to God for His love.

A FINAL WORD

The fear of failure is like stacking marbles; a very difficult task, but not any more difficult than trying to win the performance game. When we evaluate ourselves by our performance, we're ultimately going to lose, no matter how successful we are at the moment.

If we believe that our self-worth is based on our success, we will try to avoid failure at all costs. Most of us have become experts at avoiding failure. We attempt only those things in which we are confident of success. We avoid those activities in which the risk of failure is too great. We spend time around those who are not a threat to us. We avoid people who, either by their greater success or by their disapproval of us, make us feel like failures. We have trained ourselves very well!

A rat placed in a box and shocked until it huddles in one particular corner soon learns to run to that corner as soon as it is placed in the box. How much of our energy is expended avoiding the disapproving "shocks" of those around us? Even though we are meant to experience the freedom of God's love and eternal purpose, how much time do we spend huddled in a corner like a laboratory rat?

Another consequence of having to meet certain standards in order to feel good about ourselves is a rules-dominated life. Many of us know people who have a set of rules for everything, and who always place their attention on their performance. However, the focus of the gospel is on relationships, not regulations. Christ's exercise of His lordship in our lives is dependent on our attending to His moment-by-moment instruction. Focusing only on rules will relegate our lives to the prison of self-examination.

On the other hand, we may feel very good about ourselves because we are winning the performance game. We may be so talented that we are reaching virtually every goal we have set for ourselves. We can't afford to mistake this pride for positive self-worth. We must realize that God is able to bring about whatever circumstances are necessary to cause us to stop trusting in ourselves.

God intends to bring us to Himself through prayer and the study of His Word so that we can know, love, and serve Him. Sometimes, He will allow us to fail miserably so that we will look to Him instead of to ourselves for our security and significance.

Before becoming upset that God would allow you to experience failure, remember that any life less than God intended is a second-class existence. He loves you too much to let you continue to obtain your self-esteem from the empty promise of success.

Step Six
Justification

As a result of Christ's death on the cross, our sins are forgiven and God has imputed Christ's righteousness to us. Therefore, we are fully pleasing to God.

1. Read Rom. 3:19-28; 4:4-5; 5:1-11. What does it mean to be *justified*?

   _____

   _____

   _____

2. Read 2 Cor. 5:21; Col. 1:22; 3:12; and Heb. 10:14. Are you as righteous, holy, and blameless as Christ? Why, or why not?

   _____

   _____

3. Read Rom. 3:9-23; 5:6-10; and Eph. 2:1-3. Why did you need to be justified and have Christ's righteousness attributed to you? Describe God's view of you before your justification:

   _____

   _____

   _____

4. How was your justification accomplished?

   a) Rom. 3:24; Titus 3:7

   _____

   _____

   b) Rom. 3:28; Gal. 2:16

   _____

   _____

   c) Rom. 5:1; Gal. 3:24

   _____

   _____

   d) Rom. 5:9; Heb. 9:22

   _____

   _____

5. What are the results of justification?

   a) Rom. 4:7-8

   _____

   _____

   b) Rom. 5:1

   _____

   _____

   c) Rom. 5:9

   _____

   _____

d) Rom. 8:1; 33-34

_____

_____

e) 2 Cor. 5:14-15

_____

_____

f) 2 Cor. 5:21

_____

_____

g) Titus 3:7

_____

_____

6. *a)* Read Rom. 4:6-8 and Heb. 10:17. Are you remembering sins that God has forgotten? If so, why?

_____

_____

_____

b) Does remembering sin help you in any way? If so, how?

_____

_____

_____

7. How does being justified and having Christ's righteousness lead you to the conclusion: *I am completely forgiven by God, and am fully pleasing to Him?*

_____

_____

8. If your good works won't make you more pleasing to God, why should you be involved in good works? (See Rom. 6:12-13; 1 Cor. 6:18-20; Col. 3:23-24; Titus 2:11-14.)

_____

_____

_____

9. Read 1 Cor. 3:11-15. What will determine whether or not a deed will honor God? (See also Rom. 14:23 and 1 Cor. 10:31.)

_____

_____

10. Review question 1 of step 5. Using one of the occasions you listed, chart how your behavior would have been different if you had believed God's truth that *you are completely forgiven by God and fully pleasing to Him*, rather than the false belief, *I must meet certain standards in order to feel good about myself.*

    a) Situation:

    _____

    _____

    _____

    b) Belief: *I am completely forgiven and fully pleasing to God.*

    c) Thoughts:

    _____

    _____

    d) Emotions:

    _____

    _____

e) Actions:

_____

_____

11. Memorize Rom. 5:1.

Compare your answers to the following:

FOR ADDITIONAL INSIGHT

1. To be justified is to be placed in right standing with God. *Justification* is the judicial act of God by which He declares the one who trusts in Christ to be righteous. The justified person is acquitted from all guilt of sin and is declared holy, righteous, and blameless.

2. If you have trusted in Christ's death on the cross for the forgiveness of your sins, God has declared you to be perfect in His sight! If you were anything less than that, you would not be pleasing enough to Him to be His companion for eternity.

    However, justification is often stated in ways that cause it to lose its impact. We sometimes seem to say to God, "In heaven, I guess this is true, but down here in the real world, we just aren't that way." We may respond like this because we are convinced that our worth is dependent on our performance. But to God, our worth is established and secure because He has sovereignly imputed to us the righteousness of Christ.

    Suppose Christ were seated in a chair next to you, and someone asked God, the Father, "Which person do You love the most? Which person is more acceptable to You? Which person is holy, righteous, and blameless before You?" God, the Father, would respond to each question the same way: "They are equally loved, acceptable, and righteous."

3. Without Christ's righteousness, you would have no basis on which to stand before God. Before your justification, God viewed you as being unrighteous, sinful, and an enemy. You were dead in your sins, separated from God, disobedient in nature, and an object of God's wrath. Romans 3:9-20 is God's description of unjustified man. You may be thinking, *I was never really that bad.* But to God, even your best attempts at righteousness were as filthy rags (Is. 64:6). Romans 14:23 and Hebrews 11:6 also state that anything not done in faith is sin and displeases God. But take heart, the living God has seen your helplessness, and has extended justification to you through Christ's death and resurrection.

4. *a)* His grace. He gave you what you didn't deserve.
    b) Not by works (meeting certain standards)—it is His gift.
    c) Faith, a means by which you appropriate what Christ has done for you.
    d) Your justification was accomplished by the shedding of His blood.

5. *a)* Because of justification, your sin is forgiven and forgotten.
    b) You have peace with God. You are no longer considered His enemy.
    c) You are saved from His wrath.
    d) There is no condemnation remaining for you to bear.
    e) You can now live to honor Him and reflect His image.
    f) You are declared righteous.
    g) You are an heir of His eternal kingdom.

6. *a)* Satan deceives us into thinking that remembering and reliving sin is somehow a part of repentance. But this is not true! Remembering and reliving sins are the flesh's way of trying to pay for sin and control our actions. The thinking goes like this:

By remembering and reliving these sins, I inflict pain upon myself. That pain will become associated with these sins so I will never do them again. Therefore, remembering sin is helpful and good.

Why does recalling these sins cause pain? Each time you remember them, you judge yourself according to your poor past performance. The evaluation always comes out negative, and the pain of self-hatred follows. If you were not evaluating yourself by your past performance, you would probably not dredge up the painful memory of these sins.

b) Reliving sin is a destructive way of trying to produce a godly life. God's method is to forgive our sins and remember them no more (Heb. 10:17). What sins do you need to stop remembering?

7. Because you have been given the righteousness of Christ, you are just as pleasing to the Father as He is! There is nothing you can do to add to, or take away from, what Christ did for you on the cross. As a result of your justification, *you are completely forgiven and fully pleasing to God.* Although you may try to justify yourself by doing good deeds to show God that you deserve your justification, it is a vain attempt to gain what you already have. Your new life is a product of God's workmanship in which He is very pleased. As your mind is renewed by this truth, you will increasingly reflect this in your attitudes and behavior.

8. You should be involved in good works because they are an opportunity to bring honor to Christ. As you are gripped by what He has done for you, your natural response will be to honor Him in your daily life. Your good works are not a means to earn righteousness, but are a way to bring Him delight and glory. In step 7, we will look at motivations for responding in obedience to God.

9. The issue is more than just doing the "right" things. The question is, *Are you doing the right things for the right reasons?* Jesus had the most trouble with those religious people who were doing religious works for the wrong reasons. If you are honest, you probably realize that you perform many of your "good" deeds to make yourself more acceptable to others, to God, and perhaps, to yourself. But all of these "good" works will burn someday. Are you motivated to do the right things in response to what Christ has done for you? If not, it will help you to reflect more on the lostness of man, the forgiveness of Christ, and the righteousness He bought for you by His blood.

   In motivating others, we need to point people to God, to His grace, and let Him motivate them. Motivating people by guilt is an easy recourse, but it is not honoring to the Lord.

10. *Example:*

   Situation: *I failed a test.*

   God's Truth: *I am completely forgiven by God, and am fully pleasing to Him.*

   Thoughts: *I did my best under the circumstances. God can use the situation. It's not the end of the world.*

   Emotions: *Peace eventually overcame my feelings of anger and depression.*

   Actions: *Got some help in the class. Talked to my roommate about the situation; we decided that in the future, we'll both study in the library or in another quiet place.*

A FINAL WORD

Justification is the great doctrine which is the bedrock of our self-worth. *Therefore having been justified by faith, we have peace with God through our Lord Jesus Christ* (Rom. 5:1). To be justified means to be placed in right standing before God. But what exactly does this mean? Justification is the judicial act of God by which He declares us free from the guilt of sin. All the sin we will ever commit has already been forgiven. To be justified means that the blight of our sin has been removed, and that we have been completely cleansed by the blood of Christ. God sees us this way at this very moment! However, as marvelous as that is, justification means more than being forgiven. God not only forgives our sinfulness, He also provides our righteousness. Righteousness is the worthiness to stand in God's presence without fear of personal condemnation, because He has imputed the very righteousness of Christ to us.

Step Seven
Motivations for Obedience

If God is already fully pleased with us as a result of Christ's death on our behalf, then why should we desire to live for Him daily? In this step, we will identify six biblical motivations for choosing to obey God rather than live in sin, rebellion, and self-effort. We will also examine some poor motivations for obeying God.

SIX REASONS TO OBEY GOD

Love Motivates

The Christians at Corinth must have asked Paul some of the same questions we might have about obedience. He responded that the love of Christ motivates us to live for Him. Christ's death revealed the depth of His love for us. Our obedience reveals the depth of our love for Him.

> *For the love of Christ controls us, having concluded this, that one died for all...*
> *and He died for all, that they who live should no longer live for themselves, but for Him who died and rose again on their behalf.*
>
> 2 Cor. 5:14-15

Notice the word, *concluded,* in this passage. This means to analyze an issue and determine its meaning and value. In other words, Paul was saying that those who comprehend Christ's sacrifice on the cross are compelled by its immeasurable value to live not for themselves, but for Him who made the sacrifice.

True love for Christ is a response to His love for us. As we experience His love, we will find our hearts overflowing with love for Him. When we rebel against God, it is a good indication that we are deceived about some aspect of Christ's love.

Think of occasions when you have withdrawn from God, or have been angry with Him and rebellious against Him. Ask Him to reveal your thoughts about Him during those times. Then, read John 3:16-18; 17:23-24; Rom. 5:6-11; Gal. 4:5-7; Eph. 2:4-9, and reflect on His complete, tender, unconditional love for you.

Christ's love for us is our first and foremost motive for obedience. It is the solid foundation for all other motivations because it comforts our wounds, takes away our compulsion to earn love by success and approval, and gives us encouragement to follow Him.

1. *a)* Does the love of Christ compel you to obey Him? Why, or why not?

   _____

   _____

   _____

Sin Is Destructive

Among the most common responses to sin in our society are laughter and tolerance. Even many Christians seem to think that sin is "no big deal." We need to open our eyes to the obvious facts around us about the tremendous destructiveness of sin. Broken homes, hatred, bitterness, suicide, alcohol and drug abuse, sleeplessness, tension, and many other symptoms of sin are rampant.

When we sin, we grieve the Holy Spirit and block His power in our lives. As a result, we are left to our own abilities to combat the conforming pressures of the world. If we truly believed in sin's destructiveness, we would be quite afraid of it. We are deceived because sin is usually pleasurable—at least, temporarily. But the Scriptures tell us that the person who sows evil will reap evil, and the one who willingly and continually sins will destroy himself (Gal. 6:7-8). Knowing this, we should trust God's infinite wisdom by believing that He has not lied to us concerning the ultimately painful effects of sin.

2. *a)* Read the first chapter of Jonah. List the results of Jonah's choice of disobedience to God:

_____

_____

_____

_____

b) In what ways have you seen specific effects of a particular sin in your life?

_____

_____

_____

_____

c) How can viewing sin as destructive be a motivation for obedience to God?

_____

_____

Discipline from the Father

Because He truly loves us, our heavenly Father disciplines us. Discipline is proof that we have become the sons of God (Heb. 12:5-11). Although God reproves us in love when we disobey, He never punishes us in anger because Christ has removed the wrath we deserve for our sins once and for all.

If this is true, when does the Lord discipline us? Generally, God does not discipline us each time we do wrong, but only when we persist in wrongdoing. If we were quick to recognize a wrong and correct it, God would have no need to discipline us. But we must realize that when discipline does come, it is sent for correction, not condemnation. Paul wrote:

> *But when we are judged, we are disciplined by the Lord in order that we may not be condemned along with the world.*
>
> 1 Cor. 11:32

Another reason God disciplines us is to protect us from the painful effects of sin. Just as parents use discipline to teach their children that certain activities are harmful to them, our heavenly Father disciplines us to get our attention, so that He can teach us that sin is harmful to us. Whether for correction or protection, God's motive for discipline is always love, never anger or revenge. The realization that His discipline is always for our good makes us more open to the lessons He wants to teach us.

3. *a)* Do you sometimes confuse God's correction with punishment? If so, why?

_____

_____

_____

   b) How can understanding God's discipline be a motivation for you?

_____

_____

_____

God's Commands for Us Are Good

When we sin, it is usually because we doubt God's goodness. We rebel against our Creator, doubting that He who made us really knows what's best for us. This is exactly the strategy Satan used with Eve in the Garden when he said to her, *You surely shall not die! For God knows that in the day you eat from it* (the tree) *your eyes will be opened, and you will be like God, knowing good and evil* (Gen. 3:4-5). Satan convinced Eve that God was withholding a privilege from her, and she believed the lie. We often do the same in our lives today.

Rather than viewing God's commands as restrictions, we must be reminded that because God is good, His commands for us are good. God is our Creator. The Scriptures are His guidelines, given for the protection and direction of that which He created: man.

4. *a)* Read Rom. 7:12 and 1 John 5:3. How are God's commands described?

_____

_____

_____

b) Read Deut. 5:29 and 6:24. What are some results of obeying God's commands?

_____

_____

_____

c) How can viewing God's commands as good be a motivation to you?

_____

_____

_____

Our Obedience Will Be Rewarded

Our self-worth is not based on our performance and obedience; however, what we do (or don't do) has tremendous implications on the quality of our lives and our impact on others for Christ's sake. Disobedience results in spiritual poverty; a short-circuiting of intimate fellowship with the One who loves us so much that He died for us; confusion, guilt, and frustration; and an absence of both spiritual power and the desire to see people won to Christ and become disciples. On the other hand, responding to the love, grace, and power of Christ enables us to experience His love, joy, and strength as we minister to others, endure difficulties, and live for Him who has *called us out of darkness into His marvelous light* (1 Pet. 2:9). We are completely loved, forgiven, and accepted apart from our performance, but how we live is very important!

5. *a)* Read 1 Cor. 3:11-15; 2 Cor. 5:10; 1 John 4:17; and Rev. 20:11-15. According to these passages, *unbelievers* will be judged and condemned at the Great White Throne of Judgment for rejecting Christ. Though *believers* will be spared from this condemnation, we will stand before the Judgment Seat of Christ to have our deeds tested. Those deeds done for the Lord will be honored, but those deeds done for ourselves will be destroyed by fire. The Greek word to describe this judgment seat is the same used to describe the platform an athlete stands on to receive a wreath of victory for winning an event. The Judgment Seat of Christ is for the reward of good deeds, not for the punishment of sin.

This chart demonstrates some of the differences between the Judgment Seat of Christ and the Great White Throne Judgment.

	JUDGMENT SEAT OF CHRIST (1 Cor. 3:11-15)	GREAT WHITE THRONE OF JUDGMENT (Rev. 20:11-15)
WHO WILL APPEAR:	Christians	Non-Christians
WHAT WILL BE JUDGED:	Deeds	Deeds
PERSONAL RESULT:	Reward	Condemnation
ULTIMATE RESULT:	Used to honor Christ	Cast out of the presence of God into the lake of fire

b) Read 1 Cor. 9:24-27 and 2 Tim. 2:3-7; 4:7-8. How does receiving a reward become a motivation for obedience?

_____

_____

_____

Obedience Is an Opportunity to Honor God

Each time we choose to obey, we express the righteousness we have in Christ. Our performance, then, becomes a reflection of who we are in Christ.

6. *a)* Read 1 Cor. 3:16-17 and 1 Pet. 2:9. How are you described?

_____

_____

_____

b) What purposes for our lives do these passages suggest?

_____

_____

_____

7. *a)*   How much are you motivated by each of these six reasons to
    obey God? Reflect on these motivations and rate each on a scale
    of zero (no motivation to you at all) to ten (a persistent, conscious,
    compelling motivation):

    _____The love of Christ compels us to obey.

    _____Sin is destructive.

    _____The Father will discipline us if we continue
      in a habit of sin.

    _____His commands for us are good.

    _____We will receive rewards for obedience.

    _____Obedience is an opportunity to honor God.

    b)   Do any of these seem "purer" or "higher" to you? If so,
    which ones? Why?

    _____

    _____

    _____

    _____

    c)   Which of these do you need to concentrate on?

    _____

    _____

    _____

    d)   What can you do to further develop this motivation?

    _____

    _____

    _____

IMPROPER MOTIVATIONS FOR OBEDIENCE

Jesus repeatedly emphasized that His concern is not only what we do, but why we do it. The Pharisees obeyed many rules and regulations, but their hearts were far from the Lord. Motives are important! The following are some poor motivations for obeying God and their possible results.

Someone May Find Out

Many people obey God because they are afraid of what others will think of them if they don't obey. Allen went on church visitation because he feared what his Sunday school class would think if he didn't. Barbara was married, but wanted to go out with a man at work. She didn't because of what others would think.

There are problems with determining behavior solely on the opinions of others. First, there are times when no one is watching. Maybe you're on a business trip, and don't know anyone in the city. The motive to refrain from sin is missing, so you indulge in it. This happens to many Christian businessmen. A second problem is that the desire to disobey may eventually exceed the peer pressure to obey. Finally, once someone has found out you've sinned, you may no longer have a reason to obey. Sherry didn't sleep with her boyfriend for fear of what her mother would say if she found out. One day, Sherry slept with her boyfriend, and as she had feared, her mother found out. Sherry lost her motivation to obey, so she began sleeping with him regularly.

Obeying God because of others' opinions might work for awhile, but it won't honor God or set you free...and eventually, it won't work at all.

8.　*a)*　Is the fear of others' opinions a motivation for you to obey God? If it is, identify the specific sin you are trying to avoid, then review the six reasons to obey God to refresh your mind and heart about the proper motivations for obedience.

b) Which of these proper motives seems to encourage you most in regard to your specific sin?

_____

_____

_____

_____

God Will Be Angry with Me

Some people obey God because they think God will get angry with them if they don't. We've already discussed the difference in God's discipline and punishment, but to reiterate, God disciplines us in love, not anger. His response to our sin is grief, not condemnation (Eph. 4:30).

Hank was afraid that God would "zap" him if he did anything wrong, so he performed for God. He lived each day in fear of God's anger. Predictably, his relationship with the Lord was cold and mechanical.

God doesn't want us to live in fear of His anger, but in response to His love. This produces joyful obedience instead of fear.

9. If you knew that God's response to your sin was grief instead of anger, would that affect your motivation to obey Him? Why, or why not?

_____

_____

_____

I Couldn't Approve of Myself if I Didn't Obey

Some people obey God in an attempt to live up to certain standards they've set for themselves. They simply couldn't stand themselves if they didn't obey. Sadly, the idea of yielding their lives to a loving Lord is often far from their minds. They are only trying to live up to their own standards, and if they don't meet those standards, they feel ashamed. These people are primarily concerned with do's and don'ts. Instead of an intimate relationship with God, they see the Christian life as a ritual, with the key emphasis on rules. Of course, if these people succeed in keeping the rules, they often become prideful. They may also tend to compare themselves with others, hoping to be accepted on the basis of being a little bit better than someone else.

Phillip was raised in a strict church family. He was taught that cursing is a terrible sin. All of Phillip's friends cursed, but he never did. He secretly thought that he was better than his friends. The issue with Phillip was never what God wanted or God's love for him. Instead, it was his own compulsion to live up to his standards. Phillip needed to base his behavior on God and His Word, not on his own standards.

God gave us His commands out of love for us. We are protected and freed to enjoy life more fully as we obey Him.

10. *a)* What things are you not doing because you couldn't stand yourself if you did them?

_____

_____

b) What are you doing to "obey God" with the motivation of meeting your own standards?

_____

_____

_____

_____

I'll Obey to Be Blessed

God doesn't swap marbles. If our sole motive to obey is to be blessed, we are simply attempting to manipulate God. The underlying assumption is: *I've been good enough...bless me.* It's true that we will reap what we sow. It's true that obedience keeps us within God's plan for our lives. But our decision to obey should never be based solely on God's rewarding us.

Brian went to church so that God would bless his business, not because he wanted to worship God. Cheryl chose not to spread gossip about Diane, because she had told God that she wouldn't tell anybody about Diane if He would get her the promotion she wanted.

11. *a)* Do you try to make deals with God? Why, or why not?

_____

_____

_____

b) We will never be totally freed of improper motives until we're with the Lord, but what is the process of changing improper motives to godly motives?

_____

_____

_____

c) How can the Holy Spirit help you in this process?

_____

_____

Compare your answers to the questions in this step with the following:

FOR ADDITIONAL INSIGHT

1. When we love someone, we naturally look for an outlet to express that love. Along with praise, thanksgiving, telling others about Him, and other forms of service, obedience tells God that we love Him and want to honor Him.

What is your perception of God? Do you see Him as loving, strong, and kind, or as harsh and demanding? In step 15, we will specifically examine how our view of God affects our lives.

2. *a)*   Jonah's sin endangered the lives of those around him; resulted in a loss of property; caused Jonah to be unsympathetic to others; caused a loss of his personal testimony; involved others in his sin; and ultimately isolated him from God and others.

    b)   What have been the specific effects of sin on your self-concept? In your relationships? Many times, we're unable to see the full impact of sin on both ourselves and others. Ask the Holy Spirit to help you become more sensitive to the fact that sin always has a serious, negative result. As your awareness of sin's destructiveness increases, you will choose to obey more often.

    c)   Only a foolish person would intentionally do something that is harmful to himself. Viewing sin as an act of destruction makes us more aware of its negative and painful consequences.

3. *a)*   Most of us equate discipline with punishment. This misunderstanding of God's intentions causes us to fear God rather than respond to His love. We will be looking further at the fear of punishment and its effects in step 10.

    b)   God's discipline can motivate us because it is an additional expression of His love for us. He loves us so much that He doesn't want us to miss His best by continuing in sin.

4. *a)*   God's commands are described as holy, righteous, good, instructive, spiritual, and not burdensome.

    b)   If you obey God's commands, He will bless you and your children. Obedience will ultimately result in your good and in your protection.

    c)   God's commands have inherent value simply because they originate from a loving Father. God's commands are guidelines,

265

given to help us enjoy all that He has provided. They are good, and they are for our good. Therefore, they are worth obeying. Most of us have a negative attitude toward God's commands. If we believe that our worth is based on our performance, then every command is just one more thing we have to do to earn our acceptance. But if we believe that our worth is secure in Christ, then we will view His commands as helpful guidelines rather than as burdensome restrictions.

5. *b)* Although rewards are not a means for us to become more acceptable to God, they are a representation of our faithful service to Him. Rewards, then, are an honor God gives to us because we have honored Him.

6. *a)* You are of a chosen race and are a royal priest, a member of a holy nation, a person of God's own possession, and a temple of His Holy Spirit.

   b) You are to reflect His image through the way you live, and proclaim His excellencies to those around you.

7. *a)* Usually, one or two of these will stand out to each person.

   b) All of these are good and proper motivations, and in particular situations, any of them could be preeminent. However, it seems that the motivations to honor God and to express our love for Him are "higher" because they focus on Christ, and are a response to His love and majesty. In 2 Cor. 11:3, Paul writes, *But I am afraid, lest as the serpent deceived Eve by his craftiness, your minds should be led astray from the simplicity and purity of devotion to Christ.* Simple and pure devotion to Christ is our highest and best motivation for serving Him.

   c) What passages of Scripture would be good for you to study and memorize? Is there a mature Christian friend or pastor who could tell you why he or she is motivated to love and serve Christ? Is there someone you know who could encourage you on a regular basis and pray for you? What steps of obedience to the Lord do you need to take today?

8. *a)* Obeying God due to fear of what others will think is another aspect of the fear of rejection. The Lord wants you to obey *Him*, not the whims of others. Who are the people you are trying to please? What specific sin are you trying to avoid to please them? (Steps 8 and 9 will provide additional insights on the fear of rejection.) It may be that you don't show anger because your father scolded you severely when you lost your temper. But in reflecting on the proper motivations for obedience, you can choose to replace that motivation with an understanding that losing your temper dishonors God. Self-control and a proper expression of displeasure bring honor to Him.

9. If you believe that God's response to your sin is anger, you will feel alienated and bitter toward Him. However, He is genuinely concerned for your welfare and He grieves because sin is harmful to you. Realizing that He loves you and wants the best for you will prompt you to obey in response to His love. Your desire will be to honor the One who loves you.

10. *a)* Avoiding sin to meet your own standards is works-righteousness: trying to gain acceptance by adhering to a set of rules. But righteousness comes only through the gift of Christ's death and resurrection—it cannot be earned.

b) Titus 3:5 says, *He saved us, not on the basis of deeds which we have done in righteousness, but according to His mercy. . . .* When you realize that you cannot earn righteousness, no matter how strict you are, you can humbly accept the forgiveness and righteousness that Christ gives. One result is that you will become *zealous for good deeds* (Titus 2:14), not to be accepted, but to express your appreciation and desire to honor Christ.

11. *a)*   One reason you might try to make deals with God is that you have a faulty view of Him and a lofty view of yourself. Perhaps you see yourself as an equal with God, deserving the best from Him. But we are not His equals. He is the awesome, Almighty Creator; we are finite, sinful people, deserving eternal condemnation. By His grace, you are forgiven and accepted. The appropriate response to His gift of grace is not arrogance, but humility and a desire to honor Him. Yes, He is good to you and promises to provide for your needs, but He provides them as your gracious Lord and loving Father. You are the joyful recipient of His generosity.

b)   The process of changing self-serving motivations to those that will honor God may include spending time with other believers who will model the loving characteristics of God to us; exploring Scripture, perhaps looking for attributes of God as we read; expressing thanks to God for His discipline, realizing that it protects us from the destructive nature of sin; asking the Holy Spirit to help us develop an appreciation for God's commands, knowing that they are given for our welfare and spiritual growth; developing an eternal perspective, asking God to give us strength and endurance to persevere for his rewards.

c)   Being objective about our movitations to serve God is often very difficult. We must ask the Holy Spirit to enlighten us about areas of our lives where our motives are self-serving, knowing that He is faithful to guide us in truth (John 16:1, 13-14; 1 Cor. 2:10). In addition, He can lead us to others who will positively reinforce our desire to obey God with a rightful attitude. Through prayer, relationships with others, and the study of God's Word, He will enable us to increasingly experience God's love and compassion. He will lovingly convict us of improper motives for service, both in our relationship with God, and in our relationships with other people.

A FINAL WORD

Though we live with conflict between our old and new natures, Christ has freed us from the bondage of sin so that we can respond to Him in obedience. We have discussed six biblical motivations for us to be involved in good works:

1. The love of Christ compels us to obey.
2. Sin is destructive.
3. The Father will discipline us.
4. His commands for us are good.
5. We will receive rewards.
6. Obedience is an opportunity to honor God.

There are times when our feelings seem to get in the way of our obedience. We may want to indulge in some particular sin, or we may be afraid of failure or what someone might think of us. We may be selfish, or maybe just tired. But we should not hide behind bad feelings to excuse disobedience. The Lord never said pleasant emotions were a prerequisite for following Him. He said, *If anyone wishes to come after Me, let him deny himself* (and the 'right' to pleasant emotions), *and take up his cross daily, and follow Me* (Luke 9:23). This doesn't mean we should deny that we have emotions. We should express them fully to the Lord, telling Him how we feel, and then act in faith on the Word of God. Spiritual growth, character development, and Christian service should not be held hostage by our emotions. God has given each of us a will, and we can choose to honor the Lord, even in spite of our feelings.

In different situations, we will draw upon different motivations for obedience. Sometimes, we will need to be reminded of the destructiveness of sin in order to choose righteousness. At other times, we will be truly overwhelmed by God's love and will want to honor Him. Either way, it is our underlying motive which determines if our actions are done to honor God or to selfishly make us more acceptable to Him, to others, or ourselves. Elisabeth Elliot, Christian speaker and author, says, "Sometimes, 'struggling' is a nice word for postponed obedience."

a) Are you postponing obedience in any area of your life? If yes, what area(s)?

_____

_____

_____

b) What steps of action do you need to take to obey the Lord?

_____

_____

_____

As you recognize correct motives for obedience, and as you are able to identify improper motivations in your life, you may think, *I've never done anything purely for the Lord in my whole life!* You may feel a sense of pain and remorse for your inappropriate motives. But don't sink into a state of morbid introspection, demeaning yourself for your past attitudes. There are at least two perspectives that will help you focus on the Lord and grow in a godly desire to honor Him.

First, as we stated before, obedience from a right motivation is a choice. It is not based on how you feel. At any and every point in your life (like right now) you can actively, consciously choose to honor Christ. The Lord wants you to live by your godly choices, not by your fickle emotions. Ask the Holy Spirit to help you develop a sense of intensity about this choice, as Paul wrote, *...we have as our ambition...to be pleasing to Him* (2 Cor. 5:9).

Second, since your motives are usually a reflection of what you believe, they will begin to change as your belief system changes. Consistently considering and applying God's truth will have a profound and far-reaching impact on your motives. As you reject Satan's lies, you will gradually be *transformed by the renewing of your mind...*(Rom. 12:2), and will have an increasing desire to honor the One who loves you and purchased you by His own blood.

So, as an act of your will, choose to honor the Lord no matter what your emotions tell you, and consistently learn and apply the truths of God's Word so that they will begin to pervade your thoughts. Your motives won't become totally pure until you see the Lord face to face (1 John 3:2), but the better you know Him, the more you will see that He is worthy of your love, loyalty, and obedience.

Step Eight
The Fear of Rejection

Read chapter 7 in *The Search for Significance*.

This step is designed to help you understand the fear of rejection and the resulting false belief, *I must be approved by certain others in order to feel good about myself.*

1. *a)* Are you adversely affected by anyone's disrespect or disapproval? If so, list the individual(s) or group(s):

_____   _____

_____   _____

_____   _____

_____   _____

b) How does the fear of being rejected (disapproved of) by these people affect your life? Give examples:

_____

_____

_____

_____

_____

_____

2. To see how others' expectations can affect you, select one of the people you listed in question 1*a)* and answer the following:

    a) _____ would be more pleased with me if I would:
    - (1)_____
    - (2)_____
    - (3)_____

    b) _____ is proud of me when I:
    - (1)_____
    - (2)_____
    - (3)_____

    c) How does _____ attempt to get me to change by what he (or she) says and does?
    - (1)_____
    - (2)_____
    - (3)_____

    d) Things I do or say to get _____ to approve of me include:
    - (1)_____
    - (2)_____
    - (3)_____

    (Use a separate sheet of paper and repeat this exercise for each of the other people or groups you listed in question 1*a*).

3. List several specific instances when others (friends, boss, parents, children) have withheld approval, or have used criticism, silence, sarcasm, or praise to manipulate you into doing what they wanted you to do. What did they say or do? Did they succeed? Why, or why not?

*a)*_____
_____
_____

*b)*_____
_____
_____

*c)*_____
_____
_____

*d)*_____
_____
_____

4. What emotions accompanied the occasions given in question 3?

       Occasion   Emotions

*a)*_____   _____
*b)*_____   _____
*c)*_____   _____
*d)*_____   _____

5. What belief is at the root of the fear of disapproval?

_____
_____

6. *a)* How does the fear of rejection influence your moral standards (drinking, substance abuse, theft, lying, physical relationships, lifestyle)? Can you recall specific instances in your life when this fear has greatly influenced your morals? If so, list them.

_____   _____
_____   _____

_____   _____

_____   _____

b) How did the fear of rejection affect your behavior?

_____

_____

_____

7. If you run from rejection, are you really in control of your life? If not, who is?

_____

_____

8. *a)* How does the fear of rejection affect you when you want to share Christ with a friend? Do unbelievers ever use this fear to motivate you to refrain from sharing Christ with them?

_____

_____

   b) How would your zeal for evangelism be affected if you no longer depended on the approval of others for your self-worth?

_____

_____

9. How have you used disapproval, silence, sarcasm, or criticism to get others to do what you wanted them to do?

_____

_____

_____

10. Sometimes, rather than praising others because we genuinely appreciate them, we use praise as a form of manipulation. Our motive is to influence them to do something we want them to.

   a)   How do you feel when people praise you only to manipulate you?

   _____

   _____

   b)   Have you used praise to manipulate others? If so, why, and how have you used it?

   _____

   _____

   _____

   _____

   c)   How could manipulating others by praising them be considered a form of rejection?

   _____

   _____

Compare your answers with the following:

FOR ADDITIONAL INSIGHT

1.   *a)*   These individuals might include your parents, boyfriend, girlfriend, spouse, peer group, boss. God might also be on your list.

   b)   The fear of being rejected may cause us to avoid situations in which we are prone to fail or experience disapproval, and lead us to do only what we are good at doing, expecting our good performance to earn the approval of others. We also might tend to exaggerate the truth, make sure we wear or own just the right thing—whatever we think we need to do to gain the acceptance of those who are important to us.

2. For example:

    a) *My father would be more pleased with me if I called him more often, wore my hair the way he wants me to, and got a better job.*

    b) *My father is proud of me when I get a promotion, when I remember important family dates, when I win in sports.*

    c) *He criticizes me, is sarcastic with me, and sometimes ignores me.*

    d) *To gain my father's approval, I tell him only what he likes to hear; I exaggerate the truth a little; I work really hard to be a success.*

3. You probably can list far more than four occasions in which you've experienced rejection. For example: a friend's disgusted look, a professor who joked about your paper, a rejection letter from a company you wanted to work for, a dating relationship gone sour, being left out of a group function, being chosen last on an athletic team, being ignored by someone to whom you've said hello.

4. Our emotional responses in these situations may vary from slight annoyance to deep hurt, anger, and bitterness.

5. Our fear of rejection is proportional to the degree by which we base our self-worth on the opinions of others. If we believe the lie, *I am what others say I am,* the fear of rejection will plague us.

6. Some of us have established our moral standards on the approval or disapproval of others. Rather than referring to God's Word as our authority on matters of life, we have referred to people, doing what they approve of or encourage us to do. This may have led some of us to compromise our sexual purity, moral and ethical integrity, and our walk with God. God has revealed His good, acceptable, and perfect will for our lives in His Word (Rom. 12:2). We must learn to embrace and apply His truth, and refuse to believe the lie, *I am what others think of me.*

7. If you run from rejection, whomever you avoid is actually determining your actions, and is therefore your controller. As you begin to experience freedom from the control of others' opinions, your life will be increasingly focused on the Lord and controlled by Him, resulting in your growth and His glory.

8. The fear of rejection keeps many of us from sharing our faith. Unbelievers are well aware of the pain of rejection; nothing sends the message, *I don't care about you or what you have to say,* faster than it does. Sometimes, unbelievers use rejection to threaten us so that they won't have to deal with the gospel. Some examples:

   • "You don't believe that junk, do you?"
   • "How could anyone with any brains be a Christian?"
   • "Christianity is a crutch."
   • "I believe religion is a personal issue—don't talk to me about it."
   • "Only losers are Christians."

   What are they doing? They are rejecting us (inflicting emotional pain) to silence us. Becoming aware of this will give us more freedom to boldly take the initiative with others and lovingly present the gospel to them.

9. If you don't think that you use rejection to motivate others, see if any of these sound familiar:

- "If you loved me, you'd... "
- "Come on, Joe, everyone else is going."
- "You didn't know *that?*"
- "Have you heard what Susie did?"
- "If you can't do better, I'll get someone else who's more competent."
- "That's stupid!"
- "Nice shirt. Did that color cost extra?"

10. *a)* If you perceive that someone is praising you only to manipulate you, then you may very well feel used, like an object instead of a person. You may resent it. You may feel sorry for the person because you realize that he or she uses people and doesn't know how to love others.

   b) Think of a situation and ask yourself, *Why did I praise that person? Did I expect to get something out of him (or her)?*

   c) Manipulating others with praise is using them as tools to accomplish goals and rejecting them as people. Praise and appreciation can be a powerful force to build up a person, but if the goal of praise is to get someone to help us accomplish our goals, then it can be a powerful, but subtle and destructive force in his or her life.

A FINAL WORD

For whatever reason and to whatever degree we have experienced rejection, our fear of going through that pain again can affect us profoundly. We learn how to deal with physical injury early in life, but because emotional pain is sometimes perceived as a sign of weakness, and because we have not learned how to respond appropriately to this pain, we avoid it. If we are hurt, we may attempt to deny our pain by ignoring it. We may drive ourselves to accomplish tasks which we think others will approve of. Some of us can't say no for this reason. Or, we may become passive, withdrawing from others and avoiding those decisions and activities which others might criticize, or which can't guarantee success for us. Our goal in these instances is usually to avoid the pain of rejection by not doing anything which might be objectionable, but this also prevents us from enjoying the pleasures of healthy relationships and achievements.

Other behaviors related to the fear of rejection include:

1. being easily manipulated
2. being hypersensitive to criticism
3. defensiveness
4. hostility toward others who disagree with us
5. superficial relationships
6. exaggerating the truth to impress people
7. shyness
8. passivity
9. nervous breakdown

How many of these are apparent in your life?

Evaluating our self-worth by what we and others think of our performance leads us to believe that any time our performance is unacceptable, we are unacceptable as well. To some extent, virtually all of us have internalized the following sentence into our belief system, and hold to it with amazing tenacity: *I must have acceptance, respect, and approval in order to have self-worth.* This is the basic false belief behind all peer pressure.

Rejection can be communicated in a number of ways. We can easily see how criticism, sarcasm, and silence convey this message, but it may not be quite so obvious that praise can also serve as a form of manipulation and is, therefore, a form of rejection. We must ask ourselves what we are trying to accomplish when we praise someone. What is our goal? If we desire to help the person, to build him or her up, and to instill encouragement through appreciation, then praise is a godly form of communication. If, however, our desire is to get someone else to assist in accomplishing our goals, to contribute to our program, or to help us look good in front of others, then praise is a subtle but powerful form of rejection. Unfortunately, many people— including ourselves—fall prey to this manipulative praise because we so desperately want to be appreciated and will often do whatever it takes to get it from others.

If you realize that you manipulate others through praise, confess it as sin, and choose to seek their good instead of your goal. Be willing to ask, *What am I trying to accomplish?* in your interaction with others, and strive to communicate genuine, heartfelt appreciation because Christ has given them worth by sacrificing His life for them.

There are four basic levels of acceptance and rejection. Understanding these will help you understand the nature of your relationships with other people, concerning both how you are treated and how you treat others. These levels center around the question: What does one have to do to be accepted?

1. *Total Rejection:* "No matter what you do, it's not good enough." Example: relationships characterized by deep bitterness or hurt.

2. *Highly Conditional Acceptance:* "You must meet certain requirements to be accepted." Examples: most jobs, relationships with demanding people.

3. *Mildly Conditional Acceptance:* "I will be more happy with you if you do these things." Examples: most marriages, most parent-child relationships, most friendships.

4. *Unconditional Acceptance:* "I love you and accept you no matter what you do. There is nothing you can do that can make me stop loving you." (This does not mean that we can do as we please or that we are to ignore unacceptable behavior in others. Unconditional acceptance may include loving confrontation, correction, and, in some cases, discipline. The focus here is on the individual rather than his or her behavior.) Examples: God, godly relationships.

Use a separate piece of paper, and make a list of the major relationships in your life: family members, friends, people in your school, office, or church, etc. How does each of these people tend to treat you? How do you tend to treat each of them? How should you respond to each of them? How can you put fewer demands and conditions on your acceptance of them?

Step Nine
Reconciliation

God's answer to the pain of rejection is reconciliation. Christ died for our sins and restored us to a proper relationship with God. We are acceptable to God and are accepted by Him. We are not rejected! We are His.

1. *a)* Define *reconcile*. (Use a dictionary if necessary).

_____

b) Who caused the alienation in your relationship with God? (See Is. 53:6; 59:2; Rom. 3:9-12.)

_____

_____

2. Read Eph. 2:1-3 and 2 Thess. 1:8-9. How severe was the barrier between you and Holy God?

_____

_____

3. Read Col. 1:21-22. Compare your former state to your present condition:

_____

_____

_____

4. Read Rom. 5:8-11.

    a) Who initiated restoring your relationship with God?
    _____

    b) How did God reconcile you to Himself?
    _____

    c) What is your response to God? (What does *to exult* mean?)
    _____

    _____

5. *a)* What is wrong with the statement, "Thank you, Lord, for accepting me even though I am so unacceptable"?
    _____

    _____

    b) Are you currently acceptable?_____

    c) To what degree are you acceptable?_____

    d) To whom are you acceptable?_____

    e) Why are you acceptable?_____

6. If you are completely and fully accepted by the perfect Creator of the universe, why do you fear the rejection of men?
    _____

    _____

7. Read John 17:19-26 and 20:17 to see the extent of your reconciliation to God.

   a) Whom does the Father love more: Jesus Christ or you?_____

   b) How does Christ refer to you in John 20:17?_____

   c) Whom does Christ desire to be with Him for all eternity?

   _____

   d) How do these verses make you feel?

   _____

   _____

8. Can you think of recent situations in which you felt rejected, or in which someone disapproved of something you said or did? If so, list and describe your response. How would your response have been different if you had believed the truth of your total acceptance in Christ?

   a) Situation:

   _____

   _____

   _____

   Your Response:

   _____

   _____

   _____

   How Believing the Truth Would Have Changed Your Response:

   _____

   _____

   _____

b) Situation:

_____
_____
_____

Your Response:

_____
_____
_____

How Believing the Truth Would Have Changed Your Response:

_____
_____
_____

c) Situation:

_____
_____
_____

Your Response:

_____
_____
_____

How Believing the Truth Would Have Changed Your Response:

_____
_____
_____

9. Memorize Col. 1:21-22.

Compare your answers with the following:

FOR ADDITIONAL INSIGHT

1. *a)* *Reconcile* means to restore a friendship.

   b) Leon Morris, in his book, *The Atonement*, states that reconciliation implies three states: friendship, then a quarrel, then friendship again.[1] Man was responsible for the quarrel (Genesis 3 and Romans 3). Our rebellion and sin shattered our relationship with God.

2. God hates sin. As a result, you were an object of His wrath, separated and completely alienated from Him.

3. Because of your sin, you were an enemy of God. Your sin made you subject to God's wrath, but if you have trusted in Christ, you are now declared holy in His sight, without blemish and free from accusation.

4. *a)* It was Almighty God who deeply loved you and restored your relationship with Him. You were His enemy, now you are His beloved child.

   b) God reconciled you to Himself through the death of His precious Son, Jesus Christ.

   c) *To exult* means "to take great delight in." We can greatly delight in God, knowing that He loves us and that He has reconciled us to Himself.

5. You are acceptable to God! He does not just *tolerate* you. You are 100 percent acceptable to the highest judge: the perfect, holy, and righteous God Almighty. You are accepted by God for one reason: Christ has abolished the barrier and made peace with God through His blood on the cross. You have the righteousness of

Christ (2 Cor. 5:21). You can't ever be any more acceptable to God than you are now (Rom. 5:8-10; Eph. 2:14-18; Col. 1:21-22).

6. You fear rejection when you believe the lie, *I am what others think of me*, instead of believing God's truth, *I am totally acceptable and accepted because of Christ.* You will never begin to experience freedom from the fear of rejection until you realize that God has completely accepted you. If you refuse to believe God's statement, the only other option is to turn to others to meet your need for acceptance and significance, and be painfully disillusioned. The primary issue is this: Whose acceptance do you value more, God's or man's?

7. *a)* God loves you and His Son, Jesus Christ, equally! You have the same standing and the same righteousness as His Son!

b) Jesus calls you "My brother/sister" and addresses God the Father as "our Father."

c) Christ wants you with Him every day throughout eternity.

Meditate on these incredible truths until they begin to become a part of your daily thinking.

8. You might have listed something like this:

Situation:
Frank laughed at my idea in the committee meeting. (Others laughed, too.)

Your Response:
I felt deeply hurt and didn't say another word. I left as soon as the meeting was over.

How Believing the Truth Would Have Changed Your Response:

I probably would have felt hurt, then I might have asked Frank to tell me why he thought the idea was funny. (I might have laughed at the idea myself!) But I wouldn't have crawled into my shell. I would have continued to participate and would have forgotten about the incident because my sense of self-worth would not have been threatened.

A FINAL WORD

When God chose to redeem us so that we could relate to Him and rule with Him, He did not make us partially righteous, nor has He allowed for our righteousness to be marred by our poor performance. The blood of Christ is sufficient to pay for all sin. Because of His blood, we are holy and righteous before God, even in the midst of sin. This does not minimize the inherent destructiveness of sin. Instead, it glorifies the indescribable sacrifice of Christ.

There is no biblical tenet more neglected in its practical application than the doctrine of reconciliation. The Colossian reference to this doctrine reveals its application to us:

> *And although you were formerly alienated and hostile in mind, engaged in evil deeds,*
> *yet He has now reconciled you in His fleshly body through death, in order to present you before Him holy and blameless and beyond reproach. . . .*

Col. 1:21-22

Relish those last words. God sees us as *holy and blameless and beyond reproach* at this very moment. This is not merely a reference to our future standing; it describes our present status as well. It tells us something very significant: We are totally accepted by God.

This line of reasoning from the Scriptures might appear to be new, but probably would not seem so if we asked: Is there any sin so filthy that it can prevent a Christian from going to heaven? I believe most Christians would answer with a resounding NO! A believer is eternally secure; heaven is a certainty for him or her (1Pet. 1:3-5). But salvation is more than just a ticket to heaven when we die. It is the basis of a relationship. God received us into a loving, intimate, personal relationship the moment we placed our faith in Christ. We are united with God in an eternal and inseparable bond (Rom. 8:38-39). We are born of God in an indissoluble union as fellow heirs with Christ. Recognizing that there is no sin so filthy that it can make a Christian unacceptable to God is not presumptuous, but God-honoring faith in a blood-sealed warrant with the Holy Spirit, *who is given as a pledge of our inheritance, with a view to the redemption of God's own possession...* (Eph. 1:14).

On the other hand, is there anything a Christian can do to become more acceptable to God? No! If there were, then the cross would be insufficient. If we can do anything to be more acceptable to God, then Christ either lied or was mistaken when He cried out on the cross, "It is finished!" (John 19:30). If that is the case, what He should have said was, "It is almost finished, and if you live a perfect life, you and I together might make you acceptable."

Since our relationship with God was bought entirely by the blood of Christ, it is the height of pride to think that our own good works can make us acceptable to God. The Bible speaks to the contrary: *He saved us, not on the basis of deeds which we have done in righteousness, but according to His mercy...* (Titus 3:5). Christ has reconciled us to God and He allows us to experience the incredible truth, *We are totally accepted by and acceptable to God.*

What should we do when we have failed or when someone disapproves of us? A practical way of summarizing the truth we've examined is:

It would be nice if_____(my boss liked me, I could fix the refrigerator, my complexion were clear, James had picked me up on time, or...), but I'm still deeply loved, completely forgiven, fully pleasing, totally accepted, and complete in Christ.

This statement doesn't mean that we won't feel pain or anger. We need to be honest about our feelings. A statement like the one above is simply a way to quickly gain God's perspective on whatever we are experiencing. It is not magic, but it enables us to reflect on the implications of biblical truth. We can apply this truth in every difficult situation, whether it is someone's disapproval, our own failure to accomplish something, or the failure of another person.

Memorize the truth in the above statement and begin to apply it in your situations and relationships.

Step Ten
The Fear of Punishment/Punishing Others

Read chapter 8 in *The Search for Significance.*

    Steps 10, 11, and 12 form a unit that examines the fear of punishment and punishing others; the false belief, *Those who fail are unworthy of love and deserve to be punished;* propitiation; and our need to forgive others.

    This step is designed to aid you in understanding the fear of punishment and the propensity to punish others.

1.   Do you really deserve to feel good about yourself? Why, or why not?

_____

_____

_____

2.   Describe three recent incidents in your life in which you feared being blamed or punished. Why did you have this fear?

*a)*_____

_____

_____

b)_____
_____
_____

c)_____
_____
_____

3. *a)* Do you spend much time thinking about your weaknesses and failures? If so, why? (List as many reasons as you can.)

_____
_____
_____
_____

   b) What are the three most negative terms you use to describe yourself? What derogatory names do you call yourself?

_____
_____
_____

4. Does condemning yourself help you become a better person? Why, or why not?

_____
_____
_____

5. *a)* Think of a close friend or family member with whom you've had a conflict. What did you say or do to inflict emotional pain?

_____
_____
_____

    b)   What are some reasons you said or did those things?

_____

_____

_____

6.   After sinning, do you ever believe you have to feel badly about yourself before you can feel good about yourself? If so, list some of the situations in which you've done this:

_____

_____

_____

_____

7.   Do you want to go to the Father after you've sinned? If not, why?

_____

_____

_____

8.   If something goes wrong, do you assume the Lord is punishing you?

_____

9.   Does God punish His children?

_____

Review your answers with the following:

FOR ADDITIONAL INSIGHT

1. Yes, because you are God's precious son or daughter, He accepts you, loves you, and has made you complete. Because of this, no one should feel better about himself than you! You may have said no because you have failed at something very important to you. You may think that anyone who failed that badly has no right to feel good about himself. The fact is, no one *deserves* to feel good about himself. We all deserve God's wrath and condemnation, but you can feel great about yourself because Christ loves, forgives, and accepts you.

2. Perhaps you feared being blamed or punished because you didn't measure up to someone's standards. Maybe someone has threatened to punish you (either emotionally or physically) if you don't please him or her. You have this fear because the world operates under the false belief that failure must be punished. Therefore, if you've failed, you probably will conclude that you'll be punished in some way.

3. *a)* If you are preoccupied by your weaknesses and failures, you are probably often discouraged, because you believe that when something goes wrong, someone is to blame. You blame yourself and others to be sure that someone pays for the failure. This is really a system of works. If you perform well, you feel worthy of love, so you reward yourself. If you fail, you feel unworthy of love, so you blame yourself. You probably treat others the same way.

   b) We usually give ourselves demeaning names because of recurring failures. These names are distinctive for each individual, but some of these terms might sound familiar: *lazy, ugly, stupid, social klutz, unpopular, incompetent, fearful.* These may be used in comparison to someone else, like, *I'm not as pretty as*

_____. *My grades are lower than* _____. *His ideas are a lot better than mine; I'm a stupid fool.*

4.   You might think it does, but self-condemnation does not make you a better person. Using a guilt/blame motivation to perfect your performance (and thus feel good about yourself) is unscriptural and harmful to you. For a short time, blame may motivate you to perform better, but your self-concept will suffer from your condemnation. Ultimately, your self-concept is far more important than your short-term performance.

5.   *a)*   To punish others, perhaps you withdrew love, affection, and encouragement from them. Perhaps you were sarcastic or laughed at them; or, maybe you were abrupt in speaking to them. Maybe you abused them verbally, or even physically.

   b)   You probably reacted this way because you believed that *those who fail are unworthy of love, and failure must be punished.* You may have even appointed yourself to carry out the sentence of punishment.

6.   Before answering no to this question, think about the following:
   • How long should John feel badly about himself for lying to the IRS?
   • How long should Sam feel badly about himself for committing adultery?
   • How long should Christy feel badly about herself for getting drunk while her husband was at work?
   • How long should Sherman feel badly about himself because he was insensitive to his wife?
   • How long should Rick feel badly about himself for stealing from his employer?

Feeling badly about ourselves is a way of doing penance, trying to pay for our sins by our own deeds or feelings. This is performance or works-righteousness. If we believe that *those who fail are unworthy of love and deserve to be blamed and condemned*, then we probably will use feelings of guilt as a form of self-condemnation and penance. We think that if we feel badly enough for long enough (the severity and length depending, of course, on the magnitude of the sin), the sin will be forgiven, and we can go on with life.

For people with this perspective, repentance is merely a rededication to prevent failure and to avoid being embarrassed again.

Please note: I am not advocating that we should feel good about sin. Dishonoring the Lord and bringing harm to ourselves and others produce a sorrow that is right and proper. But God intends for this sorrow to be a response to the destructiveness of sin and the righteousness of Christ, not an attempt to pay for sin through penitent bad feelings. This godly sorrow is described by Paul in 2 Cor. 7:10: *For the sorrow that is according to the will of God produces a repentance without regret* (i.e. without the penance of prolonged bad feelings), *leading to salvation; but the sorrow of the world produces death* (spiritual deadness: works–righteousness).

7. If you believe that God is waiting to "lower the boom" on you, then you probably won't want to pray. No one likes to be punished, so if you believe that God's attitude toward you is anger and condemnation, you will try to avoid Him.

8. Most people have been deceived about God's character. As a result, they live in fear of what God will do to them because of their sin. But God has demonstrated His love for us on the cross when our sins were paid in full by Christ. Therefore, God doesn't punish us for our sins. He has already taken His wrath out on Christ at the cross.

9. No, God does not punish His children, but He does discipline them. Discipline is rooted in love. God disciplines us because sin is destructive, and He does not want us to self-destruct. The goal of His discipline is to restore, develop, and perfect. Punishment, on the other hand, is retaliation, and is used to impose a penalty. Christ has borne your punishment and blame for sin.

It is crucial that you understand the difference between discipline and punishment. God's discipline can be severe, but it is prompted by grief, not anger. His willingness to discipline you is indicative of His love for you.

A FINAL WORD

The proof of blame's effectiveness is that we use it so often. We often believe that we deserve to be blamed for any significant shortcoming, and think self-inflicted punishment will clear us of guilt and enable us to feel good about ourselves again.

Both self-inflicted punishment and the compulsion to punish others result from the false belief: *Those who fail are unworthy of love and deserve to be blamed and condemned.*

Paul's stepfather was a corporate executive who was driven to succeed. Nothing Paul did was good enough for him. He often laughed at Paul and called him an idiot and a wimp. Why do we use such terms to describe ourselves and others? We use them because we believe that condemnation is motivational and will provide favorable change. However, the only way this will really work is if the target will accept the message that he or she is unworthy of love.

After he betrayed Christ for thirty pieces of silver, Judas experienced such unbearable guilt that he flung the money across the temple floor and cried, *I have sinned by betraying innocent blood* (Matt. 27:4). He then went out and hanged himself! It is the common conviction of all men, even atheists, to believe that they must pay for their sins. Indeed, the need for punishment to relieve guilt and restore justice is widespread.

Without even realizing it, you probably have internalized a concept that sounds like this: *When I fail, I am unworthy of love (and when others fail, they are unworthy of love), and deserve to be blamed and condemned.*

We have been conditioned to accept personal blame or condemnation every time our performance is unsatisfactory. After reading this, some people immediately recognize this automatic response in their lives, but others do not. You may think that you are not affected by this false belief at all—but you probably are. Do you generally have an urge to find out who is at fault when something fails? Do you look for excuses when you fail?

Rather than work out our problems and objectively evaluate our performance, most of us tend to defend ourselves. Counterattack triggers counterattack. The more we criticize other people, the more defensive they usually get, and the less likely they are to admit their errors (especially to us). Criticism can lead to a counterattack from both sides, and pretty soon, it's like a volleyball game, with each person intensifying the pace while returning blame to the other person's side.

However, it is sometimes even more destructive for people to accept blame without defending themselves. Tom was becoming an emotional zombie under his wife's incessant condemnation, but instead of fighting back, he kept thinking, *Yes, Suzanne's right. I am an incompetent fool.* He was like the worn-out punching bag of a heavyweight fighter.

One of the most common problems among parents is dealing with the misbehavior of their children. It is tremendously painful for most parents to face up to the wrongdoing of their child. But a primary reason why a child's misbehavior is so painful and embarrassing is that parents tend to blame themselves for it.

Between spells of crying, Joyce said, "Mary wouldn't act like this if I'd been the mother I should have been." Dave, on the other hand, ignored his son's misbehavior with the excuse that his boy was simply "going through a stage." He rationalized his son's wrongdoing because he couldn't face the guilt of being a failure as a parent.

When their children get into trouble, parents usually alternate between blaming themselves and blaming their children. After all, someone has to be blamed. The problem in either case is not that parents are loving their child too much or too little, but that their personal significance is wrapped up in their performance as parents. Therefore, when the child does well, the parents feel good about themselves. When a child does poorly, however, they often blame each other or the child. Beneath it all is the internalized and unconscious belief: *Someone has to take the blame.*

Our worth is totally secure in Christ, so our children's success or failure, cuteness or whining doesn't affect our value in the least. We need to see our children the way our heavenly Father sees us: *deeply loved, completely forgiven, fully pleasing, and totally accepted.* Then, when they disobey, our discipline will be like the Father's discipline of us: in love, not anger. If we approach our children with an attitude of grief rather than anger when they disobey, it will make a tremendous difference! What a difference it will make if we go to our children with the attitude and words, "It's sad that you disobeyed. It was harmful to you, and I love you so much that I don't want you to harm yourself. I will need to discipline you to help you remember not to do it again. Remember, the reason I am disciplining you is that I love you so much!" ... instead of, "You've done it again, and I'll make sure you regret it! I wonder if you'll ever amount to anything!"

Responding to our children in grief instead of anger will have monumental implications on both them and us. Our children won't be afraid of us, our relationship with them won't be marred by anger, and they will be more likely to view God as a loving Father rather than as a tyrant. As parents, we will have a more accurate perception of God's love and gracious discipline, and we will be more in control of our emotions. We won't try to deny that we are getting angry at our children's misbehavior, letting our anger build and build until we explode. Instead, we will be able to express our displeasure more quickly and acceptably because it will be wholesome grief instead of unholy anger. These are powerful and welcome implications, indeed!

Propitiation

At the cross, God poured out His wrath against sin. This step will help you see that God's wrath has been satisfied; therefore, there is no need to fear punishment.

1. Define *propitiation*:

_____

_____

2. We each have had an incalculable number of sinful (disobedient, self-centered) thoughts and actions. How many sins can a Holy God overlook?

_____

3. Read Ezek. 7:8-9; Rom. 2:4-5; and Eph. 2:1-3. Does God's wrath have a specific object? If so, what is it?

_____

4. Read Gen. 19:1-26; Jer. 4:4; Ezek. 5:11-17; 23:22-30; and 2 Thess. 1:6-10. List some characteristics of God's wrath from these passages:

_____   _____
_____   _____
_____   _____
_____   _____
_____   _____
_____   _____

5.   Read 1 John 4:9-10.

   a)   Are you loved by the Father?
   _____

   b)   How do you know you are loved?
   _____
   _____

   c)   Do you *feel* loved?
   _____
   _____

6.   *a)*   Consider what it would be like to experience the wrath of
   Almighty God, and then read Is. 53:4-10. Place your name in the
   place of appropriate pronouns ("Surely He took up
   _____'s infirmities.")   The wrath that you
   deserved has been poured out on Christ.

   b)   In what ways can you express your gratitude to Christ for
   what He has done for you?
   _____
   _____
   _____
   _____
   _____

7.   The more we understand God's love and forgiveness, the more we will be willing and able to forgive others. If we think about it, the things that others do to us (ranging from acts of genuine hatred, to taking out a hard day's frustration on us, to not liking us because of the clothes we wear or the way we keep our homes) are all trivial in comparison to our sin of abject rebellion against God which He has graciously forgiven. This is why Paul encouraged the Colossian Christians to forgive each other *just as God in Christ also has forgiven you* (Eph. 4:32), completely and willingly.

a) Are there any sins (or even personality differences) in others that you have difficulty forgiving? If so, list them and confess your lack of forgiveness to God:

_____   _____

_____   _____

_____   _____

_____   _____

_____   _____

_____   _____

_____   _____

_____   _____

b) How do these compare to your sins that deserved God's wrath, but received the payment of Christ's substitutionary death?

_____

_____

_____

8.   Memorize 1 John 4:9-10.

Review your answers with the following:

FOR ADDITIONAL INSIGHT

1. *Propitiation* means "satisfaction." Theologically, propitiation refers to Christ's payment on the cross which satisfied the penalty for our sins. Christ's death propitiates, or averts, the wrath of God. God's righteous anger is directed against all sin, and therefore, against all of sinful mankind. Christ's death removed God's anger from repentant sinners.

2. God cannot overlook sin . . . not even a "little one." Even our "righteous" deeds—those deeds we do to look good in the eyes of people or to try to earn God's acceptance—are like filthy rags to God (Is. 64:6).

3. Yes. God's wrath is personal, and is directed toward the sinner and his or her sin. In fact, in Eph. 2:3, Paul describes unbelievers as simply *children of wrath*. All of us deserve God's righteous condemnation because all of us are sinners (Rom. 3:23).

4. God's wrath is swift, complete, all-consuming, terrifying, justly deserved, and is His response to sin and rebellion against Him.

5. *a)* The fact that God poured out His wrath on His Son for you is proof beyond question that He loves you.

   b) Propitiation demonstrates God's love for you.

   c) God loves you more than you know, although you may not feel loved until you take the time to meditate on this truth.
   Reflecting on God's Word will help you to replace the false belief that God wants to punish you with the truth that He loves you dearly. Spend some time thinking about the truth of Rom. 8:28-39.

6. *a)* This exercise will help you to personalize what Christ Jesus has done for you.

   b) We can express our gratitude to God directly in prayer, by studying His Word and obeying His commands, by serving Him, by forgiving others as He has forgiven us.

7. *a)* It may be difficult for you to forgive those who've hurt your feelings, gossiped about you, didn't take time to answer your questions, laughed at your mistakes, or blamed you for an error. Your list may also include people who don't dress the way you'd like them to, who don't clean up the way you'd like them to, who are more shy or more gregarious than you, who don't spend their money as you do, etc.

   b) For the comparison, look at Matt. 18:21-35. When anyone sins against you or offends you in any way, reflect on this: *There is nothing that anyone can do to me that can compare with what Christ has forgiven me for!* This will help you to gain a proper perspective on how you can truly forgive other people.

A FINAL WORD

God's plan for us is centered in the cross. To understand His plan, we must first understand the meaning of propitiation.

Prior to our spiritual birth, even our good deeds were despicable to God (Is. 64:6). If we are honest about our performance, we must admit that we have sinned thousands of times, even after having accepted Christ.

The problem with our sinfulness is that God is absolutely holy, pure, and perfect. There is absolutely nothing unholy in Him. *God is light, and in Him there is no darkness at all* (1 John 1:5). Therefore, since God is holy, He cannot overlook or compromise with sin. It took one sin to separate Adam from God. For God to condone even *one* sin would instantly defile His holiness, which He indicates by His righteous condemnation of sin (Rom. 6:23).

The Father did not escape witnessing His Son's mistreatment: the mocking, the scourging, and the cross. He could have spoken and ended the whole ordeal, yet He kept silent. Confronted with the suffering of His Son, He chose to let it continue so that we could be saved. What an expression of love! Its depth is unsearchable.

Try to recall an experience in which you were loved by someone special. That person adored you and wanted to be with you. You didn't have to perform; just being you was enough. The thought of that person selecting you to love was intoxicating. All other facets of life seemed to diminish. He or she loved you, and that love was soothing to you and satisfied many of your inner longings.

If the love of a person can make us feel this way, consider how much greater joy the heavenly Father's love can bring. We can't truly experience the love of the Father unless we realize that it supercedes any experience of being loved by another man or woman.

Frederick Faber was consumed with love for the Father. A song he wrote reveals his single-minded devotion:

> *Only to sit and think of God,*
> *Oh what a joy it is!*
> *To think the thought, to breathe the Name;*
> *Earth has no higher bliss.*
> *Father of Jesus, love's reward!*
> *What rapture it will be,*
> *Prostrate before Thy throne to be,*
> *And gaze and gaze on Thee!*[1]

One of Faber's sermons says of Christ:

Wherever we turn in the church of God, there is Jesus. He is the beginning, middle and end of everything to us... There is nothing good, nothing holy, nothing beautiful, nothing joyous which He is not to His servants. No one need be poor, because, if he chooses, he can have Jesus for his own property and possession. No one need be down- cast, for Jesus is the joy of heaven, and it is His joy to enter into sorrowful hearts. We can exaggerate about many things; but we can never exaggerate our obligation to Jesus, or the compassionate abundance of the love of Jesus to us. All our lives long we might talk of Jesus, and yet we should never come to an end of the sweet things that might be said of Him. Eternity will not be long enough to learn all He is, or to praise Him for all He has done, but then, that matters not; for we shall be always with Him, and we desire nothing more.[2]

God loves you, and He enjoys revealing His love to you. He enjoys being loved by you, but He knows you can love Him only if you are experiencing His love for you. Propitiation means that His wrath has been removed and that you are deeply loved!

Many of us have a distorted concept of the heavenly Father. We believe that God is thrilled when we accept Christ and are born into His family. But many of us also believe that He is proud of us for only as long as we perform well, and that the better our performance, the happier He is with us. We may perceive of God as being like the management in a factory. If we produce, they love us; if we don't produce, they fire us. We may believe that if we really foul up, God is going to put us on the shelf somewhere. He will take care of our most basic needs because He has obligated Himself to do that, but only the beautiful, producing Christians will enjoy His love and acceptance. This is a distorted view of our heavenly Father!

In reality, God loves us, and not a moment goes by that He isn't thinking loving thoughts about us (Ps. 40:5). We are His children, and we are individually special to Him because of Christ! Propitiation, then, means that Jesus Christ has satisfied the Father's righteous condemnation of sin by His death. The Scriptures give only one reason to explain this incredible fact: God loves you!

Step Twelve
Forgiving Others

One way we inflict punishment on those around us is by refusing to forgive them. We tend to keep score, tallying up all those times we've been wronged and all the things we don't like about another individual. We become critical. Punishing others for their failure is our way of "evening the score."

Unforgiveness is a sure way of cutting the flow of God's power in our lives. In fact, there are a number of negative consequences which often result from an unwillingness to forgive others. Before we examine these, let's look at some of the reasons why we may refuse to forgive:

Reasons for Unforgiveness

We often fail to forgive others (and ourselves) because we don't think it's possible. We forget how God has graciously forgiven all of our sins through Christ's death, and rationalize why we can't forgive. The following are among the countless excuses we make for our unwillingness to forgive ourselves and others:

- *The offense was too great.* Grant's wife had left him for another man, and he was bitter toward her. Her infidelity was too great a sin for him to forgive. But almost two years after the incident, God began to impress Grant with the idea that he should forgive his wife, *just as God in Christ also had forgiven (him)*, completely and willfully. When Grant finally did forgive her, he felt as though 100 pounds had been lifted from his back.

Roger sat shaking with anger as he recalled his wife's rape. His anger was destroying his health and his relationship with his wife. *How can any man, who really is a man, forgive such an act?* he wondered. The transient who had raped his wife had moved on, and in his perversion, had probably forgotten the incident. He was never caught. Continuing to allow the offense to produce bitterness might ultimately do more harm to Roger and his family than the destructive act of the rape.

- *He(she) won't accept responsibility for the offense.* How many people have offended us, but won't agree that they were at fault? The offense might be something slight, such as being overlooked at a social event, or something major, such as being emotionally neglected as a child. Having others agree that they've offended us isn't necessary for us to respond properly to their offense.

- *He(she) isn't truly sorry.* John pulled a practical joke on you which caused you to be late for class, and your professor refused to accept your paper because you didn't have it in on time. John doesn't see anything wrong with a little joke—he's slightly sorry, but he still thinks it was hilarious. Even if John doesn't recognize the trouble he's caused you, you can still extend forgiveness to him through Christ, and refuse to hold the offense against him.

- *He(she) never asked to be forgiven.* For whatever reason, the offender never got around to asking you for forgiveness. Are you going to withhold forgiveness until it's requested? Who is suffering, you or the offender? What would God have you do? (Read 1 Cor. 13:5 and Eph. 4:32.)

- *He(she) will do it again.* Candy's husband had been out late playing cards on every Friday night for three years. On some nights, he didn't come home. "Me? Forgive that jerk?" Candy asked. The Lord said that the number of times we're to forgive is seventy times seven . . . in other words, regardless of the number of offenses. If Candy doesn't forgive, she will be the bitter loser.

- *He(she) did it again.* David had been a horrible husband to Mandy. However, after much effort, Mandy had forgiven him for his insensitivity, his greater concern for the guys on his softball team, his lack of affection for the children, and his callous, domineering attitude. Then, David saw how poor his behavior had become. He began to change. His relationship with Mandy started to improve— until he stayed out late again with the guys. He had done it again! One mistake set the whole conflict in motion again.

- *I don't like him(her).* Generally, we don't have a great deal of appreciation for those who have wronged us. In fact, every emotion within us may call for retaliation against the creep! Only when we realize that forgiveness is an act of the will, and not of the emotions, will we choose to forgive those who have hurt us.

- *He(she) did it deliberately.* "He knew what he was doing, and he did it anyway." George had been swindled out of $10,000 by his "best friend," Hal. It had been a complex scheme which had required precise timing over a period of several months. As George sat stunned, his mind raced through those times he had been generous to Hal. He thought of how much he had loved Hal and had repeatedly trusted him. The swindle had been completely deliberate, and Hal had used him. George had been played for a sucker. Hal must be laughing at him now. Whether the offense was deliberate or not, God still wants George to forgive Hal.

- *If I forgive the offense, I'll have to treat the offender well.* Ben excused his slander of Steve by pointing out how Steve had offended him. He felt justified in destroying Steve's reputation even though most of the things he had said about Steve were lies.

  Shirley was cold to Greg, and had been for two weeks. It was her plan to punish him for two weeks because he had offended her. She would forgive him all right—as soon as she was through punishing him.

- *Someone has to punish him(her).* How often do we want God to be merciful to us and yet want Him to skin other people alive? When we don't see them suffer, we sometimes take it upon ourselves to be God's hand of vengeance.

  Charles was their pastor, but according to Gloria, he had wasted the church's money. Gloria was in charge of the church women's group. She waited patiently for God to nail Charles, but when God didn't do what she thought He should, she just knew that she was to be the divining rod for Charlie's back. Soon the church had taken sides—pro-Charles or anti-Charles. The result was that the church disgraced itself by splitting in hatred.

  Discipline is God's job. *Vengeance is Mine, I will repay*, says the Lord ... and He hasn't delegated that responsibility to us!

- *Something keeps me from forgiving.* Satan actively promotes unforgiveness. When you attempt to deal with this problem honestly, you may be in for a tremendous spiritual battle, with both confusing and conflicting thoughts and emotions. Don't be surprised if you have to resist Satan at every turn in order to accomplish the task of forgiving the offender. Forgiveness is primarily an act of the will, not a warm feeling.

- *I'll be a hypocrite if I forgive, because I don't feel like forgiving.* It's amazing how we confuse hypocrisy with obedience. We are hypocritical only if we do something for selfish gain. For instance, a hypocrite might be a politician who comes to church in order to get its members to vote for him in the next election, but who despises the church and its people. To forgive as an act of the will in obedience to the Lord's command is true spirituality, not hypocrisy.

• *I'll forgive, but I won't ever forget.* If we continue to harbor the memory of an offense, we are only fooling ourselves in thinking that we have forgiven the offender, and we will not experience any freedom. In true forgiveness, we give up the right to remember an offense or to bring it up again during arguments. (Note: This doesn't mean that when we forgive a wrong, we'll *never* think of it again. But it does mean that we won't relish the memory. Choose to think about things that are true, honorable, right, pure, and lovely [Phil. 4:8].)

• *I'll forgive, because I have found an excuse for the offense.* Hank had been very irresponsible during the early years of his marriage. His wife, Sally, had always been able to forgive him by placing the blame on his mother, who had babied Hank even after he was grown. And yet, Sally was continually angered by Hank and his mother. In fact, her volatile temper was destroying her marriage.

Sally thought that she had forgiven Hank when she had really just excused him. By blaming Hank's mother for his immaturity, she had rationalized his behavior, and had reduced her perception of his offensive actions like this:

ORIGINAL OFFENSE   REDUCED OFFENSE

After reducing each offense, Sally then forgave it. The problem was that she did not deal with the real offense, but with a distortion of it. Therefore, the real offense remained intact in spite of her efforts at "forgiveness."

When you offend someone, or when someone offends you, do you immediately look for a "reason"? If you do, you may only be rationalizing. If you come up with an excuse to the question, *Why did I forgive him (or her)?* then you have not truly forgiven the offense. You have excused it.

Results of Unforgiveness

- *Stress:* Sarah announced to the group that her husband did not deserve to be forgiven, and that she wasn't going to forgive him if it meant her life. It did. Sarah died of kidney failure. She wanted to kill her husband, but in reality she killed herself. Countless people live under extreme stress due to the bitterness and anger that result from unforgiveness.

- *Self-Inflicted Reinjury:* Robert recalled this incident: "As I drove home, flashing into my memory was a guy I played basketball with in college. He was a great antagonist of mine. He was one of the few people I have ever met whom I truly wanted to punch out. I began to remember the unkind things he did to me. Soon, anger started creeping up inside of me. I had not remembered this fellow for years, and I'm sure that he doesn't remember me at all. Yet, my reliving this event caused me a lot of pain. I had not properly dealt with it in the beginning."

  How many times are you reinjuring yourself because past offenses haunt you?

- *No More Love:* "I don't know if I can ever love someone again" is a frequent complaint from those offended by a lover. Our deepest hurts come from those we love. One way we deal with the pain of being offended is to simply withdraw, refusing to love anymore.

We often make this unconscious decision when we have not adequately dealt with an offense. We may desperately want to love again, but feel that we are incapable of it. Refusing to experience love and feeling unable to love are both devastating conditions.

- *Bitterness:* Emotions trace their lines on our faces. We think others don't notice what's going on inside, but our anger can usually be detected by even the casual observer. One person recalled seeing a neighbor go through difficulties in her marriage. Hate created such an impression on her that her face became permanently snarled. She still has that ugly look on her face. Unforgiveness produces ugliness of all sorts.

- *Perpetual Conflict:* A couple, both of whom had been previously married, received counseling several years ago. Having been hurt in their first marriage, they each anticipated hurt from their present spouse. At the smallest offense, they would each react as if their spouse were about to deliver the final blow. They were constantly on the defensive, protecting themselves from the attacks they imagined their mate would deliver. Having been offended in the past, they anticipated more hurt in the present and future, and reacted in a way that perpetuated the conflict.

- *Walls That Keep Others Out:* Strangely, many of us refuse to experience love from those who love us. We may often become anxious and threatened when personal intimacy becomes possible.

   Jane hoped and prayed that her husband Frank would come to know the Lord. This, she thought, would enable him to be more loving toward her and their children. One day, Frank accepted Christ and over time, his life began to change. He became interested in Jane, and started spending time with her and the children. He was sensitive and loving. Was it a dream come true? Instead of rejoicing, Jane deeply resented Frank for not changing sooner! *If Frank is able to love us like this now, then he's always had the ability,* she thought. She felt confused and guilty about her anger.

Jane's anger was a defense mechanism to keep distance between Frank and herself. The closer that they might get, the more pain she might experience if he reverted to his old ways. She had never truly forgiven Frank, so the bricks of unforgiveness were stacked to form a wall that kept him from getting too close. Hiding behind a wall of unforgiveness is a lonely experience.

Forgiveness Is Not Erasure

The modern idea of forgiveness is to approach an offense with a large eraser and wipe it off the books. God has never forgiven like this. For each offense, He demanded full payment. This is the reason for the cross. Beside every offense on our ledger is the blood of Christ, which has paid for our sins in full.

The Christian stands with a unique capacity for forgiveness because he or she can appropriate the forgiveness of the cross. God has forgiven us fully and completely. We, of all people, know what it is like to experience unconditional forgiveness. As a result, we can in turn forgive those around us. Think of it this way: *There is nothing that anyone can do to me (insult me, lie about me, annoy me, etc.) that can compare with what Christ has forgiven me for doing.* We gain a better perspective of others' offenses when we compare them to our sin of rebellion that Christ has completely forgiven. In Eph. 4:32, Paul writes, *And be kind to one another, tender-hearted, forgiving each other, just as God in Christ also has forgiven you.*

List ten things for which you are glad God in Christ has forgiven you. This will prime you to be willing to forgive all other offenders.

1._____   6._____
2._____   7._____
3._____   8._____
4._____   9._____
5._____   10._____

Summary of Reasons for Unforgiveness
1. *The offense was too great.*
2. *He(she) won't accept responsibility for the offense.*
3. *He(she) isn't truly sorry.*
4. *He(she) never asked to be forgiven.*
5. *He(she) will do it again.*
6. *He(she) did it again.*
7. *I don't like him(her).*
8. *He(she) did it deliberately.*
9. *If I forgive the offense, I'll have to treat the offender well.*
10. *Someone has to punish him(her).*
11. *Something keeps me from forgiving.*
12. *I'll be a hypocrite if I forgive, because I don't feel like forgiving.*
13. *I'll forgive, but I won't ever forget.*
14. *I have forgiven a lesser offense, after excusing the real offense.*

The following exercise will help you to understand biblical principles of forgiveness, and apply them to your relationships with others:

1. Read Matt. 18:21-35.

   a) How great was the debt of the king's servant?

   _____

   b) Was it possible for him ever to repay it?

   _____

2. *a)* Likewise, before you trusted Christ, how great was your debt to God?

   _____

   b) Was if possible for you to ever repay it?

   _____

321

3. *a)*   What did the servant ask for?

    _____

    b)   What did the king grant him?

    _____

4. Why was the king's servant so harsh with his fellow servant over such a small debt?

    _____

    _____

5. Read Luke 7:36-50 (especially verse 47) and compare it with the parable in Matt. 18:21-35. What is the foundation for being able to love and forgive others?

    _____

    _____

6. Read Eph. 4:32 and Col. 3:12-13.

    a)   To what degree are we to forgive others?

    _____

    b)   Describe how God has forgiven you:

    _____

7. Name some of the effects people experience when they harbor unforgiveness (attitudes toward others, their opinion of themselves, quality of relationships, etc.):

    _____

    _____

    _____

    _____

    _____

8. Do you see any of the answers to question 7 in your life? In your attitude toward others? Toward yourself? If so, describe them:

_____

_____

_____

_____

9. Is there any particular sin for which you haven't experienced God's forgiveness?

_____

_____

Review your answers with the following:

FOR ADDITIONAL INSIGHT

1. The debt of the king's servant was about $10,000,000. To put this in perspective, in his book, *Healing for Damaged Emotions*, David Seamands states that the entire annual taxes of Judea, Samaria, Galilee, Perea, and Idumea were $800,000.[1] So, the debt of the king's servant was impossible to repay—which is exactly the point!

2. Your debt to God was more impossible to repay than the servant's debt to the king. Apart from Christ, you were destined to carry this impossible debt all your life, knowing that at death you would have to give your eternal destiny to pay for it.

3. Did the servant ask for forgiveness of the debt? No. He asked for time to repay it. The king, though, had compassion and forgave him the entire debt.

4. The king's servant apparently did not believe he had been forgiven, and was trying to collect enough money to pay back the debt. He took the king's words to mean, *I'll give you a little more time. Work hard and pay me back.* But the king offered total forgiveness by cancelling the debt. The debt was GONE. He did not owe one penny of the $10,000,000. (Note that forgiveness is not experienced until it's fully accepted.)

5. Our ability to extend grace and forgiveness to others is directly related to the degree by which we have personally experienced the same.

6. We are to forgive others *just as God in Christ also has forgiven* [*us*] (Eph. 4:32). Our every thought and deed, regardless of their motives or results, have been forgiven. That forgiveness is totally unearned.

7. A lack of forgiveness may result in being harsh toward others, self-critical, demanding, guilt-ridden, resentful, finding fault, being motivated by "ought to's" (*I ought to do this; I ought not to do that*), holding grudges, and in working hard to atone for shortcomings. This is merely a partial list. See the Final Word for other results.

8. Many of us harbor ill feelings toward one or more people, but have suppressed them. We often are not consciously aware of these feelings until the Holy Spirit reveals them to us so that we can deal with them. Are there people you don't like to be around?... or whom you can't look in the eye?... or with whom you get angry every time you even *think* of them?

9. Is there something that you can't forgive yourself for having done? God the Father has forgiven you because Christ has paid for your sin. Are you refusing to forgive something God has forgiven?

Think this through carefully. Remember, the extent to which you will be able to love and forgive others is dependent on your acceptance of God's love for you and His forgiveness for *your* sins.

Use the exercise on the following pages to help you recognize any lack of forgiveness in your life, and to enable you to freely forgive as God in Christ has forgiven you.

1. Offense: List in some detail several events which caused you pain.

2. Persons to be Forgiven: List all who participated in the offense.

3. Reasons for Unforgiveness: Go through the list of reasons for unforgiveness on page 321, noting in the exercise the ones that apply.

4. Act of Forgiveness: Choose to forgive, remembering the complete forgiveness you have in Christ.

At the conclusion of the exercise, use the prayer on page 328 (or use your own) as an exercise of faith for each offense.

OFFENSE	PERSONS TO BE FORGIVEN
My brothers never had anything to do with me.	Harry, Frank

OFFENSE	PERSONS TO BE FORGIVEN

REASONS FOR UNFORGIVENESS   DATE

1, 2, 3   12-1-89
4, 5, 9

REASONS FOR UNFORGIVENESS	DATE

Dear Lord,

    *I forgive*_____ *for*
_____ (offense) *on the basis that God has freely forgiven me and commanded me to forgive others. I have the capacity to do this because Christ has completely forgiven me. I do not excuse this person's offense in any way, nor do I use any excuse for not extending forgiveness. Thank you, Lord Jesus, for enabling me to forgive.*

    I also confess that I have sinned by using the following excuses for not forgiving:

_____   _____

_____   _____

_____   _____

A FINAL WORD

Being offended by others is a frequent experience in life. We go through periods when it seems that almost everybody is "letting us down." We want freedom from being offended but the beat goes on. We are hurt by both our experience of the offense and our reliving of it. In fact, the initial pain of the wrong usually amounts to only a small fraction of the total hurt. After a while, it should become obvious to us that it is impossible to avoid being offended. However, the majority of our pain can be avoided if we will learn to deal with offenses rather than relive them countless times.

Shame

Read chapter 9 in _The Search for Significance._

    This step examines the shame that can arise from a negative evaluation of our past performance or our physical appearance. Shame is a prevailing sense of worthlessness which leads to the false belief: _I am what I am. I cannot change. I am hopeless._

1. Define _shame:_

_____

_____

2. When does shame occur?

_____

_____

3. Why does shame make an impact on our sense of self-worth? How does shame lock us into a low opinion of ourselves?

_____

_____

_____

4. Is there anything you can't keep from doing? When you've tried to stop, but then do it again, how do you feel about yourself?

_____

_____

5. List the things about your appearance or your past performance which prevent you from viewing yourself as a fully pleasing and totally accepted person:

   a) Appearance:

   _____

   _____

   _____

   _____

   _____

   b) Past Performance:

   _____

   _____

   _____

   _____

   _____

6. When people with a poor self-concept succeed at something, one would think that they would be encouraged and have a more positive outlook. But often, pessimistic people explain or minimize their success and continue in their hopelessness.

   a) Do you do this when you succeed? If so, what do you tell yourself and others?

   _____

   _____

   _____

b) Why do you say those things?

_____

_____

_____

7. What sources of input reinforce a low view of yourself?

_____

_____

_____

8. *a)* Read Ps. 139:13-16. What was God's involvement in the formation of your physical appearance and personality?

_____

_____

b) Are you a Creator critic?

_____

9. If you have a poor self-concept, what do you think it will take for you to overcome it and experience the joy and power of your new life in Christ?

_____

_____

_____

10. *a)* How do you think other people would describe you?

_____

_____

_____

b) What are their expectations of you?

_____

_____

_____

_____

    c)   How have their expectations affected your self-esteem?

_____

_____

_____

_____

Review your answers with the following:

FOR ADDITIONAL INSIGHT

1.   *Webster's Ninth New Collegiate Dictionary* defines shame as "a painful emotion caused by consciousness of guilt, shortcoming, or inpropriety; a condition of humiliating disgrace or disrepute."

2.   Shame often occurs when a failure in our performance or a "flaw" in our appearance is considered so important that it creates a permanently negative opinion about our self-worth. Even when others don't know of our failure or flaw, we may assume that their opinion of us is both poor and accurate.

3.   Shame can have a tremendous impact on us if we believe that we can never be different from what we have been. We may view ourselves as a composite of all of our past actions, and believe that we will never be able to change. Left in this hopeless state, we are likely to feel trapped in helplessness about ourselves and our future. Because much of what we do is based on our self-concept, our every action reinforces this negative perception of ourselves.

4.   Your list may include things like adultery, premarital sex, masturbation, homosexuality, alcohol or drug abuse, an eating disorder, gambling, smoking, being a "junk-food junkie," blatant

lying, exaggerating the truth, cheating, stealing, or other destructive personal habits. When you attempt to change but fail, it causes you to view yourself as a failure with no hope. You feel guilty and helpless.

5. *a)* In your appearance, anything from head to toe: height, weight, bone structure, acne, wrinkles, facial features, hair, chest, legs, feet, or teeth.

   b) Past performance: failure in your marriage or friendships; disappointing your parents; not making good grades; sloppiness; an addiction; being uncoordinated, deceitful, obnoxious, lustful, gay, adulterous, unforgiving, etc.

6. *a)* People with a poor self-concept may tell themselves:
   - *It was just luck.*
   - *I couldn't do it again.*
   - *I'm still a failure.*
   - *Stop while you're ahead, because it will never happen again.*

   b) If you tell yourself things like this, it may be because you expect failure and rejection so much that you simply can't handle success and appreciation.

7. Sources of input contributing to low self-worth may be what parents or peers actually say, or what you assume they are thinking. Your input may also come from comparing yourself with the handsome men and gorgeous women on television, in magazines, or in other forms of advertising.

8. *a)* God formed your inward parts, and He was involved in this process at conception. He has made you carefully and wonderfully. He shaped your frame. Before one day passed in your life, He

knew all that would happen, including your family background, personality type, mental capacities, and emotional makeup.

b) If you minimize your self-worth because of your appearance or your personality, you are criticizing God's unique workmanship. He is the all-wise and all-powerful Creator, and He fashioned you according to His wisdom and power. *The thing molded will not say to the molder, "Why did you make me like this," will it?* (Rom. 9:20).

9. You must first recognize that if you are evaluating yourself by your past performance or appearance, you are viewing yourself incorrectly. Your past will affect you to the degree that you evaluate yourself on the basis of previous successes or failures. Secondly, you must recognize that God has made you into a new creature through Christ's death on the cross. God says you are *deeply loved, fully pleasing, and totally accepted by Him.*

10. Others' opinions of us, either good or bad, cannot be the basis of a godly self-esteem. If their opinions of us are good, we are often led to either pride or the fear of failing and losing that good opinion. If their opinions of us are negative, we may believe them and think that we can't change. A good, proper, and godly evaluation of ourselves comes from God's Word, not other people.

A FINAL WORD

Shame occurs when a failure in our performance or a flaw in our appearance is considered so important that it solidifies a negative self-concept. Even when others don't know of our failure, we assume their opinion of us is poor, and we adopt what we think their opinion might be.

If we base our self-worth on our performance long enough, our past behavior will eventually become the sole basis of our worth. We will see ourselves with certain character qualities and flaws because that's the way we've always been. We then have unconsciously incorporated Satan's lie into our belief system: *I must always be what I have been, and live with whatever self-worth I have, because that's just me.* Interestingly, we claim only our *poor* behavior as, *That's just me.* We never hear anyone say, "That's just me; I'm so wonderful, honest, and bright."

We may think that humility is self-depreciation, but true humility is an accurate appraisal of our worth in Christ: We deserved God's righteous condemnation, yet we are recipients of His unconditional love, grace, and righteousness through Christ. We are deeply loved, completely forgiven, fully pleasing, totally accepted, and complete in Him. Thankfulness, generosity, kindness, and self-confidence constitute true humility!

Another aspect of a poor self-concept relates to personal appearance. Most of us have some aspect of our appearance that we wish we could change, but much about our appearance can't really be altered. We may not only base our self-worth on our appearance, but may tend to base our acceptance of others on their appearance, even the color of their skin. We may never be any more cruel than when we accept or reject others based on their appearance.

Are you angry with God for the way He made you? Do you compare and rank the appearance of yourself with others? If you do, you will suffer at some point in your life because there will always be someone prettier, stronger, cuter, or more handsome. Even if you are spectacularly beautiful or strikingly handsome, you will suffer because you will be afraid of losing your good looks, the basis of your self-worth.

If we insist on valuing our self-worth by our appearance and performance, sooner or later God will graciously allow us to see the futility of that struggle. The Lord never meant for us to find the fulfillment of our self-worth and significance in the opinions of others. This undeniable, unavoidable need for a sense of value was created in man by God. However, He knows we will never come to Him until we find the importance of people's opinions to be empty and hopeless. At that point, we can turn to Him and find comfort and encouragement in the truths of His Word!

What is the basis of your self-worth? Are you living by these scriptural truths or by these false beliefs?

Scriptural Truths	False Beliefs
I am completely forgiven and am fully pleasing to God.	*I must meet certain standards in order to feel good about myself.*
I am totally accepted by God.	*I must be accepted by certain people in order to feel good about myself.*
I am deeply loved by God.	*Those who fail are unworthy of love and deserve to be blamed and condemned.*
I am absolutely complete in Christ.	*I am what I am. I cannot change. I am hopeless.*

False beliefs are all a part of the enemy's insidious plan. But God has a different plan. By now, you should see that deception is a part of Satan's scheme to steal, and kill, and destroy mankind. God has His own plan for you, and it alone will bring you a stable sense of self-worth. With a godly self-worth comes a new direction and purpose: to honor the One who has laid down His life to give you security and significance.

Step Fourteen
Regeneration

This step will help you see yourself as a new creature in Christ, with new potential and new capacities. The truth that you have been made new in Him will enable you to begin developing a strong, positive self-esteem in spite of "flaws" in your appearance or past failures.

1. Do you really think that you can view yourself any differently than you always have? If not, why?

    _____

    _____

    _____

2. Read 2 Cor. 5:17.

    a) Define *regeneration:*

    _____

    b) What does your having been made a new creature mean?

    _____

    _____

3. How was your regeneration accomplished?

    a) John 1:12-13

    _____

    _____

    b) John 3:16

    _____

    _____

    c) Titus 3:5

    _____

    _____

    d) 1 Pet. 1:3

    _____

    _____

    e) 1 Pet. 1:23

    _____

    _____

4. Read Eph. 4:22-24 and Col. 3:9-10. What process do you need to go through in order to experience your new self?

    _____

    _____

    _____

5. From the passages listed on the following pages, list the characteristics of your old self and your new self:

CHARACTERISTICS OF MY OLD SELF

a) Rom. 6:6

_____

_____

_____

b) Gal. 5:19-21

_____

_____

_____

c) Eph. 2:1-3

_____

_____

_____

d) Eph. 4:17-22

_____

_____

_____

e) Col. 3:5-9

_____

_____

_____

f) Titus 3:3

_____

_____

_____

CHARACTERISTICS OF MY NEW SELF

a) Rom. 8:16-17

_____

_____

b) 2 Cor. 5:21

_____

_____

c) Gal. 5:22-24

_____

_____

d) Eph. 4:23-32

_____

_____

_____

e) Col. 2:10

_____

_____

f) Col. 3:10-15

_____

_____

g) Titus 3:1-2

_____

_____

h) 1 Pet. 1:16

_____

_____

6. Read Rom. 6:12-23 and 1 Cor. 6:9-11. How does the truth of regeneration free you from evaluating yourself by your past performance?

_____

_____

_____

7. Read 1 Sam. 16:6-7 and Ps. 139:13-16. How does the truth of regeneration free you from the shame prompted by flaws in your physical appearance?

_____

_____

_____

8. How could an understanding that you are a new creature in Christ affect your personal fitness or grooming habits?

_____

_____

_____

9. How can the fact that you have a new life in Christ affect the way you think, feel, and act?

_____

_____

_____

10. Do you use past failures, your appearance, or some other "flaw" as an excuse for not living for Christ? If so, what is your excuse? How valid is it?

_____

_____

11. Memorize 2 Cor. 5:17.

Review your answers with the following:

FOR ADDITIONAL INSIGHT

1. Much of your self-worth has probably been based on your performance and others' opinions. False beliefs have thus become the primary basis you use to evaluate yourself and the situations you face.

Belief System Based on False Beliefs	→	Ungodly Thoughts	→	Painful Emotions	→	Ungodly Actions

    Your beliefs usually influence your thoughts, emotions, and actions. False beliefs are Satan's lies, and they generate ungodly thoughts, painful emotions, and sinful actions. An ungodly performance serves to reinforce these false beliefs, which supports the conviction, *I am what I am.* You may feel trapped and hopeless to be anything different from who you are right now. Take heart! There is hope! God has made you a new creature.

2. *a) Webster's New World Dictionary* defines *regeneration* as "renewed or restored; to cause to be spiritually reborn; to cause to be completely reformed; to bring into existence again...."

    b) You have been made into a new person. At the instant of your conversion to Christ, you were born again as a new spiritual being. God creates by "fiat," that is, He makes something from nothing. Your new birth brought about more than a change of direction. It gave you a completely new nature with new capacities to reflect God's image in your daily life. This new creature resides in your body, but it is as different from your old self as a horse is from a man.

3. Your regeneration was accomplished:

a)   By the will of God.

b)   Through believing faith in Jesus Christ's death for you.

c)   By the renewing of the Holy Spirit.

d)   Through the death and resurrection of Jesus Christ.

e)   By the Word of God.

4.   The process of experiencing your new self involves three steps:

a)   Laying aside the old self—rejecting the old self's hold on you, which dictates how you think, feel, and act, and choosing to stop living in worldliness.

b)   Renewing your mind with God's truth—understanding the truth of what Christ has accomplished for you and how that gives you a new capacity to live for Him.

c)   Putting on the new self—in your thoughts, words, actions, values, and relationships.

Express the truth of your new character. Your new self can now influence how you think, feel, and act. Steps 19, 20, and 21 will aid you in the rejection, replacement, and renewal process.

5.   This exercise will help you see that regeneration has already been completed in your life. You have been transformed into a new creature. You can declare those characteristics that describe your new nature to be true of you: *I am deeply loved by God. I am completely forgiven by God. I am fully pleasing to God. I am totally acceptable and accepted by God. I am a new creation— complete in Christ.*

6.   Regeneration gives you a new beginning. No matter what you have done in the past, God has washed the guilt away and set you apart for His own use in the present. First Corinthians 6:9-11 provides a glimpse of the type of individual God can radically transform. You no longer have to think, feel, and act as false

beliefs dictate. You are now free to present yourself to God as an instrument of righteousness.

7. God was not idle during our physical formation in the womb. He was intimately involved with our creation. God fashioned each of us to be physically distinct from one another. Through regeneration, He gives each of us the capacity to reflect His image through our unique personality and appearance.

8. Our view of our self-worth is often expressed through our physical fitness and grooming habits. If we have a low self-image, our grooming habits will reflect that view. As God gives us a new sense of self-worth, it may change the way we care for ourselves. Our eating, exercise, grooming, and dressing habits are all areas in which we can glorify God. Are there any habits you need to improve in order to reflect your new nature? (Ask your spouse or a good friend.)

9. Regeneration provides you with a new system by which you can evaluate yourself and your life:

Belief System → Godly → Emotions → Godly
Based on   Thoughts   Actions
God's Truth
About You

As your mind is renewed by the Spirit of God, and as you apply the Word of God in relationships with the people of God, your life will progressively change.

10. Moses used the excuses, "Who am I? No one will listen to me! And I don't speak very well, anyway!"* to try to keep from serving the Lord. Some of us excuse our unavailability to God by

* Adapted from Ex. 3:11; 4:1, 10, NIV.

blaming our poor background; lack of education, training, or available opportunities; fears, etc. God has dealt with your excuses by making you a new person with new potential and new capacities. Write across your excuses, *I am a new creation— complete in Christ.*

A FINAL WORD

Regeneration is the renewing work of the Holy Spirit by which a person literally becomes a new creation. Our regeneration took place at the instant of our conversion to Christ. At that moment, we were given more than a change of direction; we received the impartation of new life.

The part of us that the Holy Spirit regenerated is our spirit. The Holy Spirit has energized our inner spirit with new life. Jesus called it a new birth in John 3:3,5-6, saying, *That which is born of the flesh is flesh, and that which is born of the Spirit is spirit* (John 3:6). Regeneration is the Spirit-wrought renewal of our human spirit, a transforming resuscitation so that the spirit is alive within us (Rom. 8:10).

The Holy Spirit has been joined to our human spirit, forming a new spiritual entity. A new birth has produced a new being. *Therefore if any man is in Christ, he is a new creature; the old things passed away; behold, new things have come* (2 Cor. 5:17).

Study these words carefully. Ephesians 4:24 says that our new self *has* (already) *been created in righteousness and holiness of the truth,* but we must yet *put on* this new self in order to progressively produce godly thoughts and actions—as the acorn produces an oak tree!

Section III

Application

How can I replace destructive beliefs with God's truth so that my thoughts, words, and actions reflect God's love and purpose?

Step Fifteen
Renewing Your View of God

This step will help you understand how man's concept of God has been distorted as a result of the Fall. It will also help you to begin renewing your mind with the truth of God's love, power, wisdom, and majesty.

The most tragic result of the Fall was man's alienation from his Creator. Sin separates mankind from the love and security of the Almighty. Apart from the redeeming work of Christ, man is unable to enjoy intimacy with the Father as Adam and Eve did before the Fall; in fact, he hides from God (Gen. 3:8), and his perception of God is distorted, tainted by the world and the deception of the enemy.

EXPOSING ERRORS

How accurate are your beliefs concerning God's character? Do you intimately know Him as He has revealed Himself? Or are your perceptions of Him founded on reason, experience, the human examples of parental modeling, and the ideas of others?

Taking this short test will give you some insight about your perception of God's character:

1. *a)* How do you view God?

	Always	Very often	Often	Sometimes	Seldom	Hardly ever	Never
Loving							
Faithful							
Sovereign							
Friend							
Compassionate							
All-Powerful							
Just							
Wise							

You've just recorded what you intellectually believe to be true about God. However, reactions are often a better indicator of beliefs than verbal proclamations.

b) Consider the following situations. How would you normally respond to them? How would you respond if you were convinced that God is completely loving, powerful, and wise (your *believing* response)?

(1) Your car has been stolen.

(a) Normal Response:

_____

_____

_____

(b) Believing Response:

_____

_____

_____

(2) The company where you work has been bought out by another firm. Each day, someone in your department has lost his or her job. You could be next.

(a) Normal Response:

_____

_____

_____

(b) Believing Response:

_____

_____

_____

(3) You've just lost your boyfriend/girlfriend to someone else.

(a) Normal Response:

_____

_____

_____

(b) Believing Response:

_____

_____

_____

2. Why is there a discrepancy between what you intellectually believe is true and how you react under stress?

_____

_____

3. List the factors (people, experiences, society) that have helped to shape your present view of God, and describe the effect of each on your concept of Him:

_____

_____

_____

_____

_____

Paul expressed his prayer for the Ephesians in Eph. 1:15-21. In verses 17 and 18, he asked that the eyes of their hearts might be enlightened to see God for who He is. Pause now and pray this prayer, asking God to strip away deception and show you His glory and character.

EXAMINING THE TRUTH

4. Read John 1:17-18; 14:8-10. How can you know the truth about God's character?

_____

_____

_____

5. *a)* Christ perfectly reveals the Father to us. What do each of these passages teach you about Christ?

(1) John 4:13-26, 39

_____

_____

_____

(2) John 10:11-15

_____

_____
_____

(3) John 14:2-3

_____
_____

(4) John 15:13-16

_____
_____

(5) John 17:23

_____
_____

b) Using the content of the previous passages of Scripture, write a few sentences explaining how God relates to you and feels about you.

I know that my heavenly Father...

_____
_____
_____
_____
_____

6. Read Ps. 103. In the left column, write characteristics of God the Father that you see in this Psalm. In the right column, write out what difference this characteristic makes in your life.

My heavenly Father is...   *As a result I...*

_____   _____

_____   _____

_____   _____
_____   _____
_____   _____

7. *a)* Read John 19:25-27. John recorded Christ's words on the cross, commissioning him to take care of His mother, Mary. How did John refer to himself?

_____

   b) Do you think of yourself like that? Why, or why not?

_____
_____
_____

8. Look at your answers to questions 5 and 6. Take some time to reflect on God's love and power. Praise Him for who He is and thank Him specifically for what He has done for you.

9. Tomorrow, read Ps. 145. Praise and thank God as you read each verse. Notice the characteristics of God and His activities in our lives.

Review your answers with the following:

FOR ADDITIONAL INSIGHT

1. *a)* One of the best ways to accurately determine your view of the Lord is to examine your actions. Jesus repeatedly emphasized the relationship between a man's actions and his beliefs. Matthew 12:34 says, *The mouth speaks out of that which fills the heart.* Mark 7:20-23 states: *...That which proceeds out of the man, that is what defiles the man. For from within, out of the heart of men,*

proceed the evil thoughts, fornications, thefts, murders, adulteries, deeds of coveting and wickedness, as well as deceit, sensuality, envy, slander, pride and foolishness. All these evil things proceed from within and defile the man.

b) Most people intellectually affirm that God is all-powerful, but won't trust Him to take care of the major events in their lives. Our actions are a true and accurate reflection of what we actually believe.

2. Stressful situations can produce questions in our minds regarding the character of God. Many of us freely talk about God's love when life is going well. However, when life is difficult, we often grumble and respond as if God has deserted us or hates us. It is critical that we accurately know the Lord and walk with Him in the midst of our circumstances. This requires that our knowledge of God be based on an unshifting foundation: His Word.

3. Your concept of God has probably been shaped by the opinions of others, your natural thoughts (*God wouldn't allow anyone to go to hell*), and circumstances (*How can God be good if this happened?*). We need to base our knowledge of God on His Word.

4. Jesus is the perfect representation of the Father on earth. God's Word and God's Son reveal God's character.

5. *Christ is the Good Shepherd. He laid down His life for me. When trouble comes, He won't run because He cares for me. He knows me. He has chosen me. My Father loves me like He does Jesus. He proudly calls me His friend. He wants me to be with Him for all eternity.* What an unbelievable privilege to be wanted by the Almighty God!

6. For example: *My Father has forgiven all of my sin. God Himself has removed my transgressions, as far as the east is from the west. As a result, I can be free from guilt and condemnation. No one can accuse me if God has removed my transgressions. My Father loves me—as much as the heavens are above the earth. When I begin to feel discouraged or when others reject me, I can remember the depth of God's love for me. I will never be unloved again.*

7. *a)* John called himself *the disciple whom Jesus loved.*

   b) This is just as true of you! Try introducing yourself this week to a Christian friend by saying, "I'm the disciple Jesus loves!" or, "I'm the believer who has all my needs provided for" (Matt. 6:33; Phil. 4:19). You may shock some people by doing this (so be careful about whom you say these things to), but it is important to begin verbalizing scriptural truths. Verbalizing God's Word will reinforce it in your mind and enable you to more readily replace false beliefs with His truth.

8. Tell Him how grateful you are. Tell Him why you are grateful.

9. Develop a habit of praising God and focusing on what Scripture says is true of Him. Memorizing Scripture will help you to renew your mind and will give you a true and proper knowledge of God.

A FINAL WORD

Knowing God is the most critical issue in all of life. J.I. Packer writes in his book, *Knowing God,* "Knowing about God is crucially important for the living of our lives. As it would be cruel to an Amazonian tribesman to fly him to London, put him down without explanation in Trafalgar Square and leave him, as one who knows nothing of English or England, to fend for himself, so we are cruel to ourselves if we try to live in this world without knowing about the God whose world it is and who runs it.[1]

It is critical that we accurately know the one true God. We will only follow one whom we know and trust. Satan deceives us by distorting the character of God: *If you follow and obey God, you'll be miserable. God doesn't love you because you did this. God won't accept someone like you.* By deceiving us about God's love and power, Satan robs us of the desire to love, obey, and honor Him.

Step Sixteen

Dealing with Emotional Scars

This step is designed to help you understand how God's truth can be applied to your past.

As you begin to be honest about your emotions, to reject what is contrary to God's Word, and replace it with God's truth, you will realize how significantly you have been influenced by the lies of the enemy. Many of our beliefs are lies! We live in a fallen world with fallen individuals. As a result, much of what we've learned about ourselves and the world (our "belief system") is distorted. Sadly, the world is not becoming progressively closer to the truth, but is straying farther from it. The results are tragic.

Many individuals have been raised in a broken home without one or both parents. Others have gone through a traumatic event in their lives. Some have grown up in a home environment where they've been driven to perform and have been rejected when they've failed.

Bill's parents never told him they loved him. Teresa's dad left when she was five years old. Ginger had been told she was ugly; why wasn't she beautiful like her sister? Justin's father told him he would never be successful. Peter's girlfriend was pregnant at age sixteen. Regina's teacher told her she'd never make it. Julie was looking for a job, and had been rejected three times.

Events like these (and countless others) dramatically affect our belief system. The incredibly good news is: *If any man is in Christ, he is a new creature. The old things passed away; behold, new things have come* (2 Cor. 5:17).

Can we do anything about our past? Yes and no. Obviously, we can't go back and relive it. We can never escape its negative circumstances. However, we can deal with previous poor choices and detrimental experiences so that they don't continue to influence our self-worth.

How do we deal with painful events of the past? Recovering from past wounds is not a 1-2-3-step process. Closing the chapter and relinquishing memories of hurtful experiences requires the powerful enlightenment of the Holy Spirit and our cooperation with Him. The following may serve as a helpful guide to you during this process:

1 Find a quiet place where you won't be disturbed, and ask God to reveal any particular events in your past that are significantly affecting the way you view yourself today (Ps. 139:23-24). Don't become introspective—simply ask God to point out specific instances. It may help if you limit this to a specific fear (failure, rejection, punishment, shame). For instance: *Father, show me any particular event in my life in which I experienced rejection.*

2. Briefly write out the event. Be honest in describing how you felt about it then and how you feel about it now. You may want to talk with a trusted friend about your feelings.

3. List the false beliefs which influenced your thoughts and behavior in the situation. Confess having believed Satan's deception; then, reject each lie and replace it with its corresponding truth. (See the chart at the beginning of Section II.)

4. Forgive all of those who contributed to this negative situation (Eph. 4:32). Thank God that He can use it for good in your life (Gen. 50:20; Rom. 8:28).

5. Reaffirm with God that you are free from condemnation (Rom. 8:1), and have been made a new creature in Christ (2 Cor. 5:17).

6. Ask God if there are any other incidents that He wants to bring to your memory. Allow Him to choose the best time to reveal these to you, and ask Him to help you be objective and honest about the pain of your past.

It is important to understand that the principles outlined above are to be used as *guidelines* in the process of relinquishing past painful events. Painful memories don't vanish simply because we decide we want to be rid of them. Recovering from the anguish of hurtful events in our lives requires the grace and insight of the Holy Spirit, combined with willingness, patience, persistence, time, and our application of God's Word.

This principle applies to all of the material presented in *The Search for Significance*. The truths given here and in Scripture will impact our lives only to the degree that we recognize our need for them. One man who works with a para-church organization told me that he has taught material from *The Search for Significance* nineteen times. Each time he has reviewed this material, he says, the Holy Spirit has shown him those areas of his life where he needs to apply the book's principles at a deeper level.

In our pursuit of comfort and happiness, many of us have managed to bury past instances of neglect, rejection, embarrassment, abuse, and failure. We may either deny the impact these negative instances have had on our lives, or we may escape through alcohol, drugs, sex, or unhealthy emotional attachments which make us feel good and anesthetize our pain.

Margaret, a recovering alcoholic with two years of sobriety, couldn't understand her frequent feelings of rage and occasional outbursts of anger toward men. She had experienced emotional neglect from her father as a child, and had often felt rejected by her male peers since adolescence. Her alcoholism had numbed her from the pain of these hurtful memories for a number of years. Once she regained her sobriety, she worked through a twelve-step program, and in the process, made a decision to forgive the men who had rejected her. This was a good start. But this was where Margaret stopped. She failed to recognize that the steps given to her for recovery were steps of progress which she would need to apply repeatedly to all areas of her life. And, in her attempt to avoid the sin of consciously harboring resentment, she dismissed her negative feelings and denied their existence, rather than expressing them to the Lord and allowing Him to help her work through them.

The unfortunate result of neglecting painful instances in our past is that these events continue to impact our thinking and behavioral patterns; we simply are unaware of their effect in our lives.

The story of Craig may provide a useful illustration in understanding the process of recognizing and relinquishing instances of hurt in our past.

Craig's Story
When Craig came to see me, he was suffering from deep depression. He had missed out on a promotion opportunity at work six months before, and had since become increasingly despondent and withdrawn. He felt immobilized, was losing weight, and for two months, had been sexually impotent.

I visited with Craig about his family and social relationships, his childhood, and his early adult years. He told me that he had grown increasingly distant from his father over the years, but was unable to trace this to any past event in their relationship. As we continued talking, I learned that Craig thought he related best to women because he felt readily accepted by them. With men, he told me, he felt he had to work continually at making a good impression and winning their approval. He said he was having some difficulty in expressing himself to me for that reason.

When I asked Craig about his relationship with God, I wasn't surprised to hear that he perceived Him as One who is distant and withdrawn, and that his understanding of Christianity was that of a rules-oriented lifestyle designed to promote good behavior.

At the conclusion of our meeting, I suggested that Craig begin asking God to show him any significant events from his past that were presently affecting his self-concept and his relationship with God. I also suggested that in his prayers, he focus on the areas of failure and rejection.

Craig came to see me two weeks later. He had prayed as I had suggested for several days. One morning, as he was shaving, the Holy Spirit brought to his mind a hot summer day when he was playing little league baseball. It was the championship game, the bases were loaded, and Craig was at bat. He struck out and his team lost. In front of everybody at the game, the coach yelled at him, calling him all sorts of names. But the most pain occurred when Craig's dad screamed at him from the stands, "What's wrong with you, son? Can't you even swing the bat straight?" The words hurt as much now as they did then.

I had Craig write the circumstances of the event on a piece of paper. As we discussed it over the next several weeks, he began to realize that the memory of this occasion—and others like it—were seriously affecting him.

For example, although he was a steady worker, when the pressure of his job became too intense, he withdrew. This had cost him the promotion he had wanted earlier in the year. Feeling a deep sense of shame over this and other losses, he began to fear that his wife also believed he was a failure. This had contributed to his impotency. In addition, he had become increasingly withdrawn from activities and relationships, and especially those involving other men, whose approval he desperately needed.

When Craig finally understood the full implications of this event on his self-image and subsequent choices, he was bitterly angry with both his father and his baseball coach. In fact, his first inclination was to cast the blame for all of his shortcomings on them. Gradually, however, Craig began to recognize that while his father and his coach had contributed to his perception of himself, he was responsible for his past decisions. He also realized that he was responsible for having allowed false beliefs to dominate his thinking. Craig had believed the lie, *I must be approved by certain others to feel good about myself.* He had made a wrong choice when he decided to base his value on the opinions of his father and his coach instead of the love and acceptance of God.

After we discussed this, he listed the thoughts that had resulted from those false beliefs: *I will never be able to come through in difficult situations. I am a jerk. I'm a poor son. I'll always be an athletic klutz.*

During the months that followed, Craig joined a Bible study and grew in his understanding and application of God's Word. He began to learn how to reject the lies of Satan by applying the truths of the Scripture, affirming that despite displeasing others, *he is totally accepted, fully pleasing, and deeply loved by God.*

Craig was making tremendous progress, but continued to struggle with the issue of forgiveness. It was only as he began to reflect on Col. 3:13 and Eph. 4:32, and then comprehend what Christ's death and resurrection had accomplished for him, that he was able to begin the process of forgiving his father and coach.

As he also recognized that his pain had driven him to God, enabling him to experience His presence in a new way, Craig was able to thank God for his circumstances. He began to understand why the Apostle Paul had been able to give thanks in *all* things.

Finally, Craig realized that he is a new creature in Christ, and that his worth is not dependent on the opinions of others.

My counseling with Craig began more than two years ago. I now see him only on occasion. Although he has grown tremendously in his understanding and application of the truths of God's Word, the memory of his childhood baseball failure continues to surface from time to time. When this happens, Craig has to make a conscious choice to forgive. His progress is evident in that this event no longer influences his present behavior to the degree that it once did; that he is willing to recognize the pain of this past instance; and that he is willing to crucify his former feelings of bitterness, and instead apply the principles of forgiveness to the situation.

If the mere thought of a past event creates a strong emotional reaction within you, then it is likely that this event has significantly affected your self-esteem. Not all deeply-rooted beliefs will disappear quickly. You will need to focus repeatedly on God's truth and reject your past beliefs. You may experience some emotional pain as you go through this process, but that pain will be far less than what you will experience if you continue to live by false beliefs. Don't grow weary of allowing God to transform your thinking! It will make a tremendous difference in how you handle similar situations in the future. You can learn and grow rather than plod through life, deeply hurt and scarred from the past. It's worth the struggle!

Use the following worksheets to begin dealing with any emotional scars you may have. (In completing these worksheets, you may want to reflect on the events you described in step 12.)

DEALING WITH EMOTIONAL SCARS WORKSHEETS

1. Past Event:

_____

_____

_____

_____

_____

   a) Past Feelings:

_____

_____

_____

_____

   b) Current Feelings:

_____

_____

_____

_____

   c) Thoughts About Event and People Involved:

_____

_____

_____

_____

   d) False Belief(s):

_____

_____

_____

_____

e) God's Truth(s):

_____

_____

_____

_____

2. Past Event:

_____

_____

_____

_____

a) Past Feelings:

_____

_____

_____

b) Current Feelings:

_____

_____

_____

_____

c) Thoughts About Event and People Involved:

_____

_____

_____

_____

d) False Belief(s):

_____
_____
_____
_____

e) God's Truth(s):

_____
_____
_____
_____

3. Past Event:

_____
_____
_____
_____

a) Past Feelings:

_____
_____
_____
_____

b) Current Feelings:

_____
_____
_____
_____

c) Thoughts About Event and People Involved:

_____
_____
_____
_____

d) False Belief(s):

_____
_____
_____
_____

e) God's Truth(s):

_____
_____
_____
_____

4. Past Event:

_____
_____
_____
_____
_____

a) Past Feelings:

_____
_____
_____
_____

b)   Current Feelings:

_____
_____
_____
_____

c)   Thoughts About Event and People Involved:

_____
_____
_____
_____

d)   False Belief(s):

_____
_____
_____
_____

e)   God's Truth(s):

_____
_____
_____
_____

Forgiveness

We examined many principles of forgiveness in step 12. However, as suppressed hurts from our past continue to surface, we often need to begin learning how to apply forgiveness at a deeper level.

Those of us who have been adept at denying painful instances in our lives are, at the point of discovery, much like chemically dependent persons who begin to discover their emotions at the onset of sobriety, often for the first time. For that reason, I want to devote the remainder of this step to what two authors and I have shared about forgiveness in our workbook, *Rapha's Twelve-Step Program for Overcoming Chemical Dependency.*[1]

Forgiveness is always a decision, and usually a hard one. Forgiveness and understanding are next of kin, but they're not the same.

By way of illustration, let's say that I just purchased a new car and you ask me if you can borrow it for a day. I loan the car to you, and you have the misfortune of wrecking it. Perhaps the accident occurred in understandable circumstances. Maybe it was pouring rain, the streets were slick, and someone cut in front of you. That's understandable. But "understandable" isn't going to pay for the cost of repairs to my car. That's the difference. Forgiveness is counting the cost and releasing others from the debt of what they owe.

If I really release you from this debt, I'll refrain from reminding you about my car. I won't look at you and wink each time the word *car* is mentioned in conversation. I won't tell you that I've been turning up the radio to avoid hearing the clanky noises my car is now making. Nor will I say, "It's okay, but don't ever ask to borrow my car again!" It may be prudent for me to refrain from loaning you my car, depending on your driving record, but if I am to forgive you, I must release you from even the *guilt* of the penalty you would have owed me.

If I genuinely forgive you, I'll also refrain from walking to my car blindfolded so I won't have to see the damage. Forgiveness counts the cost and then releases the offender from the penalty that is owed. Why should we forgive?

- *God commands us to forgive others through Jesus Christ.* "And whenever you stand praying, forgive, if you have anything against anyone..." (Mark 11:25).
- *We have been forgiven by God through Jesus Christ.* "And be kind to one another, tender-hearted, forgiving each other, just as God in Christ has also forgiven you" (Eph. 4:32).
- *An unforgiving spirit hurts us.* I may choose to release you from the debt of paying for my car, and you may leave the country. If I continue to be burdened by resentment, guess who's going to suffer for it? Not you ... you're in another country enjoying the culture; you're not thinking about my car and me. I'll be the one who's hurting. And if I allow it to consume me, resentment will increasingly turn me toward a path of destruction.

1. Read Matt. 18:21-35; Rom. 5:6-11; and Col. 2:13-14; 3:13. Describe the forgiveness you have in Christ. Explain what it is, how it was given, and how this affects you:

    a) Define *forgiveness:*

    _____

    _____

    b) How has God extended forgiveness to you through Christ?

    _____

    _____

    c) How does this affect you?

    _____

    _____

2. From the events you described on pages 370-374, who has offended you or harmed you? What did they do to you?

Person	Offense
_____	_____
_____	_____
_____	_____
_____	_____
_____	_____
_____	_____
_____	_____

3. What would it mean to release each person from the penalty they owe you?

Person	Result of Forgiveness
_____	_____
_____	_____
_____	_____
_____	_____
_____	_____
_____	_____

4. Have you forgiven any of these people already? If so, explain how:

Person	Application of Forgiveness
_____	_____
_____	_____
_____	_____
_____	_____
_____	_____
_____	_____

5. What have been the results of your forgiveness response...

    a) For you?

    _____

    _____

    _____

    b) For them?

    _____

    _____

    _____

6. If you have not forgiven all of the persons mentioned earlier, what are the consequences of your unwillingness to forgive...

    a) For you?

    _____

    _____

    _____

    b) For them?

    _____

    _____

    _____

7. How can you tell that you've forgiven someone?

    _____

    _____

    _____

8.   Memorize Col. 3:13:

Note: Use the worksheets on pages 370-374 as guidelines each time the Holy Spirit reminds you of your need to practice forgiveness. Don't be discouraged if the same instances often come to mind. You are making progress each time you apply scriptural principles of forgiveness at a deeper level in your life.

FOR ADDITIONAL INSIGHT

1.   *a)   Forgive,* as defined by *Webster's Ninth New Collegiate Dictionary,* means "to cease to feel resentment against (an offender)...to grant relief from payment of (a debt)."

b)   God's forgiveness has been extended to us through the saving work of His Son on the cross. We are reconciled to God through the blood of the Lamb, Jesus. Colossians 2:13-14 says: *And when you were dead in your transgressions and the uncircumcision of your flesh, He made you alive together with Him, having forgiven us all our transgressions, having canceled out the certificate of debt consisting of decrees against us and which was hostile to us; and He has taken it out of the way, having nailed it to the cross.*

c)   By assuming the guilt of our sins, Christ has avenged the righteous wrath of God. We are justified in God's sight, and as a result, we are fully pleasing to Him *despite* our sin. Through the sacrifice of His blood, Christ has reconciled us to our Creator so that we can enjoy intimate fellowship with Him.

3.   In his book, *Forgiveness,* Charles Stanley writes that three elements are essential to the process of forgiving: an injury, a debt resulting from the injury, and a cancellation of the debt.[2]

The act of forgiving requires that we look honestly at our injury, how it has affected us in the past, and how it may continue to affect us in the future.

As we deal with the hurt, anger, and grief we have experienced because of an injury, we form a basis for determining the debt we have incurred as a result of it. At this point, we may be tempted to indulge in self-pity, hatred, bitterness, and depression. We may also experience a desire to seek revenge against the one who has harmed us. Here, we must recognize that we will never be able to extend forgiveness until we have compared the gravity of our own sins with those that have been committed against us. Until we can truly comprehend the significance of our sin and the grief it brings to God and others, we can neither fully appreciate nor fully experience the cost incurred by Christ to extend forgiveness to us. Understanding the depth of His forgiveness toward us provides us with the compassion, mercy, and motivation to forgive others.

4. If you are applying the principles of forgiveness to someone who has injured you in some way, you've probably begun the process described above. This process may need to be repeated for the same incident each time it comes to mind.

Remember that forgiveness does not mean overlooking an injury or denying its painful consequences in our lives. We can never experience healing from our wounds by neglect. Just as an untreated bodily wound would have detrimental effects on our physical health, so our failure to treat injuries inflicted by others will result in further damage to our emotional, spiritual, relational, and mental well-being.

5 *a)* Our willingness to forgive others gives us an assurance that God is working in our lives through His Holy Spirit, and that we are, indeed, recipients of His generous mercy and forgiveness. Our love and gratitude for the Lord will increase as we, by being

reconciled to a previous offender, better grasp the reality and significance of our being reconciled to God through Christ. We will be freed from preoccupation with a past event, and able to focus on present matters that deserve our attention. We will experience the benefits of peace with others, enabling God to meet our needs for companionship and intimacy, and giving Him an opportunity to free us from the destructive effects of prolonged anger, self-pity, resentment, and depression.

b) There is never any guarantee that our obedience to God will effect a positive response from other people. However, it is possible that if others are aware of the injury they've caused us, our willingness to forgive them may prompt feelings and actions that reflect their gratitude. Our forgiveness response may give them a sense of joy as they experience Christ's love through us. As a result, they may not only feel comfortable and confident in our presence, but if they are Christians, they may be more highly motivated to continue serving the Lord. If they are not believers, our forgiveness may be the impetus God uses to bring them to a trusting relationship with Him. However, regardless of the response we encounter from others, we are called to extend forgiveness to anyone who injures us, whether the injury is slight or severe.

6. *a)* If you choose to withhold forgiveness from others, you are likely to become resentful. This will carry over into all of your relationships, including your relationship with God. You may become absorbed in thinking about the person who has harmed you, how this has hurt you, and how you can get even. Or, you may avoid this person, and as a result, miss out on the benefits that might accompany companionship with him or her. If your anger is prolonged and intense, it may result in severe depression or other psychosomatic problems.

b) If the person who has injured you is unaware of the harm he or she has caused you, he or she is likely to be confused by your behavior. In addition to experiencing a sense of alienation from you, this person may experience deep anxiety about you and your relationship.

7. We may never be able to completely forget the offense of another person against us. However, if we truly forgive, our perception of that individual will not be clouded by the memory of the offense. Gradually, we will be able to distinguish between the individual and his or her harmful behavior; our thoughts about that person will be increasingly characterized by love and compassion; and our desire will be to extend a blessing to him or her, rather than an insult (Rom. 12:14).

A FINAL WORD

Jesus said that He was sent by God *to proclaim release to the captives, and recovery of sight to the blind, to set free those who are downtrodden* . . . (Luke 4:18).

The Lord wants us to be freed from the bondage of past hurts and long-held grudges. For most of us, this is a process which requires that we *work out our salvation* (Phil. 2:12), in part, by replacing false beliefs with scriptural truths, and by choosing to forgive those who have hurt us.

Be patient with yourself as the Holy Spirit plays past events of your life back to you in present situations. Freedom from those instances is a journey which takes longer for some than for others. You will be making progress each time you gain an insight from your past which can affect both your present and your future. Learn to view pain as a positive motivator which can drive you toward God. Rather than running from it, allow God to use it for your good by walking through it with Him, giving Him an opportunity to remold your self-image, thinking, and behavior along the way.

The Ministry of the Holy Spirit: Dealing with Sin

Read chapter 14 in *The Search for Significance*.

This step will help you understand the Holy Spirit's ministry of convicting us of sin and guiding us into truth. You also will gain insights about confession of sin.

1. Read John 14:16-17. Why do you need a Helper?

   _____

   _____

2. What do the following passages say about the role of the Holy Spirit in teaching truth to you?

   a) John 14:26

   _____

   _____

   b) John 16:13

   _____

   _____

c) 1 Cor. 2:11-13

_____
_____

3. Read 2 Tim. 3:16-17. How does the Holy Spirit use Scripture in our lives?

_____
_____
_____
_____

4. Another role of the Holy Spirit is to convict the world concerning sin, righteousness, and judgment (John 16:8-11).

   a) What does it mean to be *convicted*?

   _____
   _____

   b) What is the purpose of the Holy Spirit's conviction?

   _____
   _____

5. Read 1 John 1:9.

   a) What is *confession?*

   _____
   _____

   b) Does confession make you forgiven?

   _____
   _____

6. Take a moment to allow the Holy Spirit to convict you of any ungodly thoughts or actions in the past week or so. List the sins that come to mind and confess them, using the outline on page 388 as a guide.

Review your answers with the following:

FOR ADDITIONAL INSIGHT

1. Christ realized that you could never live the Christian life in your own effort. Your bondage to your old nature and your unrenewed mind hinder you from understanding and applying God's truth. You may be overwhelmed with all you have studied so far in this workbook. However, it is the Holy Spirit's role, as your Helper, to enable you to understand and apply biblical truth. Depend on Him, not on your own abilities, to do this.

2. *a)* John 14:26: He will teach you all things and help you to remember what Christ has said.

    b) John 16:13: He will guide you into all truth.

    c) 1 Cor. 2:11-13: He will show you what things are from God, teaching you by combining spiritual thoughts with Scripture.

3. The Holy Spirit uses Scripture for four purposes in the believer's life:
    a) Teaching: Imparting knowledge of the truth.
    b) Reproof: Revealing areas in your life where you fall short of the truth.
    c) Correction: Getting you back on track.
    d) Training in righteousness: Helping you apply truth in the "nitty gritty" of your life: your finances, your schedule, your relationships.

4. *a)* *Convict* means to convince of error or sinfulness. The convicting work of the Holy Spirit is God's way of showing you that your thoughts and/or actions are contrary to your new nature in Christ.

   b) As we have seen, our ungodly thoughts, painful emotions, and disobedient actions usually originate in our false belief system. The Holy Spirit convicts us of ungodliness in order to (1) expose the wrongdoing; (2) expose its basis in false beliefs; (3) reestablish God's truth as the root of our thoughts and actions; (4) draw us back into a life of love and service for Christ.

   The following are some common mistakes we make when the Holy Spirit convicts us of sin:

(1) *Leaning on our own understanding.* The Lord has given the Holy Spirit to convict us of sin. The Holy Spirit needs no help in discovering what sins He wants to reveal to us
   A mature believer knows that the Father does not deal with every sin His children commit. We might go for a long period of time before the Holy Spirit puts His finger on something we should or should not be doing. Our heavenly Father knows how discouraging it would be for us to realize how far our performance is from the mark, so He begins to shape that performance by revealing a few sins to us at a time. The important issue is not that we realize all the sins we commit, but that we respond to those which He wishes to show us.
   The Holy Spirit's work of conviction begins as He reveals our obviously sinful acts to us—stealing or lying, for instance. Then, as we mature, His conviction is more often focused on sins of omission than commission—more on what we do not do than what we do.
   Some of the older saints spoke of their hearts breaking when they discovered that their motives for prayer or evangelism

weren't totally pure. It wasn't that they weren't sharing their faith or praying, but that their *motive* wasn't totally right. Won't it be wonderful when we mature to the place where this is an issue?

Avoid leaning on your own or any other person's understanding about what is sin in your life. Study the Scriptures to see what God wants for you, and listen to the conviction of the Holy Spirit.

(2) *Confusing guilt with conviction.* Review chapter 14, "Guilt vs. Conviction." You commit enough sins without having to worry about those thoughts and actions which aren't sins at all. Take your thoughts and deeds before the Lord to see what He thinks of them. Ask Him to show you which are guilt feelings and which are actually sins.

(3) *Turning conviction into condemnation.* God has declared you to be righteous, holy, and blameless. Christ bore all the condemnation you deserved at the cross. Therefore, the Holy Spirit's conviction of sin in your life is not a condemnation of you.

(4) *Not recognizing the root of sins.* Ungodly thoughts and actions are usually a reflection of the false beliefs you use to evaluate yourself. One of the Holy Spirit's goals in pointing out your sin is for you to see that you are basing your self-worth on false beliefs.

Use these points of conviction in order to identify false beliefs, reject them, and replace them with God's truth.

5. a) *Confession* means "to agree with." Confession is not dragging from our memory all the sins we've ever committed and telling them to God. Confession is agreeing with God concerning the specific sin we are convicted of. We agree with God in three ways:

(1) *Agreement*
   I sinned when I _____.
   The lie I was believing was _____.

(2) *Claiming Forgiveness*
   I am forgiven through Christ's death on the cross.

(3) *Repentance*
   I am deeply loved, completely forgiven, fully pleasing,
   totally accepted, complete in Christ. I now choose to act in
   a way that honors Him, which means I will _____

   _____.

b) Our confession does not make us forgiven. We have
forgiveness because Christ died to pay for our sins. Confession
is a means for us to *experience* our forgiveness, not a means for
us to *obtain* it. Confession should be done with an attitude of
repentance, which involves turning away from sin and turning to
God. Repentance is not a matter of feeling sorry just because we
got caught. True confession causes us to reject sin because it
grieves the Lord. Confession enables us to experience our
forgiveness and enjoy our fellowship with God.

An example of proper confession of sin:

Dear Father,
The Holy Spirit has pointed out to me that I sinned when
I (name specific thoughts and actions). *I was believing the*
lie (name specific false belief) *when I sinned. Thank you*
that I am completely forgiven, and that You choose not to
remember my sin. I reaffirm that You have declared me
to be deeply loved, completely forgiven, fully pleasing,
totally accepted, and a new creature—complete in Christ.
Amen.

6. The following points will give you some additional insights about confession:

    a)   All sin is against God. Notice how David recognized this in Ps. 51:4. He had committed adultery with Bathsheba and had then murdered her husband to cover up his sin. Although others had been affected by his sin, David recognized that its commission was primarily against God. In confronting David, Nathan the prophet asked, *Why have you despised the word of the Lord by doing evil in His sight?* (2 Sam. 12:9). Notice that the focus is on God, not David or others.

    When we have the truth of God's Word to guide us, and still choose to sin, God says we are *despising* Him. Few of us would openly tell God that we have no use for His Word, or worse, that we despise Him, yet that is actually what we are doing when we sin against Him. Perhaps if before choosing to sin, we would say to God, "I despise You and Your Word," we would be more enlightened about how sin grieves our heavenly Father.

    b)   Confession recognizes the full scope of sin. Correct confession requires that we not only recognize a specific act as sinful, but understand that the ungodly thoughts and false beliefs which generated the ungodliness are sinful as well. The excuses we might use to justify our sin are part of the ungodly thoughts that cause us to act in an ungodly manner. Narrowly defining sin as only a wrong action is misleading. We need to deal with the root of the action: the false belief.

    c)   *Confession involves accepting our forgiveness in Christ.* All too often, Christians construct a penance cycle that they believe they must put themselves through before they can feel forgiven. Once convicted of a sin, they might plead with God for forgiveness, and then feel depressed for a couple of days to show that they are really sorry and deserve to be forgiven.

This cycle is typical of "works-righteousness." The Lord Jesus died on the cross for our sins and has declared us justified. God not only forgives, He also forgets. Hebrews 10:17 says, *their sins and their lawless deeds I will remember no more.* We cannot earn our forgiveness by punishing ourselves. Confession is simply an application of the forgiveness we already have. Accepting our forgiveness allows us to move on in our fellowship with the Lord and to serve Him joyfully. God does not put us on the shelf and declare us permanently unusable because of our sin. Even after Peter's denials of Christ, he experienced forgiveness and was used powerfully by God as a leader of the church.

d) True confession involves repentance. Repentance means turning away from sin and turning instead to God. When we truly repent, we have a change of attitude about sin. In fact, because repentance involves recognizing the gravity of our sin, it should grieve us as much as it does God.

e) True confession may involve restitution. In confession, it may be necessary to make right a wrong. You may need to confess your sin to a fellow believer to ask for his or her forgiveness. You may need to pay back something you stole, or replace something you broke. Christ taught us that we should be reconciled to one another before we can move on (Matt. 5:23-24).

A FINAL WORD

The Lord Jesus realized that once He left the world, His followers would need help. The Holy Spirit, our helper and teacher, was sent to dwell within believers and to be our source of wisdom and strength. The Holy Spirit helps us to live in a way that honors Christ by convicting us of our ungodliness. Conviction allows us to deal with sin in our lives so that we can continue to experience God's love, power, and wisdom.

The Ministry of the Holy Spirit:
Living by Faith

Read chapter 11 in *The Search for Significance.*

    This step is designed to help you understand how God can empower you to live according to His truth. It might be tempting to set new biblical goals for your life and work harder to achieve them in your own efforts, but this would simply be implementing a biblical standard with the false belief: *I must meet certain standards to feel good about myself.* Failure would soon follow. We are to depend upon God's Spirit to complete the work He has started within us (Phil. 1:6).

THE HOLY SPIRIT: SOURCE OF ABUNDANT LIFE

1.   Read John 7:37-39 and answer the following questions:

    a)   *If any man is thirsty* is a metaphor for our desire and need for Christ. What does it mean to *drink* of Christ?

_____

_____

b)   In what ways are you *thirsty* for Him?

_____

_____

c)   What are some aspects of the Christian life that *rivers of living water* might symbolize?

_____

•_____

_____

d)   Jesus said that these "rivers" flow from our *innermost being*. What does this mean to you?

_____

_____

_____

2.   Read John 15:1-8. This passage contains another metaphor which illustrates that the Holy Spirit is the source of a life that honors Christ. Answer the following:

a)   Describe how a branch produces fruit (vv. 4-5):

_____

_____

_____

b)   What are some evidences of spiritual *fruit* within the believer's life?

_____

_____

_____

c)   John 15:2 says that God prunes every fruitful branch, that it may bear more fruit. What are some ways that God *prunes* us?

_____

_____

_____

d) What are some things that prevent a branch from producing fruit?

_____

_____

_____

e) What could prevent you from living a more fruitful, Christ-honoring life?

_____

_____

_____

f) Summarize Christ's teaching in these two passages (John 7:37-39 and John 15:1-8) in your own words:

_____

_____

_____

_____

_____

_____

_____

THE SCRIPTURES: BASIS OF A LIFE OF FAITH

The Scriptures are filled with facts and promises from God. Facts are statements that are *already* true of us. Promises are statements that we know *will be* fulfilled because of the trustworthiness of God. The following is a very short list of each:

Facts from God's Word

You are completely forgiven by God (Rom. 3:19-25;
Col. 2:13-14).

You are righteous and pleasing to God (2 Cor. 5:21).

You are totally accepted by God (Col. 1:19-22).

You are deeply loved by God (1 John 4:9-10).

You are absolutely complete in Christ (2 Cor. 5:17; Col. 2:10).

The Holy Spirit dwells in you (Rom. 8:9-11).

You are God's child (Rom. 8:15-16).

You are a fellow heir with Christ (Rom. 8:17).

God works all things together for good for those who love Him
(Rom. 8:28).

Promises from God's Word

Christ will never leave us (Matt. 28:20; Heb. 13:5).

He will abundantly provide for our needs (Phil. 4:19).

We will be in heaven with Him (John 14:1-3).

We will reign with Him (2 Tim. 2:12).

He will strengthen us (Is. 40:29).

He will give us His peace (John 14:27).

He will accomplish His purposes (1 Thess. 5:24).

He will enable us to give generously (2 Cor. 9:6-11).

We will be persecuted (John 15:18-21).

3. Which three of these facts and promises stand out to you? Why?
    How would trusting either that God has accomplished these facts,
    or that He will fulfill these promises, affect your life?

    a) Fact or Promise:

    _____

    _____

    (1) Why it stands out:

    _____

(2) How trusting God would affect you:

_____

_____

b) Fact or Promise:

_____

_____

(1) Why it stands out:

_____

_____

(2) How trusting God would affect you:

_____

_____

c) Fact or Promise:

_____

_____

(1) Why it stands out:

_____

_____

(2) How trusting God would affect you:

_____

_____

4. Romans 4:16-22 is an account of Abraham's faith. What things do you notice about his faith in this passage? In what promise from God was Abraham trusting? (See Gen. 15:5 and 17:5).

_____

_____

_____

_____

It is very instructive to go through a book of the Bible and identify the facts, promises, and commands listed there. In the next few days, do this exercise with Paul's letter to the Ephesians.

OBSTACLES TO LIVING A LIFE OF FAITH

Obstacles that can keep us from living a life of faith include:

- *Having the wrong purposes;* that is, living a self-centered, self-gratifying life instead of desiring to please Christ. In 2 Cor. 5:9, Paul writes, *Therefore also we have as our ambition...to be pleasing to Him.*

- *Being too mechanical.* The Christian life is first and foremost a relationship with Christ, not a list of rules. Discipline certainly has its place, but the source of *living water* (John 7:38) is our Lord.

- *Being too mystical.* Some of us wait until God has "spoken" to us before doing anything, seemingly oblivious to the clear teaching of the Scriptures to live a life of faith in Christ and His Word. There is definitely a mystical aspect to Christianity, but we must be careful not to fall into passivity. Some of us mistake our emotions as "signs from God." We tend to make decisions based on emotions instead of God's Word. We need to choose to read His Word, pray, and actively obey Him whether we sense His presence or not. God is honored by our faith in action despite our feelings.

- *Lack of knowledge about the love and power of Christ.* Sadly, many Christians are uninformed about the wealth of love and power available to them through Christ.

- *Sin clouds our fellowship with Christ.* Sin is destructive to us and dishonoring to the Lord. At its root, all sin is like Eve's rebellion in the Garden. It is the desire to be like God and to run our own lives. It is turning our backs on Christ, our Savior and source of light and life.

- *Spiritual conflict.* The *world* (the inordinate desire for success, comfort, prestige, etc. [1 John 2:15-17]); the *flesh* (the inordinate desire to gratify our sensuality, e.g., sex, overeating, alcohol, and drugs [Gal. 5:16-21]); and *Satan* (Eph. 6:10-12) all war against us with the aim of causing us to forsake the Lord and His purposes for the wanton pleasures of this life.

5. Read over these carefully. Which of these obstacles hinder you in your relationship with Christ? What can you do to begin overcoming them?

_____

_____

_____

_____

Your Response

You can claim God's promises and live a life of faith that honors Him if you:

Desire. Do you honestly desire to honor Christ and minister to others? If so...

Confess any sin (or sins). Remember, *confession* is agreeing with God that a specific sin is, indeed, sin; agreeing with Him that you are forgiven by the death of Christ; and repentance—turning to God in obedience to His Word.

Present. Then present all areas of your life to Christ as "instruments of righteousness." Paul wrote to the believers in Rome:

> *Therefore do not let sin reign in your mortal body that you should obey its lusts,*
>
> *and do not go on presenting the members of your body to sin as instruments of unrighteousness; but present yourselves to God as those alive from the dead, and your members as instruments of righteousness to God.*
>
> Rom. 6:12-13

> *I urge you therefore, brethren, by the mercies of God, to present your bodies a living and holy sacrifice, acceptable to God, which is your spiritual service of worship.*
>
> *And do not be conformed to this world, but be transformed by the renewing of your mind, that you may prove what the will of God is, that which is good and acceptable and perfect.*
>
> Rom. 12:1-2

Obey. Give thanks to the Lord for His grace and power, and continue to trust Him moment by moment. Depend on His Word. Let the Holy Spirit use you in the lives of others, and deal with any sin as soon as you become aware of it so that your fellowship with Him won't be hindered.

6. As you reflect on these principles of faith, where are you in this process? What will your next step be?

_____

_____

_____

Use the following to compare your answers and to gain additional insight from this study:

FOR ADDITIONAL INSIGHT

1. *a)* To *drink* of Christ can mean to believe in His love and power, to enjoy Him, and to be satisfied by Him.

    b) You may be experiencing a sense of thirst for Christ because you feel distant from Him; you may be grieved because some aspect of your life doesn't honor Him, or because you have committed specific sins of immorality, jealousy, worry, criticism, or anger; you may feel very dry and rigid because you live a "rules-dominated" life.

    c) *Rivers of living water* may symbolize the love, joy, and intimacy of knowing Christ; the power to be effective in evangelism and discipleship; love for the unlovely; any expression of the life of Christ flowing through the believer.

    d) This means that the "rivers" are not externally contrived. They arc from the heart—a spontaneous overflow of the very nature of Christ produced in us by the Holy Spirit. The sheer strength of the human will *can* produce changes in a life, but because the source isn't the Holy Spirit, pride is the result, instead of thankfulness and humility.

2. *a)* A branch produces fruit by allowing the water and nutrients from the vine to flow through it. The fruit is the natural, spontaneous expression of a healthy branch.

    b) Hebrews 13:15 says that a sacrifice of praise to God is *the fruit of lips that give thanks to His name.* Galatians 5:22-23 says that *the fruit of the Spirit is love, joy, peace, patience, kindness, goodness, faithfulness, gentleness, self-control*—Christian character. Throughout the New Testament and the history of the Church, we see another fruit of those who allow the Holy Spirit to produce the love and power of Christ in their lives: the salvation of many people.

c) God may prune us by allowing us to experience troubles and difficulties, sickness, failure, or reproof from either Christians or non-Christians.

d) A branch can't bear fruit if it's cut off, or if it contracts a disease, is eaten by insects, is placed in poor environmental conditions, etc.

e) Your Christian life could be hindered if your love for Christ grew cold, if you developed an inordinate desire for worldly pleasures, if you sought to gain the approval of others, if you tried to gain your significance from success, if you couldn't experience the wealth of God's love and power, if you pursued a life of abject disobedience, etc.

f) In your summary, consider the Holy Spirit's purpose to glorify Christ (John 16:14); what the Holy Spirit can produce in one's life; and what could hinder the branch from producing fruit and the thirsty person from experiencing the *rivers of living water* (John 7:38).

3. These facts and promises may appeal to you because they relate to your security, your physical needs, or your desire to minister to others.

   In your future study of God's Word, you might want to put an *F*, a *P*, and a *C* in the margin of your Bible to designate a *fact*, a *promise*, and a *command*. This will make you more aware of Scripture's personal applications.

4. Abraham's faith existed in spite of his circumstances. He did not waiver in unbelief, but was fully assured. The specific promise was that he would be the *father of many nations.*

5. It may be that only one obstacle hinders you, or that several of them are problems for you. Write down a clear, biblical remedy for each obstacle. Ask the Lord to help you. Make yourself accountable by coming back to it periodically to see how you are doing. Don't give up if you fail! Keep trusting Him to strengthen you as you follow Him.

6. We have a choice. The Lord will not force us to follow Him, but He is willing and able to fully meet our needs if we are willing to give Him the glory for the results. A life of joy, fruitfulness, strength, and influence in a needy world awaits any believer who will trust Him. D.L. Moody was an unknown cobbler when he heard someone say, "The world has yet to see what God can do through one man whose heart is completely His." D.L. Moody responded, "Lord, I want to be that man!" Moody became one of the world's leading evangelists because of his intense desire to honor Christ and be used by Him. Will you respond like D.L. Moody and say to God, "Lord, I want to be that man (or that woman)!"?

A FINAL WORD

The truth that *you are deeply loved, completely forgiven, fully pleasing, totally accepted, and a new creature in Christ* will never work its way into your thoughts, emotions, and actions through a self-improvement program. If you have been depending on your own effort to live the Christian life, stop for a moment and confess that as sin. Thank the Lord for your forgiveness in Christ, and ask the Holy Spirit to empower you to experience the truth that *you are deeply loved, fully pleasing, totally accepted, and a new creature in Christ.*

When we depend on God, will we feel His love and strength? Maybe, maybe not. Our culture would make us think that our feelings are the most important way of determining if our actions are valid. But as Christians, we have a much higher authority than our feelings. We have the truth of God's Word, and we can choose, as an act of our will, to obey Him. Our will is paramount, not our feelings. The French philosopher Fenelon said, "The essence of Christianity resides in the will." Our feelings *may* reflect the love of Christ as we forgive others, share our faith, give generously, and demonstrate other spiritual characteristics in our lives. But on many occasions, our emotions are inconsistent, unpredictable, and diametrically opposed to God's Word. Often, we refuse to obey Him because we don't *feel* like it. For example, we may be afraid to share our faith because someone might reject us, or we may continue to indulge in sin because we don't *feel* like stopping. But what about the times when we earnestly want to obey God, and our emotions say, *NO!*? Here are some possible reasons our feelings may oppose the ways of God:

1) Our sinful nature may be prompting us to disobey God. Galatians 5:17 says, *For the flesh sets its desire against the Spirit, and the Spirit against the flesh; for these are in opposition to one another....*

2) We may be experiencing spiritual conflict. Satan, our enemy, is a thief who *comes only to steal, and kill, and destroy* (John 10:10). If he can get us to live by our feelings instead of God's Word, then he will effectively steal our joy, kill our motivation to live for Christ, and destroy the consistency of our Christian testimony.

3) It may be that our negative emotions are simply the residual feelings of the fear of failure or the fear of rejection that we are in the process of overcoming by claiming God's truth.

When you choose to believe God's Word, your emotions may not follow immediately. Does that mean you aren't trusting God? No. Faith is often exercised in the context of struggle, in the midst of conflicting thoughts and emotions. A look at the people of God in the Scriptures shows that their faith was not in the absence of doubts and struggles, but in the *face* of doubts and struggles. The idea that faith is only found apart from conflicting thoughts and emotions is one of Satan's schemes to confuse and discourage you. When we trust in God, we will experience many obstacles to faith, but placing our trust in His Word—not our feelings—will see us through.

Step Nineteen
Renewing Our Minds

Read chapter 10 in *The Search for Significance.*

Steps 19-22 explain the process of laying aside the old self and putting on the new self, so that our thoughts, emotions, and actions increasingly reflect the character of Christ.

This exercise is based on 2 Cor. 10:3-5:

> *For though we walk in the flesh, we do not war according to the flesh,*
> *for the weapons of our warfare are not of the flesh, but divinely powerful for the destruction of fortresses.*
> *We are destroying speculations and every lofty thing raised up against the knowledge of God, and we are taking every thought captive to the obedience of Christ.*

Believe it or not, desire it or not, understand it or not, we are at war. Most of us don't like to think about spiritual warfare, hoping, like the proverbial ostrich with his head in the sand, that it will pass us by. The battlefield is the mind. Paul instructs us:

> *...be transformed by the renewing of your mind, that*
> *you may prove what the will of God is, that which is good*
> *and acceptable and perfect.*
>
> Rom. 12:2

Satan's goal is to keep our minds unrenewed, so that we won't be transformed. He does this by establishing fortresses of deception which produce thoughts that are against the knowledge or understanding of God. Fortresses of deception are belief systems that are reinforced over the years by the thoughts, emotions, and actions they produce. It is a self-feeding system. For instance, if a person believes that he is a failure, when he succeeds, his belief system (his fortress) will produce such thoughts as:

- *What luck!*
- *It's about time. Look at all the failure you had to go through just to get one success.*
- *How unusual for a loser like you to do something right.*

If the person fails, his belief system will produce such thoughts as:

- *I told you you'd fail.*
- *What a loser you are.*
- *You can't help it, you just can't do any better.*

Whether he succeeds or fails, the result is the same. His belief that he is a failure is reinforced.

The following exercise will teach you how to begin establishing a stronghold of truth in your mind through memorization and meditation. This mind-renewal is essential to the application of step 21: Rejecting Satan's lies and replacing them with God's truth.

ESTABLISHING A STRONGHOLD OF TRUTH

The Truth Card

A simple 3x5 card can be a key factor in helping you base your self-worth on the liberating truths of the Scriptures.

1. To make the Truth Card, use a 3x5 card. On the front, write out both the following truths and their corresponding verses from Scripture:

    I am deeply loved by God (1 John 4:9-10).
    I am completely forgiven, and am fully pleasing to God (Rom. 5:1).
    I am totally accepted by God (Col. 1:21-22).
    I am a new creation, complete in Christ (2 Cor. 5:17).

On the back of the card, write out the false beliefs listed on page 231.

2. Learn how to use the Truth Card.

    Carry this card with you continuously. Each time you are about to do a routine activity, like have something to drink, look at the front side and slowly meditate on each phrase. Thank the Lord for making you into a person who has these qualities. By doing this for the next twenty-eight days, you will develop a habit of remembering that you are deeply loved, completely forgiven, fully pleasing, totally accepted, and complete in Christ.

    If you have not already done so, memorize the supporting verses listed on the card over the next four days. Look in your Bible for other verses that support these truths and commit them to memory. Doing this will establish God's Word as the basis for your beliefs (Col. 3:16).

    Also memorize the false beliefs. The more familiar you are with these lies, the more you will be able to recognize them in your thoughts. Then, as you recognize them, you can more readily replace them with the truths of God's Word.

Properly Evaluating Yourself and Others

For in the way you judge, you will be judged; and by your standard of measure, it will be measured to you (Matt. 7:2). From this passage of Scripture, and from what we know about ourselves, we can draw the following conclusions and applications:

1. We use the same methods for judging others that we use to judge ourselves.

2. Though some of us are more reflective than others, all of us spend a great deal of time evaluating our performance.

3. We have a choice. We can use the same method we have always used to evaluate ourselves and others (Our Self-Worth = Performance + Others' Opinions), or we can adopt God's judgment (Our Self-Worth = God's Truth About Us).

4. If we want our lives to be what God has designed them to be, then we must use His truth (rather than our own opinions) as our standard of evaluation.

5. To accomplish this change in mindset, we need to apply the following action points:

    a) When we see another person (especially if this person has offended us in some way), we should think, and if possible, state verbally, "This person has great worth apart from his performance because Christ gave His life for him and, therefore, imparted great value to him. If this person has accepted Christ, *he is deeply loved, fully pleasing, completely forgiven, totally accepted, and complete in Christ.*"

b) We can tell those in our families, whom we know are Christians, "You are deeply loved, completely forgiven, fully pleasing, totally accepted, and complete in Christ."

6. As you do this, you will automatically begin to use the same system of evaluation on yourself, and thereby reinforce these truths as the basis of your own self-worth.

7. You can apply this exercise in both your own life and your family members' lives after failures. Affirmation of love and acceptance can be powerful in shaping a healthy self-concept!

Exposing Ungodly Thoughts

Our thoughts reveal what we really believe, yet it is difficult for most of us to be objective in our thinking simply because we haven't trained ourselves to be. We usually let any and every thought run its course in our minds without analyzing its worth. Is it a God-honoring thought, or is it a speculation, or a *lofty thing raised up against the knowledge of God* (2 Cor. 10:5)?

It is very helpful to be able to identify thoughts that are not honoring to God. Then, we can reject them and replace them with truth. One way of identifying such thoughts is to state what is true and see what thoughts come to mind. Hopefully, our thoughts will increasingly reflect our thankfulness to God for who He is and what He has done for us, but sometimes, we will respond by contradicting the truth.

For example, you might respond to the truth that you are fully pleasing to God by thinking, *No, I'm not! I mess up all the time; to be fully pleasing, I'd have to be perfect!* When we see it written out, we easily recognize that response as a lie. However, we seldom write down our thoughts and analyze their validity.

As a first step in this analysis, write down your thoughts in response to the four truths we've examined. (Again, they will probably be mixed: some positive, thankful, and godly, and some contradictory to the truth.)

- *I am deeply loved by God:*

  _____

  _____

  _____

- *I am completely forgiven and am fully pleasing to God:*

  _____

  _____

  _____

- *I am totally accepted by God:*

  _____

  _____

  _____

- *I am complete in Christ:*

  _____

  _____

  _____

Thoughts that contradict these truths are lies. Reject them and replace them with passages of Scripture to reinforce the truth in your mind. Here are some passages to reflect on:

- *Justification*: Rom. 3:19-24; 4:4-5; 5:1-11; Titus 2:11-14.
- *Propitiation*: Matt. 18:21-35; Luke 7:36-50; Rom. 3:25; 8:1-8; Col. 3:12-14; Heb. 2:17; 3:4-7.
- *Reconciliation*: John 15:14-16; Rom. 5:8-10; 8:15; Eph. 2:11-18.
- *Regeneration*: 2 Cor. 5:17; Gal. 5:16-24; Eph. 2:4-5; 4:22-24; Col. 3:5-17.

A FINAL WORD

Our thoughts are seldom neutral. They either reflect beliefs based on the Word of God or beliefs based on the world's values. The Lord can give us the perception we need to identify the source of our thoughts and determine if they are of Him or not. The more our thoughts are in line with God's Word, the more our actions will be honoring to Him. In fact, the purity of our thoughts ultimately determines how much our lives will honor Christ. Paul told Titus that Christ *gave Himself for us, that He might redeem us from every lawless deed and purify for Himself a people for His own possession, zealous for good deeds* (Titus 2:14).

Step Twenty
Identifying False Beliefs

This is a pivotal point in the process of understanding and applying all that has come before! So, take your time. Be honest about your emotions. Reflect on the principles brought out here, and apply them to specific instances in your life. As you do, you will probably realize that Satan's lies have controlled your life far more than you previously realized. You will probably also realize that God's love and power can progressively free you from introspection, anger, and fear, and give you a heart of thankfulness and a greater desire to live for Him.

First, you need to realize where your emotions and actions come from. Jesus said, *Out of the abundance of the heart the mouth speaketh* (Matt. 12:34, KJV). In other words, our communication (which reveals our thoughts, emotions, and the intent of our actions) comes from our hearts (our belief system). Because every situation in our lives is interpreted by what we believe, our belief system, not the situation, is the key to our response! The following diagram illustrates this process:

Situation

⇩

Belief System ⇨ **Thoughts** ⇨ **Emotions** ⇨ **Actions**

413

In addition to comprising our reactions to immediate events, our emotions are products of our family backgrounds, our past experiences and relationships, and patterns of responses. Many of us come from homes where we were not loved and affirmed as children. We may have learned to repress painful emotions because we didn't want to believe that something was wrong with our families, our source of stability and security. Some of us have become numb, unable to feel either anger or joy, hurt or love. Some of us have developed a habit of forgetting difficult instances and their accompanying pain as a defense mechanism. There are many different ways to block pain and try to gain a sense of worth, but we need to begin reversing this trend by finding someone who will encourage us to be honest about our feelings. We can use our feelings as a gauge to determine if our response to a situation is based on the truth or a lie.

Painful or distressing emotions, chiefly anger or fear, are often an indication that we are basing our self-worth on our performance or others' opinions of us. These negative emotions surface when that falsely-based self-worth has been shattered or is even threatened. There are many variations of anger and fear, including bitterness, rage, disgust, hurt, tension, withdrawal, and anxiety, but not all anger and fear are negative. Feelings are neither right nor wrong. They are signals which tell us something about our environment. We need to be honest about our emotions so that they can tell us what we need to know about our perceptions.

When our emotions are painful or distressing, we need to ask, *Why am I responding this way? Am I believing a lie? If so, which one?*

TRACING EMOTIONS TO ROOT BELIEFS

Let's suppose that someone (Bill) picked you up late, so you are late to work (or school, or church, or to a committee meeting). Your response is anger. You can trace that anger back to its root false belief in order to replace it with corresponding truths from the Scriptures.

The following is an illustration:

Situation: Bill picked you up late. You are late to work.

⇩

False Belief ⇨   *Ungodly*   ⇨ *Emotions* ⇨ *Ungodly*
                      Thoughts   *Actions*
(?)   ⬉_____ *Anger*

How do you determine the false belief responsible for your anger? Ask yourself, *Why am I angry? Am I angry because...*

- *I hate to be late* (your "certain standard"), *and my lateness makes me feel badly about myself. (I must meet certain standards...)*

- *My boss will be displeased with me because I'm late, and her opinion of me means so much. (I must be approved by certain others...)*

- *Bill failed by being late to pick me up. It was his fault, that creep! (Those who fail are unworthy of love and deserve to be punished.)*

- *No matter what I do, something always goes wrong. (I am hopeless. I can't change. I will always be this way.)*

Note that the proper response is not, *I'm not angry,* when in fact you are. Denial only compounds our problems; it is not a solution. We need to be honest with the Lord and with ourselves about our feelings.

If the situation in the above example had happened to you, what would your emotion(s) probably have been? Which false belief(s) can you trace your emotion(s) back to?

Recent Situations

Think over the past two weeks, and list five recent situations in which you have had distressing or painful emotions. Take time to reflect on the following questions about each occasion: What

415

emotion(s) were you experiencing? What were your actions? What false belief(s) were you believing?

1. SITUATION:
_____
_____
_____
_____

   a) Emotion(s):
_____
_____
_____

   b) Ungodly Action(s):
_____
_____
_____

   c) False Belief(s):
_____
_____
_____

2. SITUATION:
_____
_____
_____
_____

   a) Emotion(s):
_____

_____

_____

    b) Ungodly Action(s):

_____

_____

_____

    c) False Belief(s):

_____

_____

_____

3. SITUATION:

_____

_____

_____

_____

    a) Emotion(s):

_____

_____

_____

    b) Ungodly Action(s):

_____

_____

_____

    c) False Belief(s):

_____

_____

4. SITUATION:

_____

_____

_____

_____

a)   Emotion(s):

_____

_____

_____

b)   Ungodly Action(s):

_____

_____

_____

c)   False Belief(s):

_____

_____

_____

5. SITUATION:

_____

_____

_____

_____

a)   Emotion(s):

_____

_____

_____

b) Ungodly Action(s):

_____

_____

_____

c) False Belief(s):

_____

_____

_____

Recurring Situations

What are some recurring situations in which you frequently have painful or distressing emotions? Some of these may have shown up in the list above, and perhaps include things like: meeting new people, seeing someone whose clothes or mannerisms are different than yours, preparing for a big exam, being late, mingling at parties, being alone, spending extended periods of time with your parents, entertaining people at your home, having to clean up when your spouse or roommate leaves the dishes dirty, despairing when someone disagrees with you or is disappointed in you; being frustrated over a "flaw" in your appearance.

What recurring situations trigger anxiety, anger, fear, sarcasm, withdrawal, or nagging for you? List some of those situations in the spaces below. How do you usually respond? Which false belief is at the root of this response?

1. SITUATION:

_____

_____

_____

_____

    a) Emotion(s):

_____

_____

_____

    b) Ungodly Action(s):

_____

_____

_____

    c) False Belief(s):

_____

_____

_____

2. SITUATION:

_____

_____

_____

_____

    a) Emotion(s):

_____

_____

_____

    b) Ungodly Action(s):

_____

_____

_____

c) False Belief(s):

_____

_____

_____

3. SITUATION:

_____

_____

_____

_____

    a) Emotion(s):

_____

_____

_____

    b) Ungodly Action(s):

_____

_____

_____

    c) False Belief(s):

_____

_____

_____

4. SITUATION:

_____

_____

_____

_____

    a) Emotion(s):

_____

_____

_____

    b) Ungodly Action(s):

_____

_____

_____

    c) False Belief(s):

_____

_____

_____

5. SITUATION:

_____

_____

_____

_____

    a) Emotion(s):

_____

_____

_____

    b) Ungodly Action(s):

_____

_____

_____

c) False Belief(s):

_____

_____

_____

A FINAL WORD

This week, every time you realize that you are responding to a situation with a negative, painful emotion, stop to ask yourself, *Why?* and trace it back to its root false belief. Keep a sheet of paper with you and write down those situations, your emotions, ungodly actions, and root false beliefs. You will be using this exercise in step 21.

Step Twenty-One
Reject/Replace

Read chapter 12 in *The Search for Significance*.

In step 20, we saw how we can use our emotions to help us analyze why we respond the way we do. Painful emotions, such as anger, fear, resentment, and anxiety can show us that we are believing Satan's lies. Being honest about these and other emotions is crucial in our application of God's Word! Once we become aware of the specific lie that is affecting us, we can then apply God's specific solution to that lie from His Word—a process that often occurs best in the context of affirming relationships.

If we are not aware of the specific lie we are believing, we usually attempt to meet our need with any and every biblical truth—knowing that it is true and hoping that it will help. However, if Scripture doesn't speak powerfully to our specific need, we can become frustrated and disillusioned instead of freed and encouraged.

In this step, we will go beyond tracing our emotions to their false beliefs. We will learn how to replace insidious lies with the powerful Word of God, so that our thoughts and actions will increasingly glorify God.

Our diagram, then, looks like this:

Painful
Emotions

Recent Situations

First, let's look at the assignment from step 20. List several of the situations with the corresponding emotions, ungodly actions, and false beliefs you identified in that step. Then, write out the specific solution to the situation from the Scriptures with a passage or two. Describe how your initial response would have been different if you had believed God's truth instead of Satan's lie, and finally, complete the statement that summarizes the proper response to that situation. Look at the Final Word in step 9, or at the following example for a good understanding of the summary statement. If you don't want to use the situations you described in step 20, use any others that come to mind. The example we will use is the same as in step 20.

Example:
Situation:
- a) *Bill picked me up late.*
- b) *I was late to work.*

Emotions:
- a) *Anger at Bill.*
- b) *Fear that my boss would be upset with me.*

Ungodly Actions:
- a) *I hardly spoke to Bill all day.*
- b) *I avoided looking at my boss's eyes. I withdrew from her.*

False Beliefs:
  a) *Those who fail are unworthy of love and deserve to be blamed and condemned.*
  b) *I must be approved by certain others to feel good about myself.*

God's Truth (Passages):
  a) Propitiation: *I am deeply loved by God; therefore, I can love others with God's love* (1 John 4:9-11).
  b) Reconciliation: *I am totally accepted by God* (Col. 1:19-22).

Supposed Godly Response:
  a) *Forgive Bill; help him any way I can; offer to take my car if his isn't running well; be cheerful.*
  b) *Apologize to my boss; relax and realize that there was nothing I could do about being late this morning. Hopefully, she will understand, but if not, I need to do my work with peace and joy.*

Summary Statement:
  a) *It would be nice if Bill had picked me up on time, but he didn't. Even so, Bill is deeply loved by God.*
  b) *It would be nice if my boss really liked me and accepted me, but if she doesn't, I'm still deeply loved, completely forgiven, fully pleasing, and totally accepted by God.*

1. SITUATION:

    _____

    _____

    _____

    _____

a)   Emotion(s):

_____

_____

_____

b)   Ungodly Action(s):

_____

_____

_____

c)   False Belief(s):

_____

_____

_____

d)   God's Truth (Passages):

_____

_____

_____

e)   Supposed Godly Response:

_____

_____

_____

f)   Summary Statement: *It would be nice if...*

_____

_____

_____

2. SITUATION:

_____

_____

_____

_____

    a) Emotion(s):

_____

_____

_____

    b) Ungodly Action(s):

_____

_____

_____

    c) False Belief(s):

_____

_____

_____

    d) God's Truth (Passages):

_____

_____

_____

    e) Supposed Godly Response:

_____

_____

_____

f) Summary Statement: *It would be nice if...*

_____
_____
_____

3. SITUATION:

_____
_____
_____

a) Emotion(s):

_____
_____
_____

b) Ungodly Action(s):

_____
_____
_____

c) False Belief(s):

_____
_____
_____

d) God's Truth (Passages):

_____
_____
_____

e) Supposed Godly Response:

_____

_____

_____

f) Summary Statement: *It would be nice if...*

_____

_____

_____

4. SITUATION:

_____

_____

_____

_____

a) Emotion(s):

_____

_____

_____

b) Ungodly Action(s):

_____

_____

_____

c) False Belief(s):

_____

_____

_____

d) God's Truth (Passages):

_____

_____

_____

e) Supposed Godly Response:

_____

_____

_____

f) Summary Statement: *It would be nice if...*

_____

_____

_____

5. SITUATION:

_____

_____

_____

_____

a) Emotion(s):

_____

_____

_____

b) Ungodly Action(s):

_____

_____

_____

c) False Belief(s):

_____

_____

_____

d) God's Truth (Passages):

_____

_____

_____

e) Supposed Godly Response:

_____

_____

_____

f) Summary Statement: *It would be nice if...*

_____

_____

_____

Recurring Situations

All of us have developed patterns of responding based on our family backgrounds, our past experiences, and our personalities. These patterns can be very healthy and productive if they are based on strong, loving parents and a consistent life of honesty and courage. But the number of dysfunctional families is increasing, and the corresponding response patterns in the lives of family members are becoming more painful and destructive. The response patterns that we have developed show up in situations which tend to recur fairly often.

Use the situations you listed in step 20, or add those that have come to mind since you completed that step. Describe your response and write out the corresponding truth with Scripture passages, citing how believing God's truth can affect you if you choose to apply it in these situations.

1. SITUATION:

    _____
    _____
    _____
    _____

    a) Emotion(s):

    _____
    _____
    _____

    b) Ungodly Action(s):

    _____
    _____
    _____

    c) False Belief(s):

    _____
    _____
    _____

    d) God's Truth (Passages):

    _____
    _____
    _____

    e) Supposed Godly Response:

    _____
    _____

f) Summary Statement: *It would be nice if...*

_____

_____

_____

2. SITUATION:

_____

_____

_____

_____

a) Emotion(s):

_____

_____

_____

b) Ungodly Action(s):

_____

_____

_____

c) False Belief(s):

_____

_____

_____

d) God's Truth (Passages):

_____

_____

_____

e) Supposed Godly Response:

_____

_____

_____

    f)   Summary Statement: *It would be nice if...*

_____

_____

_____

3. SITUATION:

_____

_____

_____

_____

    a) Emotion(s):

_____

_____

_____

    b) Ungodly Action(s):

_____

_____

_____

    c) False Belief(s):

_____

_____

_____

    d) God's Truth (Passages):

_____

_____

e)   Supposed Godly Response:

_____

_____

_____

f)   Summary Statement: *It would be nice if...*

_____

_____

_____

4. SITUATION:

_____

_____

_____

_____

a)   Emotion(s):

_____

_____

_____

b)   Ungodly Action(s):

_____

_____

_____

c)   False Belief(s):

_____

_____

_____

    d)   God's Truth (Passages):

_____

_____

_____

    e)   Supposed Godly Response:

_____

_____

_____

    f)   Summary Statement: *It would be nice if...*

_____

_____

_____

5.   SITUATION:

_____

_____

_____

_____

    a)   Emotion(s):

_____

_____

_____

    b)   Ungodly Action(s):

_____

_____

_____

c) False Belief(s):

_____

_____

_____

d) God's Truth (Passages):

_____

_____

_____

e) Supposed Godly Response:

_____

_____

_____

f) Summary Statement: *It would be nice if...*

_____

_____

_____

A FINAL WORD

Hopefully, you are now gaining a better understanding of how to use your emotions to identify your beliefs, so that you can reject Satan's lies and replace them with God's truths. But do not expect perfection! You have built your existing belief system over a period of many years. You may have experienced the deep pain of a dysfunctional family background, neglect, abuse, and chronic condemnation. Belief systems do not change easily or quickly. Sometimes, replacing lies with the truth will seem easy, while at other times, it will be very frustrating.

The enemy of our soul does not want us to be freed from his lies. Expect spiritual battle, uneasy feelings, and some discouragement. But be patient and persistent! As you apply these principles, the time interval between your painful emotions and your ability to replace lies with the truth will generally become shorter and shorter. As you claim the truth of God's Word, memorizing it and meditating on it, you may even find yourself responding with godly thoughts, emotions, and actions at the outset of difficult situations!

Hang in there. Be alert and aware of Satan's lies (Eph. 6:10-12; 1 Pet. 5:8-9). The enemy will want to confuse you and muddle your thinking. The simple act of writing out your situations, emotions, and responses can be an amazingly helpful weapon in enabling you to be specific and effective in your battle. You may want to do this at a certain time every day until it becomes second nature to recognize your negative emotions, trace them back to their root false beliefs, and replace them with God's truth.

The Lord is for you! He will give you wisdom, strength, and encouragement...so keep at it!

Step Twenty-Two
Proclaiming His Excellencies

This step explains our privilege and responsibility to be Christ's ambassadors in a lost world. God has set us apart to be the light and salt of the world, and His Spirit enables us to powerfully influence those around us for all eternity. We have the ability to see the world's spiritual poverty through God's eyes and offer to it His magnificent solution.

1. According to 1 Pet. 2:9 (NIV), you are *a chosen people, a royal priesthood, a holy nation, and a people belonging to God.* What do these terms mean to you? Think of what you've learned already concerning justification, reconciliation, propitiation, and regeneration.

   _____

   _____

   _____

2. What is the result of being specifically chosen by God? (See Eph. 2:10 and 1 Pet. 2:9.)

   _____

   _____

441

3. Read Luke 19:10. What was Jesus' goal in coming to earth?

_____

_____

4. Read Matt. 4:19 and 28:18-20. As we yield our lives to God and the truth of His Word, what will we inevitably be involved in?

_____

_____

5. Reflect on what Christ has done for you. Use your Bible to make a list of as many things as possible. Then, make a parallel list of what was true of you before you trusted in Christ:

Before Christ   In Christ

_____   _____

_____   _____

_____   _____

_____   _____

_____   _____

6. Do you have a sense of gratitude for what Christ has done for you? If not, why?

_____

_____

7. Read 1 Cor. 6:19-20 and 2 Cor. 5:14-15. How does your perception of what Christ has done for you affect your motivation to communicate the gospel to others?

_____

_____

8. Do you view your unsaved family and friends as people for whom Christ died and to whom He wants to extend salvation (John 3:17-18)? If not, why?

_____

_____

_____

9. How does your perception of the lostness of those without Christ affect your desire to share your faith?

_____

_____

_____

10. To what extent has Satan deceived Christians about the lostness of people? How can you tell?

_____

_____

_____

11. Read John 17:18; Acts 1:8; Rom. 1:14-16; and 2 Cor. 5:18-20. What is your personal role in evangelism?

_____

_____

12. Who is the person you would most like to tell about Christ?

_____

Review your answers with the following:

FOR ADDITIONAL INSIGHT

1. God has chosen you [*out of the world*] to be His (John 15:19). You are special because you are His. You have "royal blood" because you are God's own son or daughter (John 1:12). You are *holy and blameless* because of Christ (Col. 1:19-22). *Once you were not a people, but now you are the people of God* (1 Pet. 2:10). God cares for you, loves you, and provides for you beyond what any earthly father does for his children. You are His and He is yours (1 Cor. 6:19-20).

2. The result of being specifically chosen by God is that you will *proclaim the excellencies of Him who has called you out of darkness into His marvelous light* (1 Pet. 2:9). Paul states in Eph. 2:10 that you are created in Christ to do good works. God has made you His ambassador, the light of the world.

3. Christ's goal was to seek and save the lost. No one took Jesus' life against His will (John 10:17-18). He willingly gave it to redeem a lost world.

4. As we follow Him, we will continue to be transformed, and will become more like Him. Therefore, we will increasingly be involved in reaching the world for Christ, because the world is on His heart.

5. Your list could look like this:

BEFORE CHRIST	IN CHRIST
enemy of God (Rom. 5:10)	child of God (1 John 3:1)
death (Rom. 6:23)	eternal life (John 5:24)
no hope (Eph. 2:12)	hope (1 Pet. 1:3-5)
separated from God (Col. 1:21)	loved (John 17:23)
guilty (John 3:36)	forgiven (Eph. 1:7)
hostile to God (Eph. 2:12-15)	peace with God (Rom. 5:1)
condemned (John 3:17-18)	not condemned (John 3:17-18)

6. If you don't have a sense of gratitude, you've probably not fully comprehended what God has done for you. Jesus said that he who is forgiven little, loves little. He who is forgiven much, loves much (Luke 7:40-47). If you understand salvation as your goodness plus Christ, you're tragically mistaken. God justifies the ungodly (Rom. 4:4-5). You were His enemy, but now you are saved by His marvelous grace.

To put things in perspective about performance, during what percentage of the time do you follow these commands?

a) Love God with all your heart, soul, mind, and strength (Mark 12:30): _____%

b) Hate the world and things in the world (1 John 2:15): _____%

c) Bless those who persecute you (Rom. 12:14): _____%

d) Set your heart and mind on the things above (Col. 3:1-2): _____%

e) Rejoice in the Lord always (Phil. 4:4): _____%

f) Do nothing from selfishness or conceit (Phil. 2:3): _____%

g) Are filled with the Spirit (Eph. 5:18): _____%

h) Let no unwholesome word come from your mouth (Eph. 4:29): _____%

i) Seek first the kingdom of God and His righteousness (Matt. 6:33): _____%

j) Demonstrate holiness in all you do (1 Pet. 1:15): _____%

Is your performance "good" enough? James wrote, *For whoever keeps the whole law and yet stumbles in one point, he has become guilty of all* (James 2:10). So even one sin makes us worthy of eternal condemnation. Our self-righteous activities cannot pacify the righteous wrath of God. It is critical that we understand all God has done for us in Christ. Don't let Satan deceive you! You were in desperate need of a Savior. Christ bore your punishment. Praise and thank Him for the rest of your life!

7. Your gratitude for what Christ has done for you motivates you to live for Him and share His love with others. Have you ever been so excited about an event, new item, or sale that you couldn't wait to tell someone? How much more should gratitude for God's love motivate you to tell others about Christ!

8. If not, you believe the world's evaluation instead of God's truth. The world says, "Oh, he is a good person," "She doesn't hurt anyone," "God wouldn't be fair to condemn them," etc.

9. If you perceive of those who are lost as "not really that bad off," you will not be burdened to share Christ with them. If you see them as objects of God's wrath and destined for eternity in the lake of fire (Rev. 20:15), you will do anything at any cost to see them reconciled to God.

10. Satan has tragically deceived us concerning the lost. Here are some of the lies he tells:
   • *Man is basically good.*
   • *People don't need Christ.*
   • *They'll have a second chance.*
   • *God is love. He wouldn't let anyone perish.*

- *They just need to treat others as they want to be treated.*
- *It doesn't matter what they believe as long as they're sincere.*

Satan uses these lies to encourage us to excuse ourselves from our personal responsibility of telling people about Christ.

11. God has personally commanded you to be a critical part of reaching His world for Christ. He has given you all you need to be an active and effective laborer in the harvest. The first step is for you to assume personal responsibility for the task.

12. Consider a family member, friend, coworker, neighbor, supervisor.

A FINAL WORD

God's heartbeat is for people. This is clearly seen by the life and death of His Son for the world. When we become God's children through Christ, we join in His purpose: to reach a world destined for an eternity without Christ because of their fallen, hardened hearts. People have *exchanged the truth of God for a lie* (Rom. 1:25), and they desperately need someone to share the truth with them. A number of Christians ignore the fact that God has called them to the harvest (John 4:35-38). They are not only disobedient, but are missing out on one of the most exciting parts of God's perfect plan for their lives. It is genuinely thrilling to follow Him and allow Him to make us into fishers of men!

Step Twenty-Three
"Why Am I Afraid to Share My Faith?"

Find a location where you are free from distractions and can concentrate on this exercise. Imagine the following scene:

You are with a close friend or family member. This person genuinely cares for you and you feel the same way about him or her. This person knows you intimately; he or she knows your strengths, weaknesses, and your most personal secrets. You both know that this is a special relationship. Unfortunately, this close friend does not know Christ. You have desired to share Christ with him or her before, but you always have backed down, fearing that you might hurt the relationship and ultimately be rejected. But now is the time. You've decided to do it. Answer the following questions as you imagine the incident occurring:

1. Can you think of any reasons why you wouldn't tell this individual about Christ? If so, what are they?

_____

_____

_____

2. Is your obedience to God in evangelism dependent upon this person's response? (In other words, are you going to share your faith with this person primarily because you think he or she will respond?)

_____

_____

3. Which are you more concerned about: this person rejecting the love and forgiveness of Christ, or this person rejecting you?

_____

_____

4. There are many proper and improper motivations for sharing Christ with people (love for Christ, the desire to honor Him, the desire to help them escape eternal destruction and live a godly life, obedience to Christ's commands; to impress other believers, guilt, to show how much you know, to have authority over someone). Which motives are compelling you to share Christ?

_____

_____

_____

_____

_____

5. Will sharing your faith make God more pleased with you? Why, or why not?

_____

_____

6. Have you shown any partiality to this person's race, sex, social status, or peer group?

_____

_____

7. How would God have you respond to your fears?

_____

_____

8. Make a list of people whom you want to tell about Christ. When would be a good time to tell each one? Pray that God will open their hearts to respond to His love.

Names   Time

_____   _____

_____   _____

_____   _____

_____   _____

_____   _____

_____   _____

_____   _____

Repeat this exercise considering the following:

You are now with a person you hardly know—perhaps someone you've just met. You want to communicate the gospel to this individual. Although you've always been uneasy about sharing Christ with strangers, you decide that now is the time. Think through each of the previous questions as the scene unfolds in your mind.

Compare your answers with the following:

FOR ADDITIONAL INSIGHT

1. You may have many reasons for not sharing Christ with this person, including the fear of rejection or the inconvenience of taking the time and effort to tell him or her.

2. Your obedience to God in evangelism should not depend on the responses of other people. In going to the cross, did Christ's obedience to the Father depend on the responses of others?

3. If fearing what the person will think of you leaves you mute, review how to deal with the fear of rejection. What is the false belief? What does God's Word say is true of you? Focus on God's truth and imagine the scene again.

4. Recognizing our true motivations for sharing Christ is often difficult. The Scriptures give many motives for sharing our faith. Some of these include the great needs of the lost (John 3:36; Eph. 2:1-3); our having been given the ministry of reconciliation (2 Cor. 5:18-20); our being commanded to go into all the world with the gospel (Matt. 28:18-20); and our love for Christ (2 Cor. 5:14-15).

    If your primary motivation for evangelism is knowing that you will feel guilty if you don't do it, you need to dwell on all that God has done for you in Christ. You also need to focus on the present and impending state of those who don't know Him. A proper understanding of these facts will fill your heart with thanksgiving, confession, urgency, and love.

    We need to remember that evangelism is not just dispensing a message. It involves helping and caring for those we tell about Christ's love. Wherever Christ preached the gospel, He also cared for the physical and emotional needs of people.

5. God accepts you for one reason: Christ's death and resurrection have made you acceptable. You can do nothing to become more acceptable to Him. However, this does not change the fact that God's good and perfect will for you is that you be His ambassador. He has given you this responsibility.

6. Do you fear rejection by some group? Or, do you look down at a group because the people in it aren't as good, or as cool, or as sharp, or as smart as you are?

7. God wants you to understand the truth about people's needs, Christ's love, and your opportunities to help others know Christ. He wants you to reject those lies that produce the fear of rejection, and focus on the truth. He wants you to sensitively and lovingly tell people about His love and forgiveness.

8. Pray regularly for two people and take the initiative to tell them about Christ.

A FINAL WORD

The fear of rejection can haunt us as we contemplate sharing the gospel, and for good reason. Christ assured us that we would be rejected. In John 15:18-25, Jesus said that the reason we are rejected is because, indeed, we are His: *If you belonged to the world, it would love you as its own. As it is, you do not belong to the world, but I have chosen you out of the world. That is why the world hates you* (John 15:18-19, NIV). Almighty God has chosen us! He has made us new, set us apart, and reconciled us to Himself. We are special and precious to Him, but we should not expect the world to be thrilled with our commitment to Christ.

Sadly, we often forget that we are special and chosen. At times, we wish that we belonged to the world. When faced with the choice of being rejected for taking a stand for Christ or going along with the world, we often choose the world. The fear of rejection is too great. But God has provided a solution for our fear of rejection! We no longer have to accept the opinions of others as the basis of our self-worth. Instead, the love and acceptance of the infinite, Almighty God frees us to live in abandonment to Him.

How many have we neglected to share Christ with because we feared rejection? As a result of the assurance we have in our standing with Christ, we can step out in faith and lovingly tell people about His offer of forgiveness. Billions of people are waiting to hear His message.

Step Twenty-Four
Building Up One Another

This step is intended to help you see that your new basis of self-worth gives you the capacity to honor God in your relationships with others.

WORLDLY RELATIONSHIPS

1. *a)* From 1 Cor. 3:1-3; 6:8; and Gal. 5:15, 19-21, list the characteristics of worldly, or *carnal,* relationships:

_____   _____

_____   _____

_____   _____

b) What effect does seeking your self-worth from your performance and others' opinions have on your relationships?

_____

_____

_____

c)   How have you used disapproval, rejection, or punishment to manipulate others? Be specific:

_____

_____

_____

_____

GODLY RELATIONSHIPS

2.   *a)*   Read Gal. 5:14; Phil. 2:1-4; and 1 Pet. 3:8-9. What are some characteristics of godly relationships?

_____   _____

_____   _____

_____   _____

b)   What effect does finding your self-worth in God's truth have on your relationships?

_____

_____

_____

c)   What does it mean to *minister* to others?

_____

_____

_____

d)   Read Rom. 15:14; 2 Cor. 3:5-6; and 1 Pet. 4:10. What makes us adequate to minister?

_____

_____

_____

3. Read Col. 4:5-6 and 1 Pet. 3:14-16. How are we to conduct ourselves with non-believers?

_____

_____

_____

4. *a)* Scripture gives believers numerous instructions for building and maintaining relationships with fellow believers. Fill in the following chart, then use this information to make personal application in your relationships:

    Example:

    • Rom. 15:7 *Wherefore, accept one another, just as Christ also accepted us to the glory of God.*

    Instruction: Accept one another

    Meaning: Receive with approval or favor

    Personal Application: *I need to be kind and accepting to Bill, even when he's in a bad mood.*

    • John 15:17

    _____

    _____

    Instruction:

    _____

    _____

    Meaning:

    _____

    _____

Personal Application:

_____

_____

• Eph. 4:32*a*

_____

_____

Instruction:

_____

_____

Meaning:

_____

_____

Personal Application:

_____

_____

• Eph. 4:32*b*

_____

_____

Instruction:

_____

_____

Meaning:

_____

_____

Personal Application:

_____

_____

• Heb. 3:13

_____

_____

Instruction:

_____

_____

Meaning:

_____

_____

Personal Application:

_____

_____

• Heb. 10:24

_____

_____

Instruction:

_____

_____

Meaning:

_____

_____

Personal Application:

_____

_____

b) We can draw many applications from these few passages, but it is difficult (impossible!) to start applying all of them at the same time. What are two or three specific applications you want to begin making today?

_____

_____

_____

c) How do you think your decisions (above) will affect your relationships with these people?

_____

_____

_____

d) For further study, see John 13:14; Rom. 12:10,16; 15:5,14; Gal. 6:2; Eph. 5:21; James 5:16.

Review your answers with the following:

FOR ADDITIONAL INSIGHT

1. *a)* Characteristics of worldly, or *carnal,* relationships include immorality, impurity, sensuality, idolatry, enmities, strife, jealousy, outbursts of anger, disputes, dissensions, factions, envyings, drunkenness, carousing, wronging and defrauding one another.

b) The world's strategy for self-worth can affect our relationships like this:

Seeking self-worth from: performance and others' opinions.
Personal goal in relationships: to meet our own need for self-worth.
Personal strategy to reach the goal: manipulation of others in order for them to enhance our performance, or to give us positive feedback about our performance.

Results in the relationship:

(1) Conflicting goals: Each person wants his or her selfish needs met by the other.

(2) Resulting fears: Fears of failure, punishment, rejection, or shame.

(3) Pain: emotional, physical, or both.

(4) Withdrawal/isolation: We seek to protect ourselves from further pain by withdrawing from others.

(5) Callousness: We build walls around us in order to protect ourselves from further pain in future relationships.

c) Lawrence J. Crabb, Jr., noted Christian psychologist, writes in his book, *The Marriage Builder,* "Whenever the goal of our behavior is essentially to change the other person—whether the change is good or bad—we are wrong." We often use disapproval or praise to manipulate others to meet our goals. We may communicate rejection verbally or non-verbally when they don't meet our goals. We may cause them to fear our punishment. We may reinforce a person's poor self-concept by our disapproval of his or her attitude or actions. Or, we may tell these people how much we appreciate them, but only because they have contributed to our goals.

2. *a)*   A godly relationship is characterized by: a love for God and for the other individual which expresses itself in action, despite one's emotions; an unselfish attitude which is communicated by seeking the other person's best interests; a unity which is maintained through conflict resolution and a like-minded purpose to glorify God in all aspects of the relationship; encouragement, sympathy, brotherly kind-heartedness, giving a blessing instead of an insult.

   b)   God uses us in one another's lives to meet specific needs at specific times. We reflect God's image; our sense of godly self-worth is reinforced as we think, feel, and act in a godly manner. We reinforce the worth of others in Christ; our ministry to others is a picture of God's ministry to them. Therefore, the truth of their worth is reinforced by our love, concern, and admonitions. Look back at the world's effects on relationships in 1*b)*. What a difference!

   c)   God chooses to meet specific needs at specific times through other believers. He equips those believers with the resources necessary to meet those needs. As you turn your focus away from your own need for significance (because your need is fully met by Christ), you are free to minister to others. Our ministry to others is a tangible expression of love that brings them to a deeper awareness of God's love and concern for them.

   d)   As a result of your completeness in Christ, God has made you adequate for the opportunities He gives you. He has gifted you with talents and resources, and has filled you with goodness and knowledge. The stewardship of your completeness in Christ is expressed through your ministry to others.

3. We are to conduct ourselves with wisdom, making the most of the opportunities we have to share Christ with others. We should speak with grace, as though our words were seasoned with salt, always ready to give a defense of our hope in Christ, behaving properly toward those outside the body of believers.

4. This study will give you a new perspective of the potential of relationships in the body of Christ.

A FINAL WORD

We often approach relationships with the desire for others to meet our personal needs for security, acceptance, and significance. Such self-centered objectives lead to a conditional love for others which is often marked by possessiveness, manipulation, jealousy, and anger.

God intends for us to rest in the knowledge that He is the source of our fulfillment, and that He will provide for our emotional, relational, and spiritual needs His way. Trusting in Him for these provisions will gradually free us to serve as models of His unconditional love and acceptance, and enable us to receive what others can give without demanding more.

Experiencing God's Purposes

We have discovered many wonderful truths in this study. We have learned that Christ has paid for our sins, averted the wrath of God, and made us dear, beloved children of God. We are people with a purpose! God's gracious love and awesome power are available to enable us to reign triumphantly with Him. We have the unspeakable privilege of representing the King of kings! Let's look more specifically at what these truths mean.

OUR CALLING

1. Read 1 Pet. 2:1-10 and list the characteristics or titles of the believer found in this passage:

    _____

    _____

    _____

    _____

    _____

2. Verse 9 says that you can *proclaim the excellencies of Him who has called you out of darkness into His marvelous light.* In what ways does Christ seem excellent to you?

    _____

    _____

    _____

    _____

3. Read 1 Cor. 10:31. Describe what it means for you to glorify Christ:

    _____

    _____

    _____

4. Read Matt. 5:13-16 and list as many characteristics of salt and light as you can think of. How are they used? What do they do? What if they were not available?

    SALT   LIGHT

    _____   _____

    _____   _____

    _____   _____

    _____   _____

    _____   _____

    _____   _____

    _____   _____

    _____   _____

5. What are some specific things you can do to demonstrate the characteristics of salt and light to the world around you?

_____

_____

_____

_____

OUR VALUES

6. Read Luke 12:15-21. Imagine a rich man living in our culture today. What things would he own? What would he do? How would he spend his time?

_____

_____

_____

_____

_____

7. Why was the rich man in Luke described as a *fool*?

_____

_____

_____

8. List the people, activities, and possessions you value most. Do each of these make you rich toward God (i.e., enhance your relationship with Him, strengthen biblical values, enable you to have a godly influence on people, encourage your family, etc.)? Why, or why not?

   a) People:

   _____

   _____

   _____

_____
_____
_____
_____

    b)   Activities:

_____
_____
_____
_____
_____
_____

    c)   Possessions:

_____
_____
_____
_____
_____
_____

9.   Think of how you spend your money and your time. Also, think of whom (or what) you really care about. In what ways do your finances, time, and affections reflect richness toward God? In what ways do they reflect selfishness and worldliness?

    a)   Finances:

_____
_____
_____
_____
_____
_____

b) Time:

_____
_____
_____
_____
_____
_____

c) Affections:

_____
_____
_____
_____
_____
_____

10. What can you do, beginning this week, to be more "rich toward God"?

_____
_____
_____
_____
_____

CHRIST IS WORTHY

The book of Revelation gives us a glimpse of the glory and majesty of the risen Christ. Chapters four and five portray a scene in heaven in which He receives praise, worship, and adoration.

11. *a)* Read Rev. 4:9-11 and 5:1-14. According to these passages, those in heaven have been completely freed from sin and its effects, so that their response to Christ is not tainted by Satan's

lies. Though you will not be completely freed from the effects of sin until you die and see the Lord face to face, how would rejecting Satan's lies and replacing them with God's truth affect your relationship with Christ today?

_____

_____

_____

_____

b) What difference would replacing Satan's lies with God's truth make in your outlook on life? Your moods?

_____

_____

_____

_____

c) What difference would it make in your relationships with other believers?

_____

_____

_____

_____

d) With unbelievers?

_____

_____

_____

_____

Review your answers with the following:

FOR ADDITIONAL INSIGHT

1. Believers are described as newborn babes longing for the truths of Scripture; choice and precious in the sight of God; living stones; a chosen race; a royal priesthood; a holy nation; a people for God's own possession; those who can proclaim His excellencies; once, not a people, now the people of God; recipients of God's mercy.

2. Christ is excellent because He is loving, powerful, and kind; He protects us and provides for us. If we view Him as a stern or an aloof taskmaster, or as a sweet but powerless person, then He won't seem very excellent to us.

3. You might have said something like this: *For me, to glorify Christ means to know Him so well and love Him so much that His very character would exude from me. I would tell everyone about how wonderful He is. I would try to make sure that He is honored in my every conversation and action....*

4. Salt: preserves, flavors, prevents food from spoiling, it has healing properties but it stings, a little goes a long way, etc. Light: shows reality, reveals dangers, guides us. Without it, we would not be aware of what is around us or be able to perceive and avoid danger.

5. You can demonstrate these characteristics by sharing the gospel with your family and friends, having a regular time of prayer and Bible study with your roommate or family, supporting missionaries, teaching Sunday school, being involved in sharing Christ with your neighbors and others in the community, etc.

6. A rich man today might have a Jaguar or Porsche. He might own two or three houses. He might spend a lot of time at a private club,

play the stock market as a hobby, and spend a lot of money on clothes, travel, excitement, and comfort.

7. The rich man in Luke was described as a fool because he valued the things of this life more than those that are eternal. His time and efforts were spent on his own pleasures, which are quickly gone, instead of giving to others and helping others to know Christ.

8. The things you value most may include your family, friends, skiing, having a comfortable life or a particular vocation, etc. These would make you rich toward God if they encouraged you in your relationship with Christ, your relationships with other believers, and your ministry in the lives of non-believers.

9. Obviously, a certain amount of your time and money goes toward providing for your physical needs and the needs of your family. But, what about beyond your needs? How about your "want list"? How do you spend extra money? How do you spend your free time? Do you consider giving to meet someone else's needs, or taking time to provide a listening ear to someone who is lonely, or giving up a tennis game for the chance to share your faith? How much time and money do you spend on entertainment (movies, TV shows, books, magazines, parties, etc.) that dishonors the Lord and sets a poor example for your family and others?

10. We can become more rich toward God through any investment we make toward His kingdom, whether it be in our personal habits or civic involvement. Some examples include prayer, Bible study, time with our family, time helping others, being an honest citizen, and supporting missionaries. Our involvement with Christ's kingdom will become more extensive as we grow with Him. Which of the above investments will you begin making for Him today?

11. *a)* Rejecting Satan's lies and replacing them with God's truths will stimulate you to sing more about Christ, pray more, believe Him more, enjoy Him more, and be more of an activist for Him and His kingdom.

b) Perhaps your outlook will be more optimistic and more pleasant.

c) Perhaps you will be less critical of others, less pushy and demanding. You will be increasingly freed from preoccupation with yourself, and will take on more of Christ's heart for people, desiring to meet their needs for encouragement, warmth, and love.

d) You will want all people, Christians and non-Christians, to experience the forgiveness, acceptance, and hope that only Christ can give.

A FINAL WORD

He is worthy! He is Lord! He truly is excellent, and He deserves all of our affections and efforts. No political causes, no persons, no material goods, no fame nor prestige can compare to the One who died and rose again on our behalf (2 Cor. 5:15). Only two things are eternal: God's Word and people. Let's live in self-abandonment, reflecting His image so that He is honored by our every conversation and action, and so that millions will know the love of Christ, which surpasses knowledge (Eph. 3:19).

Unfortunately, many of us determine our own worldly goals for our lives, and then ask, *How can Christ help me meet these goals?* He certainly is able to meet our needs, but this question misses the heart of faith: Jesus Christ is the Lord of the universe, the Savior, the King of kings, the Alpha and the Omega. He did not come just to aid us in meeting our own selfish goals. He did not come to make us feel good as we continue to pursue our own selfish interests. He came to pay for our sin of self-righteousness and to free us from pursuing our own goals, so that we can experience His love and live completely for His interests. In Luke 6:46, Jesus asked, *Why do you call me, 'Lord, Lord'*, *and do not do what I say?* If we insist on living for our own purposes and refuse to do what He says, we need to stop calling Him *Lord*. We should not be asking, *How can Christ help me meet my goals?* but, *You are the Lord, and I want to honor You! What do You want me to do?*

Even an atheist can grasp the profound implications of the lordship of Christ. C.T. Studd, a missionary to China and Africa at the turn of the 20th century, quoted an atheist he encountered:

> *If I firmly believed, as millions say they do, that the knowledge and practice of religion in this life influences destiny in another, then religion would mean to me everything. I would cast away earthly enjoyments as dross, earthly thoughts and feelings as vanity. Religion would be my first waking thought and my last image before sleep sank me into unconsciousness. I should labor in its cause alone. I would take thought for the morrow of eternity alone. I would esteem one soul gained for heaven worth a life of suffering. Earthly consequences would never stay in my head or seal my lips. Earth, its joys and its griefs, would occupy no moment of my thoughts. I would strive to look upon eternity alone, and on the immortal souls around me, soon to be everlastingly happy or everlastingly miserable. I would go forth to the world and preach to it in season and out of season. And my text would be, "WHAT SHALL IT PROFIT A MAN IF HE GAINS THE WHOLE WORLD AND LOSES HIS OWN SOUL."*[1]

At a conference at Mt. Hermon, Massachusetts, in 1888, some of the most brilliant and promising young men and women in America gathered to learn more about how they could live for Christ. During this conference, at a spontaneous prayer meeting for foreign missions, they became convinced that the desperate needs of the world and the love of Christ were compelling them to commit themselves irrevocably to Him and His cause. One hundred men and women turned their backs on wealth, prestige, and comfort to live for Christ no matter where He might lead them, no matter what the cost.

These people did not follow Christ alone. They took many others with them. Within fifty years, some 30,000 other young men and women had gone with them overseas to the mission field. The vast majority of these, too, were among the most gifted of their day and could have lived out their lives in comfort and style. But they counted all things to be loss in view of the surpassing value of knowing [and serving] Christ Jesus (Phil. 3:8).

Many years later, another group of young men and women gathered to learn how to love, honor, and serve Christ. In the spirit of the spontaneous prayer meeting at Mt. Hermon in 1888, they solemnly pledged themselves to Christ and His cause with the same abandonment as their predecessors: no matter where He might lead them, no matter what the cost. Their pledge reads,

> *In response to the incomprehensible grace of God, and realizing the urgent needs of a lost world, I pledge the entirety of my affections, time, and resources to Christ and the fulfillment of His Great Commission.*[2]

Take time to consider the wonder of the cross, that the ineffable, Almighty God became a man to die in our place. Consider the desperate needs of the world. Billions have never heard the name of Christ. Billions more have heard His name, but believe that they must earn His acceptance by self-effort. Consider the wealth of love and the awesome power of the Holy Spirit that enables us to be salt and light. Does this pledge express your heart's desire? If it does, pledge yourself to Christ and the furthering of His kingdom, write it in the front of your Bible, and join the many thousands of others who have forsaken this world for the surpassing value of knowing and following Christ. As Jim Elliot, martyred missionary to Ecuador, reflected: *He is no fool who gives what he cannot keep to gain what he cannot lose.*[3]

Notes

Chapter 7. Approval Addict

1. Lori Thorkelson Rentzel, *Emotional Dependency* (San Rafael, CA: Exodus International-North America, Box 2121, 94912.

2. C.S. Lewis, *The Four Loves* (New York: Harcourt Brace Jovanovich, Inc., 1960), pp. 91-92.

3. Lori Thorkelson Rentzel, *Emotional Dependency*, pp. 3-4. Reprinted by permission.

Chapter 9. Shame

1. Louis Berkhof, *Systematic Theology* (Grand Rapids, MI: William B. Eerdmans Pub. Co., 1941), p. 468.

Chapter 15. The Search Concluded

1. Ryrie, Charles C., Th.D., Ph.D., *The Ryrie Study Bible*, New American Standard Translation (Chicago, IL: Moody Press, 1976, 1978), p. 1710, s.v. "consider," v. 6:11.

Step 9. Reconciliation

1. Leon Morris, *The Atonement* (Downers Grove, IL: Inter-Varsity Press, 1984).

Step 11. Propitiation

1. Frederick Faber, as cited by A.W. Tozer, *The Pursuit of God* (Camp Hill, PA: Christian Publications, Inc., 1982), pp. 40-41.

2. Ibid, p. 41.

Step 12. Forgiving Others

1. David Seamands, *Healing for Damaged Emotions* (Wheaton, IL: Victor Books, 1981), p. 26.

Step 15. Renewing Your View of God

1. J.I. Packer, *Knowing God* (Downer's Grove, IL: InterVarsity Press, 1973), p. 14.

Step 16. Dealing with Emotional Scars

1. Robert S. McGee, with Pat Springle and Susan Joiner, *Rapha's Twelve-Step Program for Overcoming Chemical Dependency* (Houston, TX: Rapha Publishing, 1989, First Printing), pp. 61-64.

2. Charles Stanley, *Forgiveness* (Nashville, TN: Oliver-Nelson Books, 1987), p. 16.

Step 25. Experiencing God's Purposes

1. Norman Grubb, *C.T. Studd* (Washington, PA: Christian Literature Crusade, 1972), p. 32.

2. Campus Crusade for Christ, Camp Hoblitzell, 1984.

3. Elisabeth Elliot, *Through Gates of Splendor*, 25th Anniversary Ed., (Wheaton, IL: Tyndale House Publishers, Inc., 1986).

THE SEARCH FOR SIGNIFICANCE

Devotional

ACKNOWLEDGMENT

THE SEARCH FOR SIGNIFICANCE DEVOTIONAL

I want to thank Sandy Ballard-Rote for her excellent work and outstanding contribution to this devotional. Sandy provided editorial assistance, compiled the prayers at the end of each day, and attractively designed the layout for this book. Her efforts have added to both the contents and the appearance of this work.

INTRODUCTION

Several years ago, a study was conducted by a major seminary to determine which factors encourage spiritual growth. Many spiritual disciplines were examined, such as church attendance, regular Bible study, and prayer. One factor, however, proved to have the greatest influence in encouraging people to grow in their relationships with God: meditation. Consistent reflection on God's Word had a far greater impact than any other discipline.

This devotional is designed to stimulate and enhance that kind of consistent reflection. Each of these daily studies contains a reflection question or two and a "prayer starter" to help you express your desires, feelings, and needs to the Lord.

Some of us feel undue stress when we look at a daily devotional because we think if we don't "keep up," we are not being spiritual enough—that we are somehow failing in our walk with the Lord. Consistency is laudable and good, but don't worry if you miss a day or if your weekend journal ends in the middle of a week. The goal is to reflect on God's truth so that it sinks deeply into our hearts and minds. The pace is not as important as the depth of our reflection.

Above all, this devotional is a book of hope. I trust that God will use it to encourage you to grasp His love and grace more deeply than ever before. And too, I trust that His love will then have a profound impact on every aspect of your life!

ROBERT S. MCGEE

TRUE FREEDOM

You shall know the truth, and the truth shall make you free.

JOHN 8:32

IN THIS PASSAGE, CHRIST WAS REFERRING not only to an intellectual assent to the truth, but also to the application of truth in the most basic issues of life: our goals, our motives, and our sense of self-worth. Unfortunately, many of us give only lip-service to the powerful truths of the Scriptures without allowing them to affect the basis of our self-esteem in a radical way. Instead, we continue to seek our security and purpose from worldly sources: personal success, status, beauty, wealth, and the approval of others. These rewards may fulfill us for a short time, but they soon lead us to a sense of urgency to succeed and be approved again.

To meet these compelling needs, we drive ourselves to achieve, doing virtually anything to make people happy with us, and spend countless hours and dollars trying to look "just right." Often, we avoid situations and people where the risks of failure and rejection are high. It's a rat race that can't be won by simply running faster. We need to get off of this hopeless treadmill, and learn to apply the foundational truths that can motivate us to live for Christ rather than for the approval of other people.

Christ's death paid the penalty for our sins, and His resurrection gives us new life, new goals, and new hope. He has given us complete security and challenging purpose. These are not based on our abilities, but on His grace and the power of His Spirit. Yes, Christ wants us to be zealous and ambitious, but not about our success or status. If we understand His forgiveness and acceptance, we will pursue the right things—Christ and His cause—and we will be free to enjoy His love.

- What difference would it make in your attitude, relationships, and goals if you grasped the reality that your worth is not conditional (i.e., based on performance), but is based on the truth of the unconditional love, forgiveness, and acceptance of God?

Thank You for loving me, Father. As I become more aware of how complete I am in You, please help me to . . .

TURNING ON THE LIGHT

The Lord is my light and my salvation; whom shall I fear?
The Lord is the defense of my life; whom shall I dread?

PSALM 27:1

WE ALL HAVE EXPERIENCED THE INABILITY to be objective about our experiences, thoughts, and behavior in different circumstances. This objective "light" didn't begin to penetrate my own life until shortly after I had entered the business world. Before that time, whenever I felt the pain of rejection, the sting of sarcasm, or anything less than the complete approval of others, I tried to shrug it off. I reasoned that because of my status as a Christian, I should exude an attitude of happiness and contentment in all things. When something didn't go the way I'd hoped or planned it would, I simply told myself it didn't really matter. Though I was able to fool myself in these instances, my gloomy countenance told those who were closest to me another story.

On one such occasion, a good friend of mine inquired about what was wrong. "You seem troubled," he said. "Is anything bothering you?"

"Me? No, I'm fine."

"You don't seem fine to me," he persisted. "You're acting as though you might be depressed about something."

I stuck to my time-tested text. "No, really, I *am* fine. I guess I've just been a little pressured lately."

The truth was that an idea I'd presented in a business meeting the week before had been challenged and later, shot down. I didn't think it really mattered at first, but after hearing my friend's remarks, I began to wonder if I were being honest with myself.

Several weeks later, I phoned this friend to thank him for confronting me about my behavior. I briefly told him about the business meeting and said, "Realizing I was hurt because my idea was rejected has enabled me to be honest with the Lord about my feelings and begin working through them."

"I'm sorry about what happened," he said, "but I appreciate your honesty, and think it's great that you're doing something constructive with a difficult situation."

Over time, I began to confide in this friend about other problems I encountered. He helped me a great deal. At times, he would say, "Here's how I'd feel in your situation. I'd be angry because . . . . Do *you* feel angry?" Or, "I'd be hurt because . . . . Do *you* feel hurt?"

In the light of his honesty and love, and through the gracious work of the Holy Spirit, I began to be honest with myself and with God. The tough exterior I had developed started cracking, and I began to experience the pain I had neither wanted nor allowed myself to feel. This was hardly pleasant, but acknowledging the presence of hurt in my life was my first step toward finding comfort.

• What are some reasons people are afraid of the truth about themselves?

Sometimes being honest with You, myself, and others can be painful. Thank You, Jesus, for Your never-ending comfort. Today, I'm feeling . . .

STAYING IN THE DARK

Teach me what I cannot see; if I have done wrong, I will not do so again.

JOB 34:32, NIV

WHY DO SOME OF US LACK OBJECTIVITY? Why can't we see the reality of our lives? Why are we afraid to "turn on the lights"?

There are a number of answers to these questions, and they vary for each person. Perhaps we think that our situations are "normal," that experiencing loneliness, hurt, and anger is really all there is to life. Perhaps we want to be "good Christians," and believing that _good_ Christians don't have problems or feelings like ours, we deny the existence of our painful emotions. Perhaps our lack of objectivity is a learned response from childhood. All of us desperately want our parents to be loving and supportive. If ours aren't (or weren't), we may protect our concept of them by blaming ourselves for their lack of love, and deny that we have been hurt by their behavior.

- In what ways is "darkness" more comfortable than "light"?

- What are some ways you can tell if you are being objective or not?

- How would increased objectivity affect your life and relationships?

Father, thank You for the lessons You're teaching me about my emotions. As I strive to be more objective, I need You to . . .

CONFRONTING REALITY

Search me, O God, and know my heart;
Try me and know my anxious thoughts;
And see if there be any hurtful way in me,
And lead me in the everlasting way.

PSALM 139:23–24

HUMAN BEINGS DEVELOP ELABORATE DEFENSE MECHANISMS to block pain and gain significance. We suppress emotions; we are compulsive perfectionists; we drive ourselves to succeed, or withdraw and become passive; we attack people who hurt us; we punish ourselves when we fail; we try to say clever things to be accepted; we help people so that we will be appreciated; and we say and do countless other things.

A sense of need usually propels us to look for an alternative. We may have the courage to examine ourselves and may desperately want to change, but may be unsure of how and where to start. We may refuse to look honestly within for fear of what we'll find, or we may be afraid that even if we can discover what's wrong, nothing can help us.

It is difficult—if not impossible—to turn on the light of objectivity by ourselves. We need guidance from the Holy Spirit, as well as the honesty, love, and encouragement of at least one other person who's willing to help us. Even then, we may become depressed as we begin to discover the effects of our wounds. Some of us have deep emotional and spiritual scars resulting from the neglect, abuse, and manipulation that often accompany living in a dysfunctional family (alcoholism, drug abuse, divorce, absent father or mother, excessive anger, verbal and/or physical abuse, etc.), but all of us bear the effects of our own sinful nature and the imperfections of others.

Whether your hurts are deep or relatively mild, it is wise to be honest about them in the context of affirming relationships so that healing can begin.

- Describe your need for healing. What is your family background? How did (does) your relationship with your parents affect you? Have you experienced deep wounds, mild abrasions, or something in-between?

Please help me to have the courage to look at myself objectively—to be honest about my need to change and heal. As I try to be more like You, Jesus, please show me . . .

AT THE DEEPEST LEVEL

Surely you desire truth in the inner parts;
you teach me wisdom in the inmost place.

PSALM 51:6, NIV

MANY OF US MISTAKENLY BELIEVE THAT God doesn't want us to be honest about our lives. We think that He will be upset with us if we tell Him how we really feel. But the Scriptures tell us that God does not want us to be superficial—in our relationship with Him, with others, or in our own lives.

The Lord desires truth and honesty at the deepest level, and wants us to experience His love, forgiveness, and power in *all* areas of our lives. Experiencing His love does not mean that all of our thoughts, emotions, and behaviors will be pleasant and pure. It means that we can be *real*, feeling pain and joy, love and anger, confidence and confusion.

The Psalms give us tremendous insight about what it means to be honest with the Lord. David and other psalmists wrote and spoke honestly about the full range of their responses to situations.

- Read Psalm 51:6. Why do you think that the Lord wants us to be honest?

I realize that even before I think or speak, You already know what is in my heart. You know if my thoughts, words, and actions are honest portrayals of my feelings. I'm grateful for Your omniscience, Lord. Realizing that You already know the truth helps me to not be afraid of reaching toward deeper levels of honesty with myself. I am comforted in knowing that You are already at the next level, waiting for me to arrive. In my awareness of this, I confess . . .

PRESUMPTIONS

Through presumption comes nothing but strife,
But with those who receive counsel is wisdom.

PROVERBS 13:10

SOME PEOPLE BEGIN MOVING TOWARD HEALING AND HEALTH rather quickly. Others, however, may read and study, go to seminars and meetings—they may even be in relationships where they are loved and encouraged—but they may not see substantive change in their lives and patterns of behavior. One reason for this spiritual and emotional inertia is a sense of hopelessness. For various reasons (family background, past experiences, poor role-modeling), we may have negative presumptions which determine our receptivity to love and truth. In some cases, God's light may have revealed our pain and wall of defenses, but it may not yet have penetrated to our deepest thoughts and beliefs about ourselves. These beliefs may not be clearly articulated, but often reflect misperceptions such as these:

- God doesn't really care about me.
- I am an unlovable, worthless person. Nobody will ever love me.
- I'll never be able to change.
- I've been a failure all my life. I guess I'll always be a failure.
- If people really knew me, they wouldn't like me.

When the light of love and honesty shines on thoughts of hopelessness, it is often very painful. We begin to admit that we really do feel negatively about ourselves—and have for a long time. But God's love, expressed through His people, and woven into our lives by His Spirit and His Word can, over a period of time, bring healing even to our deepest wounds and instill within us an appropriate sense of self-worth.

- Read 2 Timothy 3:16–17 and explain how the Scriptures can affect our thinking and our lives.

When I'm feeling hopeless, God, please give me a gentle reminder of Your presence. Thinking of You—knowing that You created me—helps me to remember that I am a very special person. This makes me feel . . .

SEARCHING FOR SIGNIFICANCE

Now on the last day, the great day of the feast, Jesus stood and cried out, saying, "If any man is thirsty, let him come to Me and drink. He who believes in Me, as the Scripture said, 'From his innermost being shall flow rivers of living water.'" But this He spoke of the Spirit, whom those who believed in Him were to receive; for the Spirit was not yet given, because Jesus was not yet glorified.

JOHN 7:37–39

RELATIVELY FEW OF US EXPERIENCE THE BLEND OF CONTENTMENT and godly intensity that God desires for each person. From life's outset, we find ourselves on the prowl, searching to satisfy some inner, unexplained yearning. Our hunger causes us to search for people who will love us. Our desire for acceptance pressures us to perform for the praise of others. We strive for success, driving our minds and bodies harder and farther, hoping that because of our sweat and sacrifice, others will appreciate us more.

But the man or woman who lives only for the love and attention of others is never satisfied—at least, not for long. Despite our efforts, we will never find lasting, fulfilling peace if we have to continually prove ourselves to others. Our desire to be loved and accepted is a symptom of a deeper need—the need that often governs our behavior and is the primary source of our emotional pain. Often unrecognized, this is our need for self-worth.

- *If any man is thirsty* is a metaphor for our desire and need for Christ. What does it mean to *drink* of Christ?

- In what ways are you *thirsty* for Him?

Thank You, God, for the peace that comes from knowing I no longer need to prove myself to others. As I rest in the knowledge that You accept me totally and unconditionally, I want to praise You for . . .

THE *REAL* ABUNDANT LIFE

Put on the full armor of God, that you may be able to stand firm against the schemes of the devil. For our struggle is not against flesh and blood, but against the rulers, against the powers, against the world forces of this darkness, against the spiritual forces of wickedness in the heavenly places.

EPHESIANS 6:11–12

IN THE SCRIPTURES, GOD SUPPLIES THE ESSENTIALS for discovering our true significance and worth. The first two chapters of Genesis recount man's creation, revealing man's intended purpose (to honor God) and man's value (that he is a special creation of God). John 10:10 also reminds us of how much God treasures His creation, in that Christ came so that man might experience "abundant life." However, as Christians, we need to realize that this abundant life is lived in a real world filled with pain, rejection, and failure. Therefore, experiencing the abundant life God intends for us does not mean that our lives will be problem-free. On the contrary, life itself is a series of problems that often act as obstacles to our search for significance, and the abundant life is the experience of God's love, forgiveness, and power in the midst of these problems. The Scriptures warn us that we live within a warfare that can destroy our faith, lower our self-esteem, and lead us into depression. In his letter to the Ephesians, Paul instructs us to put on the armor of God so that we can be equipped for spiritual battle. However, it often seems that unsuspecting believers are the last to know this battle is occurring, and that Christ has ultimately won the war. They are surprised and confused by difficulties, thinking that the Christian life is a playground, not a battlefield.

- How can believing that "the abundant life is freedom from problems" be a hindrance to faith?

- How is spiritual warfare a part of the abundant life?

Father, as I grow in You, I am increasingly aware that the problems I face are accompanied by valuable lessons You want me to learn. I don't look forward to pain or misfortune, but knowing that You're there beside me, wanting to teach me something through my struggles—and that I really matter to You—helps me to not be afraid. Father, today I need You to . . .

SPECIFIC SOLUTIONS

See to it that no one takes you captive through philosophy and empty deception, according to the tradition of men, according to the elementary principles of the world, rather than according to Christ.

For in Him all the fulness of Deity dwells in bodily form.

COLOSSIANS 2:8–9

As CHRISTIANS, OUR FULFILLMENT IN THIS LIFE DEPENDS not on our skills to avoid life's problems, but on our ability to apply God's specific solutions to those problems. An accurate understanding of God's truth is the first step toward discovering our significance and worth. Unfortunately, many of us have been exposed to inadequate teaching from both religious and secular sources concerning our self-worth. As a result, we may have a distorted self-perception, and may be experiencing hopelessness rather than the rich and meaningful life God intends for us.

Whether labeled "self-esteem" or "self-worth," the feeling of significance is crucial to man's emotional, spiritual, and social stability, and is the driving element within the human spirit. Understanding this single need opens the door to understanding our actions and attitudes.

What a waste to attempt to change behavior without truly understanding the driving needs that cause such behavior! Yet, millions of people spend a lifetime searching for love, acceptance, and success without understanding the need that compels them. We must understand that this hunger for self-worth is God-given and can only be satisfied by Him. Our value is not dependent on our ability to earn the fickle acceptance of people, but rather, its true source is the love and acceptance of God. He created us. He alone knows how to fulfill *all* of our needs.

- Are you glad you are you?

- Do you have a healthy sense of self-worth?

Jesus, please show me the areas of my life where I fail to rely on You for my self-worth and, instead, look to others for acceptance. I admit . . .

A REASONABLE RESPONSE

For by grace (unmerited favor) you have been saved (rescued from spiritual death—hell) through faith (trust); and that not of yourselves, it is the gift of God; not as a result of works, that no one should boast.

EPHESIANS 2:8–9

ARE YOU TRUSTING IN YOUR OWN ABILITIES to earn acceptance with God, or are you trusting in the death of Christ to pay for your sins, and the resurrection of Christ to give you new life? Take a moment to reflect on this question: On a scale of 0–100 percent, how sure are you that you would spend eternity with God if you died today? An answer of less than 100 percent may indicate that you are trusting, at least in part, in yourself. You may be thinking, *Isn't it arrogant to say that I am 100 percent sure?* Indeed, it would be arrogance if you were trusting in yourself—your abilities, your actions, and good deeds—to earn your salvation. However, if you are no longer trusting in your own efforts, but in the all-sufficient payment of Christ, then 100 percent certainty is a response of humility and thankfulness, not arrogance.

If there is any question about whether you have conclusively accepted Christ's substitutionary death to pay for the wrath you deserve for your sins, take some time to think about the question we have examined, and reflect on His love and forgiveness. Then, respond by trusting in Christ and accepting His payment for your sins. You can use this prayer to express your faith:

Lord Jesus, I need You. I want You to be my Savior and Lord. I accept Your death on the cross as the complete payment for my sins. Thank You for forgiving me and for giving me new life. Help me to grow in my understanding of Your love and power so that my life will bring honor to You. Amen.

- On a scale of 0–100 percent, how sure are you that you would go to heaven if you died tonight?

0%__ 10%__ 25%__ 35%__ 50%__ 75%__ 85%__ 95%__ 100%__

- If you died tonight and stood before God and He asked you "Why should I let you into heaven?" what would you say?

I am overwhelmed with love for You, Lord. Your gift of salvation fills my heart with gratitude like nothing else ever could. Thank You for . . .

THE IMPACT OF FAITH

As [a man] thinks within himself, so he is.
PROVERBS 23:7

BECAUSE OUR PERFORMANCE AND ABILITY TO PLEASE OTHERS so dominates our search for significance, we have difficulty recognizing the distinction between our real identity and the way we behave, a realization crucial to understanding our true worth. Our true value is not based on our behavior or the approval of others, but on what God's Word says is true of us.

Our behavior is often a reflection of our beliefs about who we are. It is usually consistent with what we think to be true about ourselves. If we base our worth solidly on the truths of God's Word, then our behavior will often reflect His love, grace, and power. But if we base our worth on our abilities or the fickle approval of others, then our behavior will reflect the insecurity, fear, and anger that comes from such instability.

Though we usually behave in ways that are consistent with our beliefs, at times, our actions may contradict them. For example, we may believe that we are generous and gracious, when we are actually very selfish. Sometimes, our behavior changes what we believe about ourselves. If, for instance, we succeed in a task at which we initially believed we would fail, our confidence may begin to grow and expand to other areas of our lives. Our feelings, behavior, and beliefs all interact to shape our lives.

Our lifestyle is usually a reflection of what we think about ourselves. Analyze your lifestyle. Describe . . .

- The things you talk about:

- The places you like to go:

- The people you spend time with:

- Your ambitions and dreams:

- How you spend your time:

- How you spend your money:

Heavenly Father, as I search myself—my motives, priorities—to discover where I have based my self-worth, I admit . . .

DAY 12

DEVELOPING BELIEFS AT HOME

> For evils beyond number have surrounded me;
> My iniquities have overtaken me, so that I am not able
> to see;
> They are more numerous than the hairs of my head;
> And my heart has failed me.
> Be pleased, O Lord, to deliver me;
> Make haste, O Lord to help me.
> Let those be ashamed and humiliated together
> Who seek my life to destroy it;
> Let those be turned back and dishonored
> Who delight in my hurt.
>
> PSALM 40:12–14

OUR HOME ENVIRONMENT PLAYS A CENTRAL ROLE in forming our beliefs and emotions, and these can have a powerful impact on our outlook and behavior.

This truth is evident in the case of Scott. Scott grew up in a home without praise, discouraged by his parents whenever he attempted anything new and challenging. After twenty years of hearing, "You'll never be able to do anything, Scott, so don't even try," he believed it himself. Neither Scott nor his parents could later understand why he had flunked out of college and was continually shuffling from one job to another, never able to achieve success. Believing he was doing the best he could do, but suspecting he would always fail, Scott consistently performed according to his self-perception.

Separated from God and His Word, people have only their abilities and the opinions of others on which to base their worth, and the circumstances around them ultimately control the way they feel about themselves.

- List some activities, relationships, or achievements which make you feel better about yourself:

- List some activities, poor relationships, or failures which make you feel badly about yourself:

Lord, as I reflect on the home environment in which I was raised, I feel . . .

498

COMPULSIONS AND WITHDRAWAL

> ... Every one who thirsts, come to the waters;
> And you who have no money come, buy and eat.
> Come, buy wine and milk
>   without money and without cost.
> Why do you spend money for what is not bread,
>   And your wages for what does not satisfy?
> Listen carefully to Me, and eat what is good,
>   And delight yourself in abundance.
> Incline your ear and come to Me.
>   Listen, that you may live;
> And I will make an everlasting covenant with you,
>   According to the faithful mercies shown to David.

ISAIAH 55:1–3

WE ALL HAVE COMPELLING, GOD-GIVEN NEEDS for love, acceptance, and purpose. Many of us have become masters at "playing the game" to be successful and win the approval of others. Some of us, however, have failed and have experienced the pain of disapproval so often that we have given up and have withdrawn into a shell of hurt, numbness, or depression. In both cases, we are living by the deception that our worth is based on our performance and others' opinions—some of us are simply more adept at playing this game than others.

Our attempts to meet our needs for success and approval fall into two broad categories: compulsiveness and withdrawal. Some people expend extra effort, work extra hours, and try to say just the right thing to achieve success and please those around them. These people may have a compelling desire to be in control of every situation. They are perfectionists. If a job isn't done perfectly, if they aren't dressed just right, if they aren't considered "the best" by their peers, then they work harder until they achieve that coveted status. And woe to the poor soul who gets in their way! Whoever doesn't contribute to their success and acclaim is a threat to their self-esteem—an unacceptable threat. They may be very personable and have a lot of "friends," but the goal of these relationships may not be to give encouragement and love; it may be to manipulate others to contribute to their success. That may sound harsh, but people who are driven to succeed will often use practically everything and everybody to meet that need. The sad truth is that most perfectionists never are satisfied with their work, no matter how well their efforts have turned out. This perception of imperfection only fuels their compulsion to "do it right next time."

The other broad category is withdrawal. Those who manifest this behavior usually try to avoid failure and disapproval by avoiding risks. They won't volunteer for the jobs that offer much risk of failure. They gravitate toward people who are comforting and kind, skirting relationships that might demand vulnerability, and consequently, the risk of rejection. They may appear to be easygoing, but inside they are usually running from every potential situation or relationship that might not succeed.

Obviously, these are two broad categories. Most of us exhibit some combination of the two behaviors, willing to take risks and work hard in the areas where we feel sure of success, but avoiding the people and situations that may bring rejection and failure.

- Whose opinion of you do you value most?
- What is your most common response to that person?

Father, please help me to be more aware of how I may be compelling others to withdraw or "perform" as well. I admit ...

PARENTS AS MODELS

The Lord sustains all who fall,
  And raises up all who are bowed down.
The eyes of all look to Thee,
  And Thou dost give them their food in due time.
Thou dost open Thy hand,
  And dost satisfy the desire of every living thing.

PSALM 145:14–16

WHEN WE BASE OUR SECURITY ON SUCCESS and others' opinions, we become dependent on our abilities to perform and please others. We develop a *have-to* mentality: *I* have to *do well on this exam (or my security as a "good student" will be threatened); I* have to *make that deal (or it will mean that my boss will think I am a failure); My father (or mother, spouse, or friend)* has to *appreciate me and be happy with my decisions (because I cannot cope with his disapproval).*

Our self-esteem and view of God are usually a mirror of our parents' attitudes toward us. Those who are loved and affirmed by their parents tend to have a fairly healthy self-concept, and usually find it easy to believe that God is loving and powerful. Those whose parents have been neglectful, manipulative, or condemning usually seem to feel that they have to earn a sense of worth, and that God is aloof, demanding, and/or cruel.

Our parents are our models of the character of God. When we do not have that fundamental sense of feeling loved and protected by them, then we tend to base our self-worth on how well we perform and please others, instead of on what the sovereign God of the universe, our all-wise, omniscient Savior says of us.

- Is it difficult to view yourself in terms other than your performance or others' opinions of you? If so, why?

Father, please help me see myself through Your eyes, and show me . . .

DAY 15

THE SOURCE OF OUR SECURITY

For you have not received a spirit of slavery leading to fear again, but you have received a spirit of adoption as sons by which we cry out, "Abba! Father!"

ROMANS 8:15

WE DO NOT *HAVE TO* BE SUCCESSFUL OR *HAVE TO* BE PLEASING to others to have a healthy sense of self-esteem and worth. That worth has freely and conclusively been given to us by God. Failure and/or the disapproval of others can't take it away! Therefore, we can conclude, *It would be nice to be approved by my parents* (or whomever), *but if they don't approve of me, I'm still loved and accepted by God.* Do you see the difference? The *have-to* mentality is sheer slavery to performance and the opinions of others, but we are secure and free in Christ. We don't *have to* have success or anyone else's approval. Of course, it would be nice to have success and approval, but the point is clear: Christ is the source of our security; Christ is the basis of our worth; Christ is the only One who promises and never fails.

The transition from the slavery and compulsion of a *have-to* mentality to the freedom and strength of a *want-to* motivation is a process. Bondage to such thinking is often deeply rooted in our personalities, patterns of behavior, and ways of relating to other people. These patterns of thinking, feeling, and responding—learned over time—flow as naturally as the course of rainwater in a dry desert riverbed. Changing them requires time, the encouragement of others, the truth and application of God's Word, and the power of God's Spirit.

• Describe how your thoughts and beliefs have been developed. (Include the influences of society, your daily background, experiences, relationships):

Father, You are my source of security. Thank You for always being here with me. Thank You for . . .

501

THE HOLY SPIRIT

"And I will ask the Father, and He will give you another Helper, that He may be with you forever. That is the Spirit of truth, whom the world cannot receive, because it does not behold Him or know Him, but you know Him because He abides with you, and will be in you."

JOHN 14:16–17

DEEP SPIRITUAL HEALING REQUIRES GIVING ATTENTION to the whole man, to his emotional, relational, physical, and spiritual needs. The Holy Spirit is given by God to communicate His love, light, forgiveness, and power to our deepest needs. This spiritual aspect of healing is perhaps the most fundamental, because our view of God (and subsequent relationship with Him) can determine the quality and degree of health we experience in every other area of our lives.

Some of us believe that the Holy Spirit's ministry is characterized only by positive, pleasant emotions like love and joy. However, one of the miracles of the Holy Spirit's work is that of producing honesty and courage in our lives as we grapple with the reality of pain. He is the Spirit of truth, not denial, and He enables us to experience each element of the healing process as He gives us wisdom, strength, and encouragement through God's Word and other people.

• Describe the Holy Spirit's role in the healing process:

Dear Father, I am grateful for Your . . .

THE TRAP OF PERFORMANCE

If you have died with Christ to the elementary principles of the world, why, as if you were living in the world, do you submit yourself to decrees, such as, do not handle, do not taste, do not touch (which all refer to things destined to perish with the using)—in accordance with the commandments and teachings of men? These are matters which have, to be sure, the appearance of wisdom in self-made religion and self-abasement and severe treatment of the body, but are of no value against fleshly indulgence.

COLOSSIANS 2:20–23

BECAUSE OF OUR UNIQUE PERSONALITIES, WE EACH REACT very differently to this deception: *I must meet certain standards in order to feel good about myself.* As we saw in a previous chapter, some of us respond by becoming slaves to perfectionism—driving ourselves incessantly toward attaining goals.

Perfectionists can be quite vulnerable to serious mood disorders, and often anticipate rejection when they believe they haven't met the standards they are trying so hard to attain. Therefore, perfectionists tend to react defensively to criticism and demand to be in control of most situations they encounter. Because they are usually more competent than most, perfectionists see nothing wrong with their compulsions. "I just like to see things done well," they claim. There is certainly nothing inherently wrong with doing things well; the problem is that perfectionists usually base their self-worth on their ability to accomplish a goal. Therefore, failure is a threat and is totally unacceptable to them. Many high achievers are driven beyond healthy limitations. Rarely able to relax and enjoy life, they let their families and relationships suffer as they strive to accomplish often unrealistic goals.

• Why do people use performance as a measurement of personal worth?

Heavenly Father, I need to slow down today and focus on improving my present relationships. In the whirlwind activities of daily life, I confess that I get caught up with . . .

THE PIT OF DESPAIR

For we also once were foolish ourselves, disobedient, deceived, enslaved to various lusts and pleasures, spending our life in malice and envy, hateful, hating one another. But when the kindness of God our Savior and His love for mankind appeared, He saved us, not on the basis of deeds which we have done in righteousness, but according to His mercy, by the washing of regeneration and renewing by the Holy Spirit.

TITUS 3:3–5

THE SAME FALSE BELIEF (*I MUST MEET CERTAIN STANDARDS to feel good about myself*) that drives people to perfectionism also sends them into a tailspin of despair. They rarely expect to achieve anything or to feel good about themselves. Because of their past failures, they are quick to interpret present failures as an accurate reflection of their worthlessness. Fearing more failure, they often become despondent and stop trying.

The pressure of having to meet self-imposed standards in order to feel good about ourselves can result in a rules-dominated life. Individuals caught in this trap often have a set of rules for most of life's situations, and continually focus their attention on their performance and ability to adhere to their schedule. Brent, for example, made a daily list of what he could accomplish if everything went perfectly. He was always a little tense because he wanted to use every moment effectively to reach his goals. If things didn't go well, or if someone took too much of his time, Brent got angry. Efficient, effective use of time was his way of attaining fulfillment, but he was miserable. He was constantly driven to do more, but his best was never enough to satisfy him.

- Do you have to be successful in order to feel good about yourself? What would you have to be or do to feel like you are a "success"?

- In what area(s) would you *never* allow yourself to fail?

As I reflect on how I feel so driven to perform, to meet the standards of others, Jesus, I admit . . .

SETTLED ACCOUNTS

He made Him (Christ) who knew no sin to be sin on our behalf, that we might become the righteousness of God in Him.

2 CORINTHIANS 5:21

VISUALIZE TWO LEDGERS: ON ONE IS A LIST OF ALL YOUR SINS; on the other, the righteousness of Christ. Now exchange your ledger for Christ's. This exemplifies justification—transferring our sin to Christ and His righteousness to us.

I once heard a radio preacher berate his congregation for their hidden sins. He exclaimed, "Don't you know that someday you're going to die and God is going to flash all your sins upon a giant screen in heaven for all the world to see?" How tragically this minister misunderstood God's gracious gift of justification!

Justification carries no guilt with it, and has no memory of past transgressions. Christ paid for all of our sins at the cross—past, present, and future. Hebrews 10:17 says, *And their sins and their lawless deeds I will remember no more.* We are completely forgiven by God!

• Why did you need to be justified and have Christ's righteousness attributed to you?

Father, thank You for . . .

DAY 20

MOTIVATIONS FOR OBEDIENCE

Therefore having been justified by faith, we have peace with God through our Lord Jesus Christ.

ROMANS 5:1

SOME PEOPLE HAVE DIFFICULTY THINKING OF THEMSELVES as being pleasing to God because they link *pleasing* so strongly with performance. They tend to be displeased with anything short of perfection in themselves, and suspect that God has the same standard.

The point of justification is that we can never achieve perfection on this earth; even our best efforts at self-righteousness are as filthy rags to God (Isaiah 64:6). Yet, He loves us so much that He appointed His Son to pay for our sins and give to us His own righteousness, His perfect status before God.

This doesn't mean that our actions are irrelevant, and that we can sin all we want. Our sinful actions, words, and attitudes grieve the Lord, but our status as beloved children remains intact. In His love, He disciplines and encourages us to live godly lives—both for our good and for His honor.

The Apostle Paul was so enamored with his forgiveness and righteousness in Christ that he was intensely motivated to please God by his actions and his deeds. In 1 Corinthians 6:19–20; 2 Corinthians 5:9; Philippians 3:8–11, and in other passages, Paul strongly stated his desire to please, honor, and glorify the One who had made him righteous.

Some people may read these statements and become uneasy, believing that I am discounting the gravity of sin. As you will see, I am not minimizing the destructive nature of sin, but am simply trying to elevate our view of the results of Christ's payment on the cross. Understanding our complete forgiveness and acceptance before God does not promote a casual attitude toward sin. On the contrary, it gives us a greater desire to live for and serve the One who died to free us from sin.

- How does being justified and having Christ's righteousness lead you to the conclusion: *I am completely forgiven by God, and am fully pleasing to Him?*

God, as I reflect on the magnitude of Your forgiveness and unconditional love for me, I feel . . .

506

CHRIST'S LOVE

> For the love of Christ controls us, having concluded this, that one died for all, therefore all died; and He died for all, that they who live should no longer live for themselves, but for Him who died and rose again on their behalf.
>
> 2 CORINTHIANS 5:14–15

UNDERSTANDING GOD'S GRACE COMPELS US TO ACTION BECAUSE love motivates us to please the One who has so freely loved us. When we experience love, we usually respond by seeking to express our love in return. Our obedience to God is an expression of our love for Him (John 14:15, 21), which comes from an understanding of what Christ has accomplished for us on the cross (2 Corinthians 5:14–15). We love because He first loved us and clearly demonstrated His love for us at the cross (1 John 4:16–19). Understanding this will highly motivate us to serve Him.

This great motivating factor is missing in many of our lives because we don't really believe that God loves us unconditionally. We expect His love to be conditional, based on our ability to earn it.

Our experience of God's love is based on our perception. If we believe that He is demanding or aloof, we will not be able to receive His love and tenderness. Instead, we will either be afraid of Him or angry with Him. Faulty perceptions of God often prompt us to rebel against Him.

Our image of God is the foundation for all of our motivations. As we grow in our understanding of His unconditional love and acceptance, we will be better able to grasp that His discipline is prompted by care, not cruelty. We will also be increasingly able to perceive the contrast between the joys of living for Christ and the destructive nature of sin. We will be motivated to experience eternal rewards *where neither moth nor rust destroys* (Matthew 6:20). And we will want our lives to bring honor to the One who loves us so much.

• Does the love of Christ compel you to obey Him? Why, or why not?

I will try to honor You today in my actions, words, and thoughts. As I grow in my awareness of just how much You care about me, Father, and how much I care about You, I realize that I cannot grieve You without grieving myself. I give thanks to You today for . . .

SIN IS DESTRUCTIVE

For the wages of sin is death, but the free gift of God is eternal life in Christ Jesus our Lord.

ROMANS 6:23

SATAN HAS EFFECTIVELY BLINDED MAN TO THE PAINFUL, DAMAGING CONSEQUENCES of sin. The effects of sin are all around us, yet many continue to indulge in the sex, status- and pleasure-seeking, and rampant self-centeredness that cause so much anguish and pain. Satan contradicted God in the Garden when he said, *You surely shall not die!* (Genesis 3:4). Sin is pleasant, but only for a season. Sooner or later, sin will result in some form of destruction.

Sin is destructive in many ways. Emotionally, we may experience the pain of guilt and shame and the fear of failure and punishment. Mentally, we may experience the anguish of flashbacks. We may also expend enormous amounts of time and energy thinking about our sins and rationalizing our guilt. Physically, we may suffer from psychosomatic illnesses or experience pain through physical abuse. Sin may also result in the loss of property, or even the loss of life. Relationally, we can alienate ourselves from others. Spiritually, we grieve the Holy Spirit, lose our testimony, and break our fellowship with God. The painful and destructive effects of sin are so profound that why we don't have an aversion to it is a mystery!

* How can viewing sin as destructive be a motivation for obedience to God?

Looking at my own life, I can see the far-reaching effects of sin's destruction. I long to be more like who I really am in You, Lord. As we walk together today, I need You to . . .

THE FATHER'S DISCIPLINE

All discipline for the moment seems not to be joyful, but sorrowful; yet to those who have been trained by it, afterwards it yields the peaceful fruit of righteousness.

HEBREWS 12:11

OUR LOVING FATHER HAS GIVEN US THE HOLY SPIRIT to convict us of sin. Conviction is a form of God's discipline, and serves as proof that we have become sons of God (Hebrews 12:5–11). It warns us that we are making choices without regard to either God's truth or sin's consequences. If we choose to be unresponsive to the Holy Spirit, our heavenly Father will discipline us in love. Many people do not understand the difference between discipline and punishment. The following chart shows their profound contrasts:

	PUNISHMENT	DISCIPLINE
SOURCE:	God's Wrath	God's Love
PURPOSE:	To Avenge a Wrong	To Correct a Wrong
RELATIONAL RESULT:	Alienation	Reconciliation
PERSONAL RESULT:	Guilt	A Righteous Lifestyle
DIRECTED TOWARD:	Non-Believers	His Children

Jesus bore all the punishment we deserved on the cross; therefore, we no longer need to fear punishment from God for our sins. We should seek to do what is right so that our Father will not have to correct us through discipline, but when we are disciplined, we should remember that God is correcting us in love. This discipline leads us to righteous performance, a reflection of Christ's righteousness in us.

• Do you sometimes confuse God's correction with punishment? If so, why?

Heavenly Father, if there is sin in my life that I am denying, please convict me of it through the power of Your Holy Spirit . . .

HIS COMMANDS FOR US ARE GOOD

Thy word is a lamp to my feet,
And a light to my path.
I have sworn, and I will confirm it,
That I will keep Thy righteous ordinances.

PSALMS 119:105–106

GOD'S COMMANDS ARE GIVEN FOR TWO GOOD PURPOSES: to protect us from the destructiveness of sin, and to direct us in a life of joy and fruitfulness. We have a wrong perspective if we only view God's commands as restrictions in our lives. Instead, we must realize that His commands are guidelines, given so that we might enjoy life to the fullest. God's commands should never be considered as a means to gain His approval.

In today's society, we have lost the concept of doing something because it is the right thing to do. Instead, we do things in exchange for some reward or favor, or to avoid punishment. Wouldn't it be novel to do something simply because it is the right thing to do? God's commands are holy, right, and good, and the Holy Spirit gives us the wisdom and strength to keep them. Therefore, since they have value in themselves, we can choose to obey God and follow His commands.

• How can viewing God's commands as good be a motivation to you?

Thank You for Your commands, dear Lord. I need to remember that they're not dead ends, blocking my path to happiness. Instead, they are sensible routes in the journey of my life when I'm wise enough to follow them. I trust You to . . .

510

DAY 25

ETERNAL REWARDS

For we must all appear before the judgment seat of Christ, that each one may be recompensed for his deeds in the body, according to what he has done, whether good or bad.

2 CORINTHIANS 5:10

YET ANOTHER COMPELLING REASON TO LIVE FOR GOD'S GLORY is the fact that we will be rewarded in heaven for our service to Him.

Now if any man builds upon the foundation with gold, silver, precious stones, wood, hay, straw, each man's work will become evident; for the day will show it, because it is to be revealed with fire; and the fire itself will test the quality of each man's work. If any man's work which he has built upon it remains, he shall receive a reward. If any man's work is burned up, he shall suffer loss; but he himself shall be saved, yet so as through fire.

1 CORINTHIANS 3:12–15

Through Christ's payment for us on the cross, we have escaped eternal judgment; however, our actions will be judged at the judgment seat of Christ. There, our performance will be evaluated and rewards presented for service to God. Rewards will be given for deeds that reflect a desire to honor Christ, but deeds performed in an attempt to earn God's acceptance, earn the approval of others, or meet our own standards will be rejected by God and consumed by fire.

- Read 1 Corinthians 9:24–27 and 2 Timothy 2:3–7; 4:7–8. How does receiving a reward become a motivation for obedience?

Thank You, God, for . . .

511

CHRIST IS WORTHY

Whom have I in heaven but Thee?
    And besides Thee, I desire nothing on earth. . . .
But as for me, the nearness of God is my good;
    I have made the Lord God my refuge, that I may tell of
all Thy works.

PSALM 73:25, 28

CHRIST IS WORTHY OF OUR AFFECTION AND OBEDIENCE. There is no other person, no goal, no fame or status, and no material possession that can compare with Him. The more we understand His love and majesty, the more we will praise Him and desire that He be honored at the expense of everything else.

Our most noble motivation for serving Christ is simply that He is worthy of our love and obedience. The Apostle John recorded his vision of the Lord and his response to His glory:

> After these things I looked, and behold, a door standing open in heaven, and the first voice which I had heard, like the sound of a trumpet speaking with me, said, "Come up here, and I will show you what must take place after these things." Immediately I was in the Spirit; and behold, a throne was standing in heaven, and One sitting on the throne. And He who was sitting was like a jasper stone and a sardius in appearance; and there was a rainbow around the throne, like an emerald in appearance. And around the throne were twenty-four thrones; and upon the thrones I saw twenty-four elders sitting, clothed in white garments, and golden crowns on their heads. . . .
>
> And when the living creatures give glory and honor and thanks to Him who sits on the throne, to Him who lives forever and ever, the twenty-four elders will fall down before Him who sits on the throne, and will worship Him who lives forever and ever, and will cast their crowns before the throne, saying,

> "Worthy art Thou, our Lord and our God,
>   to receive glory and honor and power;
> for Thou didst create all things,
>   and because of Thy will they existed,
>   and were created."

REVELATION 4:1–4, 9–11

- How do you feel as you reflect on the passages from Revelation 4?

- Do they motivate you? Why, or why not?

Father, today I want to praise You for . . .

512

GIVING AND RECEIVING LOVE

"By this all men will know that you are My disciples, if you have love for one another."

JOHN 13:35

A SYMPTOM OF OUR FEAR OF REJECTION IS OUR INABILITY TO GIVE and receive love. We find it difficult to open up and reveal our inner thoughts and motives because we believe that others will reject us if they know what we are really like. Therefore, our fear of rejection leads us to superficial relationships or isolation. The more we experience isolation, the more we need acceptance. Psychologist Eric Fromm once wrote, "The deep need of man is the need to overcome separateness, to leave the prison of his aloneness."

The fear of rejection is rampant, and loneliness is one of the most dangerous and widespread problems in America today. Some estimate that loneliness has already reached epidemic proportions, and say that if it continues to spread, it could seriously erode the emotional strength of our country. Loneliness is not relegated only to unbelievers. Ninety-two percent of the Christians attending a recent Bible conference admitted in a survey that feelings of loneliness were a major problem in their lives. All shared a basic symptom: a sense of despair at feeling unloved and a fear of being unwanted or unaccepted.

For the most part, our modern society has responded inadequately to rejection and loneliness. Our response has been outer-directed, meaning that we try to copy the customs, dress, ideas, and behavioral patterns of a particular group, allowing the consensus of the group to determine what is correct for us. But conforming to a group will not fully provide the security we are so desperately seeking. Only God can provide that through His people, His Word, His Spirit, and His timing.

• How does the fear of being rejected (disapproved of) by people affect your life? Give examples:

Father, You made me a unique, special individual. Whenever I feel rejected by others, please hold me fast in the truth that You are satisfied with the results of Your work, and so shall I be content. Father, I trust You to . . .

THE FEAR OF REJECTION

> All who hate me whisper together against me;
>> Against me they devise my hurt, saying,
> "A wicked thing is poured out upon him,
>> That when he lies down, he will not rise up again."
> Even my close friend, in whom I trusted,
>> Who ate my bread,
>> Has lifted up his heel against me.
> But Thou, O Lord, be gracious to me, and raise me up.
>
> PSALM 41:7–10A

VIRTUALLY ALL OF US FEAR REJECTION. WE CAN FALL PREY to it even when we've learned to harden our defenses in anticipation of someone's disapproval. Neither being defensive nor trying to please another person's every whim is the answer to this problem. These are only coping mechanisms which prevent us from dealing with the root of our fear.

Rejection is a type of communication. It conveys a message that someone else is unsatisfactory to us; that he or she doesn't measure up to a standard we've created or adopted. Sometimes, rejection is willfully used as an act of manipulation designed to control someone else. Usually, rejection is manifested by an outburst of anger, a disgusted look, an impatient answer, or a social snub. Whatever the form of behavior, it communicates disrespect, low value, and lack of appreciation. Nothing hurts quite like the message of rejection.

If this is true, why do we reject others so frequently? Again, rejection can be a very effective, though destructive, motivator. Without raising a finger, we can send the message that our targeted individual doesn't meet our standards. We can harness this person's instinctive desire for acceptance until we have changed and adapted his or her behavior to suit our tastes and purposes. This is how rejection enables us to control the actions of another human being.

- How have you used disapproval, silence, sarcasm, or criticism to get others to do what you wanted them to do?

Rejection is a powerful, destructive tool. Please remind me of this fact, Lord, as I relate to those around me today. Father, I hope . . .

514

LIKE PUPPETS ON A STRING

For am I now seeking the favor of men, or of God? Or am I striving to please
men? If I were still trying to please men, I would not be a bond-servant of Christ.

GALATIANS 1:10

HOW DO YOU REACT TO THE FEAR OF REJECTION? SOME OF US project a cool, impervious
exterior, and consequently, never develop deep, satisfying relationships. Some of us are so
fearful of rejection that we withdraw and decline almost everything, while others continually
say yes to everyone, hoping to gain their approval. Some of us are shy and easily manipulated;
some of us are sensitive to criticism and react defensively. A deep fear of rejection may prompt
hostility and promote the development of nervous disorders.

Our fear of rejection will control us to the degree by which we base our self-worth on the
opinions of others rather than on our relationship with God. Our dependence on others for
value brings bondage, while abiding in the truths of Christ's love and acceptance brings freedom and joy.

* Describe a situation when someone (friend, boss, parent, child) withheld approval, or
  used criticism, silence, sarcasm, or praise to manipulate you into doing what he or she
  wanted you to do. What did this person say or do? Did he or she succeed? Why, or why
  not?

*When I think about what I just described, dear God, I feel a lot of different
emotions. Please help me to sort them out, Lord . . .*

CONDITIONAL APPROVAL

His speech was smoother than butter,
But his heart was war;
His words were softer than oil,
Yet they were drawn swords.

PSALM 55:21

MY DESIRE FOR THE APPROVAL OF OTHERS HAS OFTEN BEEN SO GREAT that I sometimes joke about having been born an "approval addict." Growing up, I had the feeling that I didn't fit in; that I was "different" from others; that there was, therefore, something inherently wrong with me. I felt inadequate and tried to win the approval of others, desperately hoping that this would compensate for the negative feelings I had about myself.

But ironically, the conditional approval of others was never enough to satisfy me. Instead, being praised only reminded me of the disapproval I might encounter if I failed to maintain what I had achieved. I was thus compelled to work even harder at being successful. I occasionally find myself falling into this pattern of behavior even now, despite my improved knowledge, experience, and relationship with God.

To see how others' expectations can affect you, answer the following:

• _____ would be more pleased with me if I would:

• _____ is proud of me when I:

• How does _____ attempt to get me to change by what he (or she) says and does?

• Things I do or say to get _____ to approve of me include:

Dear God, please help me to apply Your truths in my everyday life by ...

GOING DEEPER

I went about mourning
    as though it were my friend or brother;
I bowed down mourning,
    as one who sorrows for a mother.
But at my stumbling they rejoiced, and gathered themselves
    together;
The smiters whom I did not know gathered together against
    me,
They slandered me without ceasing.

PSALM 35:14–15

I DON'T BELIEVE THAT ANY OF US WILL GAIN COMPLETE FREEDOM from our propensity to base our self-worth on the approval of others until we see the Lord. Our God-given instinct to survive compels us to avoid pain. Knowing that rejection and disapproval bring pain, we will continue our attempts to win the esteem of others whenever possible. The good news is that because we are fully pleasing to God, we need not be devastated when others respond to us in a negative way.

As we grow in our relationship with God, the Holy Spirit will continue teaching us how to apply this liberating truth to different aspects of our lives at an increasingly deeper level. In fact, one evidence of His work within us is the ability to see new areas of our lives in which we are allowing the opinions of others to determine our sense of worth. With spiritual maturity, we will more often be able to identify these areas and choose to find our significance in God's unconditional love for us and complete acceptance of us. However, profound changes in our value system take honesty, objectivity, and prolonged, persistent application of God's Word.

• Does spiritual growth lead to more complexity or more simplicity in your faith? Explain.

Father, as I grow in Your Word, please teach me more about . . .

RECONCILIATION

And although you were formerly alienated and hostile in mind, engaged in evil deeds, yet He has now reconciled you in His fleshly body through death, in order to present you before Him holy and blameless and beyond reproach.

COLOSSIANS 1:21–22

As I TALKED WITH PAM, IT BECAME OBVIOUS THAT SHE DID NOT understand this great truth of reconciliation. Three years after she married, Pam had committed adultery with a coworker. Although she had confessed her sin to God and to her husband, and had been forgiven, guilt continued to plague her, making it difficult for her to feel acceptable to God. Four years after the affair, she still could not forgive herself for what she had done.

Sitting in my office, we explored her reluctance to accept God's forgiveness.

"It sounds as though you believe that God can't forgive the sin you committed," I said.

"That's right," she replied. "I don't think He ever will."

"But God doesn't base His love and acceptance of us on our performance," I said. "If any sin is so filthy and vile that it makes us less acceptable to Him, then the cross is insufficient. If the cross isn't sufficient for all sin, then the Bible is in error when it says that He forgave *all* your sins (Colossians 2:13–15). God took our sins and cancelled them by nailing them to Christ's cross. In this way, God also took away Satan's power to condemn us for sin. So you see, nothing you will ever do can nullify your reconciliation and make you unacceptable to God."

Our unconditional acceptance in Christ is a profound, life-changing truth. Salvation is not simply a ticket to heaven. It is the beginning of a dynamic new relationship with God. *Justification* is the doctrine that explains the judicial facts of our forgiveness and righteousness in Christ. *Reconciliation* explains the relational aspect of our salvation. The moment we receive Christ by faith, we enter into a personal relationship with Him. We are united with God in an eternal and inseparable bond (Romans 8:38–39). We are bound in an indissoluble union with Him, as fellow heirs with Christ. The Holy Spirit has sealed us in that relationship, and we are absolutely secure in Christ.

• Read Colossians 1:21–22. Compare your former state to your present condition:

Lord, I trust You to . . .

DAY 33

DECLARED ACCEPTABLE

Having also believed, you were sealed in Him with the Holy Spirit of promise, who is given as a pledge of our inheritance, with a view to the redemption of God's own possession, to the praise of His glory.

EPHESIANS 1:13–14

RECENTLY IN A GROUP PRAYER MEETING, SOMEONE PRAYED, "Thank you, God, for accepting me when I am so unacceptable." This person understood that we cannot earn God's acceptance by our own merit, but seemed to have forgotten that we are unconditionally accepted in Christ. We are no longer unacceptable—the point of the cross. Through Christ's death and resurrection, we have become acceptable to God. This did not occur because God decided He could overlook our sin, but because Christ forgave all of our sins so that He could present us to the Father, holy and blameless.

Because of reconciliation, we are completely acceptable to God and are completely accepted by God. As these passages illustrate, we enjoy a full and complete relationship with Him, and in this relationship, His determination of our value is not based on our performance.

* What is wrong with the statement, "Thank you, Lord, for accepting me even though I am so unacceptable"?

Sometimes it's hard to comprehend that I have been accepted by You, and that, because of Christ, I really am acceptable to You, Father. Thank You, for . . .

THE FINAL AUTHORITY

And in Him you have been made complete, and He is the head over all rule and authority.

COLOSSIANS 2:10

WE CAN DO NOTHING TO CONTRIBUTE to Christ's free gift of salvation; furthermore, if we base our self-worth on the approval of others, then we are actually saying that our ability to please others is of greater value than Christ's payment. We are the sinners, the depraved, the wretched, and the helpless. He is the loving Father, the seeking, searching, patient Savior who has made atonement for the lost, and has extended to us His grace and sonship. We add nothing to our salvation. It is God who seeks us out, convicts us of sin, and reveals Himself to us. It is God who gives us the very faith with which to accept Him. Our faith is simply our response to what He has done for us.

So then, our worth lies in the fact that Christ's blood has paid for our sins; therefore, we are reconciled to God. We are accepted on that basis alone, but does this great truth indicate that we don't need other people in our lives? On the contrary, God very often uses other believers to demonstrate His love and acceptance to us. The strength, comfort, encouragement, and love of Christians toward one another is a visible expression of God's love. However, our acceptance and worth are not *dependent* on others' acceptance of us, even if they are fellow believers! Whether they accept us or not, we are *still* deeply loved, completely forgiven, fully pleasing, totally accepted, and complete in Christ. *He alone* is the final authority on our worth and acceptance.

- If you are completely and fully accepted by the perfect Creator of the universe, why do you fear the rejection of men?

Heavenly Father, please help me to understand how the fear of not being accepted has affected my life. Please show me . . .

THE ROLE OF RELATIONSHIPS

Fathers, do not exasperate your children, that they may not lose heart.
COLOSSIANS 3:21

FOR MANY OF US, THE UNCONDITIONAL LOVE, FORGIVENESS, AND ACCEPTANCE of Christ seems abstract, and is difficult to comprehend. We may understand the premise of these character traits, but may still be unable to incorporate them into our personal experience. Often, we can trace this difficulty to our parental relationships.

God intends for parents to model His character to their children. According to Scripture, parents are to give their children affection, compassion, protection, provision, and loving discipline. When parents provide this kind of environment in their home, children are usually able to transfer these perceptions to the character of God, and believe that He is loving, compassionate, protective, gracious, and a loving disciplinarian. In turn, they are often able to model these characteristics to their own children.

Many of us, however, have not received this parental model of God's character. On an extremely wide spectrum, some of us have had relatively healthy relationships with our parents, while others have experienced various forms of neglect, condemnation, and manipulation. Still others have suffered the deeper wounds of sexual abuse, physical abuse, or abandonment. The greater the degree of dysfunction (or poor modeling) in a family, the greater the potential for emotional, spiritual, and relational wounds. Put another way, the poorer the parental modeling of God's love, forgiveness, and power, the greater our difficulty in experiencing and applying these characteristics in our lives.

- In what ways did your parents accurately reflect God's care, protection, and provision?

- In what ways did they misrepresent God's nature to you?

Father, please open my heart and my eyes so I may see how Your character differs from what I've seen modeled in my childhood. This may take a lot of honesty and objectivity on my part, but I want to grow closer to You, and I want to be a good role-model for my children (future children). I know I can trust You to . . .

HEALTHY VS. UNHEALTHY RELATIONSHIPS

Bear one another's burdens, and thus fulfill the law of Christ.
For each one shall bear his own load.

GALATIANS 6:2, 5

BECAUSE SO MANY OF US ARE VULNERABLE WHEN WE BEGIN allowing ourselves to experience the pain that usually accompanies growth, it is wise to have a basic understanding of healthy and unhealthy relationships.

We must first understand that while God often demonstrates His love and affirmation for us through believers and non-believers alike, His desire is that our relationships with others will enable us to know Him more fully. His work through others is, in part, to serve as a channel by which we can better understand His divine love and acceptance of us. Sadly, we are all prone to miss His message and mistake His messenger(s) as the source of our fulfillment. When this misperception is carried to an extreme, we can fall into *emotional dependency*, "the condition resulting when the ongoing presence and/or nurturing of another is believed necessary for personal security."*

In his book, *The Four Loves*, C. S. Lewis described the difference between lovers and friends:

> Lovers are always talking to one another about their love; Friends hardly ever about their Friendship. Lovers are normally face to face, absorbed in each other; Friends, side by side, absorbed in some common interest. Above all, Eros (while it lasts) is necessary between two only. But two, far from being the necessary number for Friendship, is not even the best.*

Healthy relationships are turned outward, rather than inward. Healthy relationships encourage individuality rather than conformity, and are concerned with independence, rather than emotional dependence. Healthy relationships point one's focus to the Lord and pleasing Him, rather than toward the friendship and pleasing one another.

• What are some characteristics of healthy relationships? Of unhealthy ones?

It's good to have a basic understanding of healthy and unhealthy relationships. Lord, I look to You for discernment as I apply what I'm learning to my present and future relationships. Please cross my path with fellow Christians who are seeking healthy friendships. Thank You for . . .

* C. S. Lewis, *The Four Loves* (New York: Harcourt Brace Jovanovich, Inc., 1960), pp. 91–92,

AVOIDING EMOTIONAL DEPENDENCY

Therefore, laying aside falsehood, speak truth, each one of you, with his neighbor, for we are members of one another.

EPHESIANS 4:25

HOW DO WE KNOW WHEN WE'VE CROSSED THE LINE from a healthy relationship to one that is emotionally dependent? When either party in a relationship:*

- experiences frequent jealousy, possessiveness and a desire for exclusivism, viewing other people as a threat to the relationship.
- prefers to spend time alone with this friend and becomes frustrated when this does not happen.
- becomes irrationally angry or depressed when this friend withdraws slightly.
- loses interest in a friendship other than this one.
- experiences romantic or sexual feelings leading to fantasy about this person.
- becomes preoccupied by the person's appearance, personality, problems, and interests.
- is unwilling to make short- or long-range plans that do not include the other person.
- is unable to see the other's faults realistically.
- becomes defensive about this relationship when asked about it.
- displays physical affection beyond what is appropriate for a friendship.
- refers frequently to the other in conversation; feels free to "speak for" the other.
- exhibits an intimacy and familiarity with this friend that causes others to feel uncomfortable or embarrassed in their presence.

Our relationships with one another are very important to God; so much so, that He has placed unity among the brethren as a priority in our relationship with Him (see Matthew 5:23–24). This is because God has reconciled us to Himself as a _body_ in Christ (Ephesians 2:16), and therefore intends for us to interact as _members of one another_ (Ephesians 4:25).

Pray that God will guide you to relationships which will encourage you to be honest; practice the truth of His Word; affirm you, and thereby help you develop an appropriate love for yourself; and compel you to focus on Him as the gracious provider of your needs. Eventually, your gratitude will motivate you to practice pleasing Him rather than other people.

- Do any of the characteristics of dependent relationships apply to your relationships? Which ones? What can you do about them?

Thank You for everything I've learned about dependent relationships, Lord.
As I think about my friends, family, coworkers, and other relationships,
please show me which ones I need to recognize as being emotionally depen-
dent upon me or those upon which I am emotionally dependent. Lord, I trust
You to . . .

THE FATHER'S LOVE

If I speak with the tongues of men and of angels, but do not have love, I have become a noisy gong or a clanging cymbal. And if I have the gift of prophecy, and know all mysteries and all knowledge; and if I have all faith, so as to remove mountains, but do not have love, I am nothing.

1 CORINTHIANS 13:1–2

HOW DO WE LEARN TO REJECT SATAN'S LIE, *I must be approved by certain others to feel good about myself*? How can we begin to practically apply the great truth of our reconciliation to Almighty God? The following exercise will help you begin to experience the freedom and joy of reconciliation.

The thirteenth chapter of First Corinthians describes God's unconditional love and acceptance of us. To personalize this passage, replace the word *love* with *My Father*. Then, memorize the following, and when fear comes to you, recall the love and kindness of God:

> *My Father* is very patient and kind.
> *My Father* is not envious, never boastful.
> *My Father* is not arrogant.
> *My Father* is never rude, nor is He self-seeking.
> *My Father* is not quick to take offense.
> *My Father* keeps no score of wrongs.
> *My Father* does not gloat over my sins, but is always glad when truth prevails.
> *My Father* knows no limit to His endurance, no end to His trust.
> *My Father* is always hopeful and patient.

As you memorize this passage, ask God to show you if your perception of Him is in error in any way. This will enable you to have a more accurate perception of God, and will help you to experience more of His unconditional love and acceptance.

• Describe your thoughts and feelings as you reflect on the paraphrase of 1 Corinthians 13:

When I read the thirteenth chapter of 1 Corinthians, I feel humbled, overwhelmed, grateful, joyful ...
Your Spirit fills me with love, compassion, reverence, patience ...

ASSIGNING BLAME

And so, as those who have been chosen of God, holy and beloved, put on a heart of compassion, kindness, humility, gentleness and patience; bearing with one another, and forgiving each other, whoever has a complaint against anyone, just as the Lord forgave you, so also should you.

COLOSSIANS 3:12–13

WHETHER CONSCIOUSLY OR UNCONSCIOULSY, WE ALL TEND TO POINT an accusing finger, assigning blame for virtually every failure. Whenever we fail to receive approval for our performance, we are likely to search for a reason, a culprit, a scapegoat. More often than not, we can find no one but ourselves to blame, so the accusing finger points right back at us. Self-condemnation is a severe form of punishment.

If possible, we will often try to place the blame on others and fulfill the law of retribution—that people should get what they deserve. For most of our lives, we have been conditioned to make someone pay for failures or shortcomings. When we miss a deadline at work because we didn't use our time wisely and don't want to admit it, we try to find someone else to take the blame. When a problem is partly our fault and partly someone else's, we often are quick to mention the other person's culpability.

For every flaw we see around us, we often search for someone to blame. Some of us internalize, blaming ourselves for everything and anything that anybody did wrong. Others externalize the blame, hoping to exonerate ourselves by making sure others are identified as "guilty" and punished.

- Does condemning yourself help you become a better person? Why, or why not?

Heavenly Father, today I will try not to be so hard on myself and others. As I look to You for a model of compassion, please show me . . .

DEFENDING AND BLAMING

But if you bite and devour one another, take care lest you be consumed by one another. But I say, walk by the Spirit and you will not carry out the desire of the flesh.

GALATIANS 5:15–16

ANOTHER REASON WE SEEK TO BLAME OTHERS IS THAT OUR success often depends on their contributions. Their failures are threats to us. When these failures block our goals of success, we usually respond by defending ourselves and blaming others, often using condemnation to manipulate them to improve their performance. Blaming others also helps put a safe distance between their failures and our fragile self-worth.

Whether our accusations are focused on ourselves or others, we all have a tendency to believe that someone has to take the blame. When Ellen discovered that her fifteen-year-old daughter was pregnant, she went a week without sleep, tossing and turning, trying to determine who was at fault. Was it her daughter, who had brought this reproach on the family, or was she to blame for failing as a mother? All Ellen knew was that someone had to take responsibility for the crisis.

Rather than being objective and looking for a solid, biblical solution to our problems, we often resort to either accusing someone else or berating ourselves.

* Think of a close friend or family member with whom you've had a conflict. What did you say or do to inflict emotional pain?

* What are some reasons you said or did those things?

Lord, I've said and done some things that have hurt _____ .
There was a better way of handling my emotions and I admit . . .

ONE UP—ONE DOWN

Therefore consider the members of your earthly body as dead to immorality, impurity, passion, evil desire, and greed, which amounts to idolatry. For it is on account of these things that the wrath of God will come, and in them you also once walked, when you were living in them. But now you also, put them all aside: anger, wrath, malice, slander, and abusive speech from your mouth.

COLOSSIANS 3:5–8

SOMETIMES, WE BLAME OTHERS TO MAKE OURSELVES FEEL BETTER. By blaming someone else who failed, we feel superior. In fact, the higher the position of the one who failed (parent, boss, pastor, etc.), the farther they fall, and often, the better we feel. This desire to be superior, to be "one up" on someone, is at the root of gossip.

In other situations, however, just the opposite is true. When a parent fails, a child usually accepts the blame for that failure. Even as adults, we may readily assume blame in our relationships with those in authority. We have much invested in supporting those we depend upon. This is one reason why denial is so strong in abusive families. For example, one little girl said, "I never told anybody that Daddy was molesting me because I thought that somebody would take him away from our family."

• Describe three recent incidents in your life in which you feared being blamed or punished. Why did you have this fear?

Jesus, it's not easy to stand up and accept the full responsibility of my wrongdoings. I am comforted, though, by knowing that You are pleased by my efforts to do so. Thank You for . . .

527

RESPONDING TO OTHERS' FAILURES

> And be kind to one another, tender-hearted, forgiving each other, just as God in Christ also has forgiven you.
>
> EPHESIANS 4:32

HOW SHOULD WE RESPOND IF ANOTHER FAILS? If the person who failed is a Christian, we need to affirm God's truth about him or her: *He(or she) is deeply loved, completely forgiven, fully pleasing, and totally accepted by God, and complete in Christ.* This perspective can eventually change our condemning attitude to one of love and a desire to help. By believing these truths, we will gradually be able to love this person just as God loves us (1 John 4:11), forgive him or her just as God has forgiven us (Ephesians 4:32), and accept him or her just as God has accepted us (Romans 15:7). This does not mean that we will become blind to the faults or failures of others. We will continue to see them, but our response to them will change considerably over time, from condemnation to compassion. As we depend less on other people for our self-worth, their sins and mistakes will become less of a threat to us, and we will desire to help them instead of being compelled to punish them.

• How do you normally respond to other Christians' sins and failures?

• How would you like to respond now?

Heavenly Father, teach me Your way of compassion. Please show me . . .

CONDEMNING PEOPLE FOR MISTAKES

Never pay back evil for evil to anyone. Respect what is right in the sight of all men.

If possible, so far as it depends on you, be at peace with all men.

ROMANS 12:17–18

WE TEND TO MAKE TWO MAJOR ERRORS WHEN WE PUNISH others for their failures. The first is that we condemn people not only for genuine sin, but also for their mistakes. When people who have tried their best fail, they do not need our biting blame. They need our love and encouragement. Again, we often tend to blame others because their actions (whether they reflect overt disobedience or honest mistakes) make us look like failures, and our own failure is unacceptable to us. Husband–wife, parent–child, and employer–employee relationships are especially vulnerable to one's being threatened by the failure of another. A wife gets angry with her husband for his not-so-funny joke at an important dinner party; a parent erupts at a child for accidentally spilling milk; a manager scowls at an employee because an error in the employee's calculations has made him look foolish to his supervisor. People generally experience difficulty in dealing with their _sins_; let's not compound their problems by condemning them for their _mistakes_.

A second major error we often make by condemning others is believing that we are godly agents of condemnation. Unable to tolerate injustice, we seem to possess a great need to balance the scales of right and wrong. We are correct in recognizing that sin is reprehensible and deserves condemnation; yet, we have not been licensed by God to punish others for their sins. Judgment is God's responsibility, not man's.

Jesus dealt specifically with this issue when several men decided to stone a woman caught in adultery. He told them that the person without sin should throw the first stone. Beginning with the eldest, all of the accusers walked away as they remembered their own sins (John 8:3–9). In light of their own sinfulness, they no longer saw fit to condemn the sins of another.

As this incident clearly illustrates, we should leave righteous condemnation and punishment in the hands of the One worthy of the responsibility. Our response should be love, affirmation, and possibly, compassionate correction.

- Which of these errors do you tend to make?

- How does that affect you? Your relationships?

Dear Lord, please give me the desire to encourage and build up others rather than condemn and punish them. Help me remember that "treating others how I would like to be treated" includes my responses to their mistakes and failures, too. Please let me sense Your nearness today as ...

PRIVILEGES OF SONSHIP

"You are of your father the devil," Jesus explained, "and you want to do the desires of your father."

JOHN 8:44

WORDS LIKE THESE MAKE IT EASY TO UNDERSTAND why we believe Satan's lies so readily! However, at some point in our lives, the Holy Spirit drew us to Christ, and we trusted Him to forgive us and give us new purpose and meaning in our existence. The Holy Spirit baptized us into the body of Christ, a new spiritual family, the family of God. He plucked us from the family of Satan (Colossians 1:13–14) and adopted us into God's eternal family as sons and daughters (Romans 8:15). We were cursed to die as members of Satan's family, but as members of God's family, we were granted everything pertaining to life and godliness at the very moment of our new birth. We were not forced to qualify to receive God's provisions, but instead have received the rights and privileges of sons by His grace and mercy. In one of the most famous dialogues in the Bible, Jesus explained the profound truth of regeneration to Nicodemus:

"... unless one is born again, he cannot see the king-dom of God .... That which is born of the flesh is flesh, and that which is born of the Spirit is spirit. Do not marvel that I said to you, 'You must be born again.'"

JOHN 3:3, 6–7

• What does "grace" mean to you?

• How has your understanding of God's attitude toward you changed?

Heavenly Father, thank You for ...

HONEST OR NOT?

A prudent man conceals knowledge,
But the heart of fools proclaims folly.
PROVERBS 12:23

WHEN OTHERS' OFFEND US OR INSULT US, should we tell them that they have made us angry or hurt our feelings? This question can be difficult to answer. Some psychologists tell us that we should vent all of our emotions because repression is unhealthy. Others tell us that our emotions will always be positive and controlled if we are truly walking with the Lord. We should avoid both of these extremes. Venting our anger uncontrollably is not a healthy solution, but neither is continued repression and denial.

We need a safe environment to express our emotions: a good friend or counselor who will help us get in touch with our true feelings, which we may have suppressed for years. We can also learn to express ourselves fully to the Lord and tell Him our true feelings, fears, hopes, and dreams. (The Psalms are filled with honest expressions of anger, pain, confusion, hope, and faith.) In this safe environment, we can slowly learn how to communicate appropriately with those who have hurt us. This requires wisdom because each situation and each person often requires a different form of communication.

- What factors determine how, if, how much, and when you tell someone of your hurt and anger? Who can you talk to honestly about your pain?

Christ Jesus, I don't want to run away from my emotions, and, likewise, I don't want to express myself to others who have offended me in such a way that I end up offending them. Please help me to pause long enough to assess a situation and seek Your wisdom in how to respond. I need You to . . .

A HEALTHY SENSE OF ASSERTIVENESS

But speaking the truth in love, we are to grow up in all aspects into Him, who is the head, even Christ.

EPHESIANS 4:15

AS WE LEARN TO RELATE APPROPRIATELY WITH THOSE who have hurt or injured us in some way, we will begin to develop a healthy sense of assertiveness—an important component in shaping other people's behavior toward us. For example, if others are rude, but never realize it because we passively accept their behavior in an attempt to avoid upsetting them, at least two things usually happen: We develop resentment toward them, and they never have to come to terms with their negative impact on others. They then miss an important opportunity to change, and we effectually prolong their hurtful behavior. There are appropriate and inappropriate ways of communicating our sense of anger or resentment to others, but these feelings need to be spoken—for their benefit and for ours.

We also need to remember that learning how to express our feelings appropriately is a _process_. We can't expect to respond perfectly to everyone. It takes time to express years of repressed pain. It also takes time to learn how to respond firmly and clearly. Be patient with yourself.

We have a choice in our response to failure: We can condemn or we can learn. All of us fail, but this doesn't mean that we are failures. We need to understand that failing can be a step toward maturity, not a permanent blot on our self-esteem. Like children first learning to walk, we all stumble and fall. And, just like children, we can pick ourselves up and begin again. We don't have to allow failure to prevent us from being used by God.

- Describe a "healthy sense of assertiveness."

- How much is too much? How much is too little?

Lord, as I learn how to respond to others in a proper, assertive way, please give me discernment, patience, and . . .

INORDINATE FEAR OF GOD

For we do not have a high priest who is unable to sympathize with our weaknesses, but we have one who has been tempted in every way, just as we are—yet was without sin. Let us then approach the throne of grace with confidence, so that we may receive mercy and find grace to help us in our time of need.

HEBREWS 4:15–16, NIV

THERE HAVE BEEN MANY TIMES IN MY LIFE THAT I FELT God was going to punish me by causing me to lose all that I had, either because I'd done something I shouldn't have, or because I'd failed to do something I should have. This erroneous perception of God has driven me away from Him on many occasions when I've needed Him most, and is completely contrary to the One whom Paul described as *the Father of mercies and God of all comfort* (2 Corinthians 1:3).

If we have trusted Christ for our salvation, God has forgiven us, and wants us to experience His forgiveness on a daily basis. Moses was a murderer, but God forgave him and used him to deliver Israel from Egypt. David was an adulterer and a murderer, but God forgave him and made him a great king. Peter denied the Lord, but God forgave him, and Peter became a leader in the Church. God rejoices when His children learn to accept His forgiveness, pick themselves up, and walk after they have stumbled. But we must also learn to forgive ourselves. Rather than viewing our weaknesses as a threat to our self-esteem, it is God's desire that they compel us to move forward in our relationship with Him.

- What are some reasons we may have an inordinate fear of God?

- What are some differences between a healthy respect to God and this inordinate fear?

Father, I will remind myself every morning that I have been forgiven by You. And because You have forgiven me, I can forgive myself . . .

FOR WHOM DID CHRIST DIE?

For while we were still helpless, at the right time Christ died for the ungodly. For one will hardly die for a righteous man; though perhaps for the good man someone would dare even to die. But God demonstrates His own love toward us, in that while we were yet sinners, Christ died for us.

ROMANS 5:6–8

TO UNDERSTAND GOD'S WONDROUS PROVISION OF PROPITIATION, it is helpful to remember what He has endured from mankind. From Adam and Eve's sin in the Garden of Eden to the obvious depravity we see in our world today, human history is mainly the story of greed, hatred, lust, and pride—evidence of man's wanton rebellion against the God of love and peace. If not done with a desire to glorify Him, even our "good" deeds are like filthy garments to God (Isaiah 64:6).

Our sin deserves the righteous wrath of God. He is the Almighty, the rightful judge of the universe. He is absolutely holy and perfect. *God is light, and in Him there is no darkness at all* (1 John 1:5). Because of these attributes, God cannot overlook sin, nor can He compromise by accepting sinful behavior. For God to condone even one sin would defile His holiness like smearing a white satin wedding gown with black tar.

Because He is holy, God's aversion to sin is manifested in righteous anger. However, God is not only righteously indignant about sin, He is also infinitely loving. In His holiness, God condemns sin, but in the most awesome example of love the world has ever seen, He ordained that His Son would die to pay for our sins. God sacrificed the sinless, perfect Savior to turn away, *to propitiate,* His great wrath.

And for whom did Christ die? Was it for the saints who honored Him? Was it for a world that appreciated His sinless life and worshipped Him? No! Christ died for *us,* while we were yet in rebellion against Him.

- Why is it significant to realize that Christ died for you personally and not only for "all people"? How does that make you feel?

Heavenly Father, thank You for . . .

THE FATHOMLESS LOVE OF CHRIST

> For I am convinced that neither death, nor life, nor angels, nor principalities, nor things present, nor things to come, nor powers, nor height, nor depth, nor any other created thing, shall be able to separate us from the love of God, which is in Christ Jesus our Lord.
>
> ROMANS 8:38–39

WHO CAN MEASURE THE FATHOMLESS DEPTH OF LOVE that sent Christ to the cross? While we were the enemies of God, Christ averted the wrath we deserved so that we might become the sons of God.

What can we say of our holy heavenly Father? Surely, He did not escape seeing Christ's mistreatment at the hands of sinful men—the scourgings, the humiliation, the beatings. Surely, He who spoke the world into being could have delivered Christ from the entire ordeal. And yet, the God of heaven peered down through time and saw you and me. Though we were His enemies, He loved us and longed to rescue us from our sins, and designated the sinless Christ to become our substitute. Only Christ could avert God's righteous wrath against sin, so in love, the Father kept silent as Jesus hung from the cross. All of His anger, all of the wrath we would ever deserve, was poured upon Christ, and Christ became sin for us (2 Corinthians 5:21). Because he paid the penalty for our sins, and God's wrath was avenged, God no longer looks upon us through the eyes of judgment, but instead, He now lavishes His love upon us. The Scriptures teach that absolutely nothing can separate us from God's love (Romans 8:38–39). He has adopted us into a tender, intimate, and powerful relationship with Him (Romans 8:15).

- What does it mean to "lavish love" on someone?

- Do you sense that God lavishes His love on you? Why or why not?

Thank You, God, for the love that you lavish on me. I feel . . .

LETTING GO

That, in reference to your former manner of life, you lay aside the old self, which is being corrupted in accordance with the lusts of deceit, and that you be renewed in the spirit of your mind, and put on the new self, which in the likeness of God has been created in righteousness and holiness of the truth.

EPHESIANS 4:22–24

TOO OFTEN, OUR SELF-IMAGE RESTS SOLELY ON AN EVALUATION of our past behavior, being measured only through a memory. Day after day, year after year, we tend to build our personalities upon the rubble of yesterday's personal disappointments.

Perhaps we find some strange kind of comfort in our personal failings. Perhaps there is some security in accepting ourselves as much less than we can become. That minimizes the risk of failure. Certainly, if we expect little from ourselves we will seldom be disappointed!

But nothing forces us to remain in the mold of the past. By the grace and power of God, we can change! We can persevere and overcome! No one forces us to keep shifting our feet in the muck of old failures. We can dare to accept the challenge of building a new life.

Dr. Paul Tournier once compared life to a man hanging from a trapeze. The trapeze bar was the man's security, his pattern of existence, his lifestyle. Then God swung another trapeze into the man's view, and he faced a perplexing dilemma. Should he relinquish his past? Should he reach for the new bar? The moment of truth came, Dr. Tournier explained, when the man realized that to grab onto the new bar, he must release the old one.

- What memories and wounds of the past enslave you?

- How can you let them go and build a new identity, new qualities in relationships, and a new hope?

- What sources of input reinforce a low view of yourself?

Jesus, the past has left some scars on me. Some of them are small, others are quite apparent. You know my wounds, You know my needs. It's not always easy to let go of the past, but I realize I must if You are going to be in control of my present and my future . . .

DAY 51

GRASPING GOD'S VIEW

I can do all things through Him who strengthens me.

PHILIPPIANS 4:13

OUR PAST RELATIONSHIPS MAY INVOLVE THE INTENSE PAIN OF NEGLECT, abuse, and manipulation, but if we do not begin the process of healing, we will be unable to experience the joy, challenge, and yes, the potential for failure in the present.

I have struggled with this process of change for the greater part of my life. It may have been that I was raised in a poor family. It may have been that while I was growing up, I often felt very awkward. It may have been that there were some inadequacies in my home life. For whatever reasons, I grew up with a sense of shame about myself and my circumstances.

I often felt inadequate during my childhood. I had the impression that I just didn't measure up. Others might not have thought I felt this way, but my sense of inadequacy was often intense.

Being exceptionally tall and lanky, I was uncomfortable with the way I looked, and felt out of place among my peers. My feelings of inferiority prevented me from pursuing dating relationships for a number of years. The threat of potential rejection prompted me to withdraw from social gatherings, preferring instead to spend time with the few friends I felt most comfortable with.

The truth that I am deeply loved, fully pleasing, and totally accepted by the God of the universe has taken me a lifetime to comprehend. But gradually, by studying God's Word and by experiencing loving relationships with other believers who genuinely care for me and appreciate me, I have continued to gain a better understanding of the way God values me. This has improved my sense of self-worth considerably.

• How can unrealistic expectations of "quick change" in our lives prove to be a major hindrance to our progress?

• Do you really think that you can view yourself any differently than you always have? If not, why?

Lord, I need You to . . .

537

CHANGE IS A PROCESS

"The kingdom of God is like a man who casts seed upon the soil; and goes to bed at night and gets up by day, and the seed sprouts up and grows—how, he himself does not know. The soil produces crops by itself; first the blade, then the head. But when the crop permits, he immediately puts in the sickle, because the harvest has come."

MARK 4:26–29

MANY OF MY PAST MEMORIES ARE STILL PAINFUL FOR ME, and I imagine they always will be. But through Christ, my present attitude about myself is continually changing. Knowing that I have no reason to feel ashamed has motivated me to pursue a number of challenges that I wouldn't have even considered pursuing a number of years ago. In the process, I have experienced failure and success. God has used each instance to teach me that despite my circumstances, my worth is secure in Him.

We need to be honest about the pain, the anger, the disappointment, and the loneliness of our past. We need to put ourselves in relationships that will encourage us to feel what we may have suppressed for many years. This will enable us to begin (or continue) to experience hope, and eventually, healing. Change is possible, but it is a process.

Does this seem strange? Does it seem difficult? We may have difficulty relinquishing what is familiar (though painful) for what is unfamiliar because our fear of the unknown often seems stronger than the pain of a poor self-concept. It seems right to hang on. Proverbs 16:25 says, *There is a way which seems right to a man, but its end is the way of death.*

Any change in our behavior requires a release from our old self-concept, which is often founded in failure and the expectations of others. We need to learn how to relate to ourselves in a new way. To accomplish this, we must begin to base our self-worth on God's opinion of us and trust in His Spirit to accomplish change in our lives. Then, and only then, can we overcome Satan's deception that strongly influences our self-perception and behavior.

- In what ways are you afraid of change in your life?

- Why would we tend to cling to the "painful familiar" instead of reaching, learning, and growing?

God, as I struggle to make the right choices, to grow, and heal, I am grateful to You for . . .

538

PUT ON THE NEW SELF

That, in reference to your former manner of life, you lay aside the old self, which is being corrupted in accordance with the lusts of deceit, and that you be renewed in the spirit of your mind, and put on the new self, which in the likeness of God has been created in righteousness and holiness of the truth.

EPHESIANS 4:22–24

WHEN WE TRUST CHRIST AND EXPERIENCE NEW LIFE, forgiveness, and love, our lives will begin to change. Still, regeneration does not affect an instantaneous change in the full realm of our performance. We will continue to stumble and fall at times, but the Scriptures clearly instruct us to choose to act in ways that reflect our new lives and values in Christ.

We are to *put on*, or envelop ourselves in, this new self that progressively expresses Christian character in our attitudes and behavior. We are marvelously unique, created to reflect the character of Christ through our individual personalities and behavior. Each believer, in a different and special way, has the capability to shine forth the light of God. No two will reflect His light in exactly the same way.

The truth of regeneration can dispel the specter of the past. Our sins have been forgiven, and we now have tremendous capabilities for growth and change because we are new people with the Spirit of God living in us. Yes, when we sin, we will experience its destructive effects and the Father's discipline, but our sin will never change the truth of who we are in Christ.

- Describe how to "put on the new self."

- Read Ephesians 4:22–24. What process do you need to go through in order to experience your new self?

Father, thank You for . . .

IT IS FINISHED!

"And others are the ones on whom seed was sown among the thorns; these are the ones who have heard the word, and the worries of the world, and the deceitfulness of riches, and the desires for other things enter in and choke the word, and it becomes unfruitful. And those are the ones on whom seed was sown on the good soil; and they hear the word and accept it, and bear fruit, thirty, sixty, and a hundredfold."

MARK 4:18–20

OUR REDEMPTION WAS MADE COMPLETE AT CALVARY when Jesus lifted up His eyes and cried, *It is finished!* (John 19:30), He told us that the provision for man's reconciliation with God was complete. Nothing more need be done, because the Word of life had been spoken to all mankind. Man needed only to hear the Word, accept it, and place his hope and trust in Christ.

But if the redemption we enjoy is complete, why do we so often fail to see the changes in our lives we long for? Why do we wrestle day after day with the same temptations, the same failings, and the same distractions we have always fought? Why can't we break free and move on toward maturity?

Christ illustrated the reasons for our lack of fruitfulness in the parable of the sower in Mark 4:3–20. In agriculture, productivity depends on the fertility of the soil, the climate, and the presence or absence of weeds. The reasons Christ gave for lack of fruit in the believer's life were: Satan's taking away the Word of God, persecution, and the worries of the world. For most of us, the worries of the world are the primary culprit for our lack of growth.

In the context of honesty, affirmation, and patience, we can focus on the forgiveness we have received, and reject the deception and worldly desires that choke out the Word of life. We need to base our lives on God's Word and allow His character to be reproduced within us by the power of His Spirit.

- What are some factors which are encouraging your spiritual growth?

- What factors are hindering your growth?

Dear Lord, as I identify the areas of my life that are preventing progress in my growth, I confess . . .

OUR SOURCE OF CHANGE

And I will ask the Father, and He will give you another Helper, that He may be with you forever.

JOHN 14:16

THE TRUTHS WE HAVE EXAMINED IN THIS BOOK can have tremendous implications on our every goal and relationship, but now we need to understand how to actually implement them in our lives. How can we begin to experience positive change? Jesus answered this question in His last time of intimate instruction with His disciples (John 13–16). He told them that He would soon be put to death, but that they would not be left alone. That Helper is the Holy Spirit. The Holy Spirit, the third Person of the Trinity, is God and possesses all the attributes of deity. His primary purpose is to glorify Christ and bring attention to Him. Christ said, *He shall glorify Me; for He shall take of Mine, and shall disclose it to you* (John 16:14). The Holy Spirit is our teacher, and He guides us into the truth of the Scriptures (John 16:13). It is by His power that the love of Christ flows through us and produces spiritual fruit within us (John 7:37–39; 15:1–8). This spiritual fruit is described in many ways in the New Testament, including: intimate friendship with Christ (John 15:14); love for one another (John 15:12); joy and peace in the midst of difficulties (John 14:27; 15:11); steadfastness (Ephesians 5:18–21); and evangelism and discipleship (Matthew 28:18–20).

- Describe the blend and balance of the *Holy Spirit's* responsibility and *your* responsibility for your growth.

Thank You for the guidance and peace I have from Your Holy Spirit . . .

BEARING FRUIT

I am the true vine, and My Father is the vine dresser. Abide in (live, grow, and gain your sustenance from) Me, and I in you. As the branch cannot bear fruit of itself, unless it abides in the vine, so neither can you, unless you abide in Me. I am the vine, you are the branches; he who abides in Me, and I in him, he bears much fruit; for apart from Me you can do nothing.

JOHN 15:1, 4–5

OBVIOUSLY THIS FRUIT IS NOT ALWAYS EVIDENT in the lives of Christians, but why not? As we all know, the Christian life is not an easy one. It is not simply a self-improvement program. True, we may at times be able to make some changes in our habits through our own discipline and determination, but Christianity is not merely self-effort. The Christian life is a supernatural one in which we draw on Christ as our resource for direction, encouragement, and strength. In one of the most widely-known metaphors of the Bible, Christ described the Christian life in John 15, using the illustration of a branch and a vine.

In terms of that which honors Christ, is spiritually nourishing to us, and is genuine Christian service, anything done apart from the love and power of Christ amounts to nothing. Although we may expend tremendous effort at a great personal cost, only that which is done for Christ's glory in the power of His Spirit is of eternal value.

• Describe how a branch produces fruit (John 15:4–5).

• What are some evidences of spiritual fruit within the believer's life?

I am Your child. As a part of You, I desire to . . .

THE FRUIT OF THE SPIRIT

But the fruit of the Spirit is love, joy, peace, patience, kindness, goodness, faithfulness, gentleness, self-control . . .

GALATIANS 5:22–23

As w RESPOND TO THE LOVE OF CHRIST and trust His Spirit to fill us, these characteristics will become increasingly evident in our lives. The filling of the Holy Spirit includes two major aspects: our purpose (to bring honor to Christ instead of to ourselves) and our resources (trusting in His love and power to accomplish results, instead of trusting in our own wisdom and abilities). Although we will continue to mature in our relationship with the Lord over the years, we can begin to experience His love, strength, and purpose from the moment we put Him at the center of our lives.

Are you depending on God's Spirit to teach you, change you, and use you in the lives of others? If so, continue trusting Him! If not, identify any obstructions in your relationship with Him. Are there specific sins you need to confess?

Confession means to agree with God that you have sinned and that Christ has completely forgiven you. It also means "to repent," to turn from your sins to a life of love and obedience to God.

As you continue in the process of experiencing more of God's grace, take time to reflect on His love and power. Trust Him to guide you by His Word, fill you with His Spirit, and enable you to live for Him and be used by Him in the lives of others. Abiding in Christ does not mean deliverance from all of your problems, but it will provide a powerful relationship with the One who is the source of wisdom for difficult decisions, love to encourage you, and strength to help you endure.

- Why do you need a Helper?

Father, I trust You to teach me, change me, and use me for Your purposes. Thank You for . . .

REPLACING FALSE BELIEFS

Teach my Thy way, O Lord,
>And lead me in a level path,
>Because of my foes.
Do not deliver me over to the desire of my adversaries;
>For false witnesses have risen against me,
>And such as breathe out violence,
I would have despaired unless I had believed that
>I would see the goodness of the Lord
>In the land of the living.
Wait for the Lord;
>Be strong, and let your heart take courage;
>Yes, wait for the Lord.

PSALM 27:11–14

FOR MANY OF US, THE MAJORITY OF OUR BELIEFS were formed before we became Christians; therefore, it is easy to understand why many of our actions do not reflect Christ's character. Until those false beliefs are identified, ruthlessly rooted out, and replaced with biblical convictions, our lives will continue to be filled with destructive thoughts and actions.

Because of our fallen human nature, all of us experience false beliefs which contradict God's Word. Failure to recognize them can have devastating effects on our lives.

For example, a young girl named Dawn was sent to me by her parents, who hoped I could reason with her about her promiscuous behavior. But Dawn could not understand how something that felt so good and made her so happy could be wrong.

Over the course of several weeks, Dawn began to discuss her circumstances more openly with me. She explained that her father spent so much time working that he had little time for her and her mother. Dawn had been neglected, and after several meetings together, her wall of defenses eroded and she cried, "I just want to be loved, that's all!" Her behavior had been her unconscious attempt to feel close to someone. She had enjoyed it primarily because she finally felt loved, even though most of these men were really using her and not loving her at all.

Dawn eventually joined a support group, where she met other young women who were learning about the pain of their past and their hope for the future. These women could identify with Dawn's dreams and fears. They encouraged her and each other to gain a new sense of identity based on their love for each other and the truth of God's Word. This process hasn't been easy for Dawn, but her progress is real.

• How can people affect your ability to replace false beliefs with God's truth?

I'm grateful, dear Lord, for the good role-models You have placed in my life, and I want to be a good example for others, as well . . .

REJECT/REPLACE

Finally, brethren, whatever is true, whatever is honorable, whatever is right, whatever is pure, whatever is lovely, whatever is of good repute, if there is any excellence and if anything worthy of praise, let your mind dwell on these things. The things you have learned and received and heard and seen in me, practice these things; and the God of peace shall be with you.

PHILIPPIANS 4:8–9

ONE OF THE GREATEST CHARACTERISTICS OF PERSONAL MATURITY in Christ is the ability to be honest about how we really feel about a person or situation, and the willingness to accept full responsibility for our emotional and behavioral reactions in the disturbing circumstances of life. In realizing that our circumstances aren't the cause of our self-destructive reactions, and by applying God's truths to those situations, we can gain peace and perspective.

The world need not have control over us. Our spiritual battles may be intense, but we will be able to persevere if we can begin to analyze our circumstances through God's perspective and reject the false beliefs which often control our emotions and actions. Faith in God's Word prevents us from being buffeted by difficult situations, or having to live "under the circumstances."

Identifying our false beliefs is the first step on our path toward new freedom in Jesus Christ. Once we recognize that many of our deeply-held beliefs are actually rooted in deception, we can begin using our emotions as a checkpoint to determine if we are basing our beliefs about a given circumstance on the truth or lies. Many of our painful emotions, such as fear, anger, and tension, are often the product of believing Satan's lies. Therefore, when we experience these emotions, we can ask ourselves, *What am I believing in this situation?* In almost every case, we will be able to trace our negative emotions back to one of Satan's false beliefs. We can then choose to reject the lie we have identified and replace it with the corresponding truth from the Scriptures. This process is amazingly simple, yet profound and applicable.

- What are some true and honorable things you can choose to dwell on?

- How will focusing on these things affect you?

Lord, please help me to . . .

RESPONDING TO EMOTIONS

Trust in Him at all times, O people;
Pour out your heart before Him;
God is a refuge for us.

PSALM 62:8

IN EXAMINING OUR EMOTIONS, it is important to realize that not all distressing emotions reflect deception. For example, the emotion of remorse might be the Holy Spirit's conviction leading us to repentance. Anger with someone for molesting a child or beating an elderly person is righteous anger, just as a measure of fear while driving during rush hour is entirely justifiable!

In our problem-filled world, there are at least two ways that many of us choose to deal with our emotions and surrounding circumstances. One is to shut them out completely, refusing to acknowledge their presence or to be affected by them; the other is to become enslaved to them.

Switching off our emotions can cause us to become callous and insensitive to ourselves and those around us. Unfortunately, this is just what happened to Mike.

Over the years, Mike had deadened himself to his emotions, apparently not allowing anything to bother him. He had experienced a difficult childhood, first being abandoned by his parents, and then being shuffled from one relative to another. In an effort to stop the pain, Mike learned to block out his feelings and to ignore his circumstances.

Melinda, on the other hand, wore her emotions on her sleeve. She wasn't difficult to figure out. Her flaring temper, her torrent of tears, and her jovial laughter were all indications of her rollercoaster emotions. Never knowing what to expect, Melinda's husband, Ken, became weary of trying to deal with his volatile wife.

Melinda's erratic mood swings affected her so much that they became, in effect, her lord. Her feelings seemed to be more real than anything else in her life and they clouded her perception of God and His purposes.

• In what ways do you express your emotions?

• In what ways are you enslaved to them?

Dealing with my emotions—allowing myself to feel them and responding to them in a healthy way—requires a lot of thought, effort, and guidance from You. Father, I trust You to . . .

546

EMOTIONS, A GIFT FROM GOD

> My heart is in anguish within me,
>> And the terrors of death have fallen upon me.
> Fear and trembling come upon me;
>> And horror has overwhelmed me.
>
> PSALM 55:4–5

WE OFTEN RESPOND INCORRECTLY TO THEM, but our emotions are in fact a gift from God, intended to be used and enjoyed. Emotions are signals which tell us something about our environment. They can protect us by helping us to choose appropriate behavior. We can help ourselves (and others) by encouraging honesty and by allowing ourselves to fully experience both our positive and negative feelings. Emotions help us to determine what is really going on inside. In the same way that good parents allow their children to express hurt, and experience comfort and healing when they have fallen, we can do this for ourselves and others by advocating an honest expression of emotions and by applying comfort to the hurts each of us experience. In this way, we can avoid repression and denial, and encourage an appropriate expression of our emotions—within ourselves, with others, and with God.

The inability to experience and express feelings is as dangerous to our well-being as the inability to feel physical pain. As we become aware of painful emotions and destructive behavior, we need to acknowledge these feelings and actions to God in prayer, asking Him to reveal any false beliefs that may be hindering our fellowship with Him. Then, empowered by the Holy Spirit, and encouraged by the love and affirmation of others, we can learn to cast aside our false beliefs and choose to believe the truths of God's Word.

It is necessary to first expose our root emotions and the false beliefs which are triggering them. Then, by faith, we can allow God's Word to renew our minds.

* Why are your emotions a gift from God?

Thank You, dear God, for . . .

FAMILY FORTRESSES

For though we walk in the flesh, we do not war according to the flesh, for the weapons of our warfare are not of the flesh, but divinely powerful for the destruction of fortresses. We are destroying speculations and every lofty thing raised up against the knowledge of God, and we are taking every thought captive to the obedience of Christ.

2 CORINTHIANS 10:3–5

FOR MANY OF US, OUR FAMILY BACKGROUNDS have been very painful. Alcoholism, drug abuse, divorce, workaholism, violence, or other family disorders have left us with deep emotional scars. We may feel neglected, lonely, angry, hurt, or numb. We may consequently believe that we are unlovable people who are unworthy of being cared for by others, and that God is like our parents: harsh, condemning, manipulative, or aloof. These emotions and self-perceptions form a strong fortress that has been founded on Satan's lies and communicated to us by those who were supposed to love, protect, and provide for us. Concepts like these don't vanish quickly. Often, our first step toward progress is realizing that we have been hurting for a long time, but have refused to admit it, or perhaps, that our defense mechanisms of drivenness or withdrawal have been protecting us from the reality of our pain.

Through the process of being honest and experiencing comfort from the Lord and others, these fortresses can be slowly torn down. They are overcome by *destroying speculations and every lofty thing raised up against the knowledge of God;* that is, by identifying and rejecting specific lies, and then replacing them with the truth.

- How has your family contributed to the fortress of painful, repressed emotions and faulty perceptions?

- How can this fortress be torn down?

Heavenly Father, please open my eyes, and help me to identify the issues in my life that need to be dealt with. I desire to . . .

TRUE REPENTANCE

I now rejoice, not that you were made sorrowful, but that you were made sorrowful to the point of repentance; for you were made sorrowful according to the will of God, in order that you might not suffer loss in anything through us. For the sorrow that is according to the will of God produces a repentance without regret, leading to salvation; but the sorrow of the world produces death.

2 CORINTHIANS 7:9–10

THE CORINTHIANS' EXAMPLE DEMONSTRATES REPENTANCE as a tactical weapon of our spiritual warfare. _Repentance_ means "to change"; to change one's mind, purpose, and actions. It is more than just the experience of sorrow; it is the changing of our attitude and actions when we have realized that they are sinful and dishonoring to God.

As an offensive weapon, repentance has two sharp edges. The first allows us to discern and reject false beliefs.

The second edge of repentance is the replacement of false beliefs with the truth of God's Word. By affirming God's truth about our worth, we will lodge it deep within our hearts and minds, and begin to reshape our thinking, feelings, and behavior. Then, the process of having the truth modeled to us, affirmed in us, taught to us, and applied by us over time will enable us to increasingly experience freedom in different areas of our lives.

If false beliefs remain in our minds, unchallenged and unrejected, they retain an unconscious influence on our emotions and reactions. Consequently, our warfare is a sustained and continuous battle. Every disturbing situation provides us with an opportunity to discover our incorrect thinking, to reject our world-acquired beliefs, and exchange them for the truth. This is a daily process for every Christian; only this aggressive, conscious, truth-seeking effort can reverse years of habitually wrong thinking.

• What is genuine repentance?

Thank You for the spiritual weapon of repentance. As I struggle to turn away from sin, I praise You, dear Lord, for Your endless mercy and grace . . .

RIVETED ON GOD'S WORD

> But I say, walk by the Spirit, and you will not carry out the desire of the flesh. For the flesh sets its desire against the Spirit, and the Spirit against the flesh; for these are in opposition to one another, so that you may not do the things that you please.
>
> GALATIANS 5:16–17

AFFIRMING THE TRUTHS OF THE SCRIPTURES does not mean that our natural mind will agree with what we are affirming. The Bible teaches that the natural mind is antagonistic toward God. It may be uncomfortable to reflect on the truths of God's Word because they oppose the lies of the enemy. Don't be surprised by spiritual conflict when you confront these lies with God's truths.

Realize that we can't hope to achieve spiritual growth and change through self-effort. The Holy Spirit is our Helper, and He will point out those circumstances in which we are believing Satan's lies; He will give us insight into the truth of the Scriptures; and He will give us strength to persevere in spiritual battle. Even our desire to honor Christ is due to the Holy Spirit's work in our lives. Through His wisdom and power, and through our moment-by-moment choice to follow Him, the Holy Spirit produces changes in our lives for the glory of Christ.

In order to become proficient at affirming these truths, we need to become students of God's Word, and allow its truth to lodge deep within our hearts and minds. We should make it a regular practice to meditate upon the Scriptures so that the Holy Spirit can use them to change our beliefs, thoughts, emotions, and actions.

Learn to confront each false belief with a specific truth from God's Word. Once we have identified a specific false belief, we should claim God's corresponding truth in the situation.

- How can you learn to perceive the enemy's schemes more clearly?

- How can God's truth help you in spiritual conflict?

Father, when I am confronted by one of Satan's lies, please give me the wisdom and discernment I need to battle his deception with Your truths. Please show me . . .

NO CONDEMNATION!

There is therefore now no condemnation for those who are in Christ Jesus.
ROMANS 8:1

WHEN I SHARED THIS IMPORTANT TRUTH with a troubled Christian brother, his jaw dropped and his eyes filled with tears. He looked at me incredulously and exclaimed, "You mean, all this guilt I have been carrying for so long is unnecessary? I can be free from these tormenting feelings of condemnation? Why hasn't somebody told me this before?"

The Apostle Paul has been trying to tell us just that for centuries, but few of us have listened. We feel we deserve condemnation, and we fail to realize that Christ has freed us from the guilt and condemnation our sins deserve.

Perhaps no emotion is more destructive than guilt. It causes a loss of self-respect. It causes the human spirit to wither, and eats away at our personal significance. Guilt is a strong motivator, but it plays on our fears of failure and rejection; therefore, it can never ultimately build, encourage, or inspire us in our desire to live for Christ.

- How has guilt affected you?

Christ, You have taken away my sins. You have freed me from guilt and condemnation. I feel overwhelmed by the magnitude of Your love and for-giveness for me . . .

GUILT AND CONSEQUENCES

For all have sinned and fall short of the glory of God, being justified as a gift by His grace through the redemption which is in Christ Jesus.

ROMANS 3:23–24

SOME OF US UNDERSTAND GUILT AS A SENSE OF LEGAL and moral accountability before God. We may try to distinguish it from low self-esteem by reasoning that guilt is the result of a sinful act or moral wrongdoing, while low self-esteem is derived from a feeling of social or personal inadequacy. Consequently, a lie makes us feel unaccept-able to God and brings guilt, while bad table·manners make us feel unacceptable to the people around us and bring low self-esteem.

This perspective shows some depth of thought, but it focuses on an emotional response to guilt rather than its root cause. At its root, guilt is the condition of being separated from God and of deserving condemnation for sin. Low self-esteem can be experienced by Christians or non-Christians—anyone who believes Satan's lies and feels like a failure, hopeless and rejected.

As we have determined, guilt has a restricted meaning in the New Testament. It refers only to man's condition prior to his salvation. Only the non-Christian is actually guilty before God. He has transgressed the law of God and must face the consequences. Guilt shakes its fist and says, "You have fallen short and must pay the price. You are personally accountable." Our condemnation is removed only through Christ. He took all of our guilt upon Himself when He accepted the penalty for our sins and suffered the full punishment for all sin. Because of His substitution, we need never face guilt's consequences. We are acquitted and absolved from guilt, free from our sentence of spiritual death.

• How does Christ's death on the cross deal with our guilt?

When I think about the price You paid for my sins, Heavenly Father, I feel . . .

OVERCOMING GUILT

Who gave Himself for us, that He might redeem us from every lawless deed and purify for Himself a people for His own possession, zealous for good deeds.

TITUS 2:14

MANY OF US HAVE BEEN TOLD THAT WE ARE STILL GUILTY even after we have trusted Christ to pay for our sins. And sadly, we have heard this in churches—places that should be loudly and clearly proclaiming the forgiveness and freedom found in the cross. Perhaps some people think that if they don't use guilt motivation, we won't do anything. Guilt may motivate us for a short while, until we adjust to being properly motivated. But a short period of waiting is well worth the long-term results of grace-oriented, intrinsic motivation.

Learn to identify incorrect teaching, guilt motivation, and the results of guilt in your own thoughts. Then, refuse to believe the lies any longer, and focus instead on the unconditional love and forgiveness of Christ. His love is powerful, and He is worthy of our intense zeal to obey and honor Him. The result of proper motivation is an enduring, deepening commitment to Christ and His cause, rather than the prevalent results of guilt motivation: resentment and the desire to escape.

- Think of the last time you were motivated by guilt to do something. If you had reremembered God's truth about you—that you are deeply loved, completely forgiven, fully pleasing, totally accepted, and absolutely complete in Christ—how do you think your emotions and actions would have been different?

Dear Lord, as I continue to focus on You and Your truth, please help me to . . .

GUILT AND CONVICTION

"And He, when He comes, will convict the world concerning sin, and righteousness, and judgment."

JOHN 16:8

CHRISTIANS ARE FREED FROM GUILT, but we are still subject to conviction. The Bible frequently speaks of the Holy Spirit's work to convict believers of sin. He directs and encourages our spiritual progress by revealing our sins in contrast to the holiness and purity of Christ.

Although the Holy Spirit convicts both believers and unbelievers of sin (John 16:8), His conviction of believers is not intended to produce pangs of guilt. Our status and self-worth are secure by the grace of God, and we are no longer guilty. Conviction deals with our behavior, not our status before God. Conviction is the Holy Spirit's way of showing the error of our performance in light of God's standard and truth. His motivation is love, correction, and protection.

While guilt is applicable to non-believers, and originates from Satan, conviction is the privilege of those who believe, and is given by the Holy Spirit. Guilt brings depression and despair, but conviction enables us to realize the beauty of God's forgiveness and to experience His love and power.

• What are some differences between guilt and conviction?

I am thankful for the Holy Spirit's loving conviction and guidance ...

DAY 69

RESPONDING TO FEELINGS OF GUILT

And He died for all, that they who live should no longer live for themselves, but
for Him who died and rose again on their behalf.

2 CORINTHIANS 5:15

HOW CAN WE DEAL WITH FEELINGS OF GUILT? First, we need to affirm that Christ has
forgiven us and has made us judicially righteous before God. Our sin does not result in condemnation, but it is harmful and brings dishonor to God. We can confess our sin to God, claim
the forgiveness we already have in Christ, and then move on in joy and freedom to honor Him.
The following prayer expresses this attitude:

Father, I affirm that I am deeply loved by You, that I am fully pleasing to You,
and that I am totally accepted in Your sight. You have made me complete and have
given me the righteousness of Christ, even though my performance often falls short.
Lord, I confess my sins to You. (List them. Be specific.) I agree with You that these
are wrong. Thank You for Your grace and forgiveness. Is there anything I need to
return, anyone I need to repay, or anyone I need to apologize to? Thank You.

It is important to affirm our righteousness in Christ as well as to confess our sins. God does
not need to be reminded of our right standing in Him, but we do. Therefore, we need to make
this prayer a daily experience and allow it to pervade our thoughts and hearts. As we yield to
the gentle prodding of God-given conviction, confess our sins, and affirm our true relationship with Him, we will be gradually shaped and molded in such a way that we will increasingly honor the One who *died and rose again on [our] behalf* (2 Corinthians 5:15).

We may not experience joy and freedom immediately, especially if we have developed the
painful habit of prolonged self-condemnation as a way of dealing with sin. Loving friends
who listen to us and encourage us can be an example of God's forgiveness to us. As we
become more honest about our feelings through these affirming rela-tionships, we will be able
to increasingly experience the freedom, forgiveness, and freshness of God's grace.

- How do unrealistic expectations about our feelings keep us from experiencing God's love
  and forgiveness?

Thank You, Lord, for Your unconditional love and forgiveness. Daily, I am
becoming more aware of how complete I am in You. Please help me to
continue growing in Your Spirit by showing me . . .

555

CHRIST: BEDROCK OF OUR FAITH

So faith comes by hearing, and hearing by the word of Christ.
ROMANS 10:17

WE HAVE SEEN THAT OUR RELATIONSHIP WITH GOD, our security, and our self-worth are not earned by our efforts. They are obtained only by faith. This point is so important, let's take some time to analyze what faith is.

Faith has several synonyms: *trust, dependence, reliance,* and *belief.* The focus is on the object of faith, not the faith itself. For example, if I believe that a certain chair will hold me when I sit in it, the primary issue is the construction and quality of the chair—the *object* of my faith, not the *amount* of faith I have. Even if I believe very strongly that the chair will support me, if the chair is a rotten, broken-down piece of junk, then it will break if I try to sit in it. My faith will not make it a good chair. But if the chair is of quality construction, it takes very little faith to sit comfortably in it. Again, it is the quality of the object, not the quantity of my faith, that is of primary importance.

In Christianity, Christ is the object of faith, and faith is our trust in His character and abilities. The more we know Him, the more we will trust Him. Faith, then, requires our knowing God, and knowing Him requires a relationship. To know God, we need to talk to Him through prayer, listen to His voice, see Him at work in our lives and the lives of others, and search out His will and deeds through the Scriptures He has given us.

* What are some differences between trusting in Christ and trusting in feelings? . . . or trusting in people's opinions of you? . . . or your performance?

I get my security and self-worth from my faith in Christ. The issue is the
object of my faith, not the amount of my faith.
When I reflect on Your unconditional love for me, Your forgiveness of me,
Your constant concern for me . . . I realize I have everything I need for a
healthy sense of self-worth and security . . .

COMPLETE IN HIM

For in Him (Christ) all the fullness of Deity dwells in bodily
form, and in Him you have been made complete,
and He is the head over all rule and authority.

COLOSSIANS 2:9–10

THROUGH THE GIFT OF GOD'S GRACE, WE ARE SPIRITUALLY ALIVE, forgiven, and complete in Him. In the church at Colossae, false teachers taught that "completeness" came through a combination of philosophy, good works, other religions, and Christ. Paul's clear message was that we are made complete through Christ alone. To attempt to find completeness through any other source, including success, the approval of others, prestige, or appearance, is to be taken captive through philosophy and empty deception (Colossians 2:8). Nothing can add to the death of Christ to pay for our sins and the resurrection of Christ to give us new life. We are complete because Christ has forgiven us and given us life—the capacity for growth and change.

According to the theologian, Louis Berkhof, "Regeneration consists in the implanting of the principle of the new spiritual life in man, in a radical change of the governing disposition of the soul, which, under the influence of the Holy Spirit, gives birth to a life that moves in a Godward direction. In principle this change affects the whole man: the intellect . . . the will . . . and the feelings or emotions."*

• Do you believe you have the capacity for growth and change? Why or why not?

Father, I am excited about growing and changing. The desire of my heart is to know all that You would have me to learn about myself and relating to others in a way that is honoring to You . . .

* Louis Berkhof, *Systematic Theology* (Grand Rapids, MI: William B. Eerdmans Publishing Company, 1941), p. 468.

RESPONDING TO IMPURE MOTIVES

... we have as our ambition ... to be pleasing to Him.
2 CORINTHIANS 5:9

As YOU RECOGNIZE CORRECT MOTIVES FOR OBEDIENCE, and as you are able to identify improper motivations in your life, you may think, _I've never done anything purely for the Lord in my whole life!_ You may feel a sense of pain and remorse for your inappropriate motives. But don't sink into a state of morbid introspection, demeaning yourself for your past attitudes. There are at least two perspectives that will help you focus on the Lord and grow in a godly desire to honor Him.

First, obedience from a right motivation is a choice. It is not based on how you feel. At any and every point in your life (like right now) you can actively, consciously choose to honor Christ. The Lord wants you to live by your godly choices, not by your fickle emotions. Ask the Holy Spirit to help you develop a sense of intensity about this choice.

Second, since your motives are usually a reflection of what you believe, they will begin to change as your belief system changes. Consistently considering and applying God's truth will have a profound and far-reaching impact on your motives. As you reject Satan's lies, you will gra-dually be _transformed by the renewing of your mind_ ... (Romans 12:2), and will have an increasing desire to honor the One who loves you and purchased you by His own blood.

So, as an act of your will, choose to honor the Lord no matter what your emotions tell you, and consistently learn and apply the truths of God's Word so that they will begin to pervade your thoughts. Your motives won't become totally pure until you see the Lord face to face (1 John 3:2), but the better you know Him, the more you will see that He is worthy of your love, loyalty, and obedience.

- Have you felt that your motives had to be completely pure for you to be honoring to God?

- Why is this unrealistic?

Thank You, Father, for Your patience while I grow in my desire to honor You ...

DAY 73

REALIZING OUR RECONCILIATION

And although you were formerly alienated and hostile in mind, engaged in evil deeds, yet He has now reconciled you in His fleshly body through death, in order to present you before Him holy and blameless and beyond reproach.

COLOSSIANS 1:21–22

IS THERE ANYTHING A CHRISTIAN can do to become more acceptable to God? No! If there were, then the cross would be insufficient. If we can do anything to be more acceptable to God, then Christ either lied or was mistaken when He cried out on the cross, *"It is finished!"* (John 19:30). If that is the case, what He should have said was, "It is almost finished, and if you live a perfect life, you and I together might make you acceptable."

Since our relationship with God was bought entirely by the blood of Christ, it is the height of pride to think that our own good works can make us acceptable to God. The Bible speaks to the contrary: *He saved us, not on the basis of deeds which we have done in righteousness, but according to His mercy* . . . (Titus 3:5). Christ has reconciled us to God and He allows us to experience the incredible truth, *We are totally accepted by and acceptable to God.*

What should we do when we have failed or when someone disapproves of us? A practical way of summarizing the truth we've examined is:

It would be nice if_____(my boss liked me, I could fix the refrigerator, my complexion were clear, James had picked me up on time, or . . .), but I'm still deeply loved, completely forgiven, fully pleasing, totally accepted, and complete in Christ.

This statement doesn't mean that we won't feel pain or anger. We need to be honest about our feelings. A statement like the one above is simply a way to quickly gain God's perspective on whatever we are experiencing. It is not magic, but it enables us to reflect on the implications of biblical truth. We can apply this truth in every difficult situation, whether it is someone's disapproval, our own failure to accomplish something, or the failure of another person.

Memorize the truth in the above statement and begin to apply it in your situations and relationships.

• How will utilizing this statement affect your thoughts, emotions, and behavior?

Jesus, I ask You for clarity of thought today as I apply the above statement to my everyday situations and relationships . . .

RESPONDING TO OUR CHILDREN

Fathers, do not provoke your children to anger; but bring them up in the discipline and instruction of the Lord.

EPHESIANS 6:4

WHEN THEIR CHILDREN GET INTO TROUBLE, parens usually alternate between blaming themselves and blaming their children. After all, someone has to be blamed. The problem in either case is not that parents are loving their child too much or too little, but that their personal significance is wrapped up in their performance as parents. Therefore, when the child does well, the parents feel good about themselves. When a child does poorly, however, they often blame each other or the child. Beneath it all is the internalized and unconscious belief: *Someone has to take the blame.*

Our worth is totally secure in Christ, so our children's success or failure, cuteness or whining doesn't affect our value in the least. We need to see our children the way our heavenly Father sees us: *deeply loved, completely forgiven, fully pleasing, and totally accepted.* Then, when they disobey, our discipline will be like the Father's discipline of us: in love, not anger. If we approach our children with an attitude of grief rather than anger when they disobey, it will make a tremendous difference! What a difference it will make if we go to our children with the attitude and words, "It's sad that you disobeyed. It was harmful to you, and I love you so much that I don't want you to harm yourself. I will need to discipline you to help you remember not to do it again. Remember, the reason I am disciplining you is that I love you so much!" . . . instead of, "You've done it again, and I'll make sure you regret it! I wonder if you'll ever amount to anything!"

Responding to our children in grief instead of anger will have monumental implications on both them and us. Our children won't be afraid of us, our relationship with them won't be marred by anger, and they will be more likely to view God as a loving Father rather than as a tyrant. As parents, we will have a more accurate perception of God's love and gracious discipline, and we will be more in control of our emotions. We won't try to deny that we are getting angry at our children's misbehavior, letting our anger build and build until we explode. Instead, we will be able to express our displeasure more quickly and acceptably because it will be wholesome grief instead of unholy anger. These are powerful and welcome implications, indeed!

• How can the principle of responding to children's misbehavior out of grief affect them, you, and your relationship with them?

Father, please show me . . .

560

FAITH AND FEELINGS

For the flesh sets its desire against the Spirit, and the Spirit against the flesh; for these are in opposition to one another.

GALATIANS 5:17

WHEN WE DEPEND ON GOD, will we feel His love and strength? Maybe, maybe not. Our culture would make us think that our feelings are the most important way of determining if our actions are valid. But as Christians, we have a much higher authority than our feelings. We have the truth of God's Word, and we can choose, as an act of our will, to obey Him. Our will is paramount, not our feelings. The French philosopher Fenelon said, "The essence of Christianity resides in the will." Our feelings _may_ reflect the love of Christ as we forgive others, share our faith, give generously, and demonstrate other spiritual characteristics in our lives. But on many occasions, our emotions are inconsistent, unpredictable, and diametrically opposed to God's Word. Often, we refuse to obey Him because we don't _feel_ like it. For example, we may be afraid to share our faith because someone might reject us, or we may continue to indulge in sin because we don't _feel_ like stopping. But what about the times when we earnestly want to obey God, and our emotions say, _NO!_? Here are some possible reasons our feelings may oppose the ways of God:

1) Our sinful nature may be prompting us to disobey God.
2) We may be experiencing spiritual conflict.
3) It may be that our negative emotions are simply the residual feelings of the fear of failure or the fear of rejection that we are in the process of overcoming by claiming God's truth.

When you choose to believe God's Word, your emotions may not follow immediately. Does that mean you aren't trusting God? No. Faith is often exercised in the context of struggle, in the midst of conflicting thoughts and emotions. A look at the people of God in the Scriptures shows that their faith was not in the absence of doubts and struggles, but in the _face_ of doubts and struggles. The idea that faith is only found apart from conflicting thoughts and emotions is one of Satan's schemes to confuse and discourage you. When we trust in God, we will experience many obstacles to faith, but placing our trust in His Word—not our feelings— will see us through.

• What is the relationship between faith and feelings?

• How can unrealistic expectations of our emotions be harmful to us?

Lord, please give me wisdom in knowing when my feelings are obedient to Your Word . . .

RENEWING THE MIND

> And do not be conformed to this world, but be transformed by the renewing of
> your mind, that you may prove what the will of God is, that which is good and
> acceptable and perfect.
>
> ROMANS 12:2

IT IS INTERESTING THAT WHEN THE HOLY SPIRIT gave us a new spirit, He did not give us a
totally renewed mind. Although the Spirit of Christ lives within us and enables us to evaluate
our experiences, our minds tend to dwell on the worldly thoughts of our old nature instead of
on God's truth. We are in conflict, torn between our new godly motivation to glorify Christ
and our old motivations of lust and pride. Paul recognized this conflict.

How can we grow in Christ? How can we assist in the process that will enable us to follow
Him? To change our behavior, we usually need to see others who are being honest, and who
are in the process of applying spiritual truths to their lives. In this environment, and through
our personal study of God's Word, we can reject earthly thoughts and replace them with those
that are spiritual. Solomon wrote, *As [a man] thinks within himself, so he is* (Proverbs 23:7).
Our thoughts usually affect the way we feel, the way we perceive ourselves and others, and
ultimately, the way we act. The way we think can determine whether we will live according to
God's truth or the world's value system.

• What ideas, relationships, fantasies, or desires does your mind dwell on?

• How have these thoughts affected your emotions, behavior, and relationships?

*Lord, being honest about my behavior, relationships, and feelings can be
painful sometimes. Thank You for the Holy Spirit's help and unwavering
conviction as I walk through this long journey of spiritual, relational, and
emotional growth . . .*

NEWNESS OF LIFE

Blessed is the man who trusts in the Lord, whose confidence is in Him.
JEREMIAH 17:7

THE MOMENT YOU TRUST CHRIST, many wonderful things happen to you:

- All your sins are forgiven: past, present, and future (Colossians 2:13–14).
- You become a child of God (John 1:12; Romans 8:15).
- You receive eternal life (John 5:24).
- You are delivered from Satan's domain and transferred into the kingdom of Christ (Colossians 1:13).
- Christ comes to dwell within you (Colossians 1:27; Revelation 3:20).
- You become a new creation (2 Corinthians 5:17).
- You are declared righteous by God (2 Corinthians 5:21).
- You enter into a love relationship with God (1 John 4:9–11).
- You are accepted by God (Colossians 1:19–22).

Think on the implications of these truths in your life. Then, thank God for His wonderful grace and experience *the love of Christ which surpasses knowledge* (Ephesians 3:19).

Thank You, dear God, for . . .

DETERMINING OUR WORTH

And you were dead in your trespasses and sins, in which you formerly walked according to the course of this world, according to the prince of the power of the air, of the spirit that is now working in the sons of disobedience. Among them we too all formerly lived in the lusts of our flesh, indulging the desires of the flesh and of the mind, and were by nature children of wrath, even as the rest. But God, being rich in mercy, because of His great love with which He loved us, even when we were dead in our transgressions, made us alive together with Christ (by grace you have been saved).

EPHESIANS 2:1–5

IN THE BEGINNING, GOD DECLARED THAT MAN WAS CREATED to reign with Him; however, man rejected God's truth and chose instead to believe Satan's lie. Today, man continues to reject God's truth and offer of salvation through Jesus Christ. He chooses instead to trust in his success and the opinions of others to give him a sense of self-worth, though the Scriptures clearly teach that apart from Christ, man is enslaved to sin and condemned to an eternity in hell.

Since the Fall, man has often failed to turn to God for the truth about himself. Instead, he has looked to others to meet his inescapable need for self-worth. *I am what others say I am*, he has reasoned. *I will find my value in their opinions of me.*

Isn't it amazing that we turn to others who have a perspective as limited and darkened as our own to discover our worth! Rather than relying on God's steady, uplifting reassurance of who we are, we depend on others who base our worth on our ability to meet their standards.

- Your actions and emotions are usually indicative of your belief system. Why do you do what you do, say what you say, and go where you go? How much of what you do is to honor God, and how much is to please people?

Lord, I'm thankful for the reassurance and security I find in You . . .

REJECTING THE LIE

"Behold, I have given you authority to tread upon serpents and scorpions, and over all the power of the enemy, and nothing shall injure you."

LUKE 10:19

IN SPITE OF ADAM AND EVE'S SIN, God's plan is to bring Man back to the destiny for which he was originally created—to bear His image. To accomplish this, God gives a new nature to all who believe in Christ. This new nature is able to reflect God's character and rule His creation. In Luke 10:19, Jesus spoke of the authority of this new nature.

Satan, however, continues to deceive people, including many Christians, into believing that the basis of their worth is their performance and their ability to please others. The equation below reflects Satan's lie:

SELF-WORTH = PERFORMANCE + OTHERS' OPINIONS

- Can we overcome Satan's deception and reject this basis of our self-worth? Can we trust God's complete acceptance of us as His sons and daughters, and allow Him to free us from our dependency on success and the approval of others? Rejecting Satan's lie and accepting God's evaluation of us leads to a renewed hope, joy, and purpose in life.

Father, thank You for Your total acceptance of me. I trust You to guide me out of the web of Satan's lies, and lead me away from . . .

AFFIRMING RELATIONSHIPS

> But we proved to be gentle among you, as a nursing mother tenderly cares for her own children. Having thus a fond affection for you, we were well-pleased to impart to you not only the gospel of God but also our own lives, because you had become very dear to us.
>
> 1 THESSALONIANS 2:7–8

PEOPLE SELDOM HAVE THE OBJECTIVITY AND THE COURAGE to be honest about reality in their lives without some affirmation from others. The love, strength, and honesty we find in other people are tangible expressions of those traits that are characteristic of God. A friend, a small group, a pastor, or a counselor who won't be frustrated by our slow progress—and who won't give us quick and easy solutions—is a valuable find! (Of course, it is always wise to use discretion and discernment regarding what and with whom we share. The act of sharing is a responsibility.) Pray that God will provide a person or group of persons with whom you can be open and honest, who can objectively listen to you and share with you, and who will encourage you to make real, rather than superficial progress.

- Name someone who has affirmed and encouraged you in the past:

- How did this person's affirmation affect you?

- Who is affirming you now? What affect does this person have on you?

- Do you need to find someone who will encourage and affirm you? If so, how do you plan to find that person or group of people?

I appreciate the affirmation and encouragement of others. Father, today please show me ways I can be affirming to them, too . . .

RIGHT THINKING

Thy word is a lamp to my feet, and a light to my path.

PSALM 119:105

MANY OF US ARE UNAWARE OF WHAT WE REALLY BELIEVE about God and about ourselves. We often say what we don't mean, and mean what we don't say. God's Word is our guide. And yet, we often experience difficulty in applying scriptural concepts to our lives because of the elaborate array of defenses we have structured over the years to protect ourselves. It is important to understand that Scripture can be used to identify and attack these defensive barriers, enabling us to experience an open and honest relationship with God:

> For the word of God is living and active and sharper than any two-edged sword, and piercing as far as the division of soul and spirit, of both joints and marrow, and able to judge the thoughts and intentions of the heart. And there is no creature hidden from His sight, but all things are open and laid bare to the eyes of Him with whom we have to do.

HEBREWS 4:12–13

- Describe how your thoughts and beliefs have been developed. (Include the influences of society, your family background, experiences, relationships):

- Read 2 Timothy 3:16–17 and explain how the Scriptures can affect our thinking and our lives:

As I read in Your Word today, Father, please show me . . .

TIME

> Not that I have already obtained all this, or have already been made perfect, but I press on to take hold of that for which Christ Jesus took hold of me. Brothers, I do not consider myself yet to have taken hold of it. But one thing I do: Forgetting what is behind and straining toward what is ahead, press on toward the goal to win the prize for which God has called me heavenward in Christ Jesus.
>
> PHILIPPIANS 3:12–14

IF WE WERE COMPUTERS, solutions to our problems would be produced in microseconds. People, however, don't change that quickly. The agrarian metaphors given in the Scriptures depict _seasons_ of planting, weeding, watering, growth, and harvesting. Farmers don't expect to plant seeds in the morning and harvest their crops that afternoon. Seeds must go through a complete cycle of growth, receiving plenty of attention in the process, before they mature. In this age of instant coffee, microwave dinners, and instant banking, we tend to assume that spiritual, emotional, and relational health will be instantaneous. These unrealistic expectations only cause discouragement and disappointment.

Some of us seem to respond to this environment of growth very quickly; others, after a few weeks or months; and still others, never at all. Why the difference? Why are some of us able to apply principles of growth so much more readily than others?

Some of us are in situations where one or more elements of growth are in some way missing or lacking. We may be trying to deal with our difficulties alone. We may be depending on a rigid structure of discipline for positive change, instead of blending a healthy combination of our responsibility with the Holy Spirit's enabling power. We may be expecting too much too soon, and may be experiencing disappointment with our slow results. Some of us may, in fact, be ready to quit the growth process entirely.

• Why do we often tend to expect fast results when we begin to seek growth and change in our lives?

• Why is it important for us to have Paul's process-perspective about life (Philippians 3:12–14)?

Father, I rest in the knowledge that if I stay sincerely focused upon You, I will move forward in my growth process at the pace of Your perfect timing . . .

THE LONG JOURNEY

Not that I have already obtained it, or have already become perfect, but I press on in order that I may lay hold of that for which also I was laid hold of by Christ Jesus.

PHILIPPIANS 3:12

OUR GROWTH TOWARD WHOLENESS AND MATURITY is a journey which won't be completed until we join the Lord in heaven. The Apostle Paul understood this, and saw himself as being in the middle of this process.

If Paul, the foremost missionary and writer of much of the New Testament, saw himself as being "in the process," we can be encouraged to continue in the process toward change as well. It will help to have reasonable expectations about our progress. Sometimes, we will experience flashes of insight and spurts of growth, but the process of healing and renewal will more often be slow and methodical. Our emotions, too, may occasionally be very pleasant and positive, but when God's light shines on another area of hurt in our lives, we will likely experience another round of pain and anger. Remember that healing can only continue as we put ourselves in an environment characterized by honesty, affirming relationships, right thinking, the Holy Spirit's love and power, and time.

• Describe how your emotions might change over the course of a year or two of healing:

Lord, I am thankful for the opportunities You have given me to renew myself, to learn a better way of living, and to relate well with others . . .

NEW LIFE

For we also once were foolish ourselves, disobedient, deceived, enslaved to various lusts and pleasures, spending our life in malice and envy, hateful, hating one another. But when the kindness of God our Savior and His love for mankind appeared, He saved us, not on the basis of deeds which we have done in righteousness, but according to His mercy, by the washing of regeneration and renewing by the Holy Spirit, whom He poured out upon us richly through Jesus Christ our Savior, that being justified by His grace we might be made heirs according to the hope of eternal life.

TITUS 3:3–7

REGENERATION IS NOT A SELF-IMPROVEMENT PROGRAM, nor is it a clean-up campaign for our sinful natures. _Regeneration_ is nothing less than the impartation of new life. As Paul stated in Ephesians 2:5, we were once dead in our sins, but have since been made alive in Christ.

Regeneration is the renewing work of the Holy Spirit that literally makes each believer a new person at the moment he or she trusts Christ as Savior.

In that wondrous, miraculous moment, we experience more than swapping one set of standards for another. We experience what Jesus called a new birth (John 3:3–6), a Spirit-wrought renewal of the human spirit, a transform-ing resuscitation which takes place so that the Spirit is alive within us (Romans 8:10).

• What are some characteristics of "new life"?

As I rejoice in my "new life" and Your love, Jesus, I feel . . .

THE APPROVAL ADDICT

For we are not bold to class or compare ourselves with some of those who commend themselves; but when they measure themselves by themselves, and compare themselves with themselves, they are without understanding.

2 CORINTHIANS 10:12

WE SPEND MUCH OF OUR TIME BUILDING RELATIONSHIPS, striving to please people and win their respect. And yet, after all of our sincere, conscientious effort, it takes only one unappreciative word from someone to ruin our sense of self-worth. How quickly an insensitive word can destroy the self-assurance we've worked so hard to achieve!

The world we live in is filled with people who demand that we please them in exchange for their approval and acceptance. Such demands often lead us directly to a second false belief: _I must be approved by certain others to feel good about myself._

We are snared by this lie in many subtle ways. Believing it causes us to bow to peer pressure in an effort to gain approval. We may join clubs and organizations, hoping to find a place of acceptance for ourselves. We often identify ourselves with social groups, believing that being with others like ourselves will assure our acceptance and their approval.

Many people have admitted that their experi-mentation with drugs or sex is a reaction to their need to belong. However, drugs and sexual promiscuity promise something they can't fulfill, and experimentation only leaves these people with pain, and usually, a deeper need for self-worth and acceptance.

• How does the fear of rejection affect your behavior?

Father, sometimes people and situations can be so frustrating. I need to be more concerned about what You think of me—what I'm doing, saying, thinking, feeling—instead of allowing myself to be influenced by the opinions of others . . .

RECOILING FROM LOVE

And if one can overpower him who is alone, two can resist him. A cord of three strands is not quickly torn apart.

ECCLESIASTES 4:12

INSTEAD OF BEING REFRESHED BY THE TRUTH OF GOD'S LOVE, if we have been deeply wounded, we may recoil from it, believing that we are unlovable. We may be fearful of reaching out and being hurt again. Whatever the cause, the result is withdrawal from the very idea of being loved and accepted.

Those who have received poor parental modeling need new models—loving Christian friends—to experience the love and grace of God. Through His body of believers, God often provides us with models of His love, so that our perception of His character can be slowly reshaped into one that is more accurate, resulting in a healthier relationship with Him. Then, our deep emotional, spiritual, and relational wounds can begin to heal, and we can more fully experience God's unconditional love.

Some of us are already involved in strong relationships with people who are understanding and patient with us; some of us haven't yet been able to cultivate relationships like these, and are still looking. If this is your situation, you may need to find a pastor or counselor who can help you get started, possibly by directing you to one or more believers who can minister to you. A small fellowship group or Bible study is often an excellent resource for intimate sharing, comfort, and encouragement. If you have tried to cultivate healthy relationships, but haven't found any yet, don't give up! The Lord wants all of us to be in an environment where we can experience more of His love through our relationships with other believers.

If you ask God for guidance, and are willing to continue putting forth the effort, He will lead you to some people who can provide this kind of an environment for you in His perfect time.

- What are some reasons people might be afraid of being loved and recoil from those who love them?

- Are any of these true of you? If so, which ones? How do these affect your self-esteem, your behavior, and your relationships?

Dear God, I am grateful to You for leading me to relationships that are healthy and fulfilling. I'm so comforted to know that You are aware of how vulnerable I am and will be standing beside me as I reach out to others . . .

RESPONDING TO UNBELIEVERS

But I say to you who hear, love your enemies, do good to those who hate you, bless those who curse you, pray for those who mistreat you.

LUKE 6:27–28

BUT WHAT ABOUT OUR RESPONSE TO UNBELIEVERS? Although they haven't yet trusted in the cross of Christ for the removal of their condemnation before God, Jesus was very clear about how we are to treat them. In Matthew 22:37, 39, He told His disciples to _love the Lord your God, with all your heart, and with all your soul, and with all your mind,_ and to _love your neighbor_ (both believers and unbelievers) _as yourself._ Christ didn't come to love and die for the lovely, righteous people of the world. If He had, we would all be in trouble! Instead, He came to love and die for the unrighteous, the inconsiderate, and the selfish. As we grow in our understanding of His love for us, and continue to grasp that He has rescued us from the righteous condemnation we deserve because of our sins, we will gradually become more patient and kind to others when they fail. It can be very helpful if we compare the failure or sin of others with our sin that Christ died to forgive: _There is nothing that anyone can do to me that can compare with my sin of rebellion that Christ has completely forgiven._ That should give us a lot of perspective!

* Does the passage in Luke 6 mean you should deny the heat of others' offenses toward you and excuse them? Why, or why not?

* What is the proper blend of honesty, forgiveness, boundaries in relationships, and love?

Heavenly Father, I want to obey Your Word from Matthew 22:37, 39. I do love You with all my heart, soul, and mind. Sometimes I need an extra portion of Your help, though, when it comes to "love your neighbor as yourself." If I am to become more consistent in following this command, I need to . . .

STOP BLAMING!

And He is the radiance of His glory and the exact representation of His nature, and upholds all things by the word of His power. When He had made purification of sins, He sat down at the right hand of the Majesty on high.

HEBREWS 1:3

SOME OF US HAVE A TENDENCY TO PERCEIVE OF JESUS AS OUR FRIEND, and God as a harsh disciplinarian. Yet the author of Hebrews described Jesus as *the radiance of [God's] glory and the exact representation of His nature* (Hebrews 1:3).

Studying passages like these and spending time with compassionate, forgiving Christians has enabled the Holy Spirit to reshape my perception of God over the years. I continue to experience remorse when I fail. But rather than hide from God, fearing His punishment, I more often approach Him with appreciation for what His love has accomplished for me.

Both assuming and assigning blame for failure can have a number of detrimental consequences. Many psychologists today adhere to a theory called Rational Emotive Therapy. This very helpful theory states that blame is the core of most emotional disturbances. The answer, they insist, is for each of us to stop blaming ourselves and others, and learn to accept ourselves in spite of our imperfections. How right they are! Christ's death is the complete payment for sin, and we can claim His complete forgiveness and acceptance daily.

A number of emotional problems are rooted in the false belief that we must meet certain standards to be acceptable, and that the only way to deal with inadequacies is to punish ourselves and others for them. There is no way we can shoulder such a heavy burden. Our guilt will overpower us, and the weight of our failures will break us.

The false belief, *Those who fail (including myself) are unworthy of love and deserve to be punished,* is at the root of our fear of punishment and our propensity to punish others.

• How deeply are you affected by this lie?

• How does blaming others affect you? Your relationships?

Jesus, help me to accept others today as I would want them to accept me. I need to remember that I can make mistakes just as easily as they can . . .

PROPITIATION

By this the love of God was manifested in us, that God has sent His only begotten Son into the world so that we might live through Him. In this is love, not that we loved God, but that He loved us and sent His Son to be the propitiation for our sins. Beloved, if God so loved us, we also ought to love one another.

1 JOHN 4:9–11

WHEN CHRIST DIED ON THE CROSS, He was our substitute. He took upon Himself the righteous wrath of God that we deserved. The depth of God's love for us is revealed by the extremity of His actions for us: the holy Son of God became a man and died a horrible death in our place. A passage written by Isaiah, who anticipated the coming of Christ, states:

Surely our griefs He Himself bore,
    and our sorrows He carried;
yet we ourselves esteemed Him stricken,
    smitten of God, and afflicted.
But He was pierced through for our transgressions,
    He was crushed for our iniquities;
the chastening for our well-being fell upon Him,
    and by His scourging we are healed.
All of us like sheep have gone astray,
    each of us has turned to his own way;
but the Lord has caused the iniquity of us all to fall on Him.

ISAIAH 53:4–6

- Is it hard for you to realize that you deserved the wrath of God for your sin? Why or why not?

- How do you feel when you realize that His worth has been replaced by His love for you?

Thank You , Lord, for . . .

HIS GREAT LOVE

> But God, being rich in mercy, because of His great love with which He loved us,
> even when we were dead in our transgressions, made us alive together with Christ
> (by grace you have been saved), and raised us up with Him, and seated us with Him
> in the heavenly places, in Christ Jesus, in order that in the ages to come He might
> show the surpassing riches of His grace in kindness toward us in Christ Jesus. For
> by grace you have been saved through faith; and that not of yourselves, it is the gift
> of God; not as a result of works, that no one should boast.
>
> EPHESIANS 2:4–9

BECAUSE WE ARE HIS CHILDREN, performance is no longer the basis of our worth. We are unconditionally and deeply loved by God, and we can live by faith in His grace. We were spiritually dead, but the Lord has made us alive and has given us the high status of sonship to the Almighty God. It will take all of eternity to comprehend the wealth of His love and grace.

Propitiation, then, means that Christ has satisfied the holy wrath of God through His payment for sin. There was only one reason for Him to do this: He loves us; infinitely, eternally, unconditionally, irrevocably, He loves us. God the Father loves us with the love of a father, reaching to snatch us from harm. God the Son loves us with the love of a brother, laying down His life for us. He alone has turned away God's wrath from us. There is nothing we can do, no amount of good deeds we can accomplish, and no religious ceremonies we can perform that can pay for our sins. Instead, Christ has conclusively paid for them so that we can escape eternal condemnation and experience His love and purposes both now and forever.

Christ not only paid for our sins at one point in time, but continues to love us and teach us day after day. We have a weapon to use against Satan as he attacks us with doubts about God's love for us. Our weapon is the fact that Christ took our punishment upon Himself at Calvary. We no longer have to fear punishment for our sins because Christ paid for them all—past, present, and future. This tremendous truth of propitiation clearly demonstrates that we are truly and deeply loved by God. His perfect love casts out all fear as we allow it to flood our hearts   (1 John 4:18).

• What factors can contribute to you experiencing more and more of God's love and grace?

Dear Father, there is no greater love than Yours. I am forever grateful to You for my salvation, for my freedom from guilt and condemnation, for Your unconditional love and acceptance of me . . .

THE SEARCH FOR SIGNIFICANCE

22-Day Guided Study

ROBERT S. McGEE

AND

RUJON MORRISON

Welcome to this 22-day guided study of *The Search For Significance*. As I've prepared these daily studies I've asked myself, "Where is the reader in the beginning of this study? Are there any new insights God has given me since this material was written? How can I help the reader to overcome any obstacles that might be encountered?

These helpful insights are only the first step of applying God's truth to your life. God wants us to be free. Jesus came that we might have life and have that life more abundantly.

This guide is adapted from a transcript of conversations between the author of *The Search For Significance*, Robert S. McGee, and Rujon Morrison, the Director of Rapha Retreats in Colorado Springs where people from all over the country come to work through these and other concepts in a very intense way.

A card is provided for each day of the *22-Day Guided Study*. These cards are located at the end of the study and may be cut out for use as an encouragement to you during the day. God bless you.

Day 1

We must first recognize our condition to receive help from God. Before salvation, we must recognize that we are lost before coming to Jesus for His saving grace. In the same way, we must know that we need to be healed before we come to Him. When we try to heal ourselves, typically these are simply bandaids, temporary solutions that may help us get through the day a little easier, but don't strike at the core issue causing the pain. When I lived in Houston, I had nutgrass in my lawn. Nutgrass is a weed which has little nodules at the roots. If you break off the top, the nodules remain and actually send out new shoots, resulting in more nutgrass than you had before. Maybe you've tried to deal with painful issues, some of which have been with you for many years. Have you noticed that sometimes the more you try to resolve it, the messier it gets? Recognize this fact: if we are to experience healing, we must encounter God. It is not by our own wisdom nor by our great insight that we are healed. You can see things about yourself, truths you haven't seen before, as you go through this material. But it is entirely possible for you to walk away with just more knowledge, not the emotional healing that you desire. Complete dependence upon the Lord is vital.

Two things will be helpful to you. First, recognize that our minds are deceived. The nature of deception is that when you are deceived, you don't know it. The Bible tells us that only the Spirit of God really and truly knows us. Only His light can push back the darkness, penetrate and renew our minds. Secondly, I suggest that you find a few close friends who will pray for you during this time. These friends don't need to know all the issues you are going through, they simply need to know that you desire to gain insight into your life and would like for them to pray for you over the next few days or weeks on a daily basis. A card is provided for you to give your friends a pattern by which to pray. That is Day 1—recognizing that only God's power can give us the freedom and the insight that we need.

Day 2

Robert: Our thought life is one of our greatest enemies. Today we will examine the way our thoughts can plague us from time to time. Have you ever had times when it seemed as though your mind had a will of its own; that even if you didn't want to think about a certain thing you found yourself thinking of it?

Rujon: Yes. I think a good example of that is comparing it to instant replay, reliving a situation over and over in my mind. I try to correct the things that I did wrong, determine what I should have done, or maybe I wonder what someone else is thinking and how I should respond. That can really wear me out.

Robert: Sometimes one thought leads to another, and to another, and to another. It is almost like stairs going down into a very deep, dark, black, basement. At times I have encountered days like that and I would become almost physically ill when I recognized the first thought and where it led me. We talk to ourselves about ourselves all day long. The content of that conversation has to do with how well we are doing. In other words, you are doing a critique, analyzing and scrutinizing yourself. When you were very young, you were given categories about what to think about yourself, how you value yourself and how you determine if you're doing well or not doing so well. As you grew up, everything you encountered fit into that pattern. Two people can walk into the same room with the same people present, and one will encounter a tremendous amount of rejection while the other doesn't sense that at all. Why? Because the one believed that is what the response from others would be. There was an expectation. Why was that? Early in life a pattern was set up inside. It was part of the belief system. The rejection affirmed the belief carried since childhood. The other person entered the same room and found very friendly, accepting people. Why is that? Because that is what they have learned to expect from people. We have created a system of thought, beliefs about ourselves, over and over again, thousands and millions of times. We have confirmed beliefs we acquired at a young age when we didn't have the opportunity to say, "I don't think this is right; I don't think this fits; I don't think you're correct when you tell me these things." Correcting these beliefs is like unwinding a giant ball of twine as large as your house. It is so impossible that only the Lord can do it.

Rujon: You've described a trap. If I'm caught up in this circular kind of thinking and then I try to get out of it, I'm going to end up going back to listening to myself say what I've been told about me. So are you saying that God has to break through that?

Robert: Yes, exactly. At some point, when man's wisdom runs out what we typically do is go back to the old system that we've used all our life. This sounds quite negative but it is really bad news and good news. It is too big for us to deal with, but it's not too big for God to deal with. Recognize afresh that God is the One can bring the answers you need. You may think that God is angry with you, that He may help others, but not you. But He says to you, "Taste of me and see that I am good." Take the chance that God will come through for you, giving you insights as you go through this daily study. Be very honest with Him about your fears. If you are, the idea that He won't be faithful to you will disappear.

Day 3
Robert: In our culture, unlike other cultures of the world, we want things to happen very quickly. We're very impatient. It is interesting seeing those in other cultures who are more patient than we ever thought about being. We want to be zapped. Quite frankly, it's not a lot different in our faith. We would like for God to do things instantly, but in fact it is a process. This guided study is not to be a course as much as it is to be a process. What happens in our journey prepares us for the freedom that we can experience at the end of our journey.

Rujon: So we like that quick fix, right?

Robert: All of us do. It reminds me of the story of the difference between a squash and an oak tree. When asked if they would prefer to be a squash or to be an oak tree, most people would say, "I'd rather be an oak tree." Those of us who grew up on a farm know what squash looks like at the end of the season. They are ugly, dried up, pitiful-looking plants. After they have produced their fruit they sort of dry up and blow away. But an oak tree grows strong, withstanding the storms, the winds, the dry season, the wet season, the snow, the cold. It is interesting that it only takes a few months for God to grow a squash. It takes many years to grow an oak tree. You will experience many wonderful things and enjoy tremendous growth as you go through the process of studying *The Search For Significance.* You are in a special place in your life. Don't be discouraged. God desires to break you free and bring you into freedom. It will be a process, and it will be His process.

Day 4

Robert: Think again about being on a journey. This is very important because one of the things we've learned from helping people in Rapha Treatment Centers, treating over 20,000 people, is that when a person comes into treatment, if their expectations are too low, they don't provide the effort they need to deal with their issues. If the patient's expectations are too high, they become discouraged quickly and give up. It is extremely important in the very beginning of treatment to deal with expectations. I don't want you to get discouraged when you encounter difficulties. If breaking through very patterned thought processes were easy, everyone would already have done it. You may have thoughts and patterns of thinking that you don't like, but continue to have. These are what we want to break free from. Rujon, you have a story about someone who successfully goes through that kind of process, don't you?

Rujon: Yes, I do. It's as though a man is traveling down a road and suddenly without warning falls into a deep, dark hole. It takes great effort and energy to get out. Once he's out, the journey begins again. Then suddenly, there is the hole again and he's fallen back in again. It's happened twice now. He is saying, "How did I get here? I know this place, I've been here before and I don't want to be here." He knows what it takes to get out and so he expends still more effort and energy. The journey continues and the next time, he sees the hole coming but it is as though the hole has a power of its own, drawing him in. Soon he has fallen in yet again. Does he like it in that hole? No. But the pattern repeats itself. The journey begins again and when he comes to the hole the next time, he sees it. He comes to the same place, the same street, he knows that the hole is there. He recalls the power of that hole. But this time he chooses to go down another street, a new journey.

Robert: Sometimes we end up expending tremendous amounts of energy and effort trying to get to a destination only to find that it doesn't give us what we really need. We have desires and we have needs. When people come to me for counseling, I always know what they want; they want to be happy. I know that is what you want as well. You want to be at peace with yourself, feel affirmed and loved, you want to have joy in your life. Note the difference in our needs and our desires. For example, a young man may believe that in order to get a need met, he must marry a certain young woman. He can't think of anything else but the day they will marry. If you were to ask him what his needs were, he would tell you, "I need to marry her." But what she really represents to him is a way to feel affirmed and loved. Sometimes a few years after the marriage, the same man may say that he has a great need to divorce his wife. He is still desperately trying to get his needs met. The bride he loved was unable to meet his core needs.

Rujon: The woman whose goal is to have a big diamond to wear may have to convince her husband to agree to the purchase. They might want friends to see how well they're doing financially and the diamond would demonstrate that. They may have a sense of affirmation, feeling competent and successful and having value because of owning the beautiful diamond ring. But after she gets the diamond, all she can think of is whether she might be robbed of her jewel. She had a desire, and it may have felt good for a period of time after achieving that desire, but it didn't fulfill the need. She may actually be almost trapped and enslaved by the very thing that she desired.

Robert: It is very common for someone who has achieved success in their career to find that they are now a slave to that prestigious position. There are certain core needs in your life that God wants to meet. But for many of us, it's as though we're in a room with only one door, and that door is our desire. I've talked to many Christians who will only allow God to meet their needs by fulfilling their desires. This often creates a situation where God doesn't necessarily meet the needs through the desires. ometimes He does, but often He does not. Ask God to show you what your desires are. If you're willing to, tell Him that you are content for Him to meet your needs in any way He wants. If you don't get your needs met from God, you will try to get them met in some other way, some how. If you try to meet your needs in any ways except God's ways, problems will always arise.

Rujon: Thinking of the story I told earlier of falling in the hole, it's almost as though our desires draw us in. But that hole is really a place that can only be filled by God. The lovely thing about what you're describing is that God has put some deposits into that hole which really makes it pretty uncomfortable. It brings to light this old way of having my needs met and that is a point of conflict: "Am I going to continue to look to the things that I've looked to in the past to meet my needs, or will I take the next step and trust the Lord even more."

Robert: We really don't understand how in the world God could meet these needs without fulfilling our desires. But our God is a supernatural God. I encourage you to allow Him to meet your needs apart from your desires. Ask the Lord. He will show you how this fits in your life.

Day 5

Robert: Today we want to introduce you to the essence of *The Search For Significance*. You will begin to sense that you are controlled by people and expectations and perhaps even goals which may be related to relationships in the past. All have created a belief system within you by which you evaluate yourself. This system isn't much different than the way we evaluate a vacuum cleaner. When we purchase a vacuum cleaner, we want one that looks nice. We ask, "Is it attractive? How much power does it have? How does it perform?" If it doesn't perform satisfactorily, it loses its value. If it gets banged up and is an embarrassment for us to vacuum with, it loses some of its value. We evaluate ourselves and our worth using the same method we might use in choosing a vacuum cleaner, or a car, or a refrigerator. That is really a hard way to live and it creates tremendous problems for us. Evaluating ourselves on how well we've performed is a losing formula. If you do 13 things well during the day but really mess up on one thing, you will probably go to bed thinking about the one failure. A second way we get caught is by the opinions of others, how they think we're doing, what worth they assign to us. As you go through your day, notice how much you are affected by these two issues. There are two ways by which we evaluate ourselves. One is the world system which says that our self worth and our value are based on how well we perform and others opinions of us. The other way is God's truth, basing my self worth and value on what God has declared to be true in His word. Ask God to show you how much your life is affected by Satan's negative formula of evaluation. It is my prayer that you will come to hate this formula. I encourage you to press on in the journey traveled by tens of thousands of Christians who have been where you are. We never get completely through with the process. I wrote the book you're studying, and there are still times when I get caught in the world's formula. But I know why I get caught and I know how to get free again. And I don't get caught nearly as often.

Rujon: So you want me, today, to begin to see how I get caught up in performing. You want me to recognize that though I do several things right, the one thing I failed in will really get me. The one person who makes that critical comment is the one that I think of and worry about. When I feel emotional pain, I must stop and think, "Is this about rejection, or is this about failure? Is this about fear of either of those things or fear of punishment, or has shame come up and caught me again?" If you and I are sensitive to our emotions, God will show us how this fits into the old system.

Day 6

Robert: By Day 6, you should be more sensitive to the ways you're caught in that old system of thinking. At this point, many people encounter anger. They realize that they've lived their whole life trying to please other people, or being afraid that they would fail. After jumping through the hoops all your life, you find that the formula doesn't work. It is difficult to get rid of anger without finding a place to deposit it. Often we become very angry with others, with ourselves, and even with God. One man described how, as a small child, he would dance for his uncles. They would praise him for dancing and he would dance even faster. He is in his late 30's now and he says that he has never stopped dancing. Many years ago, my wife and I went to Las Vegas on a honeymoon, not because we wanted to go to Las Vegas but because we had very little money and someone gave us the trip as a gift. We decided that it would be a sin not to gamble in Las Vegas (showing you how the mind can distort). We decided that we would only spend $20 at the slot machines. It took me two or three days, but at the end of those days, we had none of our $20 left. Even after losing the money, I really wanted to reach in my pocket and put more money after the bad money. We must recognize that we need to stop trying to achieve success using this failed formula. I want you to recognize that there will be a tremendous drive within you to try to finally win because you have so much invested in it.

Rujon: A woman told me a story of her relationship with her husband's mother. She desperately wanted the approval of her mother-in-law, who was quite the perfectionist. The younger woman would do everything she possibly could to make her home perfect in preparation for the older woman's visit. The meal was prepared and everything was ready. But her mother-in-law could always find the one thing that wasn't quite right. The more she tried to earn the approval, the more she had to do because it was never enough.

Robert: We've heard of people who are into middle age or older and are still trying to gain the approval of a parent. In some cases the parents are dead, yet something inside still tries to perform well enough to gain that approval. It shows the tremendous drive that we have to prove the world's formula that our worth is equal to what other people think of us and our performance. We need to go ahead and recognize that we're hurt and that the anger is there for a reason; it's there because of the disappointment that all we've invested hasn't been enough. It is okay to be angry. The point is that you go ahead and tell God about that anger and allow Him to deal with it.

Rujon: You said that hurt accompanies the anger, that I've not been able to make this thing work and I'm hurt because I didn't get the approval and what I was looking for in that system.

Robert: Many think that they should be able to satisfy their needs by gaining that approval. We have a need to be affirmed. We do need to be loved, accepted,

585

and received. The problem is that other people just aren't capable of providing that for us. If you could eliminate half of the rejection and half of the failure that you experience, your problem would be that the other half still exists and is painful. You may change spouses, you can change jobs, change environments, pick up tennis, and do many other things to try to achieve this, but you'll never get there. There is no one else who can change it for you. But the good news is that it is really inside you, and therefore something that you can change with God's help and insight change. We are sort of like a tube of toothpaste. This morning when I squeezed my tube of toothpaste, I wasn't surprised when toothpaste came out. From time to time, I see things come out of me that I don't like and I have a tendency to try to blame other people for it. But you see, they didn't put that in me. Only God and I can do anything about what is inside of me. He will give the insight wisdom, direction, and understanding to do this. As I travel and speak, I meet people who have worked through these truths for a number of years. They tell of gaining a sense of freedom that they never thought that they would ever be able to have. God is on your side. He wants you to be free.

Day 7

Robert: Yesterday we talked about the negative emotion of anger that you may encounter as you go through this. There is a second negative emotion which may arise, that of grief. It is easy to get caught in this. But it is time to move on with your life and not be caught between these two very destructive emotions. Grief often occurs when one realizes that much of life has been spent trying to climb the wrong hill. In fact, often we climb a hill with much energy, effort, and desire and perhaps very good intentions and other people may even have encouraged us to do it. But at the top of the hill, instead of feeling satisfaction, we see another hill that beckons us. Are you beginning to recognize that you've been attempting to go up the wrong hill? You've been trying to get your needs met in the wrong way. Unfortunately, self pity often sets in at this point. It is easy to be depressed and upset about having wasted so many years.

Rujon: We ask, "Why didn't God stop this?" or "Why didn't God tell me this sooner?"

Robert: Those are very good questions. Or "When I was very small why did He allow me to experience some of the things I experienced?" There are no good explanations for why we go through some of the things we do. The more we attempt to find the explanation, the worse we feel and the less we understand. God doesn't have to explain to us. However, what God has done is to give us an example of His love. The question "Why" can cause you much pain. Jesus chose to die for us in a very public, very demonstrative way, going through tremendous torment and grief and pain. The Lord knew that one day we would be at the place of saying, "I don't know if God really loves me because He let me go through this; I don't know why He did this." God says, "I'm not going to tell you how that fits together, but I will demonstrate that I love you at the cross.

Rujon: I'm thinking of those who are reading this who may have been through some pretty terrible things, things they didn't ask for. Whatever that was, it was so significant that Christ paid the price for that by dying on the cross; so it mattered to Him.

Robert: Yes, they matter to Him. He says He is angered by these things that happen to us, especially when we are children. He basically says that for those who mistreat children, it is better that a millstone be hung around the neck and they be tossed into the sea. Our natural mind is never going to come to a reasonable conclusion for why we went through some of our painful circumstances. When we're caught in grief and self pity, being totally consumed by the negative, hurtful things that have happened in the past, we are focused in the wrong direction, looking behind us instead of in front of us. To have freedom, we are going to have to deal with today and what is before us. At times God does want us to deal with certain things from our past, but when that happens, it won't be because we brooded and ruminated about what has happened behind us. I don't minimize the many very painful issues and traumas that some have experienced. When you struggle (and you will) with accomplishing the things in these step studies, instead of making them into a black and white rule and feeling that you can't do it or can't seem to experience it, I want you to simply go to the Lord and tell Him what you cannot do. He is the only One who can lead you to the healing and freedom that lies ahead.

Day 8
Robert: Today I want to look at an overview of *The Search for Significance* and how it plays out in your life. Years ago when I first wrote *The Search*, I started from the perspective of the issues I saw in the lives of the people I was counselling. I started with their fears and what God's solutions were for those fears. As you read this material, you will see that I take it back to the garden where Adam and Even were created as very special creatures. They were given two great tasks by God. The Bible declares that they were to first bear the image of God, to reflect God's love, His patience, His joy, His peace, all the qualities of his character. Secondly, they were to rule. We know that they walked in the garden with Him and had fellowship with Him. He provided all that they needed, just as He does for us. Yet, when Eve was deceived by the serpent, she chose to rebel and eat of the fruit. The Bible then says that Adam was not deceived, but he knew what he was doing, joining Eve in that fallen condition. We don't hear much about our fallen condition today, but the Bible is very clear about it. The Bible describes how Adam and Eve entered into a different state of living and then reproduced themselves. All

their descendants, which includes you and me, were born into a fallen race. No one had to teach us how to sin. It came to us very naturally. In order to redeem man, Jesus took the wrath of God for our sins upon Himself. What occurred at Golgotha has great significance, but what paid the penalty for your sins and my sins was not Jesus hanging on the cross; it was when God the Father placed upon Him the wrath that we deserved. Satan understands that when a person accepts the Lord Jesus Christ, they become a new creation and the Holy Spirit actually comes to live within them. They then have a great capacity for interfering with his plans. He fights back by distorting how we perceive ourselves from the very beginning of our lives. Satan taught us that all we are is what we do and what other people think of us. In *The Search For Significance* you are going to find a way of discovering specifically what that means, and how you can come to understand that what God says is true. The success you have in breaking free from this world system will be based on whether or not you accept what God says is true of you. In this process, you will learn how to lay aside these fears of performing, of rejection, of shame, of punishment. Jesus paid a tremendous price, not only so you could be with Him for eternity in heaven, but also so you could experience freedom today. Wouldn't it be tragic if you accepted God's gift of eternal life in heaven but continued to live miserably in this life? It is my prayer that over the next few days you find a tremendous discovery as you more fully appreciate the impact that salvation really is supposed to make in your life.

Day 9

Robert: It is unfortunate that much of what we learn in childhood, the first few years of our life, become the dominant patterns for the rest of our life. I once attended a baby dedication service. A toddler was on the platform with his parents and the newborn baby. When their portion of the dedication service was over, the mother tried to coax him down, but he refused. When his father took his hand to lead him out, the crying child took a bite out of his father's hand. Well, I thought to myself, if these parents don't help this child learn a different pattern, he may not be biting people for the rest of his life, but he will indeed try to be intimidating people for the rest of his life. You see, when we are born, the Bible declares that we don't have the Holy Spirit within us to guide us in how to relate to life, so the only thing that is left for us to rely upon is what comes naturally, which God says is not of Him. I am not saying that these ways are necessarily unethical or immoral, but they are just not of the Lord. What happens is that they may help us to survive our childhood, and may be very useful to us during a certain period of our life. But they also have certain very negative consequences for us. These patterns cause us all types of problems later on. There is a verse in scripture that I've always found interesting: "When I was a child, I spoke as a child, I thought as a child, I acted as a child, but now that I have become a man I have put away childish things." As we relate to life, we relate to it based on two different principles. One is fight, and the other is flight. Under flight we have what would be a withdrawing mechanism. Early in life a person may be dominated by the pattern to withdraw from conflict and withdraw from people. That may have been very useful as a child because you may have been in a very abusive situation and the way to survive is to withdraw. But now that you are 35 or 40, you use that same withdrawal mechanism and you may be causing all kinds of havoc in your life and problems in your marriage, and issues at work. You may be a very miserable and angry person because all you know to do is to withdraw all the time. Rujon, you have known people who were in a very difficult situation as children and therefore they fantasized, living in a different world.

Rujon: It is really a strong, destructive pattern that has been learned and so it seems to be the only coping mechanism that is available. It isolates people from relationships and keeps them trapped in a system that might have kept them safe before, but now really keeps them from the love and the care of those around them.

Robert: The other side is fight—and that has to do with trying to manipulate, intimidate other people, get control of other people. There are many people who feel very uneasy in their life if they are not in control. We see this all the time. Sometimes therapists are not able to live life easily because they are so used to being in control all the time. You see people who do it through intimidation. Many people don't understand why a person gets angry so easily. All you have to do is observe what the payoff is. The payoff is that it controls the behavior of a lot of other people. That may have been something that was somewhat helpful in some way as a child. Maybe it gave them the motivation or the impetus at that time. I remember a fellow who had gone to the Marine Corps and he was a rather small individual. He said, "You know, what I did when I was there was to use the anger from my childhood to give me enough energy to get through." He was coming to see me because he was also being abusive to his wife. So, here again we see something that began at one point, was later used in life perhaps to get this man through a very difficult situation, but now in his marriage he was in a real bind because it had generalized. It is difficult to keep these patterns from exploding into all kinds of areas in our lives. In other words, we can't isolate these patterns. If you take a look at *The Search For Significance*, you'll see that we learn ways of not having to deal with failure, i.e. by withdrawing. We'll see this in the upcoming days. We will find people who do not want to deal with rejection and they do so by not being around anybody. It is pretty difficult to be rejected if you aren't around anybody. On and on it goes as we see that these patterns used in childhood have created almost a platform for destruction later on in life. Today and maybe for several days, look at your life and think of the ways that you act childishly. See how you sometimes have patterns of fighting through situations or of withdrawing. See the pattern, but also recognize the consequences in your life for having this pattern. You see, many people tell me, "This is simply the way I am." It may be the way you are, but is it also causing havoc in your life. It doesn't satisfy the needs that you have. The more excuses you have for the way you are, the worse off you are. The more excuses you have the less likelihood you will deal with anything in your life. My prayer for you is that you'll learn how to live life more fully and more abundantly.

Day 10

Robert: Yesterday we talked about childhood patterns. I encourage you to take a look at your life to see how ways you learned to live as a child have turned about and may be causing some problems for you. I want to also share with you an acronym that you can use as God shows you that these childhood patterns in your life are creating problems for you. The acronym is CROP. The first word is Confession. I went to God in confession many years ago, simply admitting to Him that when He tells me that I have done something that I actually did it. It is not simply saying, "Okay, Lord, I was not honest there," or "I expressed certain wrath, or anger, or bitterness, or resentment there," as though you were going down a grocery list. Unfortunately, many Christians believe that is what confession is all about. It is also recognizing the destructiveness and the evil of that which is involved. It is recognizing that the bitterness is very evil. The best way to do that is to ask God to open your eyes to see how these patterns have created all kinds of havoc and evil in your life. I have never seen anybody really change who has not come to this conclusion.

Rujon: You know, Robert, we don't hear a lot about evil today. Can you talk a little bit about what that means?

Robert: Unfortunately, what we have done is to relegate evil to that which is immoral or unethical, or perhaps something somebody doesn't want you to do. The Bible is much more general than that. It says that we were born into an evil world, that we have an evil and sinful nature within us. If we look at the patterns that we have been talking about, they have in fact been taking away tremendous areas of individual's lives. Many people are living at such a reduced level of life, it is almost as if they are imprisoned.

Rujon: Yes, they have little freedom to experience life. Not long ago on one of our retreats, a person was taking a shower and God spoke to him. He said, "I want you see how you have been trying to be pleasing to everybody and how that's been a dominating factor in your life. Do you see how that has ruined your life and robbed you of experiencing life and how you have been dragged back and forth, here and there, because of this compulsion to be pleasing to others?" As this man recognized that it was true, he began to cry and weep. Now he saw it as evil. It was robbing him of his existence.

Robert: I hope that by the end of this study, you really recognize that these patterns and these false beliefs have robbed you so that you can come to the point of saying, "Lord, not only have I been doing this, but this is evil." The second part of this acronym CROP is Repent. Now a lot of people believe that someplace back there, they left God and went their own way. I want to tell you that if you are one of those people, God is not far from you. He is simply behind you, right behind you, and He wants you to turn and be face to face with Him. Those who encounter pain in life learn not to trust anybody. It may be difficult at the point of repentance, of bowing the knee before the Lord to say, "Lord, I accept your authority as Lord of my life." The third part of the acronym is O for Obedience. Many people think God tests them to see if they are going to be obedient or not. Let me tell you that God already knows whether you are going to be obedient. God gives us opportunities as we confess, as we repent. If God doesn't give us opportunity to be obedient, how do we know that He has done a work in our life? In fact, as you try to break free from any area of your life, God will give you an opportunity to be obedient, not because He is being mean to you, but because this is part of the process of becoming free. The last part of the acronym is Praise, being thankful to the Lord. In this way, as we become thankful to Him about all kinds of areas of our life, we will recognize more and more of his provision for us and His love for us.

Rujon: So, this is an attitude that will begin to really take on a difference in attitude and a focus.

Robert: As God breaks us free from these patterns, there is no way for us not to be thankful. There are a lot of people who talk about miracles and people getting healed of all types of physical ailments and issues. People who begin to experience God's healing emotionally cannot help but be in tremendous praise, because suddenly there is a huge weight being taken off.

Day 11

Robert: Over the next few days we will look at the four false beliefs and God's provisions to break us free from these and the effects that they have had in our lives. Now let's remember that these false beliefs are all based on a formula that my self worth, my value for myself, is based on how well I perform and what other people think of me. The first one we will deal with today will be the Fear of Failure. This fear comes from experiencing the pain that occurs when we fail. After you experience that and have failed a few times, there is a tremendous fear of failing. It is almost a conditioned response because you feel that you should be fearful of anything that would cause that much pain.

Rujon: I think with Christians it is a profound fear because many are are trying so desperately to earn the way in. One of the common things I hear is, "No matter what I do, I can't get it right."

Robert: I think that many people who go to church have no real conception of the intensity that the pastor and his family are under to perform, because not only do they have the natural demands that we place upon ourselves, they are much more highly intensified. They are supposed to somehow have avoided all the struggles. This fear of failure will lead into a very unhealthy lifestyle. It will lead us to not trying a lot of things, won't it?

Rujon: Yes, it's interesting that it's either the fear of failing, or the fear of success that we see so often.

Robert: The higher up the ladder you get, the further you can fall. It is not that one sits around and thinks about these things, plotting them out. It just happens inside of us so that there is a lot of limitation. Some people experience tremendous depression because they believe there is really not much hope. I often tell people who are really critical of people who appear to be lazy, "If you had as much hope of being successful as they have, you would probably be about as lazy as they are." There are many kids in school like this. I have two children who have certain learning disability problems and I have gone to great expense to keep their experience of school a positive one. I have seen too many children who have struggled and at some point in their educational lives, they give up because it is easier to experience failure when you don't try, than when you have really tried and still experience failure. We see this fear of failure keeping us in a prison as it were with certain boundaries. It is not really much different than those people who suffer from agoraphobia. I have seen many in counselling who could not go out of a certain environment. I remember a women that I dealt with many years ago. She had certain streets which she considered her boundaries. Inside those boundaries she was relatively happy. But if she passed a certain street, she began to become very fearful and anxious. Most of us don't have streets that keep us within a certain boundary, but we do have activities and patterns of behavior that keep us in boundaries. Think about your life and try to determine what kind of performance boundaries you have. What things will you avoid doing because it is so uncomfortable when you do?

Rujon: Robert, do you think that we could even have sort of an internal system at work so that when we begin to approach these self-made boundaries, we will sabotage breaking through them?

Robert: Oh, absolutely. The problem is not that we don't have the potential to move past those boundaries any more than the woman who I dealt with many years ago. She could have driven her car past them. It isn't that we don't have the talent or the skill or the ability to go past these boundaries. We are so caught by the pain of failure that we don't want to experience it. Therefore, we are trapped by these barriers.

Rujon: So the pain that we have experienced in the past creates these fears that keep us from moving into new things.

Robert: Yes. Remember, it goes back to the formula. "I am what I do, and if I fail, then I am going to experience tremendous pain because I am a zero." Ask the Lord to show you how you have limited your life because of this fear. As you do, you will recognize the great significance of being able to break free.

Day 12
Robert: Yesterday we looked at the Fear of Failure. Today, let's look at God's provision for that fear. Notice that Satan has taught us that we are only valuable by how well we perform. That means that you really have no inherent value just because of who you are, that if you become too old, or too sick you don't have any real value. In other words, this system treats us like machines. If I have a piece of equipment and it becomes outdated or somehow impaired so that it cannot perform, why should I keep that piece of machinery? When we have to fear failure that much, it can so dominate our lives that we can't even admit failure. Wouldn't it be nice to be able to look at your failures, recognize them as failures, but not have them so dominate life that it just destroys your days? There are some people who believe that if they fail in a certain area, they must feel miserable for the rest of the day. Some people feel that they have to feel miserable for a week, a month, or a certain length of time and some people feel like they have to feel miserable about themselves for the rest of their life. It is all based on a lie that Satan has taught us. How does God deal with this? He does it partly through Justification. In Romans 5:1, it tells that we have become justified. Justification has two real issues. One, our sin has been taken away, but second, and more importantly in some ways, is that we haven't just become neutral, but God has placed upon us the righteousness of Christ. Our sin was placed upon Him and His righteousness was placed upon us and because of this God says that we are pleasing to Him, not because of our performance, but pleasing to Him because of what Christ has done, and who we are to Him. God wants His children to recognize that they are His. Think of it, those of you who have children. How would you feel if your children didn't recognize that they were your children? Not long ago, one of my children needed something and I was happy to provide it for her because she is my child. Yet, Christians all over this world are not experiencing the meaning of being a child of God.

Rujon: So, Robert, what is the difference between this performance and, I think the word I hear you using, personhood.

Robert: Well, Rujon, if you had been born to become the next queen of England, and if you struggled with learning math, that wouldn't diminish the fact that you were going to be the next queen of England. If you didn't hit all your walking and all your speech development correctly, it still wouldn't have affected the fact of who you are. That is the important part of God wanting us to know that He has redeemed us; He has made us a new creation, we are pleasing to Him, and we are His child.

Rujon: So, you're saying that my behavior doesn't really make up who I am.

Robert: Well, our behavior can be very grieving to the Father just as our children's behavior can be grieving to us. Sin is destructive and therefore the Father grieves when He sees us caught in sin. But if one of your children really started doing all sorts of crazy things, they wouldn't cease being your child, and you wouldn't cease loving them. In fact, instead of being angry with them as many think God is with us, what you would be is very grieved to see them make these choices. It is not that our performance is unimportant, and we will deal with this at another time. But it is that He wants us to know that what Christ did was sufficient to keep us in a condition where His love is not based upon how well we perform.

Day 13

Robert: I know that many people, when hearing about performance and God making us pleasing to Him only through salvation, feel really concerned that maybe I'm talking about license, that maybe I'm talking about some form of the faith where performance doesn't matter at all, and that I just don't know what I'm talking about at all. Many Christians obey in order to be pleasing to God. I want to tell you that this is an offense to God because what Christ did on the cross was to pay for your sin so that you could be pleasing to God based on what Christ did, not based upon your performance. It is in essence telling Christ that His work on the cross was helpful, but was not complete. Yet, He said it was finished. Where does performance play its part? The Bible declares that we will reap what we sow. There are real consequences to sin in our lives, yet it takes more consistent faith to believe that sin is de-structive than any other thing. It would be sort of like this: if I said to you, "Out in back of my house, there are some mushrooms, but they are poison-ous." You might say to yourself, "Well, you know, Robert told me they were poisonous because he is saving them for himself, or he doesn't want me to enjoy those mushrooms, or I'm awfully hungry and I bet they are not really that sickening." So you went out back and dug up the mushrooms, sauteed them and began to eat. Suddenly, you became ill. You see, it was because you didn't really believe me when I told you that they were destructive and very harmful for you. Let me give you an example. God talks to us a lot about what we do with our anger and what we do with our bitterness. Over and over I meet people who don't really respond to that anger and bitterness inside them with a real fear. Yet God desires for us to feel fearful of holding onto that anger and bitterness. There are good reasons for being obedient and there are bad reasons to be obedient. Let's start with the bad ones first. One is obedience to be pleasing to God rather than relying upon what Jesus did to be pleasing to Him. The second is to be pleasing to other people. Have you heard of someone who seems to be living a totally exemplary life and suddenly seems to go off the deep end and fall deeply into immorality? In almost every case, that person wasn't living this wonderful life unto the Lord, even though everyone around him may have thought so. What they were doing was living a life unto people and soon their desire to do whatever they ended up doing overcame their concern about what other people would think. Many Christians think that they can trade with God, that they will be obedient and God will bless them in some specific manner for being obedient. God doesn't trade marbles with us. Blessed is the person who is obedient to the Lord; there is no getting away from that, but He does not say," You be obedient today and I'll bless you with some material thing, some relationship or whatever it is that is important to you." That is not who God is. There are many who like to be religious, they like to look religious, and they do it for their own sake. They have much pride in how well they behave as compared to everyone else in the world. Let's talk about some good reasons to be obedient to God. First of all, sin is destructive. Secondly, when we are disobedient, obviously we are not doing that which is obedient. God declares that His way is the best way. He declares that His path leads into life. We cannot go down a path that leads into death and destruction, and at the same time go down the path that leads into life. There is also the issue of rewards in Heaven. The Bible declares that our good deeds will be tested. Now, obviously our bad deeds don't need to be tested because on the surface they are bad. Why would God test our good deeds? It is because so many of us think that our good deeds are done under the correct motivation and God allows us to recognize that much of what we do is not with the right motivation, to glorify Him, but in response to our own issues. When we get to heaven, we will go through a judgment of our works and our good ones will be piled up. They will be tested by fire and that which remains will be formed into a crown which we can lay at the feet of Jesus. Some of us are going to be shocked because we have believed all our lives that were doing good. Performance is important and sin is destructive. It will destroy us. The Bible talks about living out our salvation in fear and trembling. Why is that? Because we are afraid to somehow lose it and blow it? No, it's because it's sort of like this: you go into your bathroom tonight and it is very dark, pitch black. You need some medicine out of the medicine cabinet and you have all these pill bottles. They feel the same in the dark. You are going to turn your light on, not because you are overcome by some great fear, but you have a deep respect for taking the wrong medicine. I find that many Christians have not recognized the deep respect they need to have for not involving themselves in sin. We are not here to tell you that your performance does not matter. God's love, because of what Christ has accomplished, transcends your sin and allows Him to love you in spite of your sin. Think about it. Think about "Why am I obedient? Am I really obedient for the right reasons?"

Day 14

Robert: Today we will look at the Fear of Rejection. Because we are personal beings, the part of our environment that causes us the greatest grief has to do with our relationships with other people. When we experience rejection, it seems to cut through right to the core of our life and really contaminate almost every area of life until we end up almost like an addict needing acceptance. Rujon, you've seen several stories of this in the retreat which are pretty dramatic. Won't you share with us some of that which you've seen?

Rujon: We had a gentleman who was quite successful in the ministry come to one of our retreats. He said that growing up, he had never, ever received any kind of approval or nurturing from his parents. He was never really told that he was loved. It always seemed to be based on what he could do and that approval then would come from other people. He carried this into his ministry and could never do enough. Whatever people wanted of him constantly put more and more pressure upon him. He finally burned out in the ministry, going into a deep, deep depression. In his story, he says that he prayed and had many other people praying that he would be delivered of this depression, but God didn't do that. God wanted to show him the root of the depression; that he had depended upon others to tell him who he was and define what he needed based on their approval. God wanted him to be free of that. It was binding him up.

Robert: How did you discover this?

Rujon: Through a very intensive exercise, he began to examine who he really thought he was and more importantly how God viewed him. He discovered that he had gotten God confused with his parents displacing how he viewed his mother and father on God. He was very angry at God, and very hurt.

Robert: We see this happen many times. I understand that he went back to his church and openly shared what had happened to him. Sometimes people get anxious about this type of openness and are put off. However, his church family was able to relate to his experience.

Rujon: That's right. This is a man of God who is willing to be honest with himself, and therefore can be trusted. There was revival in his church as people began to move into healing.

Robert: The patterns of fear and rejection have many ways they can affect us. There is much pain that can occur in life because of rejection. It cuts to the very essence of who we are, and yet we can end up as the country western song says, "looking for love in all the wrong places." Many Christians that I talk to may not be going to the honky tonk, but they do often look for love in all the wrong places. They find some other person who they think will overcome the pain that exists in their life. Sometimes they marry that person, only to find themselves very disappointed with the results. Think about this for the next day or two. Think about how much of your life has been affected by the fear of rejection. I believe that seeing that about ourselves helps us to experience what God has for us. It isn't that we don't care about anybody else anymore, but it is that we're not addicted to their approval. It is one of the most difficult addictions to break. But our God wants to break you from it so you can experience His freedom.

Rujon: Robert, I have a quote that I think is beautiful, and it goes like this, "When I kneel before God, I can stand before any man."

Robert: There is a part of us that has to experience acceptance, that was made for us to experience God's acceptance, but many Christians are not experiencing it. It is a fact, but they aren't experiencing it. The fact is that the Heavenly Father is there to fill the void within with His love and acceptance. The more we experience His love and acceptance, the less we will be manipulated by everyone else in our lives.

Day 15

Robert: What is God's solution for our fear of rejection? How does He deal with that? Let me share a personal note with you. Many years ago after going through graduate school in psychology, I held a very firm belief that God holds the solutions for man's problems. I knew first of all that God had to have solutions for my own life situations. At the time I didn't know what the solutions were because I was as addicted to the approval of others and manipulated by those around me as anybody that ever walked this earth. I would shake someone's hand and wonder if I shook it hard enough, it my hand was too sweaty, just on and on and on. I was influenced by your acceptance or rejection of me. I cannot tell you the amount of my life which was made miserable by my need to have your approval. Yet there was something in my spirit that said that God had a solution. This solution is found in Colossians 1:21-22. "Although I was at one time hostile toward God and alienated from Him, I am now forgiven and have been brought into an intimate relationship with Him." This means that He has brought me from alienation from Him into a deeply accepted relationship with Him.

Rujon: Yes, God has accepted us and He tells us that when that acceptance is fully experienced it is enough to break us free from being addicted to the approval of others. There are certain types of addictions which can be broken by other things. One example is Methadone, which is given to heroin addicts. It is absolutely sure that if you are not experiencing His love and acceptance, you will be seeking it from other people, or you will have given up on life and simply withdraw from the whole issue of living. It is difficult to describe to a blind man what a flower garden looks like. It is equally difficult for me to really describe to you how life based upon God's acceptance of you will satisfy to the point that you will be free from being addicted to having the approval of others. It is something you have to experience.

Day 16

Robert: The next false belief we want to look at has to do with blaming those who fail. The concept is that those who fail should be punished and that when we fail, we begin to fear punishment. There is something in us that has a desire to punish those around us who fail. We use the very same process on ourselves that we use on other people.

Rujon: Do you mean that if we begin to blame other people and to punish them for failure, we will do the very same thing to ourselves?

Robert: Yes, in fact some people use this to try to keep themselves in line. I can't tell you the number of people I have talked with who actually accept as much blame and rejection as they can possibly endure on the theory that if they accept this, it will cause pain within, and they will be motivated to succeed. Let me share the two ways we get motivated: one is through fear and the other is through love. Many Christians spend very little time being motivated by love, but it is very common to find Christians motivated by fear. Look at your life over the next few days and see what you do because you are afraid of criticism. Or do you do things because you fear punishment? Do you feel like others need to be punished if they fail? If there is someone that you would like to see punished because of something they have done, you will also encounter the same idea about yourself. A godly behavior is a good goal; however, punishing those who fail won't accomplish it. Punishing yourself and accepting condemnation from others will only change your behavior for a short time.

Day 17

Robert: You may ask, what is God's solution for fear of punishment? It is very interesting that when we search the scripture, we find only one solution for fear and that is that perfect love casts out fear. Two essential points are important today: one is, if you are to stop punishing and condemning yourself, you must be willing to stop condemning other people. You must begin to look at others, recognizing that they have tremendous value. In spite of performance, they are very special individuals, highly valuable to God. Look around you at those who the world would say have very little value. Choose to find value in them. When you give up your need to punish others, something very powerful happens. You will cease to punish and condemn yourself.

Rujon: I believe that at the root of this is the way we view God. I'm from Mississippi and I grew up with an image of an awesome God, sort of like the Wizard of Oz up in heaven with a giant fly swatter, just waiting to get me any time I did anything wrong.

598

Robert: I recently talked with a man who had left the ministry 15 or 20 years ago. I knew that he had gone into a lifestyle of immorality after leaving the ministry. When I asked him why he was living like this, he told me that he knew that God was so angry with him for not performing correctly that he might as well go out and enjoy himself while he was waiting for God to get him. He had spent many years waiting for God to get even with him. Many Christians live in anticipation of God's nailing them to the wall because of their failures. They don't sense a God of love and they don't have a good picture of who the Father really is. A loving father will discipline his children, but the discipline will lead to freedom from bondage. Think about it; the Heavenly Father will never deal with you from a position of wrath again because Jesus took the wrath upon Himself for our sin. All that was taken out on Jesus.

Day 18

Robert: Today we will discuss a very common experience in life, that of shame. I find that shame occurs when something happens that we just can't get over. I used to call it emotional tar. It is like walking on the seashore where an oil spill has occurred. You get tar on your feet and it is almost impossible to remove it. This is even worse. It is as though something has happened so significant that we can never get past it or be happy again. I can't tell you the number of people who have told me of things that they believe have ruined life for them. It is the concept of being ruined. Interestingly, there is nothing in scripture that speaks of this concept. You see, many times we have concluded that not even God can deal with this. However, God does not know of a situation that He cannot overcome.

Rujon: Many times I've heard people express in words or attitudes that even God can't help with this situation. There are those who have lived through events so traumatic that they believe lies about who they are based on what happened to them. At times, instead of a traumatic event, it may be a recurring message that they've heard over and over that says, "You're not lovable," and it wounds so deeply that they can't imagine recovering from it.

Robert: Once this happens, we often find ourselves around other people who reinforce the very same message over and over again. The message seems to become ingrained within the very fiber of being. Many times the individual points toward someone in their life who confirms these shame messages and they perceive that this individual is the cause of their grief. They fail to see that the problem is that they have accepted the shame. I would suggest that because of this acceptance, they would be very uncomfortable around someone who was giving them positive, affirming messages. Until this is corrected and they cease to accept the shame message, they may seem to sabotage the efforts of others to offer love and acceptance. In your retreat setting, I know that you deal with these shame messages in a very unique way. You help the individual recognize all the messages they have taken into themselves and then begin to repeat them out of their own mouth. In other words, they are repeating curses or shame messages that have been placed upon them by others. Working with these people, you find that they often realize that these are messages they received early in life and have repeated for many years.

Rujon: In the case of traumatic events, it keeps the perpetrator alive in their lives, feeding the vicious cycle. Even if the perpetrator died years ago, they may as well be alive because the individual is actually carrying the message through.

Robert: Why don't you take a look to see if you believe some experience you have gone through has ruined your life in some way? God has good news for you. There is nothing you have gone through that He can't overcome.

Day 19
Robert: What about shame? How do we break free from it? I accepted the Lord when I was six years old. At that time God did something in my life that I didn't understand; He made me a new creation. It was many years past the age of six before I recognized that I did not have to accept shame messages. The solution to the shame messages is to accept the reality of being born again, of redemption, of God making you a brand new creation. Ask God to show you how to accept that reality. The doctrinal term is regeneration. The Bible speaks to the fact that when God created the world, he did it by "fiat", that is he spoke it into being. The Bible also uses the same term when it speaks of what occurs when a person is redeemed by Him. We are declared righteous, a new creation. God did not come to clean you up, wash you up, patch you up. He came to make you brand new. You have become a new race of people, a regenerated race. True, you have the same hands and arms, and flesh and stomach, but you are brand new inside. That which is really you has been made brand new. I wish He had turned us purple with yellow polka dots or some other obvious thing so we would know we are really different. The only way for us to truly know it is to accept what he says is true of us, receive it and begin to act upon it. Then He will prove it to us.

Rujon: I thought of this example. One of the things I would love to have if I could have anything I want is a white Mercedes convertible. It is almost as though God has given me a white Mercedes convertible and put it in my garage, but I have forgotten that I have it because I've left it parked in the garage and never take it out. I don't even think about it being around anymore. I think many of us as Christians don't really understand this concept of a new spirit, that God has given us everything we need to live life as He has called us to live it.

Robert: The fact is, we have been deceived. When we're deceived, we don't know we're deceived. We have been deceived in that we don't recognize what God

600

has already done, what He is going to do, and also what is there for us to experience now.

Day 20

Robert: Today, we will take a look at forgiving others. This may seem a bit strange to you since the topic of this material is self esteem and self worth. However, I've never seen anyone get free from powerful emotional issues or really enjoy life who has not dealt with this issue of forgiving others. It is so important, that the workbook section of *The Search For Significance* covers it in depth. In that workbook section, I've listed all kinds of reasons why we don't forgive others. Some of these are that the offense is too great, they didn't ask for forgiveness, I don't like them, they did it deliberately. On and on it goes, and the excuses for not forgiving trap us into holding onto unforgiveness. It is like a spiritual cancer in life. It makes you sick and it will grow to not only involve the person you have not forgiven, but it will generalize to the point that this bitterness and anger extends to others as well. An older woman came to see me one day and said that her friends and family told her she seemed to have a lot of anger in her life, and her countenance confirmed this to me. However, she denied that she was angry at all. Another person told me that he was not angry and did not hate, but at the same time he was screaming the words, full of the emotions of anger and hate. When we harbor unforgiveness, it becomes obvious in the way we relate to others.

Rujon: One important subtlety is that we must not excuse an offense instead of forgiving it. Often when someone is in great pain because of an offense, it seems too big to forgive, so in essence they may look for a reason to reduce the quality and quantity of the offense. They have forgiven a distortion of the offense, and the real offense remains.

Robert: Forgiveness does not mean that what happened to you does not hurt. It doesn't mean that it wasn't important. It doesn't mean that they will be no consequences. For instance, there are situations where after forgiveness is done, you may need to not be around that person anymore. Forgiveness also does not mean that God considered the offense unimportant. In fact, He tells us in scripture that when we mistreat a child, it is better that a millstone were wrapped around the neck and the offender thrown into the sea. My point is that forgiveness does not mean that the event is of no consequence.

Rujon: Those from a dysfunctional family background often were devalued and feelings were not recognized. Know that it did matter to God and He will help you deal with it. But He does require forgiveness before moving on.

Robert: God gave us the Holy Spirit because we can't figure this out on our own. If we sit and contemplate, conjure, and think about it, we become more confused. We must ask the Father to show us, push back the darkness in our minds, bring to remembrance those who are to be forgiven. Then recognize that Jesus paid for all sin at the cross and that His forgiveness is what can be shared with those who have offended you. I encourage you to look very closely at that part of the workbook that has to do with forgiveness.

Day 21

Robert: Today we will look at the part of *The Search* called "The Trip In." No matter how much truth you know, until it is applied to a specific area of deception, you will not be free. I have heard many sermons that included God's truth and I left the meeting thinking that my life would never be the same because I heard this truth. However, because I didn't understand how to apply that truth specifically to areas of deception, it soon lost its power in my life. I wasn't using it as it was intended to be used. Truth is designed to be the light that shines into the darkness. One thing about light is that it always over-comes darkness. If you have a room that is totally dark and you turn on a flashlight in the next room, no matter how bright the light, it will not illumi-nate that dark room. The light must be shone into the darkness before it will illuminate. The Bible calls it laying off the old man and putting on the new, renewing the mind. All these concepts are ones that Christians hear, they know the words, but often don't really understand what it means and how it's done. One of the most important things you can do is to allow God to bring you to recognize the deceptions and falseness in your life so He can shine the truth of His words upon it. That is part of the reason He gave us emotions. They not only bring joy, but they cue us when something is going wrong.

Rujon: If you were given the opportunity to take a pill which would cause your body never to experience fever again, you would be very foolish to take the pill. Although being feverish makes you feel bad, it is also a cue that there is something wrong physically and it is time to get some help. Emotions work in the same way. Many would like to just get rid of their negative emotions, thinking their lives would be wonderful if that were possible. But life would not be wonderful because as long as there is deception, there will be a de-structive lifestyle and patterns that corrupt relationships. The negative emo-tions are there to point out that something is wrong.

Robert: This is how the "Trip In" goes. If I notice that you're sad and I ask you why you're sad, typically you would tell me of a situation. At the same time you are going through this particular situation, someone else may be going through very similar circumstances, however with a completely different emotional response. In other words, situations don't create emotions. For instance, the situation may be that I lost my job. Therefore, I feel sad. The fact is that I lost my job, the belief is that those who fail should be punished. The thoughts I have may be that I must be a rotten failure because I just lost my job. Soon I would have all these negative emotions and begin to act on them. Sometimes I may have self pity, which is very devastating because it can lead to all types of behavior which get one into much deeper trouble. God is allowing you to experience your emotions so that you can correct whatever issues exist in your life that are negative, hurtful ones. Soon you will be able to recognize what is going on inside of you and you will do a couple of things. First, you will have a basis for how to correct the issue, and secondly you won't feel so powerless about what is happening to you.

Rujon: So you're saying that we should be open to our emotions, but not ruled and governed by them. We should be aware of them, using them as an indication that something is wrong and needs to be explored.

Robert: That's right. There are two ways we can make mistakes with emotions. One is to just allow them to totally dominate us. In this way, no one has to wonder what is going on inside the person because it is so obvious, driving and controlling. The emotions absolutely dictate every feeling and activity. The second error is to ignore and block out all emotions. The person who doesn't permit the emotions may seem to be better off, but in reality may be worse off. What happened inside is still there, and it is destructive. The one who shuts himself off from emotions is dying, life is being destroyed, but there is no recognition of what is going on.

Rujon: How do we identify those who handle their emotions in this way?

Robert: Usually we see them as very rigid. They have absolute routines of life, lists for doing everything and are typically about as sensitive as stone to those around them. Their children or their spouse may be in desperate situations, but this one doesn't have a clue of what is going on. There are many who believe that if they have a list and can accomplish all that is on that list everything will be okay. These folks feel that they always act right, look right, and everyone thinks they're always in control. Yet they are just going through routines. Often these are the ones who go off into deep immorality. People scratch their heads in disbelief wondering what in the world happened. What happened is that they didn't let their emotions tell them that something was wrong. We don't identify false beliefs just to say that we know what they are. We identify false beliefs so that we can reach into what God says is true and hang onto it. Several years ago a secretary told me that her boss was just awful, immature and a pain to work for. I told her that she needed to stay on her job long enough to learn everything God wanted her to learn. We talked about the principles in *The Search For Significance* and how she could use his less than helpful behavior to discover things about herself. The situation was squeezing her and what is inside is coming out. Now it isn't right for him to do this, but at the same time he isn't responsible for what is coming out as the situation intensifies. Often we get away from relationships which are painful before dealing with the things inside that need to be resolved. Knowing everything you have learned about *The Search* is nice, but this is where you begin to make the application to obtain freedom. It is as though you are in a cell deep in a dungeon in a castle and you have a maze to go through. The cell door is open, but you're not in the sunlight yet. You have the opportunity to walk out the cell door and through the maze, into the open air of freedom. This is about applying God's truth to bring you to that freedom.

Day 22

Robert: Sometimes I take a look at *The Search For Significance* material and realize that though I have worked for years to develop it, it is really God's material. I've watched Him change thousands of lives. Over the last few days, I have shared with you some things that I hope you will find very helpful. There are many other things in this book that you will find useful. One is learning to distinguish between guilt and conviction. The tragedy we often see is that this freedom has been paid for and we have the Holy Spirit to lead us, and yet we often sit back and accept the prison of emotion and deception that capture us. This is a beginning, not an ending. I pray that you will be able to find the freedom that Christ died to give to you. This is my prayer for you. God bless you.

Dear Friend,

You are about to embark on an exciting journey, *The Search for Significance*. In order to offer you personal encouragement and direction, I have created these tapes and accompanying cards. It is my hope that these will challenge you to seek God, to find Him, and to know Him more intimately than ever before. My prayer is that you will find His love and healing, for He is Jehovah Rapha, the God who heals.

In this packet you will find twenty-two taped sessions, each accompanied by a card. Each day:

Find a quiet place.
Set aside about twenty minutes.
Listen to the tape.
Let God speak to you through the card.

You will also see a Scripture verse for each day. Find a place you see often during the day, like a mirror, refrigerator, etc., and place the card there. Reflect upon the Scripture verse. Let it both challenge and sustain you throughout the day.

May God Bless You Richly

Dear Jesus,

Today I lift up _____ to you. He/she desires to know you more, to trust you, to see you as Jehovah Rapha, The God who heals. Lord, show yourself to _____ in a way that he/she will know that You have touched, that You care.

Help _____ know your healing love. Teach _____ the things that he/she needs to see to begin to walk in the freedom that you have for him/her.

Day One

Dear Jesus:

I cannot heal myself. My mind has been darkened by deception. Only your light can penetrate and renew my mind. I am the clay. You are the potter. Have your way in my life.

Signed: _____

Date: _____

For My Friend

I am beginning an exciting journey, a journey of healing. I ask that you would pray for me daily during this time. On the back of this card is a prayer. Thank you for remembering me each day.

The Lord is faithful to all his promises
and loving toward all he has made.
The Lord upholds all those who fall
and lifts up all who are bowed down.
The Lord is near to all who call upon him.

PSALM 145: 13–14, 18

Day Two

Come to me, all you who are weary and burdened, and I will give you rest. Take my yoke upon you and learn from me, for I am gentle and humble in heart, and you will find rest for your souls.

MATTHEW 11:28–29

Lord,
In Your gentleness, teach me your ways.
Renew my mind.
Let my soul find rest in you alone.

Day Three

Healing is a process.
What are you growing today?

Day Four

Healing is a process, much like a journey. On any journey it is important to know where you are before you start. Use this card to examine your desires, take a "check-up from the heart up." How are you getting your needs met?

DESIRES
(Specific changes in your life:
marriage, new job, passing test)

JOB PROMOTION

1.
2.
3.
4.
5.

NEEDS
(love, acceptance, identity,
security, happiness)

IDENTITY, SECURITY

What is God showing you as you reflect upon your desires and needs? Can you trust Him to give you the desires of your heart?

He will be like a tree planted by the water
that sends out its roots by the stream.
It does not fear when heat comes;
its leaves are always green.
It has no worries in a year of drought
and never fails to bear fruit.

JEREMIAH 17:8

All my longings lie open before you, O Lord;
my sighing is not hidden from you.

PSALM 38:9

Day Five

CHOOSE:

1. **The World's System:** My Performance + Other's Opinions defines My Self-worth.

2. **God's Truth:** My Self-worth is based on God's Word, what God says about me.

Which system do you really believe, not just in your "head" but in your "heart?" Ask God to show you how you've been tricked by the world's system.

Day Six

But God said to Jonah, "Do you have a right to be angry about the vine?"

"I do," he said. "I am angry enough to die."

JONAH 4:9

Does your anger protect you, give you a sense of justice? Has it trapped you in bitterness and rage, not only at others, but even possibly toward God? Ask God to show you today how anger is at work in your life. Ask Him how you can "be angry and sin not."

Day Seven

Why are you downcast, O my soul? Why so disturbed within me?
PSALM 42:5

It is important to acknowledge that much time has been wasted trying to live by a formula that has only held you captive. One mountain after another has appeared, one wrong turn after another has been taken. Anger and grief have provided the fuel and kept the direction turned away from God.

Ask God to show you today the holes you have fallen in, the mountains you keep climbing, the road you've been traveling on. Then ask him to show you how to grieve, His way.

I pray also that the eyes of your heart may be enlightened in order that you may know the hope to which he has called you . . .

EPHESIANS 1:18

I was crushed . . . so much so that I despaired even of life, but that was to make me rely not on myself, but on the God who raises the dead.

2 CORINTHIANS 1:8–9

LORD,
Use my grief as a mighty force
To turn my head into the wind.
Set me on the path you have for me.
Let me experience your resurrection power.

Day Eight

My Self-worth = My performance + others' opinions of me.

My Self-worth = What God says about me.

What has God shown you over the past few days?

Day Nine

Childhood Patterns: What we learn creates dominant patterns that may often continue to control our lives.

Ask God to show you some of these patterns or behaviros and list them below. Try to place them in either the *flight* or *fight* category.

	Flight	Fight
Patterns:		
Outcomes:		

Day Ten

OVERCOMING PATTERNS

C = Confession

R = Repentance

O = Obedience

P = Praise

He worketh.

Psalm 37:5

By now, you may see God at work and be excited. Or you may say, "I don't see any results." Know that even in the darkest night, He is at work. He is faithful.

When I was a child, I talked like a child, I thought like a child, I reasoned like a child. When I became a man, I put childish ways behind me. Now we see but a poor reflection as in a mirror; then we shall see face to face.

1 CORINTHIANS 13:11

You were taught, with regard to your former way of life, to put off your old self, which is being corrupted by its deceitful desires; to be made new in the attitude of your minds; and to put on the new self, created to be like God in true righteousness and holiness.

EPHESIANS 4:22–24

Day Eleven

THE PERFORMANCE TRAP

False Belief: I must meet certain standards in order to feel good about myself.

How has your life been limited because of this fear of rejection?

__Perfectionism   __Anxiety, Fear   __Low Motivation
__Avoiding Risks   __Pride   __Addictions
__Anger, Resentment   __Depression   __Manipulation

How have you been caught in the performance trap? Ask God to reveal this to you today. It is time for a new **CROP!**

Day Twelve

THE PERFORMANCE TRAP

False Belief: I must meet certain standards in order to feel good about myself.

God's Answer: Justification.

Justication carries no guilt with it and has no memory of past transgression. Christ paid for all our sins at the cross: past, present, and future. Justification means more than the forgiveness of sins. In the same act of love through which God forgave our sin, He also provided for our righteousness: The worthiness to stand in God's presence!

You have great worth apart from your performance because Christ gave his life for you. You are of great value!

Day Thirteen

Why Am I Obedient?

Today, I ask you Lord to show me my heart. Show me the things that motivate me, even in my relationship with you.

Create in me a clean heart, Oh Lord, My God. And renew a right spirit within me.

PSALM 51:10

For it is by grace you have been saved through faith and this is not from yourselves, it is the gift of God not by works so that none can boast.

EPHESIANS 2:8–9

I am deeply loved, fully pleasing, totally forgiven, accepted, and complete in Christ.

God, teach me today to be.
To be still and hear your voice,
To be touched by your love, your acceptance.
To be free of my need to do.
Then in you
I can both be and do.

And my people shall be satisfied with my goodness, saith the Lord.

JEREMIAH 31:14

God is for me, not against me!

Day Fourteen

THE APPROVAL ADDICT

False Belief: I must be approved by certain others to feel good about myself.

How has your life been affected by the fear of rejection?

__Anger, Resentment   __Codependency   __Depression
__Hostility   __Avoiding People   __Loneliness
__Easily Manipulated   __Control   __Addictions

How has this false belief trapped you? **Think CROP!**

Day Fifteen

THE APPROVAL ADDICT

False Belief: I must be approved by certain others to feel good about myself.

God's Answer: Reconciliation.

Justification is the doctrine that explains the judicial facts of our forgiveness and righteousness in Christ.

Reconciliation explains the relational aspect of our salvation. The moment we receive Christ by faith, we:

- enter into a personal relationship with Him;
- are united in an eternal, inseparable bond with God;
- become fellow heirs with Christ;
- are absolutely secure in Christ.

Day Sixteen

THE BLAME GAME

False Belief: Those who fail are unworthy of love and deserve to be punished.

How is the fear of being punished at work in your life?

__Self-induced Punishment   __Perfection
__Bitterness   __Criticism
__Passivity   __Punishing Others

As you reflect upon each of these, ask God to show how you have been trapped by this false belief. Refer back to Day 10 and **"work your CROP."**

God has said, "Never will I leave you; never will I forsake you."
So we say with confidence, "The Lord is my helper; I will not be afraid.
What can man do to me?"

HEBREWS 13:5–6

When I kneel before God, I can stand before any man.

God, help this become true in my life.

The cup which my Father hath given me, shall I not drink it?

JOHN 18:11

Christ paid the price.
He was for me then, and will be forever!

Day Seventeen

THE BLAME GAME

False Belief: Those who fail are unworthy of love and deserve to be punished.

God's Answer: Propitiation.

Propitiation means that the wrath of someone who has been unjustly wronged has been satisfied. It is an act that soothes hostility and satisfies the need for vengeance. When Christ died on the cross, He was our substitute. He took upon himself the righteous wrath of God that we deserved. Providing His only begotten Son as the propitiation for our sin was the greatest possible demonstration of God's love for man.

Day Eighteen

SHAME

False Belief: I am what I am. I cannot change. I am hopeless.

How is shame impacting your life?

__Guilt	__Self-pity	__Withdrawal
__Self-deprecation	__Passivity	__Loss of Creativity
__Inferiority	__Isolation	__Self-destruction
__Despising Your Appearance	__Unhealthy Relationships	

What shaming messages still hold you? Ask the Lord to reveal these to you. **Think CROP!**

Day Nineteen

SHAME

False Belief: I am what I am. I cannot change. I am hopeless.

God's Answer: Regeneration

Regeneration is the renewing work of the Holy Spirit that literally makes each new believer a new person at the moment he or she trusts Christ as Savior. There is a transforming spiritual resuscitation as the Holy Spirit breathes His life within us and seals us in that new birth. The truth of regeneration dispels the specter of the past. We are to put on, or envelop ourselves in, this new self that progressively expresses Christian character in our attitudes and behavior. Today, ask the Lord to take the shaming messages you have believed about yourself and replace them with His truths. Ask Him to write you a love letter. Ask Him to make this new life and hope real to you. Let Him surprise you with the way He speaks to you. Be open to his voice.

By this love of God was manifested in us, that God has sent His only begotten Son into the world so that we might live through Him. In this is love, not that we loved God, but that He loved us and sent His Son to be the propitiation for our sins.

1 JOHN 4:9–10

If we cannot trust in the person who died for us, who can we trust?

My lover spoke and said to me,
  "Arise, my darling,
    my beautiful one, and come with me.
See! The winter is past."

SONG OF SOLOMON 2:10–11

In the midst of shame's dark hold,
God calls out and says, "Come with me."
He offers hope.
He offers love.
His truth brings life and freedom.
Will you accept His invitation?
"Come with me."

"For I know the plans that I have for you," declares the Lord, "plans to prosper you and not to harm you, plans to give you a hope and a future . . ."

"I will be found by you," declares the Lord, "and will bring you back from captivity."

JEREMIAH 29:11, 14

Day Twenty

FORGIVENESS

We don't forgive because:
- The offense was too great.
- He/she won't accept responsibility.
- He/she isn't truly sorry.
- He/she never asked to be forgiven.
- He/she will do it again.
- He/she did it again.
- I don't feel like forgiving. I'll be a hypocrite.
- I'll have to treat him/her well.
- I'll forgive, but I'll never forget.
- Someone has to punish him/her.

Forgiveness isn't:
- The offense was too great.
- He/she won't accept responsibility.
- He/she isn't truly sorry.
- He/she never asked to be forgiven.
- He/she will do it again.
- He/she did it again.
- I don't feel like forgiving. I'll be a hypocrite.
- I'll have to treat him/her well.
- I'll forgive, but I'll never forget.
- Someone has to punish him/her.

Day Twenty-One

THE TRIP IN

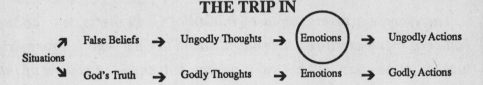

Practice this as often as you can with difficult situations you encounter throughout the day. A tool is only helpful if it is used. Ask God to help you:
- slow the process down
- see the deception
- apply the truth
- experience the freedom

Day Twenty-Two

But now Lord,
what do I look for?
My hope is in you.
PSALM 39:7

LORD,

When all I want to do is ask why,
Help me to trust instead.

When I would simply give up,
Help me to draw on your strength.

When I would be deceived by my enemy,
Help me to exercise your truths.

When I would be full of self-pity,
Help me to take hold of your joy.

When I feel unlovable,
Help me to know your unfailing love.

When I would feel confused and hopeless,
Help me put my hope in you.

Forgive us our sins
For we forgive those who sin against us.

LUKE 11:4

Therefore, I urge you, brothers, in view of God's mercy, to offer our bodies as living sacrifices, holy and pleasing to God—this is your spiritual act of worship. Do not conform any longer to the pattern of the world, but be transformed by the renewing of your mind. Then you will be able to test and approve what God's will is—his good, pleasing and perfect will.

ROMANS 12:1–2

I have great worth
because Christ gave His life for me,
and therefore,
imparted great value to me.
I am deeply loved,
fully pleasing,
totally forgiven,
accepted,
and complete in Christ.

THE SEARCH FOR SIGNIFICANCE

Small Group Leaders' Guide

LESSON 1 - OUR SEARCH FOR SIGNIFICANCE

Based on chapters 1, 2, and 4, and steps 1, 2, and 3 of *The Search for Significance,* the purpose of this lesson is for group members:

To Know: How Satan deceives Christians and non-Christians, causing almost all of us to base our self-worth on our performance and others' opinions.

To Feel: Dissatisfaction with living by Satan's lies.

To Do: Begin identifying specific deceptions in their lives.

Introduction: It is important that you help group members "break the ice" in their relationships. Introduce yourself and give a very brief explanation of how God has used *The Search for Significance* in your life. Then, ask each person to introduce himself, stating his name, occupation, etc., and follow this with a question as dignified or as ridiculous as you desire. For example, ask group members to name their favorite childhood TV star, their childhood vocational ambition, the most famous people they've ever met or would like to meet, or what kind of animal they would be if they were an animal. If those in your group already know each other fairly well, you may want to skip the icebreaker, or just do it for fun!

Hook: After the icebreaker, say to your group, "Think of your greatest achievement and your worst failure, or when you were most terribly rejected by someone. How did you feel about yourself after you had succeeded? How did you feel about yourself after you had failed or were rejected?" Give them a moment to think; then, let several people answer. To instill a sense of comfort in sharing openly within the group, avoid critiquing responses or disagreeing with them. Instead, you might say, "That's an interesting response," or you might simply thank group members for sharing.

Questions: Let's look further at self-worth and examine two systems we can use to meet this need.
1. **Step 1, no. 1.** How do you define *self-worth*?
2. **Step 1, no. 5.** There are two possible options we can choose to determine our self-worth:
   * The world's system: *Self-Worth = Performance* (what you do) + *Others' Opinions* (what others think or say about you).
   * God's system: *Self-Worth = God's Truth About You.* (If group members don't have copies of *The Search for Significance*, write the above options on a blackboard or on poster paper.)
3. What are some passages that describe what God says is true of Christians?
   a) What activities, relationships, or achieve

ments make you feel better about yourself?
   b) Whose opinions of you do you value most?
4. **Step 1, no. 3a.**
   a) Read Eph. 1:3-14. What characteristics given in this passage are true of all Christians? (List these on a blackboard or piece of poster paper.)
   b) How would deeply understanding these truths affect your sense of self-worth?

The other way we can determine our value is based on what the Scriptures say is true of us. We have looked at a small portion of God's truth as it describes us tonight (today). Overcoming the deceptions of the enemy and living in a manner that reflects the truth of who we are in Christ is a process which we will begin to examine in our next meeting together.

Assignment for Lesson 2: Read step 4 from *The Search for Significance* workbook, and answer the following questions (give your group the questions listed in lesson 2). If you do not have a copy of *The Search for Significance* book and workbook, you may purchase one here tonight (today). *Note for group leaders:* If your group appears to be noncommittal about individual study, you may want to help them to understand that they will get from the study what they're willing to give to it.

Prayer Time

Additional Activity: Sell *The Search for Significance* book and workbook to those who haven't already bought a copy.

Additional Questions:
1. **Step 1, no. 10.** Is it difficult for people to view themselves in terms other than their performance or others' opinions of them? Why, or why not?
2. **Step 2, nos. 2a), 2d.** Read Gen. 3:1-10.
   a) How did Satan tempt Eve?
   b) How did the Fall affect man's desire for significance?
3. **Step 3, no. 2.** Look at the extent to which you are affected by each false belief. Which lie affects you most? Why?

Conclusion: We have looked at two very opposite ways of gaining our sense of self-worth. One is based on the world's system. This system is comprised of Satan's deceptions, and is one through which we desperately try to perform well and please others. The paradox is that even if we succeed in our efforts to please others, we continue to feel as if we haven't done enough. Consequently, feelings of self-worth continue to elude us.

Based on chapter 5 and step 4 of *The Search for Significance.* The purpose of this lesson is for group members:

To Know: The experience of healing, hope, and health is a process.

To Feel: Encouraged that this process will make a positive impact on their lives.

To Do: Begin to incorporate the five elements required for growth and healing in their circumstances and relationships.

Hook: List the five essential elements for healing given in step 4 of *The Search for Significance* workbook on a blackboard or piece of poster paper. Then, ask your group to describe what might happen in a person's life if each of these elements were missing:
   a) Honesty
   b) Affirming Relationships
   c) Right Thinking
   d) The Holy Spirit
   e) Time
Let several people respond.

Questions:
1. **Step 4, no. 1*b*.** Read Ps. 51:6. From this passage, why do you think the Lord wants us to be honest...
   a) with Him?
   b) with others?
   c) with ourselves?

2. **Step 4, no. 2.** Think of people who have affirmed or encouraged you in the past.
   a) How did their affirmation affect you?
   b) How does a person go about finding someone who will provide support and encouragement?

3. **Step 4, no. 3.**
   a) Describe the development of our thoughts and beliefs.(Include the influences of society, family background, experiences, relationships).
   b) Have a group member read 2 Tim. 3:16–17 aloud. Then ask, "From this passage, explain how the Scriptures can affect our thinking and our lives."

4. **Step 4, no. 4.** From the following passages, what role does the Holy Spirit play in our growth and healing?

a) John 7:37–39
b) John 14:16–17
c) John 16:13–15

5. **Step 4, no. 5.**
   a) Give some reasons why we often tend to expect fast results when we begin to seek growth and change in our lives. (Write these on a blackboard or piece of poster paper).
   b) Are these realistic? Why, or why not?
   c) Why is it important for us to have a process-perspective about life?

Conclusion: Our growth toward wholeness and maturity is a journey which won't be completed until we join the Lord in heaven. The Apostle Paul understood this, and saw himself as being in the middle of this process. He wrote to the Phillipian believers:

> Not that I have already obtained it, or have already become perfect, but I press on in order that I may lay hold of that which I was laid hold of by Christ Jesus.—Phil. 3:12

If Paul, the foremost missionary and writer of much of the New Testament, saw himself as being "in the process," we can be encouraged to continue in the process toward change as well. It will help to have realistic expectations about our progress.

Remember that healing can only continue as we put ourselves in an environment characterized by honesty, affirming relationships, right thinking, the Holy Spirit's love and power, and time.

Assignment for Lesson 3: Read the Overview for Section II in *The Search for Significance* workbook, and memorize the four false beliefs and corresponding scriptural truths identified there. Also read step 5 in the workbook, and answer the following questions (give your group the questions listed in lesson 3, page 12).

Prayer Time

Additional Question
1. How can a person experience the elements of healing we've discussed to the extent that he or she needs to?
   a) Honesty
   b) Affirming Relationships
   c) Right Thinking
   d) The Holy Spirit
   e) Time

LESSON 3 - THE FEAR OF FAILURE

Based on chapter 6 and step 5 of *The Search for Significance*, the purpose of this lesson is for group members:

To Know: They are completely forgiven and fully pleasing to God in spite of failure.

To Feel: Thankful for Christ's gifts of forgiveness and righteousness.

To Do: Identify their "certain standards" or any areas in which they fear failure.

Hook: Say to your group, "As you memorized the lies given in the Overview to Section II of *The Search for Significance* workbook during the past week, which ones did you identify as being characteristic of your life? What situations were manifested by these lies? How did you respond? When did you realize that you were believing a lie?"

Let several people in the group answer.

Questions: Let's look specifically at the false belief, *I must meet certain standards in order to feel good about myself.*

1. **Step 5, no. 3.**
   a) What would you have to be or do to feel like you are a "success"?
   b) In what area(s) would you *never* allow yourself to fail?

2. **Step 5, no. 4.**
   a) What Christian activities do you use to evaluate yourself spiritually?
   b) Does performing these activities make you more pleasing to God? Why, or why not?

3. Read Rom. 3:19–25 and Titus 3:3–7.
   a) What is the basis of a right relationship with God
   b) What role do good deeds play?

4. Read 2 Cor. 5:21.
   a) Describe the righteousness of Christ.
   b) What does knowing that you have been made as righteous as Christ mean to you?

5. How might understanding and applying the truths of these passages affect...
   a) your drive for success?
   b) your self-worth?
   c) your motives?

Conclusion: It is a marvelous fact that once we trust in Christ to pay for our sins, we are completely forgiven and are considered fully righteous by God. Incorporating these truths into our conscious thinking will stimulate changes in our motivations to perform good deeds. Rather than simply adhering to certain standards to be accepted, we will be more inclined to perform good deeds in gratitude, because we are already accepted. The Apostle Paul wrote: *For the love of Christ controls us, having concluded this, that one died for all, therefore all died; and He died for all, that they who live should no longer live for themselves, but for Him who died and rose again on their behalf* (2 Cor. 5:14–15).

Assignment for Lesson 4: Continue to memorize the false beliefs given in the Overview to Section II of *The Search for Significance* workbook, and learn to identify them in your relationships and circumstances. Also read through step 6 in the workbook, and answer the following questions (give your group the questions listed in lesson 4, pages 16–17).

Prayer Time

Additional Questions
1. **Step 5, no. 5.**
   How does your desire to meet your performance standard affect your relationships with others?

2. **Step 5, no. 6.**
   a) How do you feel toward those who hinder your ability to meet your standard?
   b) How do you respond in those situations?

3. **Step 5, no. 7.**
   Some people compensate for the fear of failure by avoiding risks, while some try harder to succeed. In what ways do you compensate for the fear of failure in your life?

LESSON 4 - JUSTIFICATION

Based on chapter 6 and step 6 of *The Search for Significance,* the purpose of this lesson is for group members:

To Know: They are completely forgiven and fully pleasing to God in spite of personal failure (same as lesson 3).

To Feel: Thankful for Christ's gifts of forgiveness and righteousness (same as lesson 3).

To Do: Continue identifying their "certain standards" and begin applying the truth of justification in their lives.

Hook: Ask your group, "During the past week, were any of you able to identify the false belief: *I must meet certain standards in order to feel good about myself*? If so, how did you respond? What difference did it make when you realized that you are forgiven and pleasing to God, whether you meet your standards or not? (Or, what difference would it have made if you had realized that truth?)"

Let several people respond to each of the above questions.

Questions: Tonight (today), we're going to look at God's answer to the fear of failure and our obsession with meeting standards.

1. **Step 6, no. 3.** Read Rom. 3:9–23; 5:6–10; and Eph. 2:1–3. Describe your standing before God prior to your justification.

2. **Step 6, no. 1.** Read Rom. 3:19–28; 4:4–5; 5:1–11. What does it mean to be justified?

3. **Step 6, no. 2.** Read 2 Cor. 5:21; Col. 1:22; 3:12. How does your standing before God the Father compare to Christ's standing before Him?

4. **Step 6, no. 4.** From the following passages, how was your justification accomplished?
   a) Rom. 3:24; Titus 3:7
   b) Rom. 5:1; Gal. 3:24

5. **Step 6, no. 5.** What are the results of justification according to these passages?
   a) Rom. 4:7–8
   b) Rom. 5:9
   c) Rom. 8:1; 33–34

6. **Step 6, no. 8.** If we are completely forgiven through Christ's death on the cross, and our good deeds won't make us any more pleasing

to God, why should we obey God and be involved in good deeds?
   a) 1 Cor. 6:18–20
   b) Col. 3:23–24
   c) Titus 2:11–14

7. Do the truths we've just read in Scripture motivate you to love and serve God? Why, or why not?

8. **Step 6, no. 10.** How would your life be affected if you applied the truth of your complete forgiveness and righteousness in Christ?

Conclusion: Many of us understand that our salvation is based only on Christ's death to pay for our sins, but often, we fail to apply this incredible truth to our lives. Deep within us is an unconscious belief that we must meet one or more arbitrary standards before we can please God and have a sense of self-worth. That false belief leads to wrong goals, tension, a tendency to use people to accomplish selfish desires, anxiety, and the fear of failing to live up to our standards.

But God has provided a solution to our fear of failure! By the judicial act of justification, which we receive by faith in Jesus Christ, God has declared us free from the guilt of sin. We are completely forgiven as a result of Christ's blood, which was shed on the cross on our behalf. Not only has God forgiven our sinfulness, He also has given us Christ's righteousness: the worthiness to stand in His presence without fear of condemnation.

These are incredible truths, but they will have little impact on our lives unless we make them the foundation of our belief system. To do this, we must first learn how to identify thoughts that reflect Satan's deceptions. Our emotions serve as a checkpoint in this process. If we are filled with anger, fear, or tension, it's a good indication that we're believing Satan's lies.

The next time you experience a sense of distress, ask yourself, *Am I believing a lie? If so, which one?* Then, once you've identified the lie, reject it and replace it with the truth of God's Word.

Assignment for Lesson: Work through step 7 in *The Search for Significance* workbook. Also, pay attention to your emotions during the next week, and let them help you identify what you are believing.

Prayer Time

Based on chapter 6 and step 7 of *The Search for Significance*, the purpose of this lesson is for group members:

To Know: Proper motivations for obeying God.
To Feel: A desire to love, obey, and serve God as a result of proper motives.
To Do: Identify both proper and improper motivations for obedience to God.

Hook: Ask the group, "What is the primary reason that you obey God?" Let several people respond. "Why does that motivate you?" Let several people answer.

Questions: Let's look briefly at some of the proper motivations for obedience; then, we'll look at some of the improper motives we may have for being obedient to God.

1. **Step 7, no. 1.**
   The love of Christ compels us to obey. Read John 14:15, 21. How does obedience express love for God?

2. **Step 7, no. 2.**
   Sin is destructive. In what ways have you observed the destructiveness of sin...
   a) Internationally?
   b) Morally/Ethically?
   c) Within the family?
   d) Personally?

3. **Step 7, no. 3.**
   God will discipline us if we continue in a habit of sin.
   a) Read Heb. 12:5–11. What differences do you find between punishment and discipline?
   b) How does understanding this difference affect your relationship with God?

4. **Step 7, no. 6.**
   Obedience is an opportunity to honor God. Read 1 Cor. 6:19–20 and 2 Cor. 5:14–15.
   a) What does it mean to "honor" God?

b) What reasons do you have for wanting to honor Him?

5. **Step 7, questions 8–11.**
   Sometimes, we do what is right for the wrong reasons. Let's look at these four improper motives:
   • I couldn't live with myself if I didn't obey.
   • Other people would think less of me if they learned that I disobeyed.
   • God will be angry with me if I disobey.
   • God is obligated to bless me if I obey Him.
   a) Can you identify any of these motives in your own life? If so, which one(s)?
   b) What can you do about them?

Conclusion: God not only wants us to obey Him; He wants us to obey Him for the right reasons. Though we will never have completely pure motives until we're with the Lord in heaven, Scripture gives us plenty of good reasons to love, serve, and obey Him.

Assignment for Lesson 6: This week, think about proper motives to obey God, and see what difference they make in your life. Then, work through step 8 in *The Search for Significance* workbook for next week.

Prayer Time

Additional Questions
1. *a)* How do the improper motives given in step 7 of *The Search for Significance* reflect Satan's lies?
   b) How do they reflect poor theology?

2. What passages from Scripture help us gain the perspective we need to combat these improper motives for obedience?

Based on chapter 7 and step 8 of *The Search for Significance*, the purpose of this lesson is for group members:

To Know: They are totally accepted by God.

To Feel: Relief from the fear of rejection and thankful to God for His unconditional acceptance.

To Do: Begin to identify people and/or groups whose rejection they fear.

Hook: Ask your group the following questions, "Think of a situation in your life (recent or distant past) in which someone rejected you. What was the situation? How did you feel about it? How did you respond?" Let everyone think about these questions for a moment. Their answers will surface as they begin to respond to the questions below.

Questions: Tonight (today), we are going to look at Satan's lie: *I must be approved by certain others to feel good about myself.*

1. *a)* What are some of the many ways that people communicate rejection or disapproval? (List these on a blackboard or on poster paper.)

   b) Which are obvious? Which are more subtle?

2. What factors determine whether you feel rejected or not? (These might include your perception, background, mood, value of the other person's opinion, etc.).

3. **Step 8, no. 1.**

   a) Whose disapproval do you fear? Make a list of individuals or groups, then rank them in order based on the degree to which their disapproval affects you.

   b) How has the fear of being rejected by these people affected your attitudes and behavior?

4. **Step 8, no. 10**

   a) How do you use disapproval, sarcasm, criticism, or silence to manipulate others, so that they will do what you want them to do?

   b) What are some of the short- and long-term effects of manipulating others?

5. Read Col. 1:19–22. What is the basis of our acceptance by God?

6. What difference would it make in your relationships with the people and/or groups you listed in question 3 if you valued your acceptance with God more highly than those people's opinions of you?

Conclusion: The reason we feel the stinging pain of rejection so deeply is that we value the opinions of others more highly than the loving acceptance of God. We feel that we *must have* the approval of certain others to be secure and significant, when in fact, the only One whose approval we *must have* is God. Granted, life seems much easier when we feel approved and appreciated by others, but we need to learn to view human approval as something it would be *nice* to have, rather than as something we *must* have. There is a tremendous difference between *I must have* and *it would be nice to have* the approval of others.

Whose approval do you "have to have"? In the coming weeks, we will continue to see that we only "have to have" God's approval—and that we already have it! Our transition from unhealthy (manipulative, condemning, dependent) relationships to a healthy view of God and others is often a difficult one. As we discussed in lesson 2, that kind of growth requires a combination of honesty, affirming relationships, right thinking, the Holy Spirit, and time.

Assignment for Lesson 7: For next week, try to identify the lie: *I must be approved by certain others to feel good about myself,* in your thinking and behavior. Also, work through step 9 in *The Search for Significance* workbook.

Prayer Time

Additional Questions

1. *a)* What difference would applying the truth of reconciliation make in your relationship with God?

   b) Would you be more or less likely to obey Him? Why?

2. What difference would applying the truth of reconciliation make in how you treat others?

LESSON 7 - RECONCILIATION

Based on chapter 7 and step 9 of *The Search for Significance,* the purpose of this lesson is for group members:

To Know: They are completely accepted by God.
To Feel: Relief from the fear of rejection and thankful to God for His unconditional acceptance.
To Do: To continue identifying people and/or groups whose rejection they fear, and to continue learning how to value God's acceptance more highly than that of other people.

Hook: "Last week, we looked at the lie, *I must be approved by certain others to feel good about myself.* How did you identify that lie in your thinking during the past week? What distressing emotions, such as anger or fear, enabled you to recognize the lie? How did you respond?" Let several people answer.

Questions: Having looked at our tendency to believe that we must have the approval of others to feel good about ourselves, we're now ready to talk about our complete acceptance in Christ.

1. **Step 9, no. 2.**
   Read Eph. 2:1–3 and 2 Thess. 1:8–9. Describe man's condition apart from Christ.

2. **Step 9, no. 3.**
   Read Col. 1:19–22. What was your condition before you trusted in Christ? What is your present condition?

3. **Step 9, no. 7.**
   a) Read John 17:23–24 and 20:17. Whom does God the Father love more: Jesus Christ, or you?
   b) How does this make you feel?

4. **Step 9, no. 6.**
   If we are completely accepted by God, why do we continue to fear the rejection of men?

5. **Step 9, no. 8.**
   Think of a recent situation in which you experienced disapproval, possibly in response to criticism, a sarcastic remark, or a snub. What was your response? How might your response have been different if you had believed that you are completely accepted by Jesus Christ?

6. How would applying the truth of your total acceptance in Christ affect the way you treat family members, classmates, neighbors, friends, people at work, etc.?

Conclusion: Many of us value the opinions of one or more people more highly than God's opinion of us. In Gal. 1:10, Paul warns that we will become a slave of the one whose approval we seek; therefore, we cannot be bond-servants of Christ if we are striving to please others. Jesus Christ is the One who bought us by His death (1 Cor. 6:19–20). He is, therefore, the only One worthy of our highest love and obedience.

By more fully understanding and applying the truth of our reconciliation, or complete acceptance by God, we will begin to experience freedom from the bondage of acting to gain approval and avoid disapproval from others. With increasing freedom, we will more often choose to honor Christ, even in the face of disapproval.

As we discussed last week, *it would be nice to have* the approval of others, but if we don't, we are still deeply loved, completely forgiven, fully pleasing, and totally accepted by God through Christ.

I'm going to give each of you a 3x5 card. To help you make the distinction between *it would be nice to have* and *I have to have* the approval of others, write this statement on the card and memorize it. (Give out the 3x5 cards, and have the following written on either a piece of poster paper or blackboard):
It would be nice to have _____
approve of me, but if he/she doesn't, I'm still deeply loved, completely forgiven, fully pleasing, and totally accepted by God through Christ.

Assignment for Lesson 8: Keep this card with you and memorize this statement during the coming week. Also, work through steps 10, 11, and 12 in *The Search for Significance* workbook.

Prayer Time

Additional Question
1. Think of one person whose approval or disapproval greatly affects you. What difference would it make in your relationship with this person if you applied the concept: *It would be nice to have _____ approve of me, but if he (she) doesn't, I'm still deeply loved, completely forgiven, fully pleasing, and totally accepted by God through Jesus Christ?*

Based on chapter 8 and steps 10, 11, and 12 of *The Search for Significance,* the purpose of this lesson is for group members:

To Know: They are deeply loved by God.

To Feel: Relief from the fear of God's punishment; compassion instead of condemnation for the failures of others; thankfulness to Christ for His sacrificial death.

To Do: Begin to identify the lie: *Those who fail are unworthy of love and deserve to be blamed and condemned,* and replace that lie with the truth of Christ's strong, unconditional love.

Hook: Ask your group, "Why do we condemn ourselves and others for failure? What are some common results of condemning ourselves and others? Consider self-concept, relationships, motivation, stress levels, etc." Let several people answer.

Questions: Tonight (today), we will examine the lie: *Those who fail are unworthy of love, and deserve to be blamed and condemned,* in light of the biblical truth that God's love is unconditional.

1. **Step 11, no. 3.** Read Rom. 2:4–5. What does sinful man deserve from God?

2. **Step 11, no. 4.** List some characteristics of God's wrath from these passages:
   a) Gen. 19:1–26   b) Jer. 4:4
   c) Ezek. 5:11–17   d) 2 Thess. 1:6–10

3. **Step 11, nos. 1 and 5.**
   a) Define *propitiation.*
   b) Read Rom. 5:8 and 1 John 4:9–11. How does propitiation demonstrate God's love for us?

4. If we have been spared the righteous wrath of Almighty God because of the substitutionary death of Jesus Christ, and if we are, therefore, deeply loved by Him, why do we condemn ourselves and others for failing?

5. Step 12, nos. 1–4.
   a) How great was the debt of the king's servant?
   b) Was it possible for him ever to repay it?
   c) Before you trusted Christ, how great was your debt to God?
   d) Was it possible for you ever to repay it? (Do you really believe that? How can you know if you really believe it?)
   e) What did the servant ask for?
   f) What did the king give him?
   g) Do you think the servant understood what the king granted him?

h) Why was the king's servant so harsh with his fellow servant over such a small debt?

6. **Step 12, no. 6.** Read Col. 3:12–13.
   a) How are we to forgive others?
   b) Describe the characteristics of Christ's forgiveness of us.

7. **Step 12, nos. 7–8.**
   a) What are some of the results of not forgiving others (self-esteem, attitudes toward life and others, quality of relationships, etc.)?
   b) Is there anyone that you haven't forgiven? Take a few moments to read Matt. 18:21–35, reflect on what the passage is saying, and then choose to forgive whomever you haven't yet forgiven.

Conclusion: The forgiveness resulting from Christ's death on the cross is not ours to experience only at the initial point of salvation, but is a truth which determines the quality of our lives—our emotional, relational, spiritual and physical health—right now. God intends for us to fully experience His forgiveness, and to extend it to others as well. Yet we often condemn ourselves and others because we, like the king's servant, fail to understand the unconditional love and forgiveness that is ours through Christ. If His love covers our multitude of sins, we can forgive others for their mistakes and failures.

Assignment for Lesson 9: For next week, work through steps 13 and 14 in *The Search for Significance* workbook.

Prayer Time

Additional Questions

1. **Step 10, no. 4.** Does condemning ourselves make us better people? Why, or why not?

2. **Step 10, nos. 8 and 9.**
   a) What is the difference between *punishment* and *discipline?*
   b) What difference does it make to discipline others (children, spouse, employees, etc.) in love, rather than to condemn them for their failures?

3. What difference does it make to discipline others (children, spouse, employees, etc.) in love, rather than to condemn them for their failures?

4. **Step 11, no. 7.** What difference would it make in your life if you reflected on the following statement when others make mistakes or sin against you?
   There is nothing that anyone can do to me that can compare to my sins that Christ has forgiven?

Based on chapter 9 and steps 13 and 14 of *The Search for Significance,* the purpose of this lesson is for group members:

To Know: They are absolutely complete in Christ through regeneration.

To Feel: Relief from shame; thankful to God.

To Do: Begin to identify the lie: *I am what I am; I cannot change; I am hopeless,* in their attitudes and actions, and to begin replacing that lie with the truth of regeneration.

Hook: Tell your group, "People usually experience the painful feelings of shame when a failure in their performance or a 'flaw' in their appearance is so important that it creates a permanently negative opinion about their self-worth. What kinds of failures might cause people to feel ashamed of themselves?" Let several people respond. "What 'flaws' in their appearance might cause people to experience a sense of shame?"

Questions: Tonight (today), we will examine the lie: *I am what I am; I cannot change; I am hopeless,* with the liberating truth of our regeneration in Christ.

1. **Step 13, nos. 1 and 2.**
   a) Define *shame.*
   b) When do people usually experience shame?

2. **Step 13, no. 3.**
   How does the experience of shame affect...
   a) our self-esteem?
   b) our relationships?
   c) our work?
   d) our appearance?

3. a) Read Rom. 6:3–18. What are some characteristics of being made new in Christ? (List these on a blackboard or poster.)
   b) Read Eph. 4:17–24. From this passage, describe the process by which one can experience his or her "new self."
   c) What difference would applying these truths make in your life?

4. **Step 13, no. 8.** Read Ps. 139:13–16.
   a) What was God's role in forming your appearance and personality?
   b) Why do people struggle with the way they look?

5. **Step 14, nos. 6 and 9.** How can you specifically apply the truth of your regeneration in Christ to past failures, poor habits, or flaws in your appearance?

Conclusion: Many of us determine our value by our past performance or by our appearance, measuring our self-worth against the world's standards of success and beauty, rather than believing what God's Word says is true of us. Failures haunt us, scarring our self-concept, and we spend all kinds of time and money trying to look like the people we see in television and magazine ads. When we base our self-worth on past failures, dissatisfaction with our personal appearance, or bad habits, we usually develop the false belief: *I am what I am; I cannot change; I am hopeless.*

The liberating truth is that God has created us according to His image for His glory and purpose. By the act of regeneration, He has given us a new nature with new capacities to reflect His image in our daily lives. Regeneration gives us a new beginning, and enables us to rise above past failures to experience God's transforming love and power.

Reflect on these truths this week as you see advertisements on television, in magazines, and on billboards. The fulfillment these products promise to provide is an illusion. Success and beauty aren't the keys to happiness; Christ is!

Consider the pain and heartache experienced by the "successful" and "beautiful" people of the world. Only Christ offers unfailing love, fulfillment, and purpose in life. Let Him, not the illusion of the world, be your source of significance.

Assignment for Lesson 10: Work through steps 15 and 16 in *The Search for Significance* workbook.

Prayer Time

Additional Questions
1. **Step 13, no. 7.** What primary sources of input reinforce the idea that success and beauty should be our primary goals in life? (List these on a blackboard or piece of poster paper.)

2. Read Phil. 3:12–14. What past failures do you need to forget?

3. **Step 14, no. 7.** How can the truth expressed in Ps. 139:13–16 affect our desire to change some aspect of our personal appearance?

LESSON 10 - GOD'S LOVE AND FORGIVENESS

Based on chapter 10 and steps 15 and 16 of *The Search for Significance,* the purpose of this lesson is for group members:

To Know: The truth about God's character as demonstrated by Christ in Scripture.

To Feel: A deeper awareness of God's love and forgiveness.

To Do: Begin to identify events of the past which have contributed to a negative view of God and of themselves, and apply principles of forgiveness to the people involved in those events.

Hook: "Different people have different concepts of God. Some of these are accurate and some are not, but most of them have been spawned by events of the past.

"Describe and label (on a blackboard or piece of poster paper) several ways that people view God (like a cosmic policeman, a computer, a vending machine dispensing blessings, a Santa Claus in the sky, etc.).

"What aspects of each of these views are accurate? How are they inaccurate?"

Questions: Tonight (today), let's discuss our concept of God and how we can deal with some of the painful events of the past which may be hindering our relationship with Him and contributing to a negative view of ourselves and others.

1. **Step 15, no. 3.**
   a) What factors contribute to the development of a person's view of God?
   b) What effect has each of these had on your concept of Him?

2. **Step 15, no. 5a.** Christ perfectly reveals God the Father to us. What do each of these passages teach about Christ?
   a) John 4:13–26, 39
   b) John 10:11–15
   c) John 14:2–3
   d) John 15:13–16
   e) John 17:23

3. **Step 15, no. 9.** Read Ps. 145.
   a) What are some of the characteristics of God given in this passage?
   b) What does this psalm tell us about His activities in our lives?

4. **Step 16, no. 1.** What does each of the following passages teach about forgiveness?
   a) Matt. 18:21–35

   b) Rom. 5:6–11
   c) Col. 2:13–14
   d) Col. 3:13

5. **Step 16, no. 4.** How can you tell when you've forgiven someone?

6. **Step 16, no. 5.** What are some results of extending forgiveness to others in regard to...
   a) our concept of God?
   b) our self-concept?
   c) our relationships with other people?

7. **Step 16, no. 6.** What are some results of unforgiveness in regard to...
   a) our concept of God?
   b) our self-concept?
   c) our relationships with other people?

Conclusion: Our actions and attitudes often reflect our concept of God. If we believe that He is harsh and condemning, then we will be hard on ourselves and those around us. If we believe that He doesn't care, then we will think of ourselves as difficult to love and will fail to exercise compassion toward others. If, on the other hand, we believe that God is loving and powerful, then our lives will reflect those characteristics—in our behavior and in our attitude toward ourselves and others.

Ephesians 1:18–21 says that the love and power available to us as believers is the same as that which raised Christ from the dead. Perhaps the first step in experiencing the love of God is to be honest about our feelings, including our emotions toward Him. King David was honest with God about his hurts, fears, joys, and anger. His openness with God led to an intimate relationship with Him, so that he experienced more of God's love, forgiveness, and power.

Assignment for Lesson 11: For next week, work through steps 17 and 18 in *The Search for Significance* workbook.

Prayer Time

Additional Questions
1. What are some ways you can tell what a person really believes about God?

2. **Step 16, nos. 2–3.** Think for a moment about a particular event in your life which caused you pain. Consider your feelings, both then and now, as well as your thoughts about the people involved. What would it mean to release each person from the debt he or she owes you as a result of causing you pain?

Based on chapters 11 and 14, and steps 17 and 18 of *The Search for Significance*, the purpose of this lesson is for group members:

To Know: How the Holy Spirit operates in the believer's life to convict him or her of sin, to guide him or her into truth, and to empower him or her to live in obedience to God's Word.

To Feel: Thankful for the regenerating work of the Holy Spirit in their lives.

To Do: Trust in the Holy Spirit to act as their instructor, counselor, and source of spiritual power as they strive to live their lives for Christ's glory and honor.

Hook: "Perhaps all of us desire to honor and glorify Christ with our lives, yet it is important to remember that the Christian life is not simply a self-improvement program. Rather, it's a supernatural life in which we draw on Christ as our resource for direction, encouragement, and strength. Jesus made this very clear in the fifteenth chapter of John when He said that anything done apart from His love and power will, in the end, amount to nothing (see verses one, four, and five). Although we may expend tremendous effort at a great personal cost, only that which is done for Christ's glory in the power of His Spirit is of eternal value."

Questions: Tonight (today), we'll examine the Holy Spirit's role of convicting us of sin, guiding us into truth, and empowering us to live in a way that will bring glory and honor to the Lord.

1. **Step 17, no. 5.** Read 1 John 1:9
   a) What is *confession*?
   b) Does confession make us forgiven? Why, or why not?
   c) What does confession accomplish?

2. Why is it important to identify the false belief(s) we are believing when we sin?

3. **Step 18, no. 2.** Read John 15:1–5.
   a) Describe how we are to bear fruit.
   b) How does God *prune* us?
   c) Why does God prune us?

d) What specific characteristics does God want to produce in our lives?

4. **Step 18, no. 3.**
   a) From step 18 of *The Search for Significance,* which facts and promises from God's Word are most encouraging to you?
   b) What differences would it make in your life if you fully trusted God for these facts and promises?

5. **Step 18, no. 5.**
   a) What hinders you most in your efforts to live for Christ?
   b) What can you do about this?

6. a) Describe the Holy Spirit's role in empowering us to live a fruitful, Christ-honoring life.
   b) Describe your role in living in a way that honors Christ.
   c) How might people confuse these two roles?
   d) What can we do about this confusion in our own lives?

Conclusion: The Lord realized that once He left the world, His followers would need help. The Holy Spirit, our helper and our teacher, was sent to dwell within believers and to be our source of wisdom and strength. It is by His power that the love of Christ flows through us and produces spiritual fruit within us. It is because of His work of conviction that we can deal with sin and continue to experience God's love, wisdom, and strength.

Assignment for Lesson 12: For next week, work through steps 19, 20, and 21 in *The Search for Significance* workbook.

Prayer Time

Additional Questions
1. When should we confess sin?

2. Read Rom. 12:1–2.
   a) What does Paul urge us to do?
   b) What are "the mercies of God" in the preceding chapters? (List some of these on a blackboard or piece of poster paper.)

Based on chapters 12 and 13, and steps 19, 20, and 21 of *The Search for Significance,* the purpose of this lesson is for group members:

To Know: How to identify false beliefs, reject them, and replace them with the truth of God's Word.

To Feel: Encouraged that this process will enable them to gain increasing freedom from fear and shame.

To Do: Continue to identify, reject, and replace.

Hook: "Take a few moments to think about the past week. Did you have any painful or distressing emotions? If so, what was the emotion (anger, fear, irritation)? What situation prompted you to feel like you did? What actions accompanied your emotions? Were you believing any of the false beliefs identified in *The Search for Significance?* If so, which one(s)?"

(Note: You may want to write these questions on a blackboard or piece of poster paper, so that group members can see them easily.)

Questions: This week, we will examine how our emotions can be used to help us identify our beliefs. Then, once we have pinpointed what we believe, we can determine if we need to reject it and replace it with the truth. (On a blackboard or piece of poster paper, draw the diagram on page 426 of step 21).

1. How can our emotions reveal what it is we believe? (Make a chart with four headings, one for each of the four false beliefs: "Certain Standards," "Disapproval," "Blame," and "Shame.")

2. What emotions can result from believing each of these lies?

3. *a)* List three situations in which you had distressing emotions. (To complete this exercise, have group members turn to step 21 in *The Search for Significance*, and look at questions 1, 2, and 3. Give paper to students who don't have a workbook, and have them write six headings on each page: **Situation, Emotions, Actions, False Beliefs, God's Truth (Passages),** and **Supposed Godly Response.**)

   b) What were the emotions that accompanied each situation?

   c) What actions did you take?

   d) Which false belief(s) were you believing at the time?

4. As you continue to analyze each of those three situations, which biblical truth could you apply in response to the situation?

5. Describe how you would have responded in each situation if you had believed God's truth instead of Satan's lie.

6. What would help you to identify lies, reject them, and replace them with God's truth more quickly and effectively?

Conclusion: This is the "nuts and bolts" of renewing your mind by God's Word. It is important to remember that as Christians, we are fighting a spiritual battle (2 Cor. 10:3–5; Eph. 6:10–12). Satan's greatest weapon is deception, and his most effective strategy is to convince us that his lies are truth. But we don't have to succumb to the enemy's schemes. We can recognize his lies for what they are, and trust instead in the powerful, liberating Word of God. Jesus revealed the contrasting purpose between Satan and Himself when He said:

The thief comes only to steal, and kill, and destroy; I came that they might have life, and might have it abundantly (John 10:10).

Learn to be an expert at identifying Satan's lies, rejecting them, and replacing them with the truth of God's Word. Through that exercise, you will renew your mind and increasingly honor the Lord with your thinking and behavior.

Assignment for Lesson 13: For next week, work through steps 22, 23, and 24 in *The Search for Significance* workbook.

Prayer Time

Additional Questions

1. Feelings of fear and anger are sometimes the result of believing lies. Sometimes, however, it is good for us to experience emotions like fear and anger. How can we know when distressing emotions are good or bad for us?

2. *a)* If you identify a lie, reject it, and replace it with the truth, how quickly might your negative emotions change to pleasant feelings?

   b) Is there any guarantee that our emotions will be pleasant, even if we replace the lies we've been believing with the truth?

   c) Why do we value pleasant emotions so highly, and even determine the merit of different activities based on the emotions they produce?

Based on chapter 15 and steps 22, 23, and 24 of *The Search for Significance,* the purpose of this lesson is for group members:

To Know: They have the great privilege of representing Christ to the world and to other Christians.

To Feel: Thankful for what Christ has done for them and eager to be used by Him in the lives of others.

To Do: Communicate the gospel to a non-believer; encourage a fellow believer.

Hook: "Many of us know that as Christ's disciples, we are responsible for proclaiming the gospel to the lost of the world. Often, however, we fail to carry through with this responsibility. What are some reasons why we don't share our faith any more than we do?" (List these on a blackboard or piece of poster paper.) "In what ways are these reasons valid? How are they invalid?"

Questions: This week, we will look at the tremendous privilege we have of representing Christ to other people.

1. **Step 22, no. 5.**
   Let's make a list of things Christ has done for us, and a parallel list of our condition prior to salvation. (Write these on a blackboard or piece of poster paper.)

2. **Step 22, no. 6.**
   a) What is your honest response to the things that Christ has done for you?
   b) How do these truths affect your fear of rejection?

3. Many factors influence whether or not we choose to share the gospel with someone. Some of these might include (write out on blackboard or poster paper):
   a) the person's need for salvation
   b) your fear of rejection
   c) your ability to communicate the gospel clearly
   d) your relationship with the person
   e) time
   f) distractions
   g) other (list for the group)

   How do each of these affect what you do (or don't do) when you have an opportunity to share the gospel?

4. **Step 23, no. 8.**
   a) Write down the names of two people for whom you want to pray and with whom you want to share the gospel.

b) How will you share Christ with them?
c) When will you talk with them?

5. *a)* Who has encouraged you most in your life?
   b) How did this person encourage you?
   c) How has his or her encouragement specifically affected you?

6. **Step 24, no. 4.** Read Rom. 15:7; Col. 3:12–13; and 1 John 4:9–11. How can you personally apply these passages during the coming week? Be specific.

Conclusion: The Apostle Paul tells us in 2 Cor. 5:18–20 that God has given us the ministry of reconciliation and has made us His ambassadors to a desperately needy world. As we tell people about Christ, some will believe, some will not understand, and some will even hate us because we've told them about the love and forgiveness of Christ (see John 15:18–21). We cannot determine what others' responses to the gospel will be. We can only determine our own response: to explain the most transforming, liberating, and marvelous facts in history—or to remain silent.

Peter reminds us that as believers, we are a *chosen race, a royal priesthood, a holy nation, and a people for God's own possession, that we may proclaim the excellencies of Him who has called us out of darkness into His marvelous light* (1 Pet. 2:9).

We are people with a purpose: to represent Jesus Christ accurately, lovingly, and assertively to the world and to each other.

Assignment for Lesson 14: For next week, the last of this series, work through step 25 in *The Search for Significance* workbook.

Prayer Time

Additional Questions
1. Read Mark 1:32–39.
   a) Jesus had a sense of urgency about preaching to the lost. Why do you think He experienced that urgency?
   b) Do you have this same sense of urgency about communicating the gospel? Why, or why not?

2. Do you know someone who has a sense of urgency about sharing the gospel with those who don't know Christ? If so, how is this demonstrated in his or her life?

3. Would a sense of urgency about sharing the gospel cause you to be more sensitive or less sensitive to others? Why?

Based on chapter 15 and step 25 of *The Search for Significance,* the purpose of this lesson is for group members:

To Know: Christ is worthy of our highest ambitions and deepest affections.

To Feel: A deep desire to honor Christ in every aspect of life.

To Do: Analyze our affections, time, and finances, and determine what resources we need to yield to the Lord.

Hook: "First Corinthians 3:10–15 describes the Judgment Seat of Christ, where the deeds of believers will be judged by Christ. There, we will receive a reward for those deeds done because of our love, obedience, and service to Christ. But those deeds we've done for our own pleasure, to promote our own success, or to win the approval of others will be burned up.

"If you were to stand at the Judgment Seat today, would you be pleased with your reward? Why, or why not?"

Questions: Tonight (today), we will culminate our series by examining the rightful lordship of Christ in every area of our lives.

1. *a)* Read Mark 8:34–37. In verse 36, Christ talks about man's attempt to "gain the whole world." Describe various ways people try to "gain the whole world" in our culture today.

   b) From this passage, what is more important: the wealth of all the real estate, gold, oil, and other resources in the world, or one person's soul?

   c) Why do most people pursue only a tiny fraction of the wealth of "the whole world" at the expense of their valuable souls?

   d) Why do you and I often choose to do the same thing?

2. **Step 25, no. 6.** Read Luke 12:15–21. Imagine that "rich man" living in our culture today.
   a) What things might he own?
   b) How might he spend his time?

3. **Step 25, no. 7.** Why was this rich man described as a *fool?*

4. **Step 25, no. 8.**
   a) List the things, people, and activities that you value most.
   b) Does each of these make you "rich toward God"? For example, does each enhance your relationship with God, strengthen your biblical values, enable you to have a godly influence on others, encourage those in your family, etc ?

5. **Step 25, no. 9.** What can you do with your money, your time, and your affections to be more "rich toward God"?

6. Read Rev. 5:8–14. This passage contains three songs of praise to God. Do you enjoy praising God like this? Why, or why not?

7. How would (or how does) making Christ your Lord and honoring Him by your words and actions make a difference in...
   a) your relationship with Him?
   b) your outlook on life (your attitudes and moods)?
   c) your relationship with members of your family?
   d) your relationship with other believers?
   e) your relationship with unbelievers?

Conclusion: Christ is worthy of our highest ambitions and deepest affections! We deserved the righteous condemnation of God, yet Christ bore the penalty for our sin on the cross, and as a result, we are deeply loved, completely forgiven, fully pleasing, and totally accepted by God. There is no other person, no other cause, and no created thing that can compare to the One *who died and rose again on our behalf.*

Because of who He is and what He has done for us, it is only reasonable that we respond by living unreservedly for Him and His cause. It would be unreasonable to do anything else.

Continue to be alert to the enemy's deceptions. When you recognize his lies, replace them with the truth of God's powerful Word. The struggle is constant, and we all will fail from time to time, but God's love and strength will keep us going. As John wrote, *You are from God, little children, and have overcome them; because greater is He who is in you than he who is in the world* (1 John 4:4).

Prayer Time

Additional Questions
1. Read the atheist's quote in *The Search for Significance*, page 474.
   a) Does your life reflect the clarity and depth of these statements?
   b) Why, or why not?
   c) What do you need to do about it?

Note: If your group is beginning a new series next week on *Codependency: A Christian Perspective, Your Parents and You*, or some other material, tell them about the series and what they will be learning. Help them make the transition from this series to the next one so that they can continue to apply these concepts as they learn new ones.

Appendix 1

Father Hunger
ROBERT S. MCGEE.

McGee offers practical insight into the types of fathers we have on earth and our responses to them. *Father Hunger* addresses the child of the severely negligent father as well as the child of a loving yet imperfect father. The author's premise is that our relationship to our earthly father sets a precedent for our relationship to our heavenly Father. His treatment is one that will deeply affect your relationship with God as Abba Father.

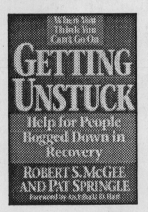

Getting Unstuck
ROBERT S. MCGEE & PAT SPRINGLE.

Although recovery is now a well sought after process, many people feel stuck between hurt and healing. The authors offer hope for those who feel trapped in the recovery process. Usually what is hindering complete recovery is their long-buried emotional wounds— wounds that they do not even know exist. Uncovering this unfinished business from the past and seeing how it affects the present can bring the sufferer out of the mud and onto the dry road of wholeness and full recovery. Includes a small group leader's guide.

Rapha Resources books and materials may be ordered by calling 1-800-460-HOPE. For more information about Rapha's treatment programs, call 1-800-847-HOPE.

Codependency
A Christian Perspective
PAT SPRINGLE.

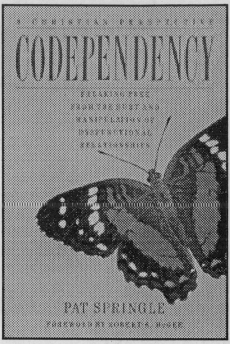

Divorce, alcoholism, drug abuse, workaholism, and similar problems are destroying the family unit and every member is affected. One of the painful affects is codependency: the compulsion to rescue and control others. A host of corollary characteristics can plague a codependent: being driven to succeed and please people, perfectionism, withdrawal, being easily manipulated, etc.

Codependency will help you recognize these painful results and offers sound, biblical processes that promise hope and healing.

The Search for Freedom
Demolishing the Strongholds that Diminish Your Faith, Hope, and Confidence in God
ROBERT S. MCGEE.

In this sequel to his best-seller *TheSearch for Significance*, Robert McGee explores what it means for men and women to be born into a fallen world where we sin and are sinned against; and he unmasks the core problem— self-protective behaviors learned in childhood. When left unchecked, these behaviors can become strongholds that control our lives, robbing us of the freedom Christ died to give us.

- The sequel to the best seller, *The Search for Significance*.

- Offers a proven plan for destroying strongholds *permanently*.

- Each chapter includes questions for individual and group study.

In his eye-opening examination of the pervasiveness of evil in our world, McGee helps readers recognize these entrenched, self-destructive patterns so that they can experience profound change in the very structure of their lives and grasp the freedom God promises.

Rapha Resources books and materials may be ordered by calling 1-800-460-HOPE. For more information about Rapha's treatment programs, call 1-800-847-HOPE.

Appendix 2

ROBERT S. MCGEE
Founder of Rapha

Dear Reader:

Many factors work together to discourage those who truly need intensive help from receiving that help. Insurance companies who attempt to save money by eliminating unnecessary medical costs, at times show little concern about those who live with intense emotional pain on a daily basis. Politicians have discovered abuses in the health care industry, but instead of true reform, they have adopted media-pleasing reform. They may have indeed reduced some the abuse, but they have done so at the expense of those who truly need help. One might compare this situation to hypothetically eliminating insurance payment for all Cesarean sections only because a small number have been performed without firm medical indication. Finally, historically there have always been the personal barriers; externally and internally we never want to admit the severity of our issues.

As I counseled in a private practice many years ago, I saw numerous people who continued to be trapped in emotional pain, seemingly not able to escape even with the help of once-a-week therapy. Seeing the need for a more intensive type of treatment, I founded Rapha in April 1986, and over 25,000 people have sought and received help since that day. I wish I could tell you that all 25,000 were success stories, but that is not so. However, results of a two-year longitudinal survey completed in 1994 indicate that over 94 percent of the patients responding not only report satisfaction with the program, but a willingness to refer friends and family to Rapha for treatment. Furthermore, over 75 percent of them indicated *their high expectations* for treatment were met. Based on these success stories and others, I believe many thousands have experienced life-long change during their time at Rapha. These folks write to me with their testimonies, come up to greet me after I speak, and openly tell me of their experiences.

For each person who received help at Rapha, there was someone who took the time and effort to encourage that first step. I've often wondered why one person would be an encourager while another would sit idly by and, perhaps, even become a hindrance. I've concluded that those who encourage others have loved enough to understand the pain and hurt of another. They have broken out of the insulated island of loneliness, have touched and been touched by another, and have found the courage to reach out and help.

On the next page, you will read a brief description of the treament programs offered at Rapha. Please look at this prayerfully. Ask God to lead you to those that need His healing touch.

Robert S. McGee

ROBERT S. MCGEE
FOUNDER OF RAPHA

640

Appendix 4

TESTIMONIALS

"Our community is fortunate indeed to have access to the outstanding Christian counseling service Rapha provides. The success of this biblically-based, Christ-centered approach to counseling is further evidence that God's principles work best in every facet of our lives."
Dr. Ed Young
Pastor of Second Baptist Church, Houston, TX

"I appreciate the commitment that Rapha has for the American teenager. Rapha's treatment program is based on a biblical perspective and brings about true healing for emotional needs."
Dawson McAllister
Author and Speaker

"I appreciate the ministry that Rapha is providing to the community as well as to the ministers and churches of the Assemblies of God in South Texas."
Rev. Howard Burroughs
Superintendent, South Texas Assemblies of God, Houston, TX

If you or someone you know is suffering from an emotional problem or substance abuse, call 1-800-847-HOPE.

"I want you to know how grateful I am to God for all you are doing. All of us who are pastors, as we sense the tremendous needs and hurts of people, are thankful for an organization like Rapha."
Dr. Charles Stanley
Pastor of First Baptist Church, Atlanta, GA

"Conferences and seminars presented by Rapha provide both evangelistic opportunities and occasions for spiritual renewal and maturity. People are drawn to these conferences, since they deal with both felt needs and biblical solutions."
Dr. Gene Getz
Senior Pastor of Fellowship Bible Church North, Plano, TX
Director, Center for Church Renewal

"I have been delighted to learn of Rapha's blend of clinical competence and scriptural authority. I believe that Rapha truly lives up to its biblical name through its God-centered caring and healing."
Dr. D. James Kennedy
Sr. Minister of Coral Ridge Presbyterian Church, Fort Lauderdale, FL

"The Christ-centered counseling available at Rapha is a great testimony to the overcoming power of biblical truth when applied to a hurting life. From the abuse recovery programs to codependency counseling and all the other services available through Rapha, they all ring freedom for those bound up in these areas because they emphasize that truth must not be only learned, but applied, in order to have effectual and lasting change upon a life for the glory of God."
Rev. Tommy Barnett
Pastor of First Assembly of God Church, Phoenix, AZ

For more information about Rapha's treatment programs, call 1-800-847-HOPE.

Appendix 5

SEMINARS

We can build our self-worth on our ability to please others, or on the love and forgiveness of Jesus Christ. Here's how you can benefit from a "Search for Significance" seminar!

- Find out how the world's system of self-worth differs from God's plan.

- Learn how our beliefs affect the way we behave.

- Discover how the drive to succeed traps us with a fear of failure and how God can replace that fear.

- Find out how God's power can overcome the fear of rejection.

- Learn how blame and shame keep us from being all God wants us to be.

- Find out how to experience forgiveness for ourselves and others.

- And more!

Search Ministries provides day, weekend, and week-long seminars. For information concerning presently scheduled events or to schedule an event,

call 1-800-460-HOPE.